P9-CSE-316

Books by Jeffrey Burton Russell

Dissent and Reform in the Early Middle Ages

Medieval Civilization

A History of Medieval Christianity: Prophecy and Order

Religious Dissent in the Middle Ages

Witchcraft in the Middle Ages

The Devil: Perceptions of Evil from Antiquity to Primitive Christianity

A History of Witchcraft: Sorcerers, Heretics, and Pagans

Medieval Heresies: A Bibliography 1960-1979 (with Carl Berkhout)

Satan: The Early Christian Tradition

Lucifer: The Devil in the Middle Ages

Mephistopheles: The Devil in the Modern World

The Prince of Darkness: Evil and the Power of Good in History

Inventing the Flat Earth: Columbus and the Historians

Dissent and Order in the Middle Ages: The Search for Legitimate Authority

Lives of the Jura Fathers (with K. and T. Vivian)

A History of Heaven: The Singing Silence

A New History of Witchcraft (with Brooks Alexander)

Paradise Mislaid: How We Lost Heaven—and How We Can Regain It

EXPOSING MYTHS ABOUT CHRISTIANITY

A Guide to Answering 145 Viral Lies and Legends

JEFFREY BURTON RUSSELL

IVP Books
An imprint of InterVarsity Press
Downers Grove, Illinois

InterVarsity Press
P.O. Box 1400, Downers Grove, IL 60515-1426
World Wide Web: www.ivpress.com
E-mail: email@ivpress.com

InterVarsity Press® is the book-publishing division of InterVarsity Christian Fellowship/USA®, a movement of students and faculty active on campus at hundreds of universities, colleges and schools of nursing in the United States of America, and a member movement of the International Fellowship of Evangelical Students. For information about local and regional activities, write Public Relations Dept., InterVarsity Christian Fellowship/USA, 6400 Schroeder Rd., P.O. Box 7895, Madison, WI 53707-7895, or visit the IVCF website at <www.intervarsity.org>.

Scripture quotations, unless otherwise noted, are from the New Revised Standard Version *of the Bible, copyright 1989 by the Division of Christian Education of the National Council of the Churches of Christ in the USA. Used by permission. All rights reserved.*

Cover design: Cindy Kiple
Images: Karl Weatherly/Getty Images
Interior design: Beth Hagenberg

ISBN 978-0-8308-3466-2

Printed in the United States of America ∞

green press INITIATIVE *InterVarsity Press is committed to protecting the environment and to the responsible use of natural resources. As a member of Green Press Initiative we use recycled paper whenever possible. To learn more about the Green Press Initiative, visit <www.greenpressinitiative.org>.*

Library of Congress Cataloging-in-Publication Data

Russell, Jeffrey Burton.
Exposing myths about Christianity: a guide to answering 145 viral lies and legends / Jeffrey Burton Russell.
p. cm.
Includes bibliographical references and index.
ISBN 978-0-8308-3466-2 (pbk.: alk. paper)
1. Christian legends—Miscellanea. 2. Superstition—Religious aspects—Christianity—Miscellanea. 3. Common fallacies—Miscellanea. 4. Apologetics—Miscellanea. 5. Christianity—Controversial literature—Miscellanea. 6. Theology, Doctrinal—Miscellanea. I. Title.
BR135.R87 2012
239—dc23

2012005242

P 19 18 17 16 15 14 13 12 11 10 9 8 7 6 5 4 3 2
Y 28 27 26 25 24 23 22 21 20 19 18 17 16 15 14 13 12

In grateful memory of

Léon-Ernest Halkin, Elinor P. Mansfield,
Marie-Louise Raffetto and Diana M. Russell

Contents

Christianity Is Stupid

Jesus and the Bible Have Been Shown to Be False

Christian Beliefs Have Been Shown to Be Wrong

Acknowledgments

My warmest and deepest thanks go to my beloved wife and vigilant editor, Pamela C. Russell. Next I thank Michael Gibson at IVP for his tireless support and many helpful criticisms. Deep thanks as well to Archbishop Chrysostomos of Etna and Brooks Alexander for the information and insights they have provided over time. I am also grateful to Joseph Amato, Giles Anderson, Stan Anderson, Art Battson, Michael Bowers, Klaus Fischer, Alan Green, Steven Gross, Hugh Feiss, Walter Kaufmann, John V. Kennedy, Steve Long, John Martinis, Tim Philibosian, Francesc and Kathy Roig, Douglas Thrower, Brian Thibeaut, Michael Tkacz, Joe Traynor, Tim Vivian and Gill Williamson. Special thanks are due to Norman Ravitch and Catherine Brown Tkacz, who each generously read an entire draft. Naturally, not all of these kind people agree with everything in the book, and factual errors are mine. Inevitably there will be errors in a book that covers so much territory, and I welcome corrections. But I hope that readers will consider the evidence as a whole.

are a non-Christian, you are invited to investigate. If you are a Christian, recall that no one ever served Jesus by suppressing the truth. If you are anti-Christian, here is an opportunity to sort fact from fiction. The goal is to dispel myths and promote reasonable understanding of the subject. Welcome all.

Chronology

(Some dates are closest approximations.)

B.C.

1200-1100: Moses

900s: Extant written fragments of Old Testament

640-609: Reign of King Josiah of Judah

600s-500s: Probable date of composition of most Old Testament books

570-495: Pythagoras, mathematician

535-475: Heraclitus, philosopher

384-322: Aristotle, philosopher

276-194: Eratosthenes, mathematician and geographer

200s: Septuagint: first complete Old Testament

200 B.C.-A.D. 70: Composition of most of Old Testament Apocrypha

200 B.C.-A.D. 100: pseudepigrapha; apocalyptic literature

106-43: Cicero, philosopher

100s (about): Dead Sea Scrolls

37-4: Reign of Herod the Great, King of Judea

25 B.C.-A.D. 45: Philo, Jewish philosopher

4 B.C.: Likely date of birth of Jesus

A.D.

35-107: Ignatius of Antioch, theologian

37-100: Josephus, historian

49: Council of Jerusalem

50-90: New Testament written

54-68: Reign of emperor Nero, persecutor

60-90: Gospels written

60-130: Papias, theologian

61-112: Pliny the Younger, correspondent

66-70: Revolt of Jews against Romans

69-155: Polycarp, theologian

70: Destruction of Jerusalem by Romans

81-96: Reign of emperor Domitian, persecutor

85-165: Ptolemy, geographer

90: Rabbis exclude Christians from the synagogues

100s-600s: Church fathers and mothers, Christian writers

100s: Rabbis exclude Apocrypha from Old Testament

110: Suetonius, Roman historian

115-200: Lucian of Samosata

130 (about): General agreement on canon of New Testament

130-200: Irenaeus, theologian

130s-200s: Christian "apocrypha"

150: Tatian, theologian

150: Theophilus of Antioch, theologian

150-250: "Christian" Gnosticism

150-215: Clement of Alexandria, theologian

156-157: *The Martyrdom of Saint Polycarp*, hagiography

160-225: Tertullian, theologian

160: Death of Marcion, heretic

161-180: Reign of emperor Marcus Aurelius

170-236: Hippolytus, liturgist

175 (about): Athenagoras, theologian

180: First known written use of the word "Trinity"

185-254: Origen, theologian

200s: Known manuscripts of substantial parts of New Testament

200s onward: Sign of the cross in universal use

200s-700s: Development of Apostles' Creed

217-222: Reign of Pope Calixtus I

251-356: Anthony, monastic

258: Death of Cyprian of Carthage, bishop

284-305: Reign of emperor Diocletian

290-346: Pachomius, monastic

300s onward: Special veneration of Mary the mother of Christ

300s onward: Christmas becomes important holiday

300s: First known complete New Testaments

300s: *Codex sinaiticus*, manuscript of large parts of Old Testament

300s: Icons become common

300s onward: Assumption of Mary common belief

300s: Term "pope" commonly used for bishops

312-313: Toleration of Christians proclaimed in Roman Empire

325: First Council of Nicaea

325-381: Nicene Creed formed

330-395: Gregory of Nyssa, theologian

339-397: Ambrose, theologian

345-420: Jerome, translator of Bible

346-399: Evagrius of Pontus, theologian, psychologist

347-407: John Chrysostomos, theologian

354-430: Augustine of Hippo, theologian

367-382: Canon of New Testament finally settled

379-395: Reign of emperor Theodosius the Great

380-430: Athanasian Creed

381: First Council of Constantinople

395: Christianity declared official religion of Roman Empire

400s onward: Vast numbers of New Testament manuscripts in many languages

400s: Slavery terminally declines in Roman Empire

400s: Origin of seven deadly sins and seven gifts of the Holy Spirit

410: Sack of Rome by Visigoths

410-417: Pope Innocent I

431: Council of Ephesus

440-461: Reign of Pope Leo I the Great

451: Council of Chalcedon

481-511: Reign of King Clovis, who converts the Franks

500-545: Dionysius the Little establishes A.D. dating

500s onward: Immaculate Conception of Mary common belief

500 (about): Dionysius the Areopagite, contemplative

553: Second Council of Constantinople

570-649: John Climacus, contemplative

570-632: Muhammad, prophet

580-662: Maximus Confessor, contemplative

589: King Recared converts Visigoths to Catholicism

590-604: Reign of Pope Gregory I the Great

600s: Penitentials rank sins according to their gravity

600s: Most Christians live in Africa and Asia, which is conquered by Muslims

632: Muhammad's conquest of western Arabia

661 (about): Muslims conquer Syria, Egypt and Iraq

673-735: Bede, historian

675-754: Saint Boniface, missionary

680: Third Council of Constantinople

700s-800s: Iconoclasts

700s: Few slaves in Europe

715-731: Reign of Pope Gregory II

731-741: Reign of Pope Gregory III

732: Frankish King Charles Martel stops Muslim invasion

750: Muslim empire stretches from present southern France to Pakistan

771-814: Reign of Charlemagne

787: Second Council of Nicaea

788: Pope Hadrian I declares Charlemagne "the new Constantine"

780-804: Charlemagne conquers the Saxons

800: Pope Leo III crowns Charlemagne emperor

800s: Masoretic (Hebrew) texts of most of Old Testament

800-1300: Era of Muslim mathematics and philosophy

800s-1000s: Marriage gradually considered a sacrament of the church

800s onward: Partial translations of Bible into English

989: Prince Vladimir of Kiev converts Russia

1000s-1200: Numerous heresies

1000s onward: Title "pope" reserved exclusively in the West to bishop of Rome

1032-1045: Reign of Pope Benedict II

1033-1109: Saint Anselm, philosopher

1048-1054: Reign of Leo IX, who launches papal reform movement

1054: Schism divides Western and Eastern churches

1056-1106: Reign of German emperor Henry IV

1073-1085: Reign of Pope Gregory VII

1079-1142: Abelard, philosopher

1080s-1090s: Muslims close Jerusalem to Christians

1088-1099: Reign of Pope Urban II

1090-1153: Bernard of Clairvaux, contemplative

1096-1291: Crusades

1100s: Rise of cities, education

1100s: Private confession established in Catholic church

1115-1180: John of Salisbury, legal theorist

1135-1202: Joachim of Fiore, millenarian

1168-1263: Robert Grosseteste, theologian, experimenter

1181-1226: Francis of Assisi

1184: Pope Lucius III orders bishops to search out heretics

1198-1216: Reign of Pope Innocent III

1200-1280: Albertus Magnus, theologian, botanist

1204: Constantinople sacked by crusaders

1212: Children's crusade

1215: Fourth Lateran Council

1217-1274: Bonaventure, contemplative

1225-1274: Thomas Aquinas, theologian

1233: Pope Gregory IX establishes papal inquisitors

1252: Pope Innocent IV allows inquisitors to use torture

1260-1328: Meister Eckhart, contemplative

1265-1321: Dante, poet

1275-1342: Marsilius of Padua, political theorist

1285-1347: William of Ockham, philosopher

1294-1303: Reign of Pope Boniface VIII

1296-1359: Gregory Palamas, contemplative

1300-1358: Jean Buridan, experimentalist

1323-1382: Nicolas Oresme, experimentalist

1330-1384: John Wycliffe, theologian

1340 (about): *The Cloud of Unknowing*, contemplative work

1342-1417: Julian of Norwich, contemplative

1372-1415: Jan Huss, dissenter

1377-1417: Great schism in papacy

1380-1392: John Wycliffe's followers translate Bible into English

1400s-1800s: Christian slave traders

1400s: Conciliar movement in Catholic church

1401-1464: Nicholas of Cusa

1435: Pope Eugenius IV excommunicates Europeans enslaving Canary Islanders

1441: First African slaves imported to Europe by a Portuguese ship

1452: Pope Nicholas V gives permission to enslave Muslim and pagan prisoners

1453: Fall of Constantinople to Turks

1462: Pope Pius II condemns slavery

1462: King Henry IV of Castile requests Pope Pius II to authorize inquisition in Spain

1473-1543: Nicolaus Copernicus, mathematician

1478: Spanish inquisition established

1483-1546: Martin Luther, Protestant reformer

1491: Extant globe of Earth

1492: Columbus discovers America

1492: Muslim rule eliminated from Spain

1494-1536: William Tyndale translates Bible into English

1500s: Abuse of indulgences

1500s-1600s: Wars between Protestants and Catholics

1500s-1800s: Alliance of churches and monarchies in Europe

1500s-1700s: "Witchcraft"

1505-1560: John of the Cross, contemplative

1507-1549: Reign of King Henry VIII of England

1509-1564: John Calvin, theologian

1515-1582 Teresa of Ávila, contemplative

1517: Beginning of Protestant Reformation

1521: Excommunication of Martin Luther

1521: Radical Thomas Müntzer arrives in Wittenberg

1523-1525: Ulrich Zwingli preaches in Zurich

1534: William Tyndale uses the term "popery"

1536: John Calvin's *Institutes of the Christian Religion* published

1537: Pope Paul III condemns enslavement of Native Americans

1538-1584: Charles Borromeo, theologian

1542: Pope Paul III centralizes a single inquisition in Rome as the Holy Office

1542-1621: Robert Bellarmine, theologian

1543: Publication of Copernicus' work on the solar system

1545-1563: Council of Trent

1546: Word "Puritan" coined

1548-1600: Giordano Bruno, philosopher

1548-1617: Francisco Suárez, theologian

1552-1634: Sir Edward Coke, jurist

1556: Pope Paul IV orders Jews of Rome segregated in a ghetto

1558-1603: Reign of Queen Elizabeth I of England

1561-1626: Francis Bacon, philosopher

1582-1610: Catholic translation of Bible into English

1562-1633: George Abbot, a translator of the King James Bible

1564-1642: Galileo, mathematician and astronomer

1571-1630: Johannes Kepler, astronomer

1591: Pope Gregory XIV condemns enslavement of Native Americans

1600: Giordano Bruno burned as a heretic

1600s-1900s: Catholic Jansenism

1603-1625: Reign of King James I of England

1604-1611: Translation of King James Bible

1609-1611: Galileo's astronomical discoveries

1611: Publication of King James Bible

1611: Galileo honored by Pope Paul V

1623-1644: Reign of Pope Urban VIII, who condemns all slavery

1618-1648: Thirty Years War

1619: First African slaves imported to British colonies in North America

1632: Galileo's *Dialogue* published

1632-1704: John Locke, philosopher

1633: Galileo found guilty of heresy and placed under house arrest

1642-1691: George Fox, contemplative

1643-1727: Isaac Newton, mathematician, philosopher

1643: Presbyterian Westminster Confession

1686-1761: William Law, contemplative

1686: The Holy Office (the Roman inquisition) condemns slavery

1688: English Bill of Rights

1689: Baptist Confession

1694-1778: Voltaire, writer

1700s: Origin of phrase "fairy tale"

1703-1791: John Wesley, Protestant leader

1711-1776: David Hume, philosopher

1712-1778 : Jean-Jacques Rousseau, founder of Romanticism

1725: First appearance of the word "science" in a modern sense

1729-1781: Gotthold Ephraim Lessing, biblical critic

1740-1814: Marquis de Sade, sadist

1743-1826: Thomas Jefferson

1750: Beginning of the Enlightenment

1752-1840: Johann Friedrich Blumenbach, racist writer

1754: John Woolman leads Quakers against slave trade

1759-1833: William Wilberforce, antislavery advocate

1770-1831: Georg W. F. Hegel, philosopher

1771: Massachusetts outlaws importation of slaves

1772-1829: Friedrich Schleiermacher, theologian

1776: American Declaration of Independence

1787: Society for the Abolition of the Slave Trade founded in England

1789: French Revolution

1798-1886: Robert Benton Seeley, millenarian

1800s-1900s: Industrial revolution

1800: Term "Caucasian" invented for white people

1800-1882: John Nelson Darby, millenarian

1801-1885: Anthony Ashley Cooper Lord Shaftesbury, millenarian

1802-1885: Victor Hugo, writer

1803: Denmark outlaws slave trade

1807: United Kingdom outlaws slave trade

1807: Racist *Short System of Comparative Anatomy*

1808: United States outlaws slave trade

1809-1882: Charles Darwin, biologist

1810-1883: Thomas Rawson Birks, millenarian

1810-1888: Asa Gray, botanist

1815: Pope Pius VII demands abolition of slave trade

1818: Netherlands outlaws slave trade

1818-1883: Karl Marx, communist philosopher

1823-1892: Joseph Ernest Renan, biblical critic

1824-1881: David Friedrich Strauss, biblical critic

1825-1895: Thomas H. Huxley, Darwin's publicist

1828: Washington Irving's fictional Columbus

1839: Pope Gregory XVI sends pastoral letter condemning slavery to U.S. Catholics

1831: France outlaws slave trade

1833: American Anti-Slavery Society founded

1833: United Kingdom abolishes slavery

1833: First use of the word "scientist"

1842-1910: William James, psychologist

1844: Racist *On the Natural History of the Caucasian and Negro Races*

1844: End of world predicted by William Miller

1844-1900: Friedrich Nietzsche, philosopher

1848: France abolishes slavery

1848: Assembly of Frankfurt declares full equality for Jews

1853: First woman ordained in America

1854: Independent Latin America completes abolition of slavery

1854-1941: Sir James Frazer, anthropologist

1854: Pope Pius IX defines doctrine of the Immaculate Conception of Mary

1856-1939: Sigmund Freud, psychiatrist

1859: Charles Darwin publishes *Origin of Species*

1861: Racist *Elements of Medical Zoology*

1861: Seventh-Day Adventists founded

1865: United States abolishes slavery

1865: Term "relativism" appears

1869-1870: Catholic First Vatican Council

1870-1924: Nikolai Lenin, Soviet dictator

1870: Infallibility of the pope in faith and morals declared

1873: Term "anti-Semitism" coined

1880-1956: H. L. Mencken, satirist

1886: Spain abolishes slavery in Cuba

1886-1968: Karl Barth, theologian

1888: Brazil abolishes slavery

1889-1945: Adolf Hitler

1890s: Elizabeth Cady Stanton edits *The Woman's Bible*

1892-1971: Reinhold Niebuhr, theologian

1893-1963: C. S. Lewis, writer

1895: Fundamentalist movement begins

1900s: Century of vicious dictators

1900s-2000s: Arab-Jewish struggles

1904-1990: B. F. Skinner, psychologist

1906: Albert Schweitzer's *Quest of the Historical Jesus* published

1906: Pentecostalism begins in Los Angeles

1906-1945: Dietrich Bonhoeffer, pastor and martyr

1914-1918: First World War

1915: Revival of Ku Klux Klan

1915-1968: Thomas Merton, contemplative

1918- : Billy Graham, evangelist

1920s: George McCready Price founds Young Earth Creationism

1924-1990: Penal codes against Christianity in the Soviet Union

1931: Term "physicalism" appears

1933: Hitler comes to power

1933: Concordat between Pope Pius XI and Hitler

1934: Barmen Declaration

1934-1996: Carl Sagan, scientist

1935: Nazis arrest seven hundred Protestant ministers

1937: Pope Pius XI issues encyclical denouncing Nazism

1937: Hitler's new (neopagan) religion established

1938: Yuletide replaces Christmas in Nazi Germany

1939-1945: Second World War

1941-1945: Holocaust

1945-1946: Nag Hammadi manuscripts discovered

1947-1960: Dead Sea Scrolls discovered

1949: Paul Blanshard publishes *American Freedom and Catholic Power*

1950: Pope Pius XII defines doctrine of Assumption of Mary

1958-1963: Reign of Pope John XXIII

1960s: Civil rights movement

1961: *The Genesis Flood* by Whitcomb and Morris

1962-1965: Catholic Second Vatican Council

1962: Saudi Arabia abolishes slavery

1965: World Council of Churches declares anti-Judaism unchristian

1965: Mutual excommunications of Eastern and Western churches canceled

1970: *The Late Great Planet Earth* by Hal Lindsey

1978-2005: Reign of Pope John Paul II (Karol Wojtyla)

1981: Mauritania abolishes slavery

1992: Rehabilitation of Galileo as orthodox

2005- : Reign of Pope Benedict XVI (Josef Ratzinger)

2008: Benedict XVI rejects all discrimination against Jews

Christianity Is Dying Out

1. Christianity is uncool and old-fashioned.

Fashionably elite people are supposed to be atheists. As a result, Christianity is uncool in much of contemporary Western society. Human beings are egocentric, and if God exists, one's own ego is not the center of the universe. In many circles—the field of social psychology, as one example—someone who takes Christianity seriously can provoke mockery or even anger from others in the circle. Humans are very tribal, and religious belief is a good way to get oneself kicked out of certain tribes. When it comes to matters of religious belief, many people think they are making up their own mind when in reality they are simply going along with the group, whether the group is Christian or atheist. In a materialist, consumerist society, belief in the transcendent (something beyond our senses) is difficult to maintain, and people find it pleasanter not to believe than to be ridiculed.

Christianity is old-fashioned in the sense that it has been around for almost twenty centuries. On the one hand, that might indicate that it has something going for it and is always being renewed. On the other hand, the general revulsion against all traditional culture since the 1960s has produced a Western society contemptuous of the old and eager to consume whatever seems new. In an extroverted society that venerates change, there is a fear—almost an existential terror—of being left out. In school one is required to learn science but not critical thought, and that lack allows strident voices to demand assent to current orthodoxies and the suppression of dissent.[1]

To a thoughtful person, the question is not whether Christianity is unfashionable or old-fashioned. The question is whether it is true. At the very

[1]Robert Wuthnow, *Religion and Science Debate: Why Does It Continue?* ed. Harold Attridge (New Haven, CT: Yale University Press, 2009), pp. 155-77.

least, one must consider whether it is a system that is sufficiently coherent and evidence-based to be respected even by those who disagree with it.

2. Christianity is outdated and dying out.

Whether we think Christianity is outdated depends on our point of view, and our point of view is influenced by where we live. If we live in Europe or on the U.S. coasts, we are more likely to be unbelievers, and we coastal folk attribute that to our superior intelligence. If we live in Nigeria, Korea or China, Christianity seems a new and liberating idea. The Pew Forum on Religion and Public Life reports that sub-Saharan Africa is the world's "most religious area." The percentage of people who say religion is very important to them ranges from ninety-eight percent in Senegal to sixty-nine percent in Botswana, compared with fifty-seven percent in the United States and much less in Europe.[2] Atheists attribute the growth of Christianity in Asia and Africa to the alleged ignorance of people in developing societies.

Point of view regarding religion also depends on age. In Western society, young people's views of Christianity mostly range from indifferent to negative.[3] A survey of Canadian teens showed that about twenty percent read the Bible or other religious scriptures at least monthly, as opposed to forty-three percent who checked their horoscopes monthly.[4] Many people born and bred in a world of designer labels regard Christianity as just another brand name, along with Buddhism, New Age, humanism and so on.[5]

In the United States, the American Religious Identification Survey indicates that from 1990 to 2008, the proportion of the population identifying themselves as Christians declined by eleven percent, while the proportion unaffiliated with any religion rose by seven and a half percent. The category "no religion" now exceeds every denomination except Catholic and Baptist.[6] That is a big change in less than two decades. However, the 2008 survey also shows that ninety-two percent believe in

[2]"Sub-Saharan Africa Is World's 'Most Religious' Area," *Christian Century*, May 18, 2010, p. 19.

[3]David Kinnaman and Gabe Lyons, *unChristian: What a New Generation Really Thinks About Christianity* (Grand Rapids: Baker, 2007), p. 28.

[4]"Sub-Saharan Africa," *Christian Century*, p. 9.

[5]Kinnaman and Lyons, *unChristian*, p. 223.

[6]Cathy Lynn Grossman, "Most religious groups in USA have lost ground, survey finds," *USA Today*, published March 9, 2009, updated March 13, 2009, <www.usatoday.com/news/religion/2009-03-09-american-religion-ARIS_N.htm>.

some kind of universal spirit, seventy-four percent believe in life after death, and seventy-nine percent believe in contemporary miracles. And though many are apatheists (from "apathy") who don't think it matters whether God exists or not, forty-one percent even of the unaffiliated say religion is important in their lives.[7] Most of the "no religion" respondents are of the "I don't care" variety, while only four percent identify themselves as atheists or agnostics.[8]

The term "agnostic" was coined in 1870 by Thomas Huxley, who came to be known as "Darwin's bulldog." It has two basic senses: "I don't know but I'd like to find out," and "I don't know, I don't think I can know, and therefore I don't care to examine the evidence." Unlike agnostics, however, most "no religion" people feel they just haven't found the right religion for them. A recent Gallup poll of U.S. residents asked respondents whether religion was "an important part" of their daily life. Nationwide, sixty-five percent said it was.[9]

In Western society overall, belief in God is declining. In Great Britain, only forty percent of people believe in God, and the figures are similar in Australia, Canada and continental European countries, with the smallest percentage of believers found in the formerly Communist countries of Eastern Europe (except Russia, where belief appears to be growing).[10] The so-called "new atheists" have gained attention in the last decade despite the fact that their arguments are not new but more than a century old. In elite circles in Europe and the United States it is considerably more respectable to be an atheist than to be a Christian. There has been a marked shift in the default position from belief in God to unbelief. This is particularly true in academia, law and mainstream media. Rejection of Christianity is considered sophisticated, and some just say, "Well, I don't believe it, and neither do my friends," as if that were an argument. This is surfing on the wave of atheism rather than looking under the froth and foam.

---

[7]"U.S. Religious Landscape Report II," event transcript, published June 23, 2008, <www.pewforum.org/US-Religious-Landscape-Survey-Report-II.aspx>.

[8]Eric Gorski, "America: A Nation of Religious Drifters," Associated Press, May 2, 2009, reporting on the Pew Foundation's 2009 report "Faith in Flux: Changes in Religious Affiliation in the U.S."

[9]Adelle M. Banks, "God big in South, not so much in New England and Pacific Northwest: New Gallup results," *Christian Century*, March 10, 2009, pp. 14-15.

[10]Andrew Greeley, *Religion in Europe at the End of the Second Millennium: A Sociological Profile* (New Brunswick, NJ: Transaction, 2003).

Also, many Christians belonging to elite tribes don't dare admit their belief for fear of losing status, alienating friends, suffering job discrimination or being banished from the tribe. In some areas of the world, notably the Middle East, Christians undergo literal banishment and actual death.[11]

Christianity is dying in the sense that many Western Christians no longer believe in the historical, traditional Christianity based on the Bible and the creeds.[12] Christian Tradition is "the whole of the explicit and implicit truths contained in Scripture and transmitted through the church."[13] Society's move toward inclusivity makes no distinction between Christianity and other religions—a position that is philosophically impossible no matter how warmhearted it may feel. The only way all religions can be equal is if all are equally meaningless. How much can we water down our beliefs without losing our identity? Are all "stories" equally true? When a community accommodates and includes every different belief, does it stand for anything at all? Saying that everybody has a different story and that no story is privileged over any other leaves every religion groping for the lowest common denominator, and it ends in evaporation. Inclusivity is empty fare for the spiritually hungry—which is an important reason why undemanding churches are fading.

Christianity is a way of life. People can be put off by it because it demands that they examine their lives both intellectually and spiritually—and then act.[14] As a result, most people in Western societies these days are "practical atheists": they think and act as if there were no God. Those people who do say they believe in God have a variety of ideas about God's nature and what their relationship to him is. Only a minority believe in the established Christian view of Jesus Christ as the unique Lord who is fully God and fully human. By repeatedly comparing Christian beliefs with belief in fairies and leprechauns, atheists have often been successful in intimidating those who do believe from speaking out. In short, Christianity

---

[11]Dale Gavlak, "'Religicide' in Iraq," *Christianity Today*, February 2011, pp. 13-16. Collin Hansen, "The Son and the Crescent," *Christianity Today*, February, 2011, pp. 19-23, addresses the differences between Muslim and Christian views of Jesus.

[12]Kenda Creasy Dean, "Almost-Christian Formation of Teens: Faith, Nice and Easy," *Christian Century*, August 10, 2010, pp. 22-27.

[13]Angelo Di Bernardino, ed., *Encyclopedia of the Early Church* (New York: Oxford University Press, 1992), p. 495.

[14]David Bentley Hart, *Atheist Delusions: The Christian Revolution and Its Fashionable Enemies* (New Haven, CT: Yale University Press, 2009), p. 236.

has become the countercultural view in Europe, Canada, Australia and elite America. It requires both thought and courage to resist the materialist trend. It's surprising that more people haven't declared themselves atheists, for if one converts to atheism from Christianity, one doesn't have to do anything, but converting from atheism to Christianity requires commitment and action. Atheism has been called tone-deaf, colorblind, even nature-challenged. Atheism is like the human eye, which sees only a tiny part of the electromagnetic spectrum. For atheists, the rest of the spectrum is just not there.[15]

"Antitheism" is a term describing outspoken opposition to God, as opposed to mere atheism, which simply posits that there is no God.[16] Antitheists regard moderates as cowards. They do not tolerate respect for belief in God at all. They regard religion as totally false and therefore evil. Antitheists are atheists with an agenda. They put themselves in a privileged position, loading the burden of truth onto theists by assuming that atheism is right until proved otherwise. Phillip Johnson and John Mark Reynolds observe that "theists are expected to produce proof, including proof that no naturalistic solution to the problem of creation is possible. Atheists need only to publish suggestions."[17] Antitheists, says Ian Markham, are fundamentalists with "an unambiguous assertion of a worldview in which the authors are entirely confident that they are right."[18]

Overt hostility to religion centering on hostility to Christianity has grown since September 2001, because antitheists claim that religious people are particularly prone to terrorism.[19] Antitheists oddly believe both that Christianity is dying and that it constitutes a frightening threat. This self-contradictory view stems mainly from the misconception that religion

[15]As for recent views by scientists, Stephen Hawking and Leonard Mlodinow, *The Grand Design* (New York: Bantam, 2010), argue against the existence of God on the basis of the currently fashionable M-Theory (a development of string theory in physics), but the opposite is argued by Hugh Ross, *Beyond the Cosmos: What Recent Discoveries in Astrophysics Reveal About the Glory and Love of God,* 3rd ed. (Orlando: Signalman, 2010).

[16]Christopher Hitchens, *Letters to a Young Contrarian* (Cambridge, MA: Basic Books, 2001), p. 55.

[17]Phillip E. Johnson and John Mark Reynolds, *Against All Gods: What's Right and Wrong About the New Atheism* (Downers Grove, IL: InterVarsity Press, 2010), p. 66.

[18]Ian S. Markham, *Against Atheism: Why Dawkins, Hitchens, and Harris Are Fundamentally Wrong* (Malden, MA: Wiley-Blackwell, 2010), pp. 7, 32.

[19]See not only the popular books of the "new atheists"—Richard Dawkins, Daniel Dennett and Sam Harris—but also the tone of the American Humanist Society (for example, the May/June 2009 issue of *The Humanist*).

is in conflict with science. In fact, science is not at odds with religion; it's only the metaphysics of physicalism that is at odds with religion.[20]

Metaphysics, according to Carlos Eire, is "thinking about what [lies] beyond (Greek: *meta*) the physical order and [gives] it its structure and its existence."[21] I use the term "metaphysics" in its primary sense: as the American Heritage Dictionary defines it, "the branch of philosophy that examines the nature of reality." The fact that many people associate metaphysics with the occult is the result of the degradation of real metaphysics in the 1900s. "Supernatural" has also acquired connotations of weirdness, but basically it means anything beyond the ordinary course of nature.

Physicalism (a word coined in 1931) is a metaphysical view maintaining that all statements not relating to physical science are meaningless; every phenomenon in nature is known to be the result of a combination of physical/chemical causes and randomness. Atheists point out that ninety-three percent of the members of the prestigious National Academy of Sciences espouse no religion. However, the percentage of American scientists as a whole espousing religion (forty-one percent to forty-five percent) changed little in the eighty years between 1916 and 1996.[22] The most vociferous attacks on Christianity have come not from scientists but from propagandists such as Marx, Lenin, Stalin, Hitler, Shaw, Darrow, Nietzsche, Sartre and Ayn Rand. When one searches for concentrations of atheists in modern universities, one finds them disproportionately in the social sciences rather than in the physical sciences.[23]

At the same time that Christianity is declining in the West, it is rapidly rising in Asia, Africa and South America. Compare the more than eighty percent of Nigerians (Muslims as well as Christians) who believe in life after death with the less than twenty-five percent in Estonia. Almost fifty percent of sub-Saharan Africans are now Christian, compared with ten percent around 1900. The total number of Christians in the world is increasing rapidly, and there may be a hundred million "crypto-Christians" worldwide who do not dare declare their belief for fear of persecution.[24]

---

[20]Benjamin Wiker, *The Catholic Church and Science* (Charlotte, NC: Tan Books, 2011).

[21]Carlos Eire, *Very Brief History of Eternity* (Princeton, NJ: Princeton University Press, 2010), p. 38.

[22]John C. Lennox, *God's Undertaker: Has Science Buried God?* (Oxford: Lion, 2007), pp. 16-17.

[23]Jeffrey Burton Russell, *Paradise Mislaid: How We Lost Heaven and How We Can Regain It* (New York: Oxford University Press, 2006), pp. 111-14.

[24]Philip Jenkins, "The Crypto-Christians," *Christian Century*, July 14, 2009, p. 45.

Thus the idea that Christianity is dying out is obviously false, and it can hardly be outdated if so many people keep coming to it. The view that it is outdated comes from the unfounded belief that new ideas are always better than old ideas, and also from a false analogy between religious knowledge and scientific technology. The analogy is false in a number of ways. First, scientific technology is a completely different way of viewing the world from theology, so advances in one do not necessarily affect the other. (It is also questionable whether the increased complexity, specialization and idiosyncrasy of theology since the Enlightenment is an advancement at all.) Second, fundamental Christian faith is more person-based than knowledge-based: it consists of commitment to the person of Jesus Christ.

Antitheists rejoice that disbelief is growing but fear that belief is growing faster. Christians rejoice that belief is growing but are concerned about its increasing departure from its roots.[25]

3. Christianity is boring.

Many people, especially younger ones, feel that Christianity is boring. Usually this feeling arises from weak impressions in church. Church seems boring if we don't understand what is going on and don't try to find out. It seems boring if the services use words or music we don't like. However, there are many churches to choose among, from almost silent services to boisterous singing and dancing, and from the most conservative to the most radical, so that a person can almost design a church for himself or herself—and some do. New congregations keep springing up, and Americans switch churches at an increasing rate.

Many churches are not at all boring; one might, for example, sample Orthodox churches with their beautiful art and rich liturgies. When people say that church is boring they often mean they find other entertainment more fun. But church isn't supposed to be a form of entertainment. Christianity is about what I can do for others. In the current me-oriented society, however, we demand instead what Christianity can do for us. President Kennedy's exhortation "Ask not what your country can do for you, but what you can do for your country" echoes as from a distant land.

---

[25]See Markham, *Against Atheism*, pp. 54, 145, and Francis S. Collins, *Language of God: A Scientist Presents Evidence for Belief* (New York: Free Press, 2006), p. 4.

Churches aside, is Christianity itself boring? Some congregations present bland versions of Christianity that are spiritually and intellectually undemanding. What is missing is not just beauty of language and music but something more fundamental: "the loss of the expectation of God's presence, or more precisely, God's dangerous presence."[26] Christianity is not a feel-good religion; its founder died in agony. The real meaning of Christianity is to transform our lives, and pastors know we tend to resist that. Another reason it may seem boring is that we imagine we already know all about it; we have heard about the baby in the manger once or twice too often. In my experience of college students and faculty, however, many people know virtually nothing about Christianity. A few years ago in my university there was an outpouring of sarcastic correspondence asking what "Christ is risen" means. Someone wrote, "What, Moses is sleeping in and Muhammad hasn't gone to bed yet?" Still another reason is a widespread feeling of "Why bother? There are lots of stories like that in other religions and cultures too." This ignores the fact that the Christian story is based on actual evidence.

Here are the basics of Christianity: One day a young woman who had not had sexual intercourse gave birth to a living, fully human being. He had powers beyond those of other people. He healed victims of incurable diseases and even brought some of the dead back to life. He told people that he had come to change the world and make them fully understand themselves so that they could be truly happy. He told them that God was more likely to prefer the poor and humble to the rich, powerful and famous. Jesus favored the poor and weak not because they were poor and weak, which is no virtue, but because the poor and weak were mistreated and oppressed by the rich and powerful. The rich and powerful people hearing Jesus were first suspicious and then enraged. They seized him and tortured him to death. They buried him. A few days after Jesus died he was truly alive again, walking, talking and eating. He went away, having promised that he would be present again at the end of the world. Many thought he must have had a unique connection with God; soon millions of people believed in him, and today nearly four billion Christians and Muslims are waiting for him to return.

[26]Thomas G. Long, "Expect a Whirlwind," *Christian Century*, February 22, 2011, p. 49.

We may choose to disbelieve Christianity, but it is not boring in itself. If it were, it could scarcely have persuaded billions of people over twenty centuries. Such people have not, for the most part, led boring lives. For example, Dietrich Bonhoeffer was a Lutheran pastor and professor in Germany who in his twenties stood up against the Nazis and those who were riding the Nazi wave; he went to England in 1934 but returned in 1935 to fight the Nazis on their home ground. He was fired from his professorship (excluded from his tribe), and his seminary was closed. When the war began, he was safely in America but chose to return again to Germany to continue his dangerous struggle; he was imprisoned in 1943 and hanged in 1945. The numbers of men and women who have suffered and died for Christ and continue to do so is vast. Obviously none finds it boring.

4. Christianity is a fairy tale.

The great psychologist Sigmund Freud (1856-1939) called Christianity a "fairy tale." The phrase derived in the 1700s from the French *conte de fées* ("story about fairies") and has now become shorthand for a story that is both false and silly. We hear remarks such as "I don't believe in the tooth fairy, Santa Claus, the Easter bunny, or Jesus." Such a remark about religion is parallel to an equally childish statement about science, such as "I don't believe in intergalactic crab monsters or molecular biology." Christianity is based on historical evidence that is open to evaluation.

For me, Christianity is the opposite of childish. As a child I learned that God didn't exist before I learned that Santa Claus didn't exist. My parents told me at an early age that only stupid people believed in God, and I accepted that until I examined the evidence. Again, we should distinguish point of view from bias: point of view develops according to evidence; bias refuses to adjust to evidence. Whatever view we hold must always be revised in accordance with the evidence. Antitheists imagine that Christians believe in a big daddy or mommy who will be nice to them when they are good and punish them when they are naughty. Such people ignore the central event of Christianity—the life and death of God's own son—and the multitudes of Christians who have painfully died for their faith. They also ignore the innumerable brilliant scientists, philosophers, writers and others who have believed and now believe in Christ. It's true that some people are childish in their belief in Christianity, but others are childish in their belief in atheism.

Freud's followers preferred the term "folk tale" to Freud's "fairy tale." Is Christianity a collection of folk tales? Some have claimed that the New Testament accounts are written versions of tales that gradually arose about Jesus before and after his death. The difference between the New Testament and folk tales is that the narratives about Jesus focus on a real person and were composed shortly after his death on the basis of eyewitness evidence. Folk tales are about fictional beings without known origins. Whatever the New Testament narratives are, they are certainly not folk tales. On the other hand, a number of fictional accounts about Jesus and his followers popped up in at least the second century and continue to proliferate today. Most make no pretense at being true and are accepted as fiction, like novels about other historical characters. Some claim to present the "real, secret truth." The Christian community has always discerned between the fictional and the historical and between what is open and what is secret. Christianity has no room for secrets and is neither fairy tale nor folk tale.[27]

5. Christianity is confusing.

Christianity is often confusing to the outsider and even to the insider. We often hear different things in different denominations, different churches and different college courses. Where do we go for a straight answer? The evidence. Christianity is a relatively coherent system about which historical facts exist. Anything else isn't really Christianity. If we plunge immediately into the deep end of the pool in the midst of diverse theological arguments, we quickly become confused and discouraged.

So here is the core: Christianity means faith in the person of Jesus Christ, who is both divine and human, who died to restore our free will, and who rose from the dead as evidence for his God-nature. Faith is dynamic interaction with God. There are two types of faith: one is intellectual assent to a proposition or system; the other is moral assent in personal trust. One type of faith is belief that Christ rose from the dead, or that Christianity as a system is true. The other type of faith is commitment

[27]Sigmund Freud, *Future of an Illusion* (New York: Liveright, 1928).

to Christ as a person in whom we have absolute trust. Both types are necessary, though the latter is deeper; the will is more fundamental than the intellect.[28] When both are seen clearly and acted upon firmly, Christian faith is not confusing.

6. Christianity is a superstition.

People often say that Christianity is just another superstition. But from the earliest use of the words, "superstition" and "religion" meant two different things. The dictionary defines the former as "an irrational belief . . . maintained by ignorance of the laws of nature or by faith in magic or chance" and characterized by "a fearful and abject state of mind resulting from such ignorance." By the way, there is no more connection between the words "superstitious" and "supernatural" than there is between "superstructure," "superglue" and "supermarket." Christians do believe that God is supernatural (Latin *super natura*, "above nature"), and Paul Davies defines a supernatural event as one that "has no complete explanation from within science alone."[29] A better definition of "superstition" is a belief that is not based on a coherent worldview. A coherent worldview is one based on basic principles and that does not contain contradictory beliefs. Traditional Christianity is coherent.

People think Christianity is superstitious because they see Christians doing things they don't understand and may appear to be superstitious in nature. It is true that Christian practices can be superstitious if one thinks they have power in themselves. Crossing oneself, raising one's hands in the air, speaking in tongues, reciting prayers, genuflecting or answering an altar call may help people open themselves to God, but they have no intrinsic efficacy, no power in themselves. Probably the most common superstition among Christians is that if we pray for something, God will (or ought to) grant it to us. The deeper Christian view is that sincere prayer always does good to the one who is praying by bringing God closer and deeper into his or her heart. God is attentive to our prayers, but he re-

---

[28]Russell, *Paradise Mislaid*, pp. 1-16; the apostle Paul's letter to the Romans, chapter 4, presents faith as involving both trust and examination of evidence. See also Rick Kennedy, *Faithcraft and Humility in Classical and Christian Liberal Arts* (forthcoming).

[29]Paul Davies, *Cosmic Jackpot: Why Our Universe Is Just Right for Life* (Boston: Houghton Mifflin, 2007), p. 79.

sponds according to his will for the good of the cosmos, including things and events we often personally do not desire.[30]

Superstitions have no place in any coherent worldview. A Christian and an atheist would both be superstitious in believing that a black cat crossing one's path is a bad omen. But there is a very common superstition that loses both atheists and Christians billions of dollars in casinos and lotteries every year: the idea of luck. It is true that an event can be lucky or unlucky for a given person. When I was ten, my father tried to teach me not to gamble by showing me how easy it is to lose money. He gave me a half-dollar and told me to put it into a slot machine. I put in the half-dollar, pulled the lever, and a dozen half-dollars clattered out. That was a lucky event for me, though not for my father. It was pure chance with nothing mysterious about it. But when a person believes that he or she is intrinsically a lucky—or unlucky—person, that's a superstition.

Common sets of beliefs, however superstitious, can promote social cohesion. Doing a dance may not produce rain, but it brings the village together. Working for "progress" may not improve human nature, but it strengthens social ties among activists. Christian leaders and communities have often acted on the superstition that repressing freedom of thought advances the cause of Christ. But socially valuable superstitions can have horrific effects. In Nazi Germany the majority believed the superstition that Hitler would bring about a thousand years of happiness for the German people. This socially useful belief strongly united the German people—and brought them, along with millions of others, to ruin. The mainstream view in any society is not necessarily the best, an obvious truth that is frequently forgotten.

7. CHRISTIANITY IS A MYTH.

The basic meaning of "myth" is a traditional story about gods or heroes: Athena sprang from the brow of Zeus; Hercules slew the hydra. Most religions—along with most political and social groups—have their myths, but religions are not themselves myths. Christianity is far too complex an intellectual and social system to be a myth. It may include myths, as with certain saints' lives, but it is not a myth itself. Myths characteristically occur in some

---

[30]Rodney Clapp, "Superstitious Prayers," *Christian Century*, March 8, 2011, p. 45.

other dimension and lack historical basis. Christianity, on the other hand, is based on the life of a historical figure—Jesus—in a certain place and time. A secondary meaning of "myth" is a fake, fraud or fiction. Again, Christianity is too complex, ancient and minutely examined to be fake. It has, however, been argued that its basic premises are false, and such arguments must be seriously examined in the light of the evidence.[31]

8. Christianity is magic.

Apart from the foggy notion that Christianity is magical in itself, there are a number of specific Christian actions that some people think of as magical. One is prayer. But only a child or a fanatic believes that prayer for *n* is going to produce *n* by cause and effect. In Christianity, prayer works in the sense that it puts the one praying into closer relationship with God. It sometimes may produce the exact result asked for, but rarely, or at least very indirectly over time. Prayer and meditation are entirely different from magic.[32] The magician tries to cause *q* by *p*; the Christian, on the other hand, only hopes for *q*. Christians do not properly try to hold deity to a contract ("I give to you to cause you to give to me") but rather seek to interact with deity in harmony with divine will.

Another action common among some Christians is thought to be magical not only by atheists but also by other Christians: the consecration of the bread and wine in Holy Communion. The idea is that the use of certain words and actions causes Christ to be present. But even in the traditions with the strongest emphasis on the presence of Christ, the consecration is offered as a prayer request. For example, a pre–Vatican II Catholic missal (Mass-book) says, "We pray thee, God, be pleased to make this same offering wholly blessed, to consecrate it and approve it."

Technology is actually closer to magic than religion is. Magic and technology have the same basic purpose: do one thing in order to cause another thing.[33] One person sacrifices a chicken to make his crops grow; another

[31]Mircea Eliade, *Myth and Reality* (New York: Harper and Row, 1963). The idea that Jesus is a myth is even less believable than it was a hundred years ago. James F. McGrath, "Fringe View," *Christian Century*, November 15, 2011, pp. 12-13.

[32]Richard J. Foster and Gayle D. Beebe, *Longing for God: Seven Paths of Christian Devotion* (Downers Grove, IL: InterVarsity Press, 2009), p. 169.

[33]Lynn Thorndike, *History of Magic and Experimental Science* (New York: Columbia University Press, 1923-1956).

spreads fertilizer on the field instead. Whether a given action "works" or not is obviously important, but the point here is not the result but the method. With both magic and technology, the idea is that if we perform action *p*, we expect *q* to result. The connection is mechanical; it is cause and effect. Technology and magic attempt to control nature; Christianity attempts to be in harmony with nature, God and reality.

9. CHRISTIANITY IS ANTISCIENTIFIC.

This is a widely held belief, but if it were true there wouldn't be so many scientists who are Christians. Science and religion are not at odds. The issue is not between science and religion but between two metaphysical worldviews. View *a* is that there is no such thing as the supernatural—nothing beyond the reach of scientific investigation. View *not-a* is that there is a spiritual reality beyond or above nature. These are two irreconcilably opposite worldviews.

The falsehood comes when materialists assert that *a* is a statement of science. In plain fact, *a* is not a scientific statement at all but a simple assertion of faith and commitment to the materialist worldview.

One of these two positions—*a* or *not-a*—must be true and the other false. The worldview of some contemporary deconstructionists that *a* and *not-a* can both be true (or both false) is a mind-dissolving fantasy arising from the current revulsion against reason and evidence in our postmodern society. Our belief as to which is true depends on our worldview, and the best worldview is one that is most open to the evidence. What we believe does not affect exterior reality. At present, the evidence points strongly to the view that there is directionality and purpose in the universe and that they derive from outside the physical universe.[34]

---

[34]Henry F. Schaefer, *Science and Christianity: Conflict or Coherence?* (Athens, GA: Apollos Trust, 2003).

Christianity Is Destructive

10. Hitler was a Christian.

The idea that Adolf Hitler (1889-1945) was a Christian, just a bad one, is a common myth. A number of current atheist writers have said that Hitler was a Christian. True, Hitler was born a Catholic Christian, just as Stalin was born an Eastern Christian, but neither of them took Christianity seriously after their early youth, and both worked covertly and overtly to destroy it.

Hitler's views were shaped by nationalism, militarism, nihilism, Wagnerian Romantic neopaganism and social Darwinism, which consisted largely of racist ideas of improving humanity by exalting the strong and destroying the weak. Hitler was obsessed by antisemitism. He loathed Jews, and he also despised Christianity, partly because of its Jewish roots and partly because it taught love and forgiveness rather than power. He believed that Christianity had weakened the German nation and thus contributed to its loss in World War I.

After coming to power in 1933, Hitler tolerated the churches until he had a firm grip on society, which he had fairly well established by 1934-1935. At the same time, he promoted a new sort of religion that mixed a small amount of Christianity with a great deal of neopaganism. By 1937 this new faith had attracted more than a million adherents; it allowed people to feel they were being spiritual and at the same time supporting the Führer. Martin Bormann, one of Hitler's closest and most influential aides, declared that National Socialism and Christianity were irreconcilable, and Hitler himself said that Christianity was a religion of fools and "old women." Hitler declared, "The heaviest blow that ever struck humanity was the coming of Christianity. . . . The deliberate lie in the matter of religion was introduced into the world by Christianity."[1]

[1]David Aikman, *Delusion of Disbelief: Why the New Atheism Is a Threat to Your Life, Liberty, and*

Christian youth movements, both Protestant and Catholic, were suppressed and replaced by the Hitler Youth. From 1938 the term "Yuletide" was preferred to "Christmas," and carols and nativity scenes were barred from schools. Hitler's intent was to suppress all loyalty in society except that which focused on himself and the Nazi Party. Hitler was the absolute source of all authority and could not tolerate any other sort of allegiance. To say "Heil Hitler" was an act of faith commitment. The term *heil* was not only a greeting; it also implied salvation. The traditional German word for Christ is *Heiland*: the Savior.

Given Hitler's inherent antipathy toward Christianity, the reaction of the churches to his programs was notably pathetic.[2] In 1933, at the beginning of Hitler's reign, Pope Pius XI naively signed a concordat (formal agreement) with the Nazis, which he soon regretted. The Protestant Barmen Declaration of 1934, which reaffirmed that Christ is above all earthly rulers, had little effect. There were a few great heroes, such as the Protestant pastor Martin Niemöller, who spent years in a concentration camp, the priest Maximilian Kolbe, who was fatally injected at Auschwitz, the Catholic farmer Franz Jägerstätter, who was beheaded, and the Protestant pastor Dietrich Bonhoeffer, who was hanged in prison. In 1935 the Nazis arrested seven hundred Protestant ministers for opposing racism, and that example served as a chilling deterrent.

In 1937, Pius XI issued the encyclical *Mit brennender Sorge* ("With burning concern") denouncing Nazi atrocities, oppression of the churches and Nazism itself as fundamentally unchristian. He ordered the encyclical to be read from all Catholic pulpits in Germany on March 21 of that year, but by then it was too late. On the whole, Catholic and Protestant leaders posed only a weak and ineffective opposition to the persecution of the Jews and political dissenters, even to the suppression and corruption of their own churches. The churches were dupes of salami tactics, acquiescing in the gradual slicing away of their liberties.

Pursuit of Happiness (Carol Stream, IL: Tyndale, 2008), p. 131.

[2] Susannah Heschel, *Aryan Jesus: Christian Theologians and the Bible in Nazi Germany* (Princeton, NJ: Princeton University Press, 2008); Klaus P. Fischer, *History of an Obsession: German Judeophobia and the Holocaust* (New York: Continuum, 1998); Michael C. Thomsett, *German Opposition to Hitler* (Jefferson, NC: McFarland, 1997).

11. The Inquisition Executed Millions of Heretics and Witches.

It is commonly believed that the inquisition executed millions of innocent women for witchcraft. But what actually was "the inquisition"? Most inquisitions throughout history have had nothing to do with religious belief. The Latin word *inquisitio* is most simply translated as "inquest" or "formal inquiry." There have been uncounted multitudes of economic, political and legal inquests from ancient times to today. So the word "inquisition" refers to a variety of processes and is not limited to religion.[3]

When religious inquests became common after 1000, they inquired into a wide number of subjects. A bishop would conduct an inquest into whether the priests of his diocese were literate (did they know Latin), honest (were they pocketing parishioners' contributions or selling the sacraments), celibate (did they have lovers) or nepotists (were they giving positions to relatives). Along with such queries came the question of whether the clergy were teaching traditional Christianity or ignorantly preaching their own fantasies. The latter could be corrected by education. But there was also the question of whether they were teaching unorthodox ideas deliberately. Clergy and laity deemed to be intentionally teaching false ideas were called "heretics" (members of factions; see 1 Cor 11:19) and it was the bishop's responsibility to control them.

Beginning in the early eleventh century and increasing through the twelfth and thirteenth centuries, a number of heresies arose—and an increasing number of opinions were declared heretical. On the one hand, growing education and developing commerce encouraged the formulation of individual opinions and helped groups propagate their views along trade routes. Thus there really was more diverse opinion after 1000 than before. On the other hand, the efforts of the popes, especially Gregory VII (r. 1073-1085) and his successors, to enforce a moral and intellectual reform of the church centralized at Rome led to the designation of an increasing number of beliefs as heresies. So heresies increased in two ways: diversity of opinion grew, and so did condemnation of diversity.

Concerned about the growth of the two heresies with the greatest

---

[3]Edward Peters, *Inquisition* (Berkeley: University of California Press, 1988); James B. Given, *Inquisition and Medieval Society* (Ithaca, NY: Cornell University Press, 2001).

number of followers (Catharism and Waldensianism), Pope Lucius III in 1184 ordered bishops to search out the heretics in their dioceses and turn them over to the secular authorities for punishment.[4] The secular authorities, concerned with maintaining public order, were usually happy to comply. Then in 1233 Pope Gregory IX established papal inquisitors in areas where heresy was getting beyond the control of the bishops. Inquisitorial procedures did not allow the accused to hear the charges against them or to know who was testifying against them. In 1252 Pope Innocent IV allowed inquisitors to use torture.

However, even when these inquisitions were at their most active, acquittals occurred and the assigned penalties varied from public recantation of errors and fasting to fines, imprisonment and confiscation of property. The famous penalty of burning at the stake was seldom invoked—although even once was too often. There was as yet no "inquisition" in the sense of a centralized office or organization conducting the investigations. On the other hand, the procedures used by the inquisitions, originally inconsistent, gradually became more standardized.

Through the fourteenth and the fifteenth centuries, inquisitions under papal mandate became rarer. But in 1542 Pope Paul III, fearful of Protestantism, revived them and for the first time centralized them in Rome under the auspices of the Holy Office, or Roman inquisition. Unlike the earlier inquisitions, the Holy Office could pursue heresy anywhere in the world under the authority of the pope. In one of the great blots on Christianity—or at least Catholicism—the philosopher Giordano Bruno was burned at the stake in 1600. Bruno has sometimes been hailed as the "first martyr for science," but he was not executed for his scientific views. Rather, he was put to death for being a pantheistic heretic, believing that the universe and God were identical.

In Spain, at the request of King Henry IV of Castile, Pope Pius II in

---

[4]Waldensians (Waldenses) were followers of Valdes (Waldo); they believed that laypersons had the right to preach, which caused them to be condemned as heretics in 1184. Waldensianism took on many forms through the years, contributed to Reformation ideas later, and still exists in small pockets. Catharism was a truly radical dualist heresy; it too had several forms, but its central ideas were that matter was evil and spirit good; Jesus was a spirit whose body was illusory, so that he neither died on the cross nor rose again; sex was evil because it entombed pure spirits in evil bodies; the Old Testament God was really the Devil because he created matter; and redemption consisted of learning how to free the spirit from the body. It was formally condemned as a heresy in 1215.

1462 authorized an inquisition into the activities of Jewish converts who were suspected of reconverting to Judaism. In 1478 Pope Sixtus IV established the infamous Spanish inquisition at the behest of the monarchs Ferdinand and Isabella. This inquisition was strongly centralized and acted as an arm of the Spanish monarchy. In the process of restoring Spain to rule by a Christian monarchy after its long domination by Islam, its rulers felt threatened by Jews and Muslims more than by heretics, so the chief targets of the Spanish inquisition were Jews and Muslims reverting to their religions—a crime considered both political and religious.

The Renaissance, not the Middle Ages, invented the witch hunts, which are the classic historical example of mass paranoia and delusion. During the 1500s and 1600s, most of northwestern Europe (not Spain, Portugal, southern Italy or eastern Europe) was gripped by terror of a vast satanic conspiracy of witches out to destroy Christian society. This conspiracy was a fantasy. There was never a witch cult devoted to Devil worship. It never existed. Yet during the Renaissance alleged witches were condemned and lynched, usually by local authorities, throughout France, northern Italy, Germany, the Low Countries and eventually England, Scandinavia and America. In the rare cases where the accused were allowed to appeal their sentences to higher authorities, such as bishops, the inquisition itself, universities and the Parlement de Paris (the French supreme court), many convictions were overturned. It has recently been statistically shown that the inquisitions actually acted as a brake on the witch craze.[5]

Modern propagandists have vastly exaggerated and inflated the harm done by inquisitions against witchcraft. The facts, as established by serious historians, show that the total number of alleged witches executed over two and a half centuries was about sixty thousand. About a third of the executed were men. Few of the executions were ordered by inquisitions; most were ordered by local authorities, and many of them were mob lynchings. In northwestern Europe, Protestant and Catholic regions were almost exactly equally involved in prosecutions of alleged witches. In Spain, home of the Spanish inquisition, there were hardly any witch trials; the Spanish inquisition was finally abolished in 1834.[6] Torture of any

[5]"Witchcraft," *New Encyclopaedia Britannica* (Macropaedia, 2002), 25:92-93.

[6]Jeffrey Burton Russell and Brooks Alexander, *History of Witchcraft: Sorcerers, Heretics, and Pagans,* 2nd ed. (New York: Thames and Hudson, 2007).

single person, let alone so many, is by Christian principles an intolerable sin. Still, inflating numbers for purposes of propaganda is also wrong.

12. Christians are intolerant fanatics.

Many people believe that Christians are intolerant fanatics, and of course intolerant Christian fanatics have always existed. People who are supposed to follow the Prince of Peace and the Good Shepherd often act less like sheep than hyenas. The illogic comes in going from the particular to the general: some Christians are intolerant; therefore all Christians are intolerant. The word "fanatic" derives from Latin *fanum*, a "temple" or other sacred place, and originally meant a person driven crazy by his or her beliefs. In practice we tend to define a fanatic as anyone who believes anything more than we do. True fanaticism has certain characteristics: closed-mindedness, anger and intimidation. There are fanatical Christians, fanatical atheists, fanatical Muslims, fanatical Marxists, fanatical Hindus—you name it, it has its fanatics.

A certain amount of intolerance is built into any ideology. A Marxist group is unlikely to be tolerant of Catholic bishops; a feminist group is unlikely to be tolerant of pro-lifers; an evangelical group is unlikely to be tolerant of atheist neo-Darwinists. It is not at all clear that religious ideology is more prone to intolerance than secular ideologies, as the subjects of Stalin and Mao learned the hard way. Over 110 million people were killed by antireligious governments during the twentieth century.

It might seem that polytheism (worship of many gods) would be more tolerant than other ideologies, since polytheists accept a variety of gods and can assimilate new deities and new ideas. Greco-Roman polytheism was famously syncretistic (combining religions). It had no problem in adopting other people's deities into its own pantheon. For example, the Greeks and Romans incorporated the Egyptian god Re with their own god Zeus-Jupiter, so that Zeus-Jupiter-Re (and many other combinations) could be worshiped together comfortably. Still, even polytheists riot, persecute and kill in defense of their religions. The medieval Mongols were polytheists. The polytheist Roman authorities from Nero (r. 54-68) to Diocletian (r. 284-305) persecuted Christians, whose refusal to accept polytheism and worship the emperor as god was considered treason.

Monotheistic religions do have a built-in higher level of intolerance. If there is only one God, then worshiping any other entity (or none) is a mortal mistake. Monotheists believe that polytheists (and atheists) who deny the oneness of God are working against the truth. This might seem intolerant, but it is simple logic. You can't be a monotheist and a polytheist at the same time, because they are mutually exclusive.

Some form of cohesion around central beliefs and practices is necessary for survival, as the Jews have proved by retaining their identity over the centuries. Intolerance of other religions is often less strong than intolerance of dissenters within one's own religion, when one feels betrayed by friends and allies. As the Old Testament makes clear, the ancient Israelites were extremely intolerant of fellow Hebrews who lapsed into idolatry. Such lapses often resulted in banishment or death. But ignorant charges have been leveled against the Old Testament. A recent movie scoffed at the idea of "God's jealousy," assuming that the term implies an analogy to the jealousy of a spouse. In fact "jealousy" is related to "zeal" (Greek *zelos*), and its meaning is "vigilant in guarding something," as in "I am jealous of my good name."

The essential point of Christianity is that God became fully human uniquely in Jesus Christ. The New Testament presents Jesus himself as speaking and acting as God. Jesus said that he is "the way, and the truth, and the life" (Jn 14:6). He said that "those who eat my flesh and drink my blood abide in me, and I in them" (Jn 6:56). From early on Christians wondered whether anyone who did not accept Christ could be saved. There was a spectrum of opinions on the question. At one end was the strict view that no one who did not accept him explicitly could be saved. At the other end was the view that in time everyone would be saved. Origen (185-254) and other universalists believed that because Christ came to save all, he would at the end of the world gather all to him.

Early Christians were well aware that many people did not accept Christ. They were in contact with polytheists, some of whom persecuted them. They were also in contact with Jews who did not accept Christ and, from 600 onward, Muslims who acknowledged Christ as a great prophet and even messiah but denied his divinity. Christians also had to consider those who lacked the opportunity to accept Jesus because they never heard of him, either because of geographical distance and isolation or because they had lived before his time. This consideration moved Christianity toward the middle of the spectrum. Most theologians agreed that the Israelite patriarchs and prophets of the Old Testament belong to the body of Christ even though they could not have known about Jesus during their lifetimes. Next it was allowed that virtuous pagans who lived before Christ were also gathered to him. Then it was allowed that virtuous nonbelievers in different lands who had never heard of Christ but pursued a life directed toward love and truth would also be part of his body. But what of those who, having actually heard the good news, rejected Christ and continued to do so? Most Christians agreed that if these accepted him at the end they too would be saved. But they also agreed that those who persisted in denying him to the end of their lives could not enter God's kingdom, for they had deliberately chosen to separate themselves from him.

That left most Christians with the question of how much unbelief was permissible. Clearly the priority was to convert unbelievers by reason, preaching and example. But what if these failed? Was it better to kill unbelievers in this life than to permit them to lose eternal life in the other, more real, world? That question opened the gates of intolerance in dealing with non-Christians. Charlemagne (r. 771-814) gave the conquered Saxons the choice of accepting Christ or being put to death, and at various times Christians have killed other Christians as well as Jews, Muslims, and heretics.

The word *tolerate* has a grudging connotation, as in "I can barely tolerate my neighbor's dog yapping at night." The word appears only twice in the Bible (Esther 3:8; Rev 2:20). Jesus did not teach toleration of people; he taught love for everyone. Toleration in its positive sense characterizes most contemporary Christianity, and Christians can translate that into positive love. The Catholic Second Vatican Council (1962-1965) prescribed that no one should ever be prevented from following his or her conscience (a reasonable judgment as to the moral quality of an act). Educated Christians realize that sincere seekers in other religions have a longing for goodness and truth implanted in them by the Holy Spirit. They agree that most religions can learn from one another. But that hardly means that Christians should cease persuading others to Christ. As one writer puts it, "Is conversion a legitimate goal in dialogue? Yes. It is perfectly legitimate for believers who take seriously the exclusive claims of their religion to try to persuade others of the truth they proclaim."[7] On the assumption that adherents of other re-

[7]Chawkat Moucarry, "A Lifelong Journey with Islam," *Christianity Today*, March 2010, pp. 38-41. *Conversio* in its classical Christian sense means a complete transformation of life (Greek

ligions actually believe in their religions, it may be impossible to understand other religions without actually believing in one's own. It's helpful to assume the honest sincerity of the other person and to begin with what we have in common rather than where we differ.

Some secularists say that anyone who believes that "there are inferior religions is a right-wing extremist."[8] Do they honestly believe that Satanism and Buddhism are equally valid? Some people who identify themselves as Christians argue that Christians should not convert people from other religions and should apologize for trying to convert others to Christ. Such a position directly contradicts both the Bible—specifically Christ's command to preach to all nations—and Tradition. It cannot be considered Christian in any meaningful sense (see Mt 24:14; 28:19; Mk 13:10; Lk 24:47).

According to surveys, young non-Christians feel that Christians who try to convert them do not listen humbly and lack genuine interest in them as individuals.[9] Still, Christians who believe that God works in and through many other religions also believe that Christ is the unique "way, and the truth, and the life" (Jn 14:6), the only passage to complete fulfillment. If one really does believe that, then it seems loving to share the truth with others. Atheists may claim that each person has value, but the claim is based on no underlying principle; it's merely a statement flung into the face of a meaningless cosmos. Without a basis in principle, any person's claim, no matter how fervently expressed, may be denied by any other person. Christians affirm the principle that each person has inherent value because each person is made in the image of God. Tolerance says, I'll put up with you if I have to. Love says, I'm listening to you.

13. Religion causes more war and suffering than atheism does.

This is one of the main antitheist myths. It is deliberate disinformation.[10] Antitheists contend that Christianity, along with Islam and other religions,

---

metanoia), as in the change from caterpillar to butterfly. Thus Christians can convert to deeper Christianity.

[8]Timothy Keller, *Reason for God: Belief in an Age of Skepticism* (New York: Dutton, 2008), p. 7.

[9]David Kinnaman and Gabe Lyons, *unChristian: What a New Generation Really Thinks About Christianity* (Grand Rapids: Baker, 2007), p. 68.

[10]William T. Cavanaugh, *Myth of Religious Violence: Secular Ideology and the Roots of Modern Conflict* (Oxford: Oxford University Press, 2009).

is the chief cause of war and suffering. They argue that it is an essential part of religions to promote or at least tolerate wars and other evils. Remove religion, and we remove the most important obstacle to overall Progress. Though recognizing that most Christian individuals are not directly involved in mayhem, they contend that even those not directly involved support the killers whether they intend to or not. Since Christianity is an evil in itself, all Christians deserve blame. The New Testament, taken with the Old Testament, upholds a wrathful and cruel deity. Granted, some Christians actually do good, but they do so despite their Christianity.

The antitheists see the true face of religion in the crusades, the inquisition, the wars between Protestants and Catholics in the 1500s and 1600s, and the Arab-Jewish struggles of the twentieth and twenty-first centuries. Christians have in fact caused much suffering in the world, as have adherents of other religions. Religious tensions were involved in the hostilities in Israel and Palestine, Ireland, Sri Lanka, Pakistan and India, Nigeria, Iraq, and Bosnia. It can also be argued that evil done by Christians is more shameful than that done in the name of other ideologies, because it directly contradicts the love and forgiveness taught by Christ.

But even in religious wars, religion usually has been a cover for secular power or for ethnic and tribal hatreds. The long civil war in Sri Lanka looked like a clash between Hindus and Buddhists but was more an ethnic war between Tamils and Sinhalese. The religious war in Ireland was much less about the authority of the pope or the queen than about generational hostilities between families.[11] The civil war in Rwanda was entirely tribal. The Thirty Years War (1618-1648) in Europe was less about religion than it was about the power of rulers protecting their turf. The proof is that the war ended only when it was agreed that each ruler could enforce his own religion in the territories he ruled. The conversion of England to Protestantism had much less to do with theology than it did with the personal, political and economic needs of Henry VIII (r. 1507-1549) and his daughter Elizabeth I (r. 1558-1603). Even in this century, more terrorist acts are secular than religious in origin.[12]

---

[11]Terry Eagleton, *Reason, Faith, and Revolution: Reflections on the God Debate* (New Haven, CT: Yale University Press, 2009), p. 141.

[12]John Micklethwait and Adrian Wooldridge, *God Is Back: How the Global Revival of Faith is Changing the World* (New York: Penguin: 2009), p. 309.

Individual atheists, like Christians and other people, often do good, but atheist rulers such Lenin, Hitler, Stalin, Mao Zedong and Pol Pot tortured, starved and murdered more people in the twentieth century than all the combined religious regimes of the world during the previous nineteen centuries. This is not an exaggeration. By the modest estimates of a BBC "war audit" in 2004, atheist rulers killed as many as 110 million people—at least sixty million in the Soviet Union and its satellites, forty million in China, fifteen million in Nazi Germany, two million in Cambodia and five million elsewhere.[13]

Antitheist repression was so successful in the Soviet Union that under the penal code of 1927 you could get ten years' hard labor in a concentration camp for teaching your child the Lord's Prayer.[14] No one can say the exact number of people killed and ruined by atheists, and numbers are numbing. It's more vivid to concentrate on the suffering of an individual such as Anne Frank or the victims that Solzhenitsyn memorializes.[15] The cruelest rulers of the past century aimed at the destruction of religion. Pol Pot learned his atheism in Paris among French existentialists.[16]

The atheist response to these facts is to concede that some atheist leaders were vicious—but it wasn't their atheism that made them vicious. However, all these atheist totalitarians were determined to destroy religion for the simple reason that they knew it competed with their own claims to total authority and power. Violent ideological programs of all sorts have something in common: they whip up hatred and indignation, they repress differing opinions, they strive to annihilate opposition, and they look for scapegoats to dehumanize people. Recently antitheists have taken to describing Christians as leeches, insects, viruses, toxins, vermin and plague-carrying rats. This is reminiscent of the situation in Rwanda, where the genocidal Hutu labeled the Tutsi as "cockroaches."[17]

The antitheist argument boils down to this: a Christian who does evil does so because he or she is a Christian; an atheist who does evil does so

---

[13]Tina Beattie, *New Atheists: The Twilight of Reason and the War on Religion* (Maryknoll, NY: Orbis, 2007), p. 79.

[14]Aikman, *Delusion of Disbelief*, pp. 111-12.

[15]Aleksandr Solzhenitsyn, *Gulag Archipelago*, 3 vols. (New York: Harper and Row, 1974-1978).

[16]Aikman, *Delusion of Disbelief*, p. 127.

[17]David Berlinski, *Devil's Delusion: Atheism and its Scientific Pretensions* (New York: Crown Forum, 2008), p. 185; Beattie, *New Atheists*, pp. 14-15.

despite being an atheist. The absolute reverse could be argued, but either way it's nothing but spin. The obvious fact is that some Christians do evil in the name of Christianity and some atheists do evil in the name of atheism. The solution is to put Christ above the world and love above power.

14. Corrupt clergy show that Christians are hypocrites who do more harm than good.

In 2009 a Pew poll of religious opinions showed that many Christians are leaving churches and that about half of those who have become unaffiliated cited a belief that religious people are hypocritical, judgmental and insincere.[18] Christians are commonly judged to be hypocrites who proclaim their moral superiority to others. Of course, the reality is that almost everyone is a hypocrite because almost everybody fails to live up to their own standards. The only people free of hypocrisy are those who have no standards to live up to. And if one judges others for being judgmental, one is being judgmental oneself. On the other hand, if Christians are just as hypocritical as everyone else, what is the advantage of being a Christian?

The word "hypocrite" comes from the Greek for "actor," someone who pretends to be what he is not. A particularly noxious sort of hypocrite is one who condemns others for immoral actions that he is doing himself. In Christian churches, the existence of so many perverted priests and self-promoting evangelists is a repulsive scandal. Most priests and preachers are genuine, but the valid question is why many are not. Some Christians are total failures at being Christian.

Often people abandon Christ because of painful experiences with Christians as children. But many others are influenced by movies and television, where Christians—especially clergy—are increasingly portrayed as either evil or stupid.[19]

Most Christians fail most of the time to meet the high demands that Christ places on them, but so long as they recognize their faults and try to remedy them, and so long as they do not boast of their virtue, they are no more hypocritical than most people. Recently even the traditional Christian teaching of "hate the sin, love the sinner" has been called hypo-

---

[18]"Faith in Flux: Changes in Religious Affiliation in the U.S.," published April 2009, <www.pewforum.org/newassets/images/reports/flux/fullreport.pdf>.

[19]Philip Jenkins, "Losing Their Religion," *Christian Century*, February 22, 2011, p. 61.

critical, yet it exactly expresses the democratic idea that no human is without sin. God loves everyone; therefore no one ought to judge another person. A person's good qualities are a gift from God, rather than the product of one's virtue.

A candidate for worst person in the world is someone who uses Christianity as a cover for his or her own vices. Since in our society it is Christians who make the most points about moral standards, they stand out most obviously when they do wrong. The church is a human institution, and there has never been any uncorrupted human institution. But the defense to those outside the church that "you're just as bad as we are" is no defense: Christians can properly be asked to hold themselves accountable to their own higher standards.

Many people reject the idea that there are such things as sin and evil. They despise believing that one can be personally responsible for failure, loathe the possibility that they can be at fault, and hate the idea that there are standards by which they might be judged. So they use the handiest weapon they can find against Christianity: the accusation of hypocrisy. On the other hand, any Christian with a holier-than-thou outlook is flouting Christ, for Jesus could not tolerate self-righteous hypocrites.

Does believing in Christianity make us act better? That depends on who we are. A great many atheists behave more admirably than a great many Christians. Would the atheists behave even better if they became Christians? Would the Christians become worse if they became atheists—or perhaps better? The failure of humans to live up to the values they assert is virtually universal. But since Christianity asserts the very highest values, it must make its case. If Christ freed humans to be able not to sin, as Christians claim, shouldn't Christians live demonstrably better lives than those who reject Christ?

Since Christianity is based on devotion to Christ and his commandment to love God with our whole heart and our whole soul and our whole mind, and to love our neighbor as ourselves,[20] why haven't things gotten better since his time on earth? After all, Christ "brought the God of Israel to the nations."[21] The truth is that there are simply too many variables for us to

[20]Jesus said that this commandment, based in the Old Testament, was the greatest of all the commandments. Mt 19:19; 22:37-39; Mk 12:30-33; Lk 10:27. See also Rom 13:8-9; Gal 5:14; Jas 2:8.
[21]Benedict XVI, *Jesus of Nazareth* (New York: Doubleday, 2007), p. 116.

answer the question satisfactorily. The world is not divided into two simple categories, "non-Christian" and "Christian." For one thing, embracing Christianity is not always the same as embracing Christ. Some overtly non-Christian people are doubtless closer to Christ than many churchgoers.

Whether true belief in Christ makes a person better is hard to approach statistically. In any survey the weight of each value would have to be determined beforehand. For example, the survey would have to determine whether "pro-choice" or "pro-life" was morally a better position. There is, however, one obvious good that has been measured statistically: charitable activity. A recent survey on giving showed that religious people (including Christians, Jews, and Muslims) are more generous than nonreligious people. Ninety-one percent of religious people give money while 66 percent of secularists do. Religious people engage in volunteer activity at a rate of 67 percent, secular people at 44 percent.[22] Another quality that truly religious people can have in greater abundance than secularists is gratitude. Wrapped in angry demands and a sense of entitlement, we as a society have lost the knack for gratitude that liberates us from self-centeredness. It is hard to be grateful to a purposeless universe of purely random and mechanical events. Love and gratitude need relationship between conscious beings.

15. CHRISTIANITY SUPPORTED BLACK SLAVERY.

Although slavery is abominable, many Christians supported the slavery of Africans, especially in the Caribbean, Brazil and the United States. It is well known that many of the founders of the United States, such as Washington and Jefferson, had slaves and that most Southern Christians supported the institution. Slavery of African-Americans was brutal exploitation and dehumanization and is a curse on American society.

How much Christianity itself condoned slavery is open to question. Slavery existed worldwide at the time of Christ in almost every country. The Apostles Saints Paul and Peter instructed slaves to obey their earthly masters (Eph 6:5; Col 3:22; Tim 6:1; 1 Pet 2:18) and masters to treat their slaves justly and fairly (Col 4:1). Pro-slavery Christians in America used these texts to declare that slaveholding was consistent with revelation. Anti-slavery Christians explained that Paul was speaking to a specific au-

[22]Arthur C. Brooks, "Religious Faith and Charitable Giving," October 1, 2003, <www.hoover.org/publications/policy-review/article/6577>.

dience at a specific time so that the text had no current application. They noted that being a slave in Greco-Roman times was quite unlike the slavery of Africans in the Americas. Being a slave in the Roman Empire could lead not only to freedom but also to educational, governmental and economic influence and sometimes even to political power. Most important, anti-slavery Christians observed that the emphasis of the New Testament is on liberation, and Paul himself states that masters and slaves are equally important to Christ (Eph 6:9). Paul's first letter to Timothy specifically condemns slave traders as egregious sinners (1 Tim 1:10). A large proportion of the converts to Christianity in the first and second centuries were slaves; obviously they found in the Christian community a marked improvement in their condition.

Two questions arise: the role of slavery worldwide and how slavery played out in the history of Christianity. Slavery is almost universal in the history of human societies. Greeks and Romans, Arabs and Africans, Aztecs and Mayans, Chinese and East Indians, blacks and whites, Christians, Muslims, Jews, Hindus, Buddhists, Confucians, Native Americans, polytheists and monotheists, and atheists—all had slaves at one time and another. The usual source of slaves was enemies captured in war; these were either exploited by their captors directly or sold on to others to be exploited. Their children were usually considered slaves as well. Raids, kidnapping and sentences for crime also yielded slaves. From the oldest records of civilization down into the twenty-first century, slavery has existed. It continues to exist today when people are still enslaved—literally, not figuratively—in sweatshops, in the so-called sex industry, and even as domestics. Women and children suffer most. Slavery exists not only in developing nations but also in the West, including the United States, where it thrives illegally underground.

The almost universal existence of slavery does not excuse Christians from their part in it, particularly because of their supposed devotion to Jesus Christ, who never condoned it and who preached the equality of all humans before God. What is the historical record of Christians in regard to slavery? There were large numbers of Christian slave traders and slave holders from the 1400s to the late 1800s. How did that happen?

Let's begin with the history of Christianity in its first few centuries. The greatest numbers of Christians were located within the Roman

Empire. Greco-Roman society had been based on slavery, but by A.D. 400, when the empire was fairly well Christianized, slavery was in terminal decline. Many factors were involved: the end of Roman conquests deprived the conquerors of new supplies of vanquished people to enslave, and the Germanic peoples who had settled in the empire did not have slaves. Christians, who at least before 300 were mostly poor, seldom had slaves either.

Christian theologians and other Christian writers clearly did not take Paul's writings as promoting slavery: they gradually and successfully pressed for greater rights for slaves. Christians recognized slaves' marriages as binding. Slaves took part in all Christian worship with no distinction between them and free persons. Slaves served as clergy, even occasionally as bishops. There were no barriers to marriage between slave and free. However, slavery was such an ancient, established institution that before 300, Christians, while demanding the good treatment of slaves, seldom denounced the institution as a whole. After 300, the moral pressure to fully emancipate slaves continually mounted. Gregory of Nyssa (330-395) condemned the whole institution.[23] Augustine (354-430) in the West and John Chrysostomos (347-407) in the East preached that slavery was a sin.

By 700 there were few slaves in Europe other than in marginal societies such as that of the pagan Vikings. Much agricultural labor was provided by serfs on manors. Serfs, resembling sharecroppers more than slaves, usually had their personal rights guaranteed by law though even they were not allowed to leave the large manorial estates without permission. Muslim areas retained slavery into modern times: Saudi Arabia abolished it in 1962 and Mauritania in 1981. Muhammad himself owned slaves. Muslim society not only enslaved many of its white subjects but also imported black slaves from sub-Saharan Africa. The best estimates (no one kept exact figures) put the number of African slaves taken north and east by Muslims and the number taken west by Christians as roughly equal for the whole period from the 700s to the 1800s—probably more than fifteen million each, a gruesome total.

Since slavery was rare in medieval Europe, it was seldom a matter even of discussion. Theologians condemned slavery when they did think about

---

[23]David Bentley Hart, *Atheist Delusions: The Christian Revolution and Its Fashionable Enemies* (New Haven, CT: Yale University Press, 2009), pp. 176-82.

it. Thomas Aquinas (1225-1274) declared it contrary both to natural law and to the fact that Christ died for all humans equally. Although medieval Europe was largely free of slavery, that situation began to change in the 1400s with the expansion of Spanish and Portuguese colonization. As the famous sociologist Rodney Stark observes, morality was shoved aside whenever slavery was immensely profitable.[24]

Although slaves of many nationalities were common around the Mediterranean Sea, the first African slaves were shipped as chattels to Europe by a Portuguese ship in 1441. In 1452, Pope Nicholas V gave permission to enslave Muslim and pagan prisoners: the first official Christian approval of slavery. But in 1462 Pope Pius II declared slavery a *magnum scelus* ("great crime"). By the early 1500s slavery was common in the Spanish and Portuguese colonies. Native Americans were enslaved first, but they proved uneconomical because they often escaped or succumbed to imported European diseases, so vast numbers of slaves began to be imported from sub-Saharan Africa. The first African slaves arrived in British American colonies in 1619, on a Dutch ship docking at Jamestown, Virginia. They were at first treated much like indentured servants, but the expansion of tobacco and cotton made field labor necessary to landowners, and slaves became personal property like a horse or a chair.

The beginnings of abolition can be seen almost as far back as the revival of slavery. Christianity—what Stark calls "moral fervor"—was the main source of the movement. In 1435 Pope Eugenius IV excommunicated Europeans enslaving inhabitants of the Canary Islands, an early territory of the Spanish and Portuguese. In 1537, Pope Paul III condemned the enslavement of any American Indians and demanded that they be freed. The Jesuit theologian Francisco Suárez (1548-1617) developed the idea of inalienable rights such as life and liberty inherent in every human being. In 1591, Pope Gregory XIV repeated the condemnation of the enslavement of Indians. Pope Urban VIII (1623-1644) condemned all slavery of Africans, Native Americans, or anyone. In 1686 the Holy Office (the Roman inquisition) condemned slavery.

All these condemnations were squarely against the economic interests of Catholic Spain and Portugal. Some Catholic clergy attempted to put

---

[24]Rodney Stark, *For the Glory of God: How Monotheism Led to Reformations, Science, Witch-Hunts, and the End of Slavery* (Princeton, NJ: Princeton University Press, 2003), pp. 291-365.

these condemnations into practice. The movie *The Mission* (1986) presents an accurate picture of what happened when the Jesuit order set up an independent republic for the Guarani Indians in order to protect them from slavery by Spanish and Portuguese colonists. The slaveholders complained bitterly to the Spanish and Portuguese governments, which quickly expelled the Jesuits from their dominions. The Jesuits working with the Guarani were killed along with the Indians they were trying to protect.

Beginning in about 1750 Christian opposition to the slave trade got new life, especially among Protestant Evangelicals. In 1754 John Woolman led the Quakers in launching a campaign against the slave trade in America, and by 1771 Massachusetts outlawed the importation of slaves. In England, John Wesley (1703-1791), the founder of Methodism, was involved with the Society for the Abolition of the Slave Trade, which was founded in 1787 by an evangelical Anglican Member of Parliament, William Wilberforce (1759-1833). Protestant Denmark outlawed slave trading in 1803, the United Kingdom in 1807, the United States in 1808, the Netherlands in 1818. Meanwhile in 1815 Pope Pius VII demanded the abolition of the trade, and in 1839 Pope Gregory XVI (r. 1831-1846) sent a pastoral letter to American Catholics condemning all slavery.

All of these actions were based on the conviction that slavery is contrary to Christianity. French abolitionism was informed by both Christian and Enlightenment ideas of the rights of man, and France abolished the trade in 1831. Meanwhile, some American admirers of the Enlightenment such as Thomas Jefferson continued to hold slaves. Washington freed his slaves at his death; Jefferson did not. Many Enlightenment figures in Europe, such as Voltaire, Montesquieu, Mirabeau and Burke, continued to condone slavery, while others, including Adam Smith, Diderot, Turgot, Samuel Johnson and Condorcet, condemned it. Despite the outlawing of the overseas slave trade by the United States, domestic slave trading continued as cotton became the South's staple industry and men, women and children were sold down the Mississippi River to the expanding cotton fields in the Deep South.

After the abolition of the slave trade, the abolition of slavery itself was next on the Christian agenda. In 1833 the American Anti-Slavery Society was founded, the majority of its membership being Protestant clergy. In the same year the United Kingdom abolished slavery. France outlawed it in 1848. In the Latin American republics slavery was abolished over the period from 1803 to 1854. The last Christian holdouts were Spain, which abolished slavery in Cuba only in 1886, and Brazil, which waited until 1888. The United States, despite strong abolitionist sentiment, did not secure the abolition of slavery until 1865 at the end of the Civil War. Stark is right that only when the economics of slavery weakened could Christian morality triumph; however, the record shows that without Christianity, slavery would have persisted longer—perhaps much longer. Christian ideas of justice and equality were at the heart of the civil rights movement of the 1960s, which was led by both African-American and white Christians. As two writers observe, "Its leadership was almost entirely composed of clergymen, many of them with highly traditional theological views."[25]

16. Christianity consists of "thou shalt nots."

Prohibited activity isn't what Christianity is about, but a lot of people, both Christians and non-Christians, think that it is. Important as the Ten Commandments are, they are not the center of Christian teaching. Most Christians regard Christ as leading to true freedom rather than his promoting legalisms.

Generations of stern priests in the confessional and ranting preachers in the pulpit helped create the common image of killjoy, wet-blanket Christianity. Scolding about sin burnt a negative image into children and adolescents, particularly in regard to sex. Teaching about sex in the nineteenth and early twentieth centuries centered on what we ought not to do rather than what we ought to do, so a lot of Christians emerged from adolescence with a sense of religion as a sinister force restraining and condemning their instincts. Their negative view has become an ingrained cliché in modern culture.

When the Vatican issued a statement urging Christians to participate positively in narrowing the gap between rich and poor, preventing waste and pollution, and striving for energy efficiency, the media's reaction was to flip the statement to fit the negative cliché. The event was reported with headlines such as "Vatican updates its thou-shalt-not list"[26] and "Thou

---

[25]Micklethwait and Wooldridge, *God Is Back*, p. 97.

[26]Associated Press, "Vatican Updates Its Thou-Shalt-Not List," Newsvine, March 10, 2008,

shalt not . . . forget to recycle: From the folks who brought you the Inquisition comes a new set of deadly sins."[27] Both Protestant and Catholic leaders have been moving to embrace the environmental movement, but the media's response makes it appear that many of its members would rather mock Christians than agree with them about anything.

The negative commandments of the Bible are outweighed by a greater number of "you shalls," including "You shall love the Lord your God all your heart, and with all your soul, and with all your strength, and with all your mind; and your neighbor as yourself," which Jesus later affirmed was the basic message of religion (Lev 19:18; Deut 6:4-5; Lk 10:27). Jesus repeatedly stated that his message was love more than law. The word "joy" appears in the New Testament more than fifty times, the word "love" more than two hundred and twenty. In the Old Testament, "love" occupies four columns of the concordance (an index of words in the Bible) as opposed to slightly more than one for "hate." Christianity's essence is not restriction but freedom. This freedom does not mean license to do whatever one feels like but rather freedom to open oneself to reaching one's full potential in compassionate energy.

Christianity is not primarily a religion of rules. It is a religion of relationship to a person, Jesus. This relationship requires acting in ways consonant with love of God and love of neighbor. Churches, being human, have tended to draw up detailed sets of rules. The need is for creative balance between anarchy and autocracy, between prophecy and order. To live, any organization needs to balance the prophets and trailblazers with the conservatives who keep the truth clear and the organization together.

17. CHRISTIANITY STUNTS SELF-DEVELOPMENT AND PERSONAL HAPPINESS.

Many people feel that Christianity is an obstacle to personal fulfillment. The old evangelical call "There's room for you at the foot of the cross" lacks appeal in a consumerist society.

The word *happy* derives from "hap," meaning chance or luck, whereas the Christian view of happiness is the complete fulfillment of a person's

---

<www.newsvine.com/_news/2008/03/10/1356304-vatican-updates-its-thou-shalt-not-list>.

[27]Barry Gottlieb, "Thou Shalt Not . . . Forget to Recycle," *Los Angeles Times*, March 17, 2008 <articles.latimes.com/2008/mar/17/opinion/oe-gottlieb17>.

potential as a human being: fulfillment as an individual, in society and in God. That state of being is joy, or "intense and especially ecstatic or exultant happiness," as the *American Heritage Dictionary* defines it. The Christian view welcomes not only spiritual pleasures but sensual ones as well. Sex, food, drink, sports, music and nature: all are to be enjoyed. Christianity (along with most other religions and philosophies) observes that when the search for pleasure isn't limited by reason, happiness is decreased rather than increased. For example, Christians believe that although "hooking up" may produce temporary social gratification and status as well as physiological and psychological pleasure, it militates against the lifetime happiness of partnership, love, commitment and trust. As pleasures and worries increase, they tend to crowd God out. It's the difference between grabbing what seems good and receiving the substantial good.

To materialists this is plain nonsense, pie in the sky, what Marxists call false consciousness. A materialistic and ego-centered culture finds repugnant the idea that Christianity is primarily about what we can do for others and Christ and only secondarily about what it can do for us.[28] If it isn't me-centered, what use is it? Increasingly in a culture that is also media-driven, preferences are based on superficial, and often erroneous, ideas. Fashion is a form of herd instinct that's difficult to resist. Self-gratification is the hallmark of contemporary culture. And many churches present Christianity so weakly that people think God's job is to boost their own self-esteem.[29]

If we believe that our ego is everything, we have effectively annihilated the universe for ourselves, and our ego finds itself eternally alone with itself in the void. The French poet Victor Hugo (1802-1885) described how the ego may at last realize its desolation and make a final effort to regain reality in the shape of the one last star in the vast emptiness. "Toward the star trembling pale on the horizon he pressed, leaping from one dark foothold to another. He ran, he flew, he cried out: Golden star! Brother! Wait for me! I am coming! Do not die yet! Do not

[28]The word "egotism" appeared by 1714 and "egoism" by 1785; by 1800 both words implied conceit or selfishness. "Egotistical" appeared by 1825. The positive idea of "the ego" as self-awareness appeared (as a translation of Freud's *ich,* German for "I") in 1910.

[29]Kenda Creasy Dean, *Almost Christian: What the Faith of Our Teenagers Is Telling the American Church* (New York: Oxford University Press, 2010).

leave me alone. . . . And the star was dying beneath his anguished stare . . . and the star went out."[30]

Those who serve others or a higher cause are more likely to be happy than those who pursue personal fame and fortune, and gratitude is an important element in happiness. The firmer one's faith, the more optimistic and less depressed one tends to be. I am privileged to have known a man who suffered terribly in both Nazi and Communist concentration camps and who came to forgive and live a life marked by kindness and gratitude. Love and gratitude are keys to harmony.

It's a common belief that a person's relationship with God is primarily, or even exclusively, an individual one, but the traditional view of Catholics, Orthodox and many Protestants is that community is the center of worship. From the first century onward, the community Eucharist (Greek *eucharisto*, "to thank")—Holy Communion or the Lord's Supper—was a distinguishing and determining practice of Christian worship. The "Lord's Supper" (Greek *kyriakon deipnon*) is the earliest term for this ritual (1 Cor 11:20). Individualism is rooted in the Protestant Reformation of the sixteenth century, when the emphasis of worship shifted from the sacramental to the biblical. With that shift, individuals could worship God by reading the Scriptures for themselves. Most Protestants hold that this ought to accompany rather than replace congregational worship, and for centuries Protestants were faithful in church attendance with the expectation that the Bible would be explained to them by the preacher.

In the twentieth century, an idea developed that each person could fully understand the Bible all by himself or herself. This notion is neither traditional nor biblical. Human beings are social animals. Though both the Old and New Testaments tell of prophets withdrawing into solitude for a time, it was always with the purpose of helping the community. The word "church" comes from the Greek *ekklesia*, meaning an assembly or congregation. Except for the most extreme hermits, even the monks of the desert worshiped together. Pope Benedict XVI asks, "How could the idea have developed that Jesus' message is narrowly individualistic and aimed only at each person singly? How did we arrive at this interpretation of the 'salvation of the soul' as a flight from responsibility for the whole, and how

---

[30]Victor Hugo, "La Fin de Satan," in *Poésie*, ed. B. Leuilliot (Paris: Laffond, 1972), 3:216-301.

did we come to conceive the Christian project as a selfish search for salvation which rejects the idea of serving others?"[31] It may be that commitment to others is a necessary ingredient of happiness.[32]

Many people consider themselves "spiritual" with no need for "organized religion." But "organized religion" is a pleonasm—both words convey the same meaning. Throughout time religion has by definition been organized. Latin *religio* meant community worship for ancient polytheists, Jews and Christians. By breaking with organization, people break with community. People say, "I want to think for myself." The problem is that no one is uninfluenced by the thought of others. If we listen to the radio or watch TV, if we have friends, if we go to classes or the movies, if we get information from magazines or newspapers or the Internet, if we see billboards, we are constantly being told what to believe, and we need a sharpened skill of discernment to sort out the true from the false, the dubious from the well-established. If we lack discernment based on objective values, somebody is eventually going to impose his or her values on us. To really be free one cannot close oneself off from evidence; one must be aware of the options and evaluate them. Increasing ignorance of cultural facts is a great boon to exploiters of every sort.

In our culture there has been a great revulsion against traditions of all kinds (except the most trivial, such as the descending ball on New Year's Eve). Tradition is considered hidebound, stifling and authoritarian rather than salutary, sane and whole. Tradition can certainly take rigid forms, but its deep meaning is open, not closed. Christian Tradition (Latin *traditio*, Greek *paradosis*) literally means "handing over" and refers primarily to the revelation of Christ to the apostles (Greek *apostoloi*, "those who are sent out") and then to the church for meditation on that revelation throughout the centuries. Rather than the idea of any one person, Christian Tradition is the accumulated knowledge and wisdom established over a period of two thousand years. As Pope John Paul II wrote, "The appeal to tradition is not a mere remembrance of the past; it involves rather the recognition of a cultural heritage which belongs to all of humanity."[33] Christian Tra-

[31]Benedict XVI, *Spe salvi* ("Saved in Hope"; San Francisco: Ignatius Press, 2007), part 16.
[32]Chuck Colson, "Lost Art of Commitment," *Christianity Today*, August 2010, p. 49. Douglas John Hall, in "Cross and Context," *Christian Century*, September 7, 2010, pp. 34-40, shows how Americans have turned the virtue of hope into a smiley face of easy happiness.
[33]Pope John Paul II, *Fides et ratio* ("Faith and Reason"), 1998, part 7, para. 85.

dition is a living body of truth encompassing past, present and future. Its accumulated wisdom is more likely to be true than what we contemporaries invent for ourselves.

Many people believe that if we get rid of traditions—and the past in general—humanity will arise clean and new and wholesome, free and equal and generous. The concept originated with Jean-Jacques Rousseau (1712-1778), whose influential novel *Emile* was "a treatise on the natural goodness of man, intended to show how vice and error are foreign to his constitution. . . . The first movements of nature are always right; there is no original perversity in the human heart."[34]

However, the idea of humanity's innate goodness and belief in our general, universal, overall Progress (allowing for a few ups and downs) is widely believed because it is comforting, not because it is true. It is the great superstition of our age. It has led to many improvements—such as the abolition of slavery—but it has also led to ignorant and bloody revolutions and the most repressive tyrannies. Most of the vicious dictators of the twentieth century persuaded their people (and sometimes themselves) that they were making a better world. The greatest "problem with the myth of progress is . . . that it cannot deal with evil."[35] Legislating for an idealized future distracts us from trying to lighten suffering where we encounter it. Only if there is a purpose drawing the cosmos toward its goal can there be Progress, and then only by understanding what the goal is.[36] The myth of Progress is "the pseudo-theological . . . great god of modern ideologies" that blinds us to the reality of radical evil and thus enables it to flourish.[37]

Historically Christianity is less focused on personal fulfillment, self-esteem or self-development than on following Christ and loving and serving God and neighbor, and on responding to the beauty of God's love with gratitude. If one has even a single moment of pure happiness and joy, then one's life is worth living. It might even be said that even if only one creature ever had only one moment of joy, the universe would

---

[34]Alan Jacobs, *Original Sin: A Cultural History* (New York: HarperCollins, 2008), p. 149.

[35]N. T. Wright, *Surprised by Hope: Rethinking Heaven, the Resurrection, and the Mission of the Church* (New York: HarperOne, 2008), p. 85.

[36]Dale A. Russell, *Islands in the Cosmos: The Evolution of Life on Land* (Bloomington: Indiana University Press, 2009).

[37]Tracey Rowland, *Ratzinger's Faith: The Theology of Pope Benedict XVI* (Oxford: Oxford University Press, 2009), p. 39.

be worth creating. Happiness doesn't always produce gratitude, but gratitude always produces happiness.

18. Christianity is insensitive to other beliefs.

Many people feel that Christians are insensitive to those with other beliefs. Of course, lots of other people are insensitive, too, but Christians run a special risk of appearing so because they believe Christ calls them to convert others. When people believe that Christians befriend them only to get something out of them—agreement or conversion—open dialogue is virtually impossible. If one side in a discussion is absolutely certain that they are right, the discussion becomes a sermon, lecture or rant. In a real dialogue, each party is willing to listen and learn from the other. Unlike adherents of some persuasions, Christians are always enjoined to treat others with loving respect. Most other religions have insights that Christians can admire and learn from, and Christians have found people more willing to listen to them if they listen to others. Everyone, Christian or not, is more true to truth by granting the presumption of good will to the other side, even when it doesn't seem evident.

Christians cannot believe that all religions are equal, because they believe that Christ is God, and it's impossible for Christ both to be God and also not to be God. The only way that all religions can be equal is if they are all meaningless. On the other hand, Christians can learn from people of other faiths; they can love them; they can listen to them; they can refrain from condescending to them or judging their ultimate relationship to God or even Christ. Many people who are not Christians are surely closer to Christ than many who claim to be Christians. Only Christ knows. The bottom line, though, is that Christians believe Christ to be the unique and ultimate fulfillment of humanity. To believe otherwise is not to be Christian.

19. Christianity is mainly about sin.

Christianity is mainly about love, forgiveness and gratitude. Still, Christianity does teach the reality of sin, an unpopular idea in a culture where self-esteem is paramount. Many people declare that there is no such thing as sin.

For Christians, the essence of sin is deliberately choosing to advance oneself above the rightful needs of others, thereby separating oneself from God, moral reality, community and ultimately oneself. Sin is arrogant: it says Important Me, Pointless You. In a just and harmonious world, hurting other people would be something we would not do and would not even want to do. But obviously we do not live in a just and harmonious world. According to Christianity, sin rips the fabric of reality. A crime consists of breaking a public law, whereas a sin consists of breaking the relationship with God and neighbor. Secular ethics assume that hurtful behavior can be corrected or even avoided by improving society. Christianity recognizes a fatal flaw deep in humanity that can be healed only by the free choice of the good.

The core reality of this fatal flaw is asserted again and again in both the Old and New Testaments. Humans are alienated from God—from the true, the good and the beautiful. For Christians, the purpose of God's becoming human in Jesus Christ was to break down the barriers of alienation and open wide the door to love and gratitude. Putting it more traditionally: to save humans by breaking their bondage to sin.

In the Bible, sin is both communal and individual. The community as a whole, including the Christian community, sins through lack of love. This was the emphasis of the early church, where confessions of both communal and individual sin were made openly in the churches. Public, communal confession was gradually replaced during the Middle Ages by private confession to a priest, a custom that became established by the twelfth century. Penances (Latin *poenae*, "punishments") were assigned, but the sins were not made public and confessors were obliged by church law not to reveal them. A valid confession included recognizing and confessing sins, making up for them, and asking for Christ's mercy—essentially turning oneself over to Christ—in helping the sinner cease to sin.

Jesus never issued a catalog of sins according to their gravity: both the greatest and the least of sins were forgiven by turning the character toward the good. The early Christian community, like most other communities, recognized that some faults are worse than others: insulting my neighbor is a sin, but murdering or enslaving him is obviously a much graver sin. The Christian community believed that both community and individual had to be burnt clean from their sins before being able to enter into the full presence of God. It seemed to follow that worse sins needed more purging than lesser ones. The idea of making up for sins originally centered on the sinner's going to the person he has hurt and repairing the damages.

As the church grew larger, and as cases were often complicated by the involvement of numerous parties, personal reconciliation became less frequently possible, so a set of rules were gradually developed. Personal reconciliation was still the center, but making up for the sin became more complex and impersonal. Beginning in the 600s, lists called "penitentials" ranked sins according to their gravity and specified the penances appropriate for each. From the 1100s, these rather mechanical books went out of use and were replaced by confessional handbooks that gave the confessor (the person to whom one confessed) latitude in assigning penances. By the 1100s, the confessor was almost always a clergyman. Having confessed, the penitent person was assigned penances, which ranged from the mildest, involving prayers, to the rare extreme such as whipping.

Indulgences—exemptions from penance—were used from the eleventh century, but in the 1500s a drastic abuse of confession crept in: the sale of these indulgences. The idea was that if one could do penance through prayer, pilgrimage and other acts, why not through money? The church approved the sale of indulgences in order to raise money for the rebuilding of St. Peter's cathedral in Rome. One could buy indulgences for one's relatives and friends as well as for oneself.

Incensed by the abuse of indulgences, Protestants condemned them and argued that a church that could approve such things must be false. Protestants then rejected the need for private confession, affirming that an individual could confess directly to God and explicitly emphasizing that God alone, without the intermediary of a priest, had the power to absolve from sin. From the late twentieth century, private confession has become rarer in Catholic churches, while a number of Protestant churches have adopted it in circumstances where an individual requests it. Recently most denominations have preferred long-range "spiritual direction" of individuals over quick "confession," but that requires a high proportion of directors, and few churches of any denomination have nearly enough.

The church has historically distinguished between lesser sins and mortal (deadly) sins. The traditional but never official "seven deadly sins" go back in one form or another to at least the 400s. They are usually listed as pride (arrogance), avarice, lust, envy, gluttony, anger and sloth. At certain times, as in the 1100s when capitalism was beginning to emerge, some argued that avarice ought to head the list in place of pride. Ordinarily, pride and arrogance were considered the worst because they were the original sin of Satan and of Adam and Eve.

Opposed to the "seven deadly sins" and also going back at least to the 400s were the "seven gifts of the Holy Spirit": wisdom, understanding, counsel, fortitude, knowledge, piety and respect for the Lord (derived from Is 11:2). These are called gifts than rather than virtues, because virtue is regarded as something an individual has within himself and can consequently boast of (as the ancient heroes of epics did). Boasting, along with pounding the pulpit, thumping the lectern, and shaking condescending fingers, are signs of self-righteousness, one of the things Jesus disliked most. In Christianity, any goodness that a person has is a free gift from God. The opposite of sin, Christians believe, is peace, forgiveness and gratitude.

20. CHRISTIANITY IMPEDES PROGRESS.

The predominant superstition of our times is Progress. Belief in lowercase progress is reasonable, for in specific fields such as electrical engineering, plumbing or surgery, progress can be made toward definable goals. But people often believe in overall Progress, as in "The Progress of Humanity." This is a superstition. Upper-case Progress implies progress toward a capital-G Goal. Without a goal you can have no progress.

If you set out for Seattle, then every minute you are closer to Seattle you are closer to your goal. But if you have no goal, every minute you are closer to Seattle is pointless and no progress at all. What, then, is the capital-G Goal? Enlightenment progressives such as Washington and Jefferson maintained that "life, liberty and the pursuit of happiness" were self-evident human rights, yet they did not apply them to slaves. And in many societies, these goals have not seemed self evident at all.[38]

The frightening question about the Progress of humanity is, who decides what it is? Hitler and Lenin believed in "Progress." So do a number of contemporary intellectuals. Here's one current example: "The direction

---

[38]Matt Ridley, in *The Rational Optimist: How Prosperity Evolves* (New York: Harper, 2010), argues that material prosperity increases with time, but that prosperity does not correlate closely with other values.

of history, as set by basic dynamics of cultural evolution, pragmatically pushes people toward useful doctrines that, wonderfully enough, contain elements of moral truth."[39] That would be wonderful indeed, if there were anything meaningful in the sentence. Of course, the author assumes he knows what "moral truth" is, and unsurprisingly it looks like the currently fashionable "correct" worldview.

Terry Eagleton challenges the idea of Progress: "At the peak of his assurance, Enlightenment man finds himself frighteningly alone in the universe, with nothing to authenticate himself but himself. His dominion is accordingly shot through with a sickening sense of arbitrariness and contingency, which will grow more acute as the modern age unfolds."[40] Eagleton discredits "the ideology of Progress, for which the past is so much puerile stuff to be banished to the primeval forests of prehistory. . . . Those who hope to sail into that future by erasing the past will simply find it returning with a vengeance."[41] The natural goodness of humanity is an illusion based neither in history nor biology, and the empty center of most Progressivism is the delusion that radical evil does not exist. Progressivism can become utopianism, which always sacrifices liberty for its ends, as Stalin did. Those who deny evil will be overtaken by it.

Secularists seeking a rational future have replaced the Christian view of the kingdom of God at the end of the world with the idea of the perfect society at the end of the world.[42] The idea of Progress has produced countless hideous cruelties by those who, like Lenin and Mao and ideologues today, are eager to force others to accept their ideological definition of the good society. These definitions are in constant flux owing to the fact that they rest on the power exerted by pressure groups instead of being based on universal principles such as truths we hold to be self-evident. On the many occasions when Christians themselves have used violence for what they felt were good ends, they were not behaving as Christians. In Christianity the end does not justify the means.

One of the lesser faults of Progress is that we assume previous civilizations didn't know anything more than what we happen to have dis-

---

[39]Robert Wright, *Evolution of God* (New York: Little, Brown, 2009), p. 286.

[40]Eagleton, *Reason, Faith, and Revolution*, p. 82.

[41]Ibid., p. 90.

[42]Norman Cohn, *Pursuit of the Millennium*, 2nd ed. (New York: Oxford University Press, 1970).

covered about them. It might be worth pondering the fact that ancient Egyptian civilization lasted more than three thousand years, whereas the United States is still working on 250.

A few of the specific charges against Christianity currently being bandied about are that it keeps people down and submissive (like Nelson Mandela), it's fascistic (like Mother Teresa), and it opposes political pluralism (like John Kennedy and Jimmy Carter). Christianity does breed tyranny sometimes, but also democracy: the ideals of Thomas Jefferson (1743-1826) descend in a direct line from those of John Locke (1632-1704), Sir Edward Coke (1552-1634), Marsilius of Padua (1275-1342), John of Salisbury (1115-1180) and Pope Gregory VII (1073-1085).

Change is not necessarily change for the better: Germany changed from a democratic republic in 1932 to a racist tyranny in 1934. Those who espouse Progress today might recall that belief in Progress was at its height a hundred years ago just at the beginning of the century that produced the most horrible events of history. For an exhaustive list of the people killed (not including those maimed, tortured, imprisoned and bereaved) during the years from 1910 to the present, see David Berlinski's tally.[43] Berlinski concludes that the "excess of stupidity" over the past century hardly inclines one to believe in overall Progress.[44]

Even so, Christians have a notable record of social constructiveness, including the creation of orphanages and universities; abolition of slavery; developments in science, natural law, women's rights and civil rights; advocacy for the rights of the poor; growth of democracy, and the struggle against poverty and oppression. Many humanists and other nonreligious people have worked for the same ends without recognizing that their basis is the Christian idea that the world ought to look as much like the kingdom of God as possible. Even the *Economist* magazine occasionally admits that religious people play major roles in alleviating suffering.[45] Charity is the fulfillment of the commandment to love our neighbor as ourselves, and Christians have always expressed that charity in hospitals, schools, famine relief and many other ways.

---

[43]Berlinski, *Devil's Delusion*, pp. 22-24.

[44]Ibid., p. 25.

[45]"Kingdoms of This World, and Otherwise: The Rich, the Poor, and Their Advocates," *The Economist*, January 25, 2007, <www.economist.com/node/8602944>.

21. Christianity supports war and the death penalty.

The misconception springs partly from those who identify Christianity with political neoconservatism and partly (and oddly) from those hating pro-life views. Since allegedly correct people know that Christianity is bad, they can't believe that Christians support anything good. They hate to admit any overlap between correctness and Christianity. Therefore if it is correct to oppose war and the death penalty, then they assume that Christians are in favor of them. Such misconceptions are not only illogical and tendentious; they are contradicted by the evidence.

Categorizing Christians by their political beliefs is a fallacy common to people who think primarily in political terms. They don't understand that Christianity is not based in politics and therefore fits categories of neither left nor right. Personally, I enjoy getting solicitations from both Left and Right organizations. Christianity has no political agenda because Jesus Christ made it absolutely clear that he rejected political agendas. Christianity and politics are fundamentally different ways of viewing the world; all connections between them are temporary.

During the first two centuries, faithful Christians in the Roman Empire followed Christ's mandate for peace, often refusing to serve in the army and being imprisoned or executed as a result. When the Roman Empire converted to Christianity in the 300s, most Christians turned from witnesses against imperial power to supporters of it. The empire began to seem less like the antichrist than a divine vehicle for spreading the gospel, so "onward, Christian soldiers."[46] From that time on, Christian thinkers tried to limit war by distinguishing between unjust war and just war. Theories varied, but the main criteria for a just war were that it had to be (a) declared by a legitimate authority, (b) in a just cause (defensively), (c) waged for the purpose of advancing good, (d) waged by limited means: noncombatants were not to be harmed, and (e) the victors must restore justice and not advance their own power beyond its original scope.

Of course the theory hardly worked in practice. The theory assumes absolute criteria for justice, but in practice it was too easy for belligerents

---

[46]The word "gospel" derives from Old English *godspell,* meaning "good news" (Greek *euangelion*).

to define legitimate authority, just cause, good, and limited means in whatever way suited their own purposes. By the late twentieth century the theory had faded enough for powers to flout these rules grossly and repeatedly. Newscasters still express especial outrage when women and children are killed in a bombing. Their outrage derives from Christianity: before Christ, the torture, murder and enslavement of women and children was normal in war. One Viking warrior was mocked by his colleagues as "the children's man" because he refused to kill babies.[47]

During the Middle Ages the church made occasional efforts to limit wars of Christians against one another. Although the idea spread and significant limitations on warfare were achieved, the plan was eventually scuttled by the unwillingness of rapacious warriors to submit to church rules. Also, from the time of Urban II (r. 1088-1099), popes usually considered wars against non-Christians to be just. The European Wars of Religion in the 1500s and 1600s are often justifiably cited as an example of the warlike behavior of Christians. Religion, however, was a façade for the struggle for political power among the princes, and the wars ended in the submission of religious power to secular power. The result was the creation of the modern state free from religious control and responsible to nothing other than itself.[48] It was "the first phase of a new age of territorial and (ultimately) ideological wars, nationalist and (then) imperialist wars, wars prompted by commerce, politics, colonial interests, blood and soil."[49]

The impracticability of the just war theory has always led some Christians to adopt pacifism on the model of Jesus himself. Christians today are divided on the subject, though most hold some degree of just war opinion. They often cite the struggle against the Nazis as conclusive evidence that some wars can be just, even though the Allies as well as their enemies honored the ideal of limited war by ignoring its principles. It's hard to reconcile the destruction of civilian cities such as Dresden and Hiroshima with the principle of just war. Neither Christ nor essential Christianity condones the taking of life under any circumstances, but historically most Christians have acquiesced in doing so. Despite this record, the civil rights

---

[47]Jeffrey Burton Russell, *Medieval Civilization* (New York: Wiley, 1968), p. 187.
[48]Hart, *Atheist Delusions*.
[49]Ibid., p. 97.

and antiwar movements of the 1960s were enthusiastically supported by many Christians and counted Christians among their leaders: Catholic leaders such as Father Theodore Hesburgh of the University of Notre Dame marched in civil rights protests hand in hand with Protestant leaders such as the Reverend Martin Luther King Jr.

One of the most divisive issues today is abortion. It is said that Christians are wicked to oppose abortion, and so they surely must hold wicked views on war and capital punishment as well. Some Christians do support war and capital punishment, just as other Christians oppose them. But a consistent Christian view, supporting the protection of human life at all the natural stages of life beginning at conception, is opposed to war, capital punishment, abortion and infanticide. During the eugenics craze of the late nineteenth and early twentieth century, many American and British scientists and politicians joined their German counterparts in arguing for the selective improvement of the human race by culling those they considered unfit in order to promote racial progress. This often meant the plan to advance allegedly superior Caucasian and especially northern European genes; this is where Hitler's ideas came from. The main and most effective opposition to the eugenics program came from Christians.[50] And now that eugenics has been revived under the euphemism of genetic engineering, it still does.

22. Christianity favors the rich.

The rich have often supported Christianity when it's to their advantage. Christians often allow themselves to be co-opted by the rich and powerful, a prime example being the alliance of the churches with the monarchies in Europe from the 1500s into the 1800s. The rich are usually powerful people with the ability to secure preferences for those who support them, including church leaders. Bishops and other Christian leaders were often appointed by the powerful and sometimes became rich and powerful themselves. With such connections, churches often found themselves ignoring the Gospels. This was one of the important grievances of the Protestant Reformation of the 1500s, though Protestant rulers such as Henry VIII (r. 1507-1549) proved even greedier than their Catholic counterparts.

[50]Richard Weikart, *From Darwin to Hitler: Evolutionary Ethics, Eugenics, and Racism in Germany* (New York: Palgrave Macmillan, 2004); Jacobs, *Original Sin*, pp. 248-50.

Christianity itself favors the poor. The Gospels are clear. Mary's song to God, after the Archangel Gabriel has announced to her that she would give birth to the Christ, is:

> My soul magnifies the Lord. . . .
> He has scattered the proud in the thoughts of their hearts.
> He has brought down the powerful from their thrones,
> and lifted up the lowly;
> he has filled the hungry with good things,
> and sent the rich away empty. (Lk 1:46-53)

In his Sermon on the Mount Jesus declares, "Blessed are you who are poor, for yours is the kingdom of God. Blessed are you who are hungry now, for you will be filled" (Lk 6:20-21) and "Blessed are the meek, for they will inherit the earth" (Mt 5:5).[51] One of Jesus' best-known sayings is that "it is easier for a camel to go through the eye of a needle than for someone who is rich to enter the kingdom of God" (Mt 19:24; Mk 10:25; Lk 18:25). Although Jesus went on to say that God could save even the rich, Christianity has an intrinsic preference for the poor. The idea is not that the poor are inherently less sinful than the rich but that the rich are more easily distracted by their possessions and self-satisfied about their worldly success. Recent popes and Protestant leaders have criticized capitalism as a system that overvalues materialism at the expense of spirituality and often at the expense of the poor.[52] A system in which profit is the ultimate purpose of humanity in unchristian: the equal dignity of humans demands an end to excessive inequality. Socialism has its own evils: Christianity rejects a system that subordinates individual conscience to collective power. In the early twenty-first century some congregations promoted the idea that accepting Jesus and Christianity would help us become successful in this world. This is not the Christianity of Jesus, who clearly said that his kingdom was not of this world or from this world (Jn 18:36).

23. CHRISTIANITY IS ANTI-ENVIRONMENT.

This is a frequent misunderstanding.[53] It's based on a certain reading of

---

[51]The word "meek" has two quite different meanings in English: (1) patient and gentle, and (2) submissive. The original Greek *praeis* has the first meaning only.

[52]Micklethwait and Wooldridge, *God Is Back*, pp. 249-50.

[53]Gilbert F. Lafreniere, *Decline of Nature* (Bethesda, MD: Academica Press, 2007).

the book of Genesis, on the alleged record of Christianity over time, and on the current beliefs of some Christians that the end of the world is at hand. Properly understood, Christianity supports most ecological aims.[54]

First, Genesis. "God said to [Adam and Eve], 'Be fruitful and multiply, and fill the earth and subdue it; and have dominion over the fish of the sea and over the birds of the air and over every living thing that moves upon the earth'" (Gen 1:28). The original words in Hebrew and Greek can be taken to mean "dominate," in the sense of exploit, or "rule over," implying responsibility for good governance. Many recent Christians have interpreted the text to mean that humans are "earth-keepers," or stewards of the planet. Nonetheless, the text has more often been taken to mean that humans may exploit nature for human benefit.

Counter to this interpretation is the love of nature expressed in the biblical Song of Songs and the book of Daniel, to name two examples. Daniel says, "Angels and heavens bless the Lord; sun and moon; stars of heaven; showers and dews; winds, fire, and heat; frost and cold; ice and snow; night and day; light and darkness; lightning and clouds; mountains and hills; springs, seas, and rivers; fish and birds; animals wild and tame, bless the Lord" (Dan 3).[55] Jesus said, "Consider the lilies of the field, how they grow; they neither toil nor spin, yet I tell you, even Solomon in all his glory was not clothed like one of these" (Mt 6:28-29; see also Lk 12:27). In the thirteenth century Saint Francis of Assisi and his Franciscans found God in the "beauty of created things, in the variety of light, shape, and color in simple, mixed, and even organic bodies, such as stars and planets, stones and metals, plants and animals."[56]

Next the Christians. Christians, Jews, Chinese, Africans and everybody else had little thought for the preservation of nature when humans were few and surrounded by vast deserts, jungles, forests and mountains teeming

---

[54]Scott Sabin, "Whole Earth Evangelism," *Christianity Today*, July 2010, pp. 26-29.

[55]Daniel 3 in the Septuagint (Greek Old Testament). Most Protestant Bibles separate out parts of Daniel and place them in the Apocrypha under "additions to the Book of Daniel." However, it has now been shown that most of these sections are not additions but were part of the original. See Catherine Brown Tkacz, *Aletheia: The Authority of the Greek Old Testament* (Etna, CA: Center for Traditionalist Orthodox Studies Press, 2012); Tkacz, "Susanna and the Pre-Christian Book and Daniel: Structure and Meaning," *Heythrop Journal* 49, no. 2 (2008): 181-96.

[56]Jeffrey B. Russell, "Glory in Time," *Soundings* 22 (1991): 43-58. See Richard Bauckham, *Living with Other Creatures: Green Exegesis and Theology* (Waco, TX: Baylor University Press, 2011).

with wild animals and other threats. Taming these threats was a universal human desire and practice. During the Roman Empire, when Christianity first arose, nothing distinguished Christians from other Romans in their environmental actions, though in theory Christianity did disenchant nature from the spirits who polytheists thought dwelled in it.

It was only beginning with the population boom of the twelfth century and the growth of cities that Europeans began serious clearing of the wilderness. The Catholic order of Cistercian monks made it their business to clear forests and swamps so as to turn them to productive agricultural use. Then, as western Europeans moved gradually into the wilder eastern and northern sections of Europe, more and more land was turned over to fields and commerce. Even so, the Europe of 1812 looked much more like the Europe of 1212 than it did that of 2012. It was only with the industrial revolution of the nineteenth and twentieth centuries that large-scale deformation of the environment began, and few historians would care to argue that Christianity caused the industrial revolution. The mover of industrialization was not Christ, but Mammon.

Next, the end of the world. Over the past few decades an increasing number of Christians have subscribed to Dispensationalist views that the end of the world will happen very soon and that it will mean not only the end of humanity but of all of nature, at least on Earth.[57] One corollary of this view was that this meant humans should gratefully use up natural resources as quickly as possible. Dispensationalist views are held by a growing number of Christians, but traditional Protestants and Catholics have joined humanists and others in condemning pollution and its cause: the exploitation of nature and of people.

No informed person denies that humanity has deformed the environment, but one has only to look at the deforestation of ancient Greece and China, neither of them even remotely Christian, to realize that the correlation between Christianity and the deformation of nature is terribly weak. The universality of human destructiveness toward the environment has recently been made clear by Jared Diamond.[58] Although Christians

---

[57]Sharan Newman, *Real History of the End of the World: Apocalyptic Predictions from Revelation and Nostradamus to Y2K and 2012* (New York: Berkley, 2010), pp. 279-283. Ian S. Markham, *Against Atheism: Why Dawkins, Hitchens, and Harris Are Fundamentally Wrong* (Malden, MA: Wiley-Blackwell, 2010), pp. 129-34.

[58]Jared M. Diamond, *Collapse: How Societies Choose to Fail or Succeed* (New York: Penguin, 2006).

have done their share of polluting, there is nothing in Christianity itself that lends itself to doing so.

A person who believes that the universe is the creation of God, who loves beauty, may be more inclined to protect the beauty of the universe than one who believes that the universe is a cosmic accident. Physicalists believe that nature is blind and can have no purpose. If nature is blind, then a pestilential swamp is as good as the Sierra. A few materialists have semi-deified Nature and Earth recently, bestowing on them some preemptive rights, an idea inconsistent with their materialist principle that nature has no purpose or meaning.[59]

24. Christianity is anti-sex.

Saint Augustine (354-410) did take a dim view of sex after overindulging in it during his youth. However, the idea that original sin was sexual in nature is a misconception (pun intended) of many Christians as well as people who hold other beliefs. The idea of original sin is found in Israelite thought well before Christianity, as in Psalm 51:5: "Indeed, I was born guilty, a sinner when my mother conceived me." The sin of humanity as represented in Adam and Eve was not lust but pride: the free-will decision to choose their own will over God's by seeking forbidden knowledge. Even theologians such as Augustine who were strict about sex agreed on this point. Adam and Eve enjoyed free and unrestricted sex in Eden; it was only after their act of disobedience that they became ashamed of it.

The positive attitude of Christianity toward sex is clear when contrasted to the Gnostic and Manichean dualist doctrine that the body is intrinsically evil. According to dualists, the body was designed by an evil creator for the purpose of entrapping and imprisoning pure spirits in disgusting matter. For Christians, the body and its functions are created good in themselves. Sex as an expression of love is good in itself and a spiritual good when partners surrender themselves to one another freely. It is only when we mismanage sex that sin enters in.

Nowhere in the New Testament did Jesus disparage sex. He condemned only abuses of sex. Jesus held that marriage was a spiritual as well as sexual

---

[59]Robert Sirico, ed., *Environmental Stewardship in the Judeo-Christian Tradition* (Grand Rapids: Acton Institute, 2007).

union that could not properly be broken. The Apostle Saint Paul was more concerned than Jesus about sexual abuses, mostly because of his experience of people's behavior in Corinth, the Las Vegas of the Roman world. Although Paul said that celibacy was a higher state than marriage, he approved marriage, and early Christianity on the whole continued its positive attitude toward marital sexuality. Christian thinkers frequently took marital sex as a metaphor and model for the union of Christ and the church or of the human soul with God. However, marriage was not considered a sacrament of the church before the ninth century and was formalized as such only from the twelfth century onward.

Reservations about sex originated in the 300s and increased from that point forward. One reason was the continued sexual laxity of late Roman society, which sometimes provoked distaste for sex in reaction. The emigration of Christian hermits and monastics from the cities into deserted areas from the fourth century onward was in part an effort to avoid the material and sexual temptations of urban society. And though Christianity was never dualist, there was a certain influence of the dualist idea that the body is the source of sin. Augustine was a convert from dualism and, though later condemning it, continued to bear some of its traces. Augustine believed that although sin was not originally sexual, it was transmitted sexually (using modern terms, he might have said genetically). Augustine's ideas eventually "tangled [original sin] with revulsion toward sexuality."[60]

The only generalization that can be made about Christian attitudes toward sex over two millennia is that there was a spectrum from the happily and joyfully accepting to the sternly and fearfully restrictive. They have ranged from acceptance of sexual behaviors far beyond the limits set by the Bible to mistrust of almost any sexual activity. Very generally speaking, sexuality and the body were more accepted in the Middle Ages than later. Although Luther was accepting of sex, other Protestant Reformers and their followers took a harsher view. The rise of puritanical Jansenism in the Catholic church from the 1600s to the 1900s also treated sex with such excessive strictness that many people found sexual repression almost synonymous with the church. In perspective almost every society—including Samoa, which both scholars

[60]Alan Jacobs, *Original Sin: A Cultural History* (New York: HarperOne, 2008), p. 66.

and Samoans know that Margaret Mead famously misrepresented—has firm rules about sexuality.

25. Christianity is anti-choice.

Everyone in the United States knows about the fierce opposition between the "pro-choice" and "pro-life" parties, which evokes lots of shouting, pressure politics and worse. Pro-choice is code for a woman's right to abort a fetus, pro-life for a concern for unborn children.

It's helpful to step back and extract the idea of "choice" from the abortion debate and get down to what the word actually means: "the power, right, or liberty to choose," according to the dictionary. "Freedom to choose" is another way of putting it. The core of Christian moral teaching is that each person has the free will to choose among moral options. But many people yield their freedom to the crowd to which they belong. The Christian affirmation of the freedom of each human individual is a sharp contrast to the atheist-materialist view that the actions of a person are determined by a combination of genetic and environmental factors. The materialist view is that we do not have any freedom to choose whatsoever; we have only the illusion of freedom. We have no real choice at all. Materialism is anti-choice in the most fundamental way.

The use of the code phrase "pro-choice" exclusively for abortion also obscures the fact that many pro-choice advocates are not in favor of free choice in other matters. Many who declare that a woman has the right to choose whether to bear a child do not believe in a woman's right to choose where her child goes to school or a woman's right to choose whether to join a union.

Now let's examine abortion. The history of Christian attitudes toward abortion is complex and can be treated only briefly here.[61] In Roman society as a whole both abortion and infanticide were permitted. Neither is mentioned in the New Testament, and there is no known Christian document from the first century A.D. relating to abortion. After A.D. 100, as Christianity was establishing its moral principles in contrast to permissive society, abortion was considered the unlawful taking of human life. Influential early Christian writers such as Athenagoras (about A.D. 175), Clement of Alexandria (150-215), Tertullian (160-225), Ambrose (339-

[61]On abortion see Micklethwait and Wooldridge, *God Is Back*, pp. 328-29.

397), Jerome (345-420), Augustine (354-430) and Chrysostomos (347-407) all condemned it, and opposition to abortion became one of the hallmarks of Christianity in the Roman Empire. It remained a hallmark of Christianity well into the 1900s.

Still, there were doubts both in practice and in theory. The practical doubt lay in the fact that despite moral and theological objections, many Christians did have abortions throughout history. The number of such actual abortions is of course impossible to determine. The theoretical doubt lies in the difficulty of deciding at what point a fetus is considered a human life. Until recently there was no established scientific evidence about that question, and theologians differed. A standard if by no means universal idea was that life began at quickening, that is, when the mother can feel the movement of the child within her. Another criterion was viability, the point when a child could survive outside the womb.

In the twentieth century biological science determined that an embryo has its own complete and unique DNA from the time of conception. Meanwhile, from the late part of that century, society and law expanded the legality of abortion, and many churches have moved in that direction as well. Much disagreement remains both among churches and in secular law as to the point in fetal development when abortion should cease to be permissible. Some say abortion is impermissible from the moment of conception; others permit the killing of a child even in the process of delivery; others set various time limits, such as twenty-four weeks into the pregnancy. Another debate centers on special circumstances such as incest, rape and the mother's health.

Though the question of abortion is currently debated along religious lines, it need not be. A zygote has the DNA it will have when it is on its deathbed. An agnostic professional biologist once asked me, "If the fetus isn't alive, what is it? And if it is alive, what kind of life does it have if it isn't human life?" Suppose the whole debate could be restructured around this question: Under what circumstances is the taking of human life permissible? That might help pro-life Christians to admit that on some issues, such as capital punishment and war, Christians have often judged that the taking of human life is justified. It might help pro-choice people admit that abortion involves taking a life that is biologically human. Both sides might then replace shouting with reasonable discussion.

26. Christianity is sexist.

Sexism is "discrimination based on gender, especially discrimination against women," the dictionary tells us. The first supposedly sexist passage in the Bible is found in the book of Genesis, where God creates Eve out of Adam's body to be a "partner," "companion" or "assistant" (Gen 2:18). Which of those words is the best translation is uncertain, but the text goes on to assert that the husband will rule over the wife. Equality is implied in the idea that a man and a woman shall be united as one flesh. However, because Eve was the first to be deceived by the serpent, both Jewish and Christian scholars often considered women more vulnerable to sin than men (Gen 2:18–3:19; compare 1 Pet 3:7).

Some current writers portray women in the Old Testament as silent, passive victims of patriarchal repression and ignore the evidence that they were often quite otherwise. The Old Testament presents a number of articulate female heroes such as Esther, Susanna, Judith, Ruth and Hannah.[62] These Old Testament women were widely venerated by both the Eastern and Western churches before the Protestant Reformation.[63] In the New Testament too women were of great importance: the sisters Mary and Martha, the women at Christ's tomb, John the Baptist's mother Elizabeth and, above all, Mary the mother of Jesus. In the New Testament texts, all of which were composed by men, women repeatedly outshone men in their devotion to Jesus: those who remained with him at his execution were mostly women, and those who first saw him after his resurrection were women. It can be argued that the Gospels favor women over men.

Saint Paul the Apostle is blamed for sexism in Christianity on account of passages such as this: "Women should be silent in the churches. For they are not permitted to speak, but should be subordinate, as the law also says. If there is anything they desire to know, let them ask their husbands at home. For it is shameful for a woman to speak in church" (1 Cor 14:34-35). When encountering passages like these, Christians have the choice of taking such an admonition as true for all time or as moored in the custom of that time, which segregated men and women in synagogues and congregations. The Apostle Saint Peter's comment that men are weak but

---

[62]Catherine Brown Tkacz, "Are Old Testament Women Nameless, Silent, Passive Victims?" *This Rock*, December 2006, pp. 6-11.

[63]Catherine Brown Tkacz, "Women as Types of Christ," *Gregorianum* 85 (2004): 278-311.

women weaker (1 Pet 3:7) is also to be read in the context of a society in which a woman had a practical need to be under the protection of father, husband or other male relative, conditions that seldom apply in contemporary Western society.

Besides, Paul upholds the equality of men and women, as in, "The wife does not have authority over her own body, but the husband does; likewise the husband does not have authority over his own body, but the wife does" (1 Cor 7:4; compare Mt 19:4-5; Mk 10:7). Paul's letters also show that women were in positions of notable power and influence in the early Christian community (Acts 16, 18, 21; 1 Cor 16:19; Phil 4:2-3). The last chapter of his letter to the Romans is full of praise for women: Phoebe, Aquila, Priscilla, Mary, Julia, Persis, Tryphena, the mother of Rufus, and Tryphosa (Rom 16:1-16). This was a remarkable change in the Near Eastern environment. In the Jewish Temple, the women's court was behind the men's and thus farther from the sanctuary, whereas in Christian congregations women and men were at equal distance from it. It was also a change from Roman law, under which a man had the right to execute his wife or children. When Paul is read in context, claims that he promoted sexism prove unreasonable.

The absolute, unlimited spiritual equality of men and women has been affirmed throughout Christianity.[64] The argument that Christianity is the origin of sexism in Western culture ignores the fact that almost all cultures have been and still are sexist. For example, Muslim and Asian societies, barely touched by Christianity, have a much more sexist record. By comparison, the early Christian community stands out in its affirmation of equality. The current idea of women's rights derives from modern feminism, but its historical basis is the fundamental Christian belief in the equality of the sexes. Margaret E. Köstenberger describes three major movements in Christian feminism. The first, in the nineteenth century, focused on advancing the voice of women in the churches. The first woman pastor in America (a Congregationalist) was ordained in 1853. Women founded or cofounded the Salvation Army and the Women's Christian Temperance Union (the WCTU may sound quaint now, but it played an important role in populist politics up through the 1920s). In the

[64]Patricia Ranft, *Women and Spiritual Equality in Christian Tradition* (New York: St. Martin's Press, 1998).

1890s Elizabeth Cady Stanton edited *The Woman's Bible*. The second movement, influenced by secular feminists in the 1960s and 1970s such as Betty Friedan and Gloria Steinem, subtracted Christianity from Christian feminism. The third movement, beginning in the 1990s, has been centered on historical and theological evidence, reemphasizing the Christian roots of gender equality.[65]

In the early Christian community women played an important role: there were women deacons such as Phoebe (Rom 16:1). Women deacons remained important up into the sixth century, though the higher offices of *presbyteros* (elder or priest) and *episkopos* (overseer or bishop) seem to have been reserved for males. One justification for this reservation is the fact that the apostles were all men. However, they were also all Jews, a criterion for high office that the Christian community had dispensed with by A.D. 100. Women continued to be excluded from ordination into the twentieth century, and they remain excluded in some churches, notably the Catholic and Orthodox. Some women today consider this appropriate; others consider it sexist. The recent growth in numbers of women ministers in Protestantism is particularly striking in Pentecostal churches, whose overall growth in the past half-century is astonishing. As Micklethwait and Wooldridge observe, "Pentecostals have already done more for feminism in Africa and Latin America than Betty Friedan."[66]

Emphasizing the issue of priests and bishops also obscures important facts. Monastic women had increasing influence from the fifth century through the Middle Ages. Their advice was treasured, and in the Middle Ages abbesses—leaders of convents, or monasteries for women—sometimes wielded considerable economic and political power. Many women monastics (nuns) were from noble families and had their own political as well as spiritual networks. Also, a large proportion of saints are female. A common misunderstanding is that the church creates saints. It does no such thing. Saints (Latin *sancti*, *sanctae*) are people who in their lives have turned their characters toward God to such a degree that they are with him. In canonizing people, the church only recognizes that they are with God. All people who are united in Christ, both past, present and

[65]Margaret Elizabeth Köstenberger, *Jesus and the Feminists: Who Do They Say That He Is?* (Wheaton, IL: Crossway, 2008).

[66]Micklethwait and Wooldridge, *God Is Back*, p. 356.

future, are saints (see Mt 27:52; Acts 29:10; Rom 15:25-31). From at least the fifth century, the saint deemed vastly higher than all other saints, female or male, was Mary the mother of Christ, and that is true among the Eastern Orthodox even more than among Roman Catholics. Some recent scholars have inconsistently disparaged the veneration of Mary's power at the same time as they've dismissed her role as passive and ineffective.[67]

Feminism began in the late nineteenth century, and feminist theology has been developing since the 1960s. Feminists observe that the image of God in most people's minds has been masculine, pointing specifically to the formula of the Trinity as "Father, Son and Holy Spirit" and to the incarnation of God in a male, Jesus. They object to the use of the pronoun "he" for God, arguing that it excludes the female. Alternative pronouns all create problems: "they" clearly implies polytheism or at least tritheism; "she" makes a specific ideological point, which the traditional "he" does not; "it" deprives God of personality. Thoughtful Christians have always known that God both includes and transcends gender.

Eastern Orthodox believers think that Western Christians are overzealous in trying to pin down definitions of God. A different approach is the apophatic tradition (Greek *apophasis*: "denial, negation"), strong in the Eastern church and also a strong undercurrent in the West. It emphasizes that no human words or concepts can ever correspond to the ultimate reality that is God. As the prophet Isaiah reports, "My thoughts are not your thoughts, nor are my ways your ways, says the LORD. For as the heavens are higher than the earth, so are my ways higher than your ways and my thoughts than your thoughts" (Is 55:8-9). Human understanding cannot plumb the depths of the divine, so we cannot presume that our formulations restrict the meaning of God. Christians might consider this when quarreling over one formulation or another.

It might help if "He" were again capitalized, distinguishing between God and any male "he." It would also help to see that part of the problem is imposed by the English language. Greek distinguishes between "human" (*anthropos*) and male human (*aner*), as Latin distinguishes between "human" (*homo*) and male human (*vir*), and as German distinguishes between "human" (*Mensch*) and male human (*Mann*), but English has always

[67]Jaroslav Pelikan, *Mary Through the Centuries: Her Place in the History of Culture* (New Haven, CT: Yale University Press, 1996).

used "man" to include both sexes, as in Charles Darwin's *The Descent of Man*. Therefore, traditionally English-speaking churches have used the phrase "God became man." Many churches correct this misunderstanding by using more accurate language such as "became human." The fact that Jesus' sex was male does not mean that his gender was restricted. At one point he used a female simile for himself: "How often have I desired to gather your children together as a hen gathers her brood under her wings" (Lk 13:34-35). Christianity has always affirmed that Jesus was a fully human person, and as fully human he includes both the female and the male. At any rate, no language changes the actual nature of God. No sensible definition of God limits him by a pronoun appropriate to creatures.

27. Christianity is homophobic.

It is not yet possible to write a word on this subject that doesn't offend somebody. People wave banners that say, "You're for us or against us." Teachers have been fired for raising questions about these issues. Even discussion of homosexual rights is quickly judged offensive, even intolerable.[68] It would, however, be irresponsible to omit an entry on the subject. I try for objectivity, but I know different people will be offended by different parts of the entry, and I regret that. I offer just one observation. The tendency to demonize "the other" is universal, but a fundamental moral principle of Christianity is that each Christian approach every other person with open understanding and sympathy, no matter how much they disagree. An offense against charity is always a sin. Still, one can also consider what is most charitable for society as a whole.

The dictionary defines the word "phobia" as "an intense, abnormal, or illogical fear of a specified thing." To insist that all who consider homosexuality immoral are phobic ignores that there are calm, normal and logical reasons for questioning homosexual behavior, whether such reasons turn out to be well-founded or not. Scientific evidence indicates that homosexuality may be more chemical than choice, and almost everyone has experienced at least some degree of pansexual attraction. It is curious, though, that the same people who insist that reality is socially constructed also insist that homosexuality has mainly physical causes.

[68]Georg Neumayr, "Error Enjoys All the Rights," *Catholic World Report*, August/September 2010, p. 1.

A poll states that 91 percent of young non-Christians perceive "present-day Christianity" as "antihomosexual."[69] It is thought that the Bible condemns homosexuality. The first thing to note is that the term "homosexuality" is anachronistic when applied to the Bible. Homosexuality by any name is barely mentioned in the Old Testament. The original story of the cities of Sodom and Gomorrah is found in Genesis 19:1-11. The clearest references are in the book of Leviticus, which condemns a wide variety of sexual behaviors, among which homoerotic behavior is only one (Lev 18–20). Homosexuality is mentioned not at all in the Gospels, and only vaguely in a few passages of the Epistles. The Apostle Saint Paul says the law is for "the unholy and profane, for those who kill their father or mother, for murderers, fornicators, those practicing unnatural sex, slave traders, liars, perjurers" (1 Tim 1:9-10). He condemns "fornicators, idolaters, adulterers, male prostitutes, those practicing unnatural sex, thieves, the greedy, drunkards, revilers, robbers" (1 Cor 6:9-10). His letter to the Romans is specific in condemning homosexual acts in both sexes (Rom 1:26-27). It is conceivable that Paul was condemning only casual sex, rather than committed relationships, which may have been unknown or unseen in his day.

In the Bible, homosexual practice is merely one of legions of sins. For example, the Bible condemns adultery vastly more frequently than homosexuality, yet humanity has never been categorized and lumped into adulterers or non-adulterers, or into perjurers or nonperjurers. There is no biblical reason to categorize humanity into "gay" and "straight." Nowhere in the Bible is homosexuality singled out as especially wrong. Everyone—homosexual and heterosexual—is a sinner.

However, there is presently a lot of phobia about Paul on account of his comments about sex, which are usually taken out of context. But Paul is the author of what Gandhi called the most beautiful statement about love in any tradition: "Love is patient; love is kind; love is not envious or boastful or arrogant or rude. It does not insist on its own way; it is not irritable or resentful; it does not rejoice in wrongdoing, but rejoices in the truth. It bears all things, believes all things, hopes all things, endures all things. Love never ends" (1 Cor 13:4-8). Love—charity—is always a virtue. A heterosexual Christian for whom homosexuality is only one of

---

[69]Kinnaman and Lyons, *unChristian*, p. 93.

hundreds of issues may not understand that a homosexual of either sex may feel, especially when experiencing bullying, defined by his or her sexuality. It is a common human trait to see everything through the lens of one's chief concern. Jews, African-Americans, Christians, Marxists, homosexuals, Muslims, feminists and atheists all have tinted lenses. It is impossible to wear no lenses at all, but the less tinted our glasses, the more clearly we will see.

Nor was Christian tradition after Paul clear on homosexuality. The early church theologians made few references to it. Early codes for penances included homosexual activity, along with hundreds of other actions requiring repentance. Late Roman law, influenced by both pagan philosophers and the Bible, regarded sodomy as illegal, a tradition in law followed into the late twentieth century. Evidence offered for homosexual marriage in Christian Tradition is unpersuasive. No known society, past or present, has allowed same-sex marriage. On the other hand, many cultures have often accepted polygamy (it is still practiced in some places).[70] The argument for polygamy therefore seems stronger than the argument for same-sex marriage. Some argue that just because no same-sex marriages have existed is no reason that they should not today, any more than the fact that all societies have had slavery means that slavery is all right today. But slavery is an inherent evil; marriage between a man and a woman is an inherent good. The Christian principle has been that sexuality is best expressed in heterosexual marriage, which exists for loyalty, child-rearing, and mutual love and commitment.

Christians today have vastly divergent views on the subject. Some believe that charity outweighs biblical texts. Some believe the biblical texts should be ignored altogether. Some note that the evidence pointing to physical causes of homosexuality was obviously unknown to "culture-bound" biblical writers. Some continue to believe that the traditional views of the Bible need to be reaffirmed. In all of this, more heat than light has been generated. However offended people on one side or the other may be, the Christian view of homosexuality is an open question. Neither side has the right to prevent the other from making its argument. To condemn all views against homosexual behavior as homophobic is itself hate speech. It

---

[70]Philip Jenkins, "One Man, One Woman?" *Christian Century*, January 26, 2010, p. 45.

is one thing to argue that homosexuality is normal and acceptable, quite another to prevent others from arguing the opposite. Whatever view one takes, neither judging nor censorship is just. What Jesus condemned most of all was self-righteousness.

28. CHRISTIANITY IS ANTISEMITIC.

Is it possible to be a Christian and an antisemite? Historically, yes; morally and theologically, no. Contemporary Christians should know enough about the results of antisemitism to eradicate it from their thoughts.[71] Jesus, Mary, Joseph and the apostles were all Jews. One doesn't cease to be a Christian by being antisemitic any more than one ceases to be a Christian by being a murderer, but antisemitism, like murder, is a sin. Jews sometimes unduly interpret criticisms of the state of Israel as antisemitic, but Christians should bear in mind that up to the middle of the twentieth century, Jews in the United States and the United Kingdom were subjected to severe prejudice in housing, clubs, businesses and universities. Before World War II, they were often excluded as students and usually excluded as faculty. However, extending the term "antisemitism" too broadly, like extending "sexism" too broadly, weakens its meaning.

Though Christianity is not itself antisemitic, large numbers of Christians have been antisemites. Antisemitism is a raw topic that covers some of the most horrific events of all time. Even addressing it as simply and briefly as possible, the following points need to be considered: (1) the definition of "antisemitism," (2) the nature of Israelite religion in the first century A.D., (3) Jesus and earliest Christianity, (4) relations between Christians and Jews from A.D. 100 to 1050, (5) relations between 1050 and 1700, (6) relations between 1700 and 1945, and (7) current relations.

The fundamental difference between Christians and Jews is that the former believe that Jesus is the divine Messiah and the latter deny it, so disagreement is inevitable. Though many recent Jewish scholars have found value in the New Testament, the Jewish tradition is to deny that the

[71]The term is usually spelled "anti-Semitic," but I follow the daughter of the late Abraham Heschel, a scholar of extraordinary wisdom and spirituality, Susannah Heschel, *Aryan Jesus* (Princeton, NJ: Princeton University Press, 2009), in using the more sensible spelling. Anti-Communism assumes the existence of Communism; anti-Catholicism assumes Catholicism and so on, but there's no such thing as "Semitism." Besides, the term "anti-Semite" itself was coined by a racist.

New Testament is revealed by God.[72] Jews resent the Christian belief that it fulfills the Old Testament and even more the belief of a few Christians that the New Testament makes the Old Testament outdated. The view (never held by most Christians) that the New Testament replaces the Old is called supersessionism.

The term "anti-Semitism" was coined about 1873 by Wilhelm Marr, the German founder of the League of Anti-Semites. It is a strange term in that Arabs as well as Jews are Semitic. Perhaps it was invented as a euphemism for "hatred of Jews." It is more shocking to hear "she hates Jews" than to hear "she is antisemitic." This coinage marks a shift in Christian attitudes toward Jews from anti-Judaism, which is opposition to Jews on religious grounds, to racist opposition to Jews.

Antisemitism is hatred of Jews on racial, ethnic and cultural grounds. It scarcely existed before the 1850s. As late as 1848 the Assembly of Frankfurt in Germany declared that Jews had full equality on the Enlightenment basis of the universal rights of man. In the 1860s and 1870s, however, biologists came to believe that the human race, rather than being one, was divided into subspecies, some of which were higher than others. By 1879 pseudoscientific antisemitism was common in intellectual circles. It proclaimed that biologically different "races" of humans existed and that these could be ranked according to their biological superiority. Scientists and publicists, especially anthropologists and social psychologists, designated Northern Europeans as the leading "race" and ranked others in a descending scale beneath.

From there to Hitler the road was open. Eugenics declared that the human species must advance and preserve itself from degradation by discouraging weaker and "lesser" persons and races. Antisemitism was the product of bad science and frenetic nationalism, not of Christianity. But scientific antisemitism was quickly passed down to an anti-Judaic public all too ready to accept it. Theological anti-Judaism provided fertile ground for the growth of extreme Judeophobia, and large numbers of anti-Judaic Christians easily absorbed racist antisemitism.

Ancient Israelite religion was centered on the Temple in Jerusalem, where the ark of the covenant was kept and where Israelites came to

---

[72]One such distinguished contemporary Jewish scholar is Jacob Neusner, who values the New Testament.

worship and sacrifice to the Lord. In the first century after Jesus, when the Roman Empire dominated the Middle East, there were a number of factions among the Jewish people: Sadducees, who emphasized Temple worship; Pharisees, who emphasized obedience to the laws of the Torah; Zealots, who wanted to overthrow Roman rule by force; Essenes, representing ascetic withdrawal from society; and Christians. All these were forms of Jewish religion. The followers of Jesus formed one of a number of Jewish factions all opposed to one another. Jesus and the apostles were Jews intensely loyal to the Hebrew Bible; Jesus quoted it frequently. However, Jesus and his followers outraged other Jews in a number of ways, especially in the claim that Jesus and God were one, an idea that to others was hideous blasphemy.

Events in the 60s and 70s A.D. radically changed the configuration of these Jewish factions. The disastrous revolt of the Jews against the Romans in 66-70 ended in the destruction of the Temple, the scattering (diaspora) of the people, and the elimination of all the factions except the Pharisees and the followers of Jesus. Though in the beginning these two had sometimes worshiped together, by the end of the first century they had split. The Pharisees regarded the followers of Jesus as blasphemous heretics while the followers of Jesus condemned the Pharisees for refusing to acknowledge Jesus as the Messiah. From the Pharisees, with their emphasis on obedience to the law, came the rabbinic, Talmudic tradition that became known as Judaism.[73] By A.D. 90 the rabbis had excluded Christians from the synagogues.

The New Testament, which was written about A.D. 50-90, contains many hostile comments about "the Jews"—for example, "Jesus . . . did not wish to go about in Judea because the Jews were looking for an opportunity to kill him" (Jn 7:1). Although such comments were directed only at Jews who did not accept Christ, many have called them antisemitic, which is an anachronistic distortion. Almost all (if not all) the New Testament writers were Jewish (see Jn 8:31). The Apostle Saint Paul insisted that "all Israel will be saved . . . for the gifts and the calling of God are irrevocable" (Rom 11:28-29).

[73]The Talmud consists of the oral tradition called Mishnah and the commentaries on it. There are two Talmuds, the Palestinian and the Babylonian, produced over the fourth to the seventh centuries of the Christian Era.

The question really is whether the hostile New Testament texts are anti-Judaic. There are two answers. The first is that they are not hostile to the Jewish people or to Jewish religion in general. Christianity is a Jewish religion. The second answer is that the texts are hostile to the anti-Christian Jewish factions including the Sadducees and eventually the Pharisees, with whom Judaism was becoming specifically identified. The term "Christianity" did not exist in the first century, when the term "Judaism" was only beginning to have its modern denotation.[74] The enduring problem was that New Testament texts were understood by later Christians as condemning all Jews.

Generally speaking, Jews and Christians usually got along reasonably well for centuries, until about 1050. In Europe, churches and synagogues existed together in towns—sometimes the synagogue was taller than the church—and Christian scholars consulted rabbis about the text and interpretations of the Hebrew Bible. Jews and Christians lived peaceably together. Obviously there were many exceptions to this peace and quiet, one of the most notorious being the enraged sermons of John Chrysostomos at Antioch in 387. John's anger was not directed at Jews as such but rather at Christians who attended services in synagogues. But just as the Gospels eventually came to be viewed as hostile to all Jews, Chrysostomos' sermons were quoted and mined extensively by later preachers against Judaism. Other Christian writers, such as Augustine, claimed that the kingdom of God could not come until all the Jews were converted and that the continued existence of unbelieving Jews was delaying the kingdom. Yet Augustine's views on the Jews were much more complex and positive than has usually been understood.[75]

On the other side, Jews tended to combine hatred and contempt in their attitudes toward Christians, whom they regarded as superstitious blasphemers. There are passages in the Talmud that condemn Jesus as an idolater and justify his execution; Jewish folklore held that Jesus was a magician, the bastard spawn of Mary impregnated by a coarse Roman soldier. Some rabbis conflated Jesus with Haman, the evildoer in the book

---

[74]Donald Harman Akenson, *Saint Saul: A Skeleton Key to the Historical Jesus* (Oxford: Oxford University Press, 2000), pp. 146-70.

[75]Paula Fredriksen, *Augustine and the Jews: A Christian Defense of Jews and Judaism* (New York: Doubleday, 2008).

of Esther. The fundamental dissonance remains that Judaism requires specific rejection of Jesus as Messiah. But because of the dominance of society by Christians, Jewish harm to Christians was heavily outweighed by Christian harm to Jews.

In the eleventh century, the relative peace that existed earlier was shattered. The reasons are many, but the most important was the papal reform movement that began in 1048. This movement corrected abuses in the church such as ignorance, thievery and sexual misconduct among the clergy. At the same time it sought to clarify and establish orthodox teaching and thus condemned heretics and Jews. It was thought that a perfect society was a fully Christian society and that Jews were blocking its way. Tensions increased, and the turning point was the crusades, which began in 1096. The crusades were aimed at liberating Jerusalem and the Holy Land from Islam, but public rage soon turned against "infidels" in northern France and Germany, and many Jews were massacred and synagogues destroyed—usually despite efforts on the part of the civil and ecclesiastical authorities to stop the riots and massacres.

From that time on, relations between Christians and Jews were embittered. Christians were determined to isolate the Jews so as to prevent them from "contaminating" Christians. Like heretics, Jews were considered carriers of religious plague. In 1215, the Fourth Lateran Council under Pope Innocent III ordered Jews to wear clothing or badges identifying themselves as Jews, a custom revived by Adolf Hitler. Catholic, Protestant and Orthodox preachers and writers often taught severe anti-Judaism, with the result that the general population attributed hideous (and preposterous) deeds to Jews, such as poisoning wells, kidnapping and eating Christian children, and violating the Christian sacraments. England, France, Spain and Portugal expelled unconverted Jews from their territories.

During the tensions generated by the Reformation of the 1500s, Catholics and Protestants found themselves in agreement that Jews were evil. In 1556 Pope Paul IV ordered the Jews of Rome to be segregated in a ghetto; Martin Luther (1483-1546) recommended burning down Jewish houses and synagogues, the destruction of Jewish books, and the execution of rabbis who continued to teach Judaism.

As late as the twentieth century, Russia combined anti-Judaism and anti-semitism, encouraging the tsars to use the Jews as scapegoats for political and economic problems. The tsars, hostile to any group that did not support them as rulers over all aspects of society, were Eastern Orthodox and regarded religious dissent as a threat to their authority. Although Jews played a prominent part in early Communism, by 1930 Stalin had resumed hostility to Jews.[76] The church did nothing in either the tsarist or the Soviet period to help the Jews. The reason was a combination of ancient anti-Judaism with the brutal fact that when political and economic stress is high, most people, including Christians, will scapegoat minorities.

In Europe beginning about 1750, many of the rationalist writers of the Enlightenment broke with the old anti-Judaism, but by that time many Jews had departed or had been isolated in ghettos, and most Christians had already been taught to hate them. From the 1870s onward, pseudoscientific racism provided a different rationale for hating Jews. Intellectual leaders scorned anti-Judaism but began to teach racist antisemitism. The populace, already steeped in anti-Judaism, eagerly embraced the new rationale.

Antisemitism was worse than anti-Judaism. Jews could escape anti-Judaism by converting, but there was no way of escaping antisemitism based on ancestry. Before the triumph of antisemitism and eugenics, unconverted Jews could—and did—assimilate to wider society and often attained high degrees of economic and political influence. Almost all Jews supported the nations in which they lived during the First World War (1914-1918); many served willingly in the armed forces. After the war, however, the Germans sought scapegoats for their defeat, and they targeted the Jews. The "final solution" was the Holocaust, the murder of most of the Jews in Europe by the Nazis. Centuries of Christian anti-Judaism united with biological racism to enable this horror. Two centuries of assimilation into European culture from the 1740s to the 1930s were not enough to save the Jews from the Holocaust of the 1940s.

Christians would do well to understand that the Jews were in exile from their homeland for twenty centuries and that they therefore have a passionate connection to their roots, a connection that makes conversion to Christianity seem treasonous. What seems stubborn to some Christians seems survival to Jews. There are more than two billion Christians

---

[76]Robert Service, *Stalin: A Biography* (Cambridge, MA: Belknap Press, 2004).

in the world and only fifteen million Jews; which religion is at greater risk is obvious. In America, where by 1890 waves of Jews were fleeing to escape Russian pogroms, nativist and nationalist reaction resulted in a deadly cocktail combining Christian anti-Judaism, scientific racism and envy of the successful.

One might think that the Holocaust would be enough to eradicate antisemitism and anti-Judaism, but it was not. Many Jews, having seen the failure of assimilation, founded a new Jewish state in the Middle East, a state that at times has repressed Christian as well as Muslim Palestinians. In Europe and America, hatred of "the Christ-killers" continued to meld with the irrational fear that Jews headed a vast conspiracy secretly wielding worldwide power.

Most Christian denominations have been putting an end to anti-Judaism. In 1965 the mainly Protestant World Council of Churches declared anti-Judaism to be fundamentally unchristian. Popes John XXIII (1958-1963) and John Paul II (1978-2005) were insistent on this point, and in 2008 Benedict XVI rejected all attitudes of contempt or discrimination against Jews. The consensus of most contemporary Christian leaders is that Jews are the people to whom God first revealed himself and that although Jews are free to convert by choice, no one should proselytize them.

A new spin has been placed on Christian-Jewish relations by the phenomenal recent growth of the radical doctrine of Dispensational eschatology (study of the end of the world). Dispensationalists predict that the nation of Israel must grow to extend from Egypt to the Euphrates and that an atomic war must take place before Christ can come again. Supported by some radical Jewish Zionists, Dispensationalists passionately support the state of Israel. They believe that all of the Holy Land is properly Jewish, that the establishment of Israel in all that land is necessary before the second coming can occur, and that at the end Christ will leave the Earth in the hands of an Israeli state while leading Christians to heaven.[77]

On the other hand, there is a marked anti-Zionist movement on the political left that views the Palestinians as victims and the Jews as op-

[77]Mark Noll, *Scandal of the Evangelical Mind* (Grand Rapids: Eerdmans, 1994), pp. 117-37; Stephen Spector, *Evangelicals and Israel: The Story of American Christian Zionism* (New York: Oxford University Press, 2010).

pressors, causing thoughtful Jews to fear a new outbreak of antisemitic activity. Recently the Jewish Anti-Defamation League has argued that Christians should not even invite Jews to convert.

29. Christianity is racist.

Jesus said, and the apostles confirmed, that the truth of Christianity was to be preached to all people of every nation. The earliest Christians were mostly Near Easterners and Africans. There is no evidence of racial discrimination against blacks or any other racial groups in early Christianity. The Apostle Saint Paul was firm: "There is no longer Jew or Greek, there is no longer slave or free, there is no longer male or female, for you are all one in Christ Jesus" (Gal 3:28). The New Testament does not mention the color of people's skin.

The bizarre idea that the Bible curses black people derives from tortured readings of Old Testament texts such as Genesis 9:18-27, in which Noah curses his son Ham and Ham's son Canaan, decreeing their slavery to Ham's brothers. In the nineteenth century, Christian racists made the connection Ham = slave = black, even though the Bible makes no mention of Ham's color. Racists conflated this passage with Genesis 4:15, where the mark put on Cain by the Lord was believed, again without any evidence, to be black skin. Such readings were nothing more than rationalizations for racism. Christianity lacks reference to race: it regards Adam as the common ancestor of all humans and Christ the Savior of all humans. The idea that Christianity is white man's religion made sense for a limited time in particular regions, such as the West Indies or the U.S. South, where misery was inflicted on millions for the wealth of a few, and where slaves were encouraged to seek release in another world rather than liberty in this one. Even there, the growth of African-American churches was impressive.[78]

During the nineteenth century, pseudo-Christian racism was eclipsed by pseudoscientific racism. The bizarre term "Caucasian" for white people was introduced by the German Johann Friedrich Blumenbach (1752-1840) in about 1800. He was followed by William Lawrence, who wrote *Short System of Comparative Anatomy*, published in 1807; South Carolinian

[78]Micklethwait and Wooldridge, *God Is Back*, p. 68.

Josiah Clarke Nott, *On the Natural History of the Caucasian and Negro Races*, 1844; and Robert Thomas Hulme, *Elements of Medical Zoology*, 1861. There were allegedly three principal varieties of race: Caucasian, Mongolian and Ethiopian. This is why the current knowledge that all races sprang from the same African roots (monogenism) is so socially important: it affirms the unity of the human race and refutes previous scientific belief that different races had different origins (polygenism).[79]

In the mid-nineteenth century, pictures showing the "evolution" from ape to Anglo-Saxon were common. Such ideas became common in America, providing pro-slavery and even moderate leaders with an excuse to condone the exploitation of African-Americans. Even the celebrated moderate Stephen Douglas proclaimed in an 1858 debate with Abraham Lincoln that "I positively deny that he [the Negro] is my brother or any kin to me whatever."[80] So prevalent were such unchristian ideas in American society that they leached into Christianity. Two rationalizations—the pseudo-Christian and the pseudoscientific—reinforced one another. The failure of Christians to recognize the full humanity of all races preceded the failure of scientists to do so; together they allowed the enslavement of Africans as well as the subjugation, exile, degradation and near extermination of Native Americans and Australian Aborigines.

After abolition, the next great struggle against racism began in the late 1950s: the civil rights movement. Enlightenment ideas surrounding the rights of man had a role in the movement, and so did Christianity. Most of the civil rights leaders were Christians and based their opposition to racism on Christian grounds. There were more Christian marches for civil rights in the 1960s than secular ones.

It's a belief on college campuses today that Christianity is opposed to multiculturalism. This is understandable when college "multicultural" programs exclude only one culture: Christianity. For centuries Christians have debated the degree to which European cultural religious practices should be exported to other regions. Such exports have had limited success, and most Christian missionaries now adapt the religion to the culture

---

[79]Ronald L. Numbers, in *Religion and Science Debate*, ed. Harold W. Attridge (New Haven, CT: Yale University Press, 2009), pp. 25-27. There is no evidence that white people originated anywhere near the Caucasus Mountains.

[80]Jacobs, *Original Sin*, p. 207.

whenever central doctrinal matters do not arise.[81] Of course, a few Christians still haven't realized that racism is totally contrary to Christianity.

30. Christianity is antidemocratic.

Christianity is itself attached to no political system or ideology, though it has often been used for political purposes from the time of Constantine's Roman Empire through the European monarchies of the 1500s to 1700s to Franco's Spain in the 1900s. The only connection of Christianity with politics—and it is an important one—is to see that God's justice is done on earth. The authority of a just ruler is to be obeyed and respected; an unjust ruler is to be ignored or, if necessary, resisted.[82] When rulers are both unjust and powerful, most people, including Christians, are in practice afraid not to yield. Yet some Christians bravely resist. It was Christians who overcame the injustice of the Roman emperors; the Jesuits tried to stop the colonial exploitation of indigenous South Americans; Christians brought about the abolition of the slave trade; Dietrich Bonhoeffer struggled against Nazi injustice; Martin Luther King Jr. led the civil rights movement; Pope John Paul II was a major force in liberating Europe from Communism.

The Christian ideal of equality is based on the principle that every person has inherent, inalienable rights because he or she is made in God's image; because of this, every human being is entitled to justice. Christians believe that each person—past, present and future, in every time and place—is of equal value to Christ. Equality is an idea that developed not among Chinese, Hawaiians, Hindus, Romans, Egyptians, Japanese, Incas or Greeks, but from Judaism and Christianity. The political world, on the other hand, whether based on dictatorship, democracy or special interests, is based on getting, retaining and expanding power. Any form of government, including democracy, can become a disaster when it substitutes the demands of special

---

[81]Dana Lee Robert, *Christian Mission: How Christianity Became a World Religion* (Malden, MA: Wiley-Blackwell, 2009).

[82]Both the English Bill of Rights of 1688 and the American Declaration of Independence in 1776 relied on the medieval right of resistance to unjust rule advanced by such theorists as John of Salisbury and Marsilius of Padua. John wrote, "To kill a tyrant is not only licit but fair and just." Ewart Lewis, ed., *Medieval Political Ideas* (New York: Knopf, 1954), pp. 276-77. Also see John Witte Jr., and Frank S. Alexander, eds., *Christianity and Law: An Introduction* (Cambridge: Cambridge University Press, 2008).

groups for actual justice for individuals. "Liberty and justice for all" is a motto often negated by powerful interests of all sorts.

31. Christianity is a religion of reward and punishment.

It is said that Christians believe because they fear hell and hope for heaven. Christians are thought to hoard up good deeds to outbalance their bad deeds and so earn the right to go to heaven. Some Christians do think that way, or used to when they were children. Humanists as well as Christians like to believe that they are good people. But what can "I am a good person" possibly mean? That I'm not as bad as someone else? Historically, psychologically and biologically, the words make no sense.

Reward and punishment are not the reason that most people believe in Christ. Essential Christian teaching focuses on God's grace, love and mercy and the joy of participating in it. (Grace is the gift of God to humans enabling them to respond with faith.) The Eastern church says that the purpose of Christianity is *theosis* or *theopoiesis*, emptying oneself of self and being filled with God.[83] Christians hope that Christ will give them faith to transform them from within and that the transformation will manifest itself in their outward behavior. Most Christians have believed that any good that they do is the action of Christ within them rather than their own virtue.

Difference of opinion about the relative importance of grace, faith and works has always existed among Christians. Whatever the emphasis, Tradition holds that a person's character is formed over a lifetime. Response to love leads a person toward communion with God; rejection of love leads to separation from God. Christianity teaches that life is the opportunity to open up to a life of love and gratitude. Reward and punishment are beside the point.[84]

32. Christians believe in Christ because they are afraid of death.

It's said that Christians believe in God and heaven because they're afraid of death. Human fear of death is almost universal. But other religions have

---

[83]T. F. Torrance, *Trinitarian Faith* (London: T & T Clark, 1991), p. 188.

[84]Jeffrey Burton Russell, *Paradise Mislaid: How We Lost Heaven and How We Can Regain It* (New York: Oxford University Press, 2006), pp. 8-9.

alternative ideas of afterlives and surviving death, and some seem pleasanter than those of Christianity. Christianity asserts that every person forms his or her own character and is responsible for that character in this life and in eternity. Although the grace of God is offered to all, some reject it and eternally estrange themselves from God. Hindus and Buddhists believe in reincarnation and fear no such estrangement, and atheists rely on the comfort of simply being annihilated.[85]

Christians believe in Christ because they believe that he is the way, the truth and the life that leads us toward harmony with God, the cosmos, living creatures, other humans and ourselves. They believe that he brings us to love, reconciliation and gratitude and that his love is eternal and persists in our life and after our death. Christians call death an enemy that is naturally to be feared. But they also consider the death of the body only a "first" death. Christians believe that this bodily death brings them fuller life—unless they choose not to love and so bring about the "second" death, the death of the soul, which is the eternal loss of God. The real terror is the judgment that may sentence us to that second death. Thus being Christian makes one more afraid of death than being a Hindu, Buddhist, or atheist, and therefore the idea that being Christian allows you to escape that fear is false.

33. Christians need a crutch.

Christians are often said to believe because they need a crutch. Unless a person is willing to agonize hourly in the actual conviction that his or her life is really and truly meaningless, everyone needs a crutch—a basis of support—of some kind. But Christianity is often singled out and demeaned as a faith for the weak and psychologically disabled. This view has influenced intellectuals from the time of the philosopher Friedrich Nietzsche (1844-1900), who said that God was dead and that Christianity was an unhealthy slave morality and the religion of the weak. Karl Marx (1818-1883) denounced Christianity as a means to distract people from their real economic problems by belief in a fantasy reality beyond the earth. Nikolai Lenin (1870-1924) proclaimed that

[85]John Casey, *After Lives: A Guide to Heaven, Hell, and Purgatory* (Oxford: Oxford University Press, 2009); D. Z. Phillips, *Death and Immortality* (London: Macmillan, 1970); Harold Coward, *Life After Death in World Religions* (Maryknoll, NY: Orbis, 1997).

Christianity was a drug that enabled people to tolerate oppression. Sigmund Freud (1856-1939) thought that the Oedipus complex was at the root of all religions.

Christianity can be a crutch. Belief that one will go to heaven is reassuring. So is the belief that God is with us at all times and hears our prayers. The sense of a warm spiritual companion through life is comforting. It's also sometimes a relief to complain and rage against God. It's more pleasant to believe that the cosmos is being guided to a goal that is good than that it is meaningless. On the other hand, Christianity is based on the life and death of Jesus, and on the belief in personal responsibility, the reality of sin, and divine judgment. As the New Testament says, "'The Lord will judge his people.' It is a fearful thing to fall into the hands of the living God" (Heb 10:30-31).

Atheism can also be a crutch. In atheism there is no intrinsic morality, so how to behave is purely a matter of personal choice. At best it means setting artificial standards for oneself. At worst it means acting without regard to others. One of the few truly consistent atheists of all time was the Marquis de Sade (1740-1814). In an intrinsically relative, valueless world, Sade argued, the only sensible thing to do is to seek your own personal pleasure. Whatever we feel like doing is good for us. If we enjoy torturing, fine. If others don't, they don't have to participate, but they have no right imposing their views on us. Crime can be more exciting than sex, Sade said, and a sex crime is the best of all. The greatest pleasure derives from torture, especially of children, and if one degrades the victim the delight is enhanced. Sade's fellow atheists recoiled in disgust at this extreme reduction of their belief, but disgust is not a moral principle.

Besides, the threshold for disgust has been waning. As Alan Jacobs points out, nothing makes people more comfortable than lowering the threshold of unacceptable behavior.[86] If there are no intrinsic moral restraints, none that we don't invent for ourselves, then we have no reason to condemn anybody, including ourselves. A meaningless universe is, well, meaningless. And that lets us do whatever we feel like doing so long as we can get away with it. The most persuasive argument for

[86]Jacobs, *Original Sin*.

atheism is its permission to do whatever we feel like doing.[87] The extreme expression of this behavior is found in sociopaths—people lacking any conscience or empathy at all.[88]

Atheists and humanists avoid relativist disgust by clinging to ideas that sound soft and benevolent, such as "equality," but which have no basis other than religious tradition. Secularists have failed to construct a plausible system of universal ethics that does not rely on baseless assumptions; rejecting relativism, they put up a false front against it and readily fall into relativism themselves.[89]

Another crutch for atheists is just going along with the crowd, whatever the crowd may be. It's uncomfortable to be banished from the tribe for raising doubts. It's convenient to believe that you have no free will and that everything you do is the result of a combination of genetics, upbringing, and chemicals in your brain. No one can blame you. The Big Bang made you do it. Finally, if one is relieved of the burden of convincing others through evidence and reason, one uses the crutch of arrogance and sarcasm to impose one's opinions instead of honestly considering those of others.

34. Christianity is immoral.

Recently, the cover of a magazine asked, "Did Christianity cause the crash?"[90] In fact, a tide of anti-Christian propaganda is holding that "Christianity caused ____" (fill in anything you don't like). The only good thing about it is that Christians can learn how Jews have felt for centuries. Antitheists believe that Christians who do good are either not really Christians or else do good despite their Christianity: Christians cannot do good on the basis of their beliefs, because their beliefs are bad.[91] They also think Christianity is immoral: it supports war, denies rights to minorities, pits itself against science and blocks progress. The antitheists attack all religions but focus on the three most prominent—Judaism, Christianity

[87]James S. Spiegel, *The Making of an Atheist: How Immorality Leads to Unbelief* (Chicago: Moody Press, 2010); Paul C. Vitz, "The Psychology of Atheism," in *A Place for Truth*, ed. Dallas Willard (Downers Grove, IL: InterVarsity Press, 2010), pp. 135-52.

[88]Martha Stout, *Sociopath Next Door* (New York: Broadway Books, 2005).

[89]Markham, *Against Atheism*, pp. 33-36.

[90]*The Atlantic*, December 2009.

[91]Christopher Hitchens, *God Is Not Great: How Religion Poisons Everything* (New York: Twelve, 2007), pp. 173-93; Jacobs, *Original Sin*, pp. 266-69.

and Islam—and their prime target is Christianity. They fail to note that in Europe and America Christians originated hospitals, orphanages, schools and universities. Humanists fail to recognize that their humane values come from Judeo-Christian religion. And one may ask what Christian oppression actually exists in contemporary America: the one that controls universities? The one that controls business and finance? The one that controls the media? The one that dominates the public schools? The one that runs the government? The one that conducts foreign policy? Where is all this hateful oppression anyway?

Immorality is sometimes distinguished from amorality (the lack of any kind of morals), but a more important distinction is between immorality and illegality. Many things are illegal without being immoral—double parking, for example—and many things are immoral without being illegal—for example, paying yourself hundreds of times more than your employees. Sometimes, as in Nazi or Soviet society, it is even illegal not to be immoral: you are obliged by law to inform on your neighbor. Illegality depends on whoever is in control of the state. Immorality is quite different: it means violating a fundamental code of behavior.

Morality and religion don't necessarily go together. In many other cultures, religion has to do with offending or placating gods who are themselves morally ambivalent. The first religion to tie morality inextricably to divine law was Israelite monotheism. An old question asks whether rape and murder are wrong because God says so or whether God condemns rape and murder because they are wrong. Judeo-Christian morality dissolves the difference: some actions are good and some evil by both natural and divine law. Even Christianity is not primarily about morality but about God's love for humanity expressed in Jesus. A recent study of the sense of fairness in societies showed that fairness correlates significantly with participation in religion.[92]

To be moral or immoral requires a free choice. Bacteria, ants, pelicans and robots can be neither moral nor immoral, because they are programmed to act exactly the way they do. Most atheists think that humans, like pelicans or robots, are programmed by genetics and circumstances to do exactly what they do. Having no freedom of choice, we are incapable of

---

[92]"Fair Play," *The Economist*, March 20, 2010, pp. 88-90.

either morality or immorality. Now, if there is no such thing as immorality, Christianity can't be "immoral." What antitheists really mean by saying that Christianity is immoral is that they believe Christianity is opposed to certain values that they think are good.

Christians believe that morality is living in harmony with the divine law found in the "two books": the Bible and nature. In the Bible the truth is revealed in words; in nature it is revealed through mathematics and research into the universe.[93] A principle is a basic truth from which consistent ideas and behavior proceed, and Christians believe that their primary principle is the truth of the two revelations.

In contrast, atheist and humanist morality can have no principle.[94] Dostoevsky's Ivan Karamazov notes that if God does not exist, everything is permitted. If a humanist wants to do good, how does he or she know what is good? If the response is that human nature is basically good, the evidence of both biology and history is counter to the claim. Further, to assert that "man is good" requires some Good by which to measure good. If there is no perfect Good, secularists have no principle on which to base their ideas of what is good. Humanists imagine that the world, once purged of religion, would adopt their own vague, liberal morality, but why would it? Why assume that such a world would embrace compassion, equality, or freedom?[95] Those ideas come from Christianity.

Secularists have been trying to establish secular moral codes without the principle of the Good and have repeatedly failed. Without this basis, ethics become relative, and "a simple 'I disagree' or 'I refuse' [or 'I am offended'] is enough to exhaust the persuasive resources of any purely worldly ethics."[96] I once heard a witness in a child-rape trial say, "Who's to say what's right or wrong in this round world?" The effort of secularism to create a principle in the welter of relativism is like pulling oneself up by one's own bootstraps. The very point of relativism is that it doesn't have a principle: everybody chooses his or her own values. Relativism therefore means that morals

[93]Josef Zycinski makes the point that "the mind of God" in modern physics is mathematical rather than Platonic; he traces the change back to the seventeenth century: *God and Evolution: Fundamental Questions of Christian Evolutionism* (Washington, DC: Catholic University of America Press, 2006), p. 176.

[94]The latest effort to establish atheist morality is Sam Harris, *Moral Landscape: How Science Can Determine Human Values* (New York: Free Press, 2010).

[95]Hart, *Atheist Delusions*, pp. 4-6.

[96]Ibid., p.15.

become a matter of fashion or else are imposed by a self-appointed authority. The atheist Jürgen Habermas and Pope Benedict XVI agreed in a debate that "there had to be some value system."[97] But any value system man creates will be dissolved by man. What evidence is there of moral progress, unless by "moral progress" one means that certain things one personally admires have recently become more common? Relativism and materialism are antithetical to one another, but the two converge in denying a principle of morality based on anything other than personal or cultural preference.

This degrades the "very notion of freedom, its reduction in the cultural imagination to a fairly banal kind of liberty," and the result is both triviality and monstrosities like eugenics.[98] Our own will, based on nothing but itself, feels any limitation on its choices to be intolerable. Any reasonable system of belief, any principles, must be avoided because they interfere with our illusion of absolute freedom, an illusion that ironically leaves us open to infinite manipulation. "The inviolable liberty of personal volition" cannot permit any "standard of the good that has the power (or the right) to order our desires toward a higher end. . . . Choice [seems] to exercise an almost mystical supremacy over all other concerns."[99] The result is "an abyss, over which presides the empty power of our isolated wills. . . . The original nothingness of the will gives itself shape by the use it makes of the nothingness of the world—and thus we are free."[100]

Atheists argue that a coherent morality can be created out of evolutionary principles. They argue that overall the process of evolution rewards altruistic behavior over selfish behavior, breeding more and more altruism into the species. However, there seems to be more evidence against this idea than for it. Allowing it for the purpose of argument, the most it can do is account for the inclination that people have to protect their children, not the moral duty to do so. If we don't abandon our child, fine; if we just don't feel like protecting her, we have no moral duty to keep her. If a Nazi shoves a Jew into a gas chamber, we can say, "That makes me feel bad," or "I find that inappropriate behavior," or "I'm offended," or even "That is unhelpful to evolutionary development," but we

[97]Micklethwait and Wooldridge, *God Is Back*, p. 137.
[98]Hart, *Atheist* Delusions, pp. 226-27.
[99]Ibid., p. 22.
[100]Ibid., p. 105.

have no basis for saying, "That behavior is immoral." We can argue all day with the Nazi or call him all sorts of names, but we can offer no principle on which to dispute his choice.

Sade argued, consistently with his atheism, that without basic moral principles behavior is simply a matter of choice. If you prefer dining to raping, okay, so long as you don't prevent him from raping.[101] If you don't like killing Jews, fine, but on what basis do you interfere with the preference of others to do so? The rights of the victim? Without a moral principle there is no basis for assigning rights to the victim—or anyone else. The idea that evolution, when defined as being without purpose and goal, can produce a basis for moral action is illogical, unfounded and frankly impossible. Under some circumstances, violent xenophobic behavior fits with evolutionary development better than altruistic behavior. The horrors of post-Christian behavior are no longer speculation but already being realized.[102]

If there is no absolute standard of morality, then there is no standard by which individual and social moralities can be judged. No standard at all. And this means, for deconstructionists and radicals, that the dominant morality will be determined by domination, power and force. The only real alternative to absolute morality is imposition of a manmade morality on a public intimidated by power and deluded into thinking that their choices are their own. The arrival, persistence and success of new elites who operate by repression and intimidation will continue.

Humanists and other secularists affirm that causing others unnecessary suffering is bad, but they cannot explain on what basis it should be considered bad. If one insists that there is no principle on which to base morality other than human preferences, then one has destroyed the possibility of moral truth and abandoned morality to either personal preference or to the dictates of power groups. Ian Markham calls this a "cozy atheism" that bases its morality on Judeo-Christian values while claiming not to. Values without principle are simply products of whoever is in power. If God goes, morality goes. Although the antitheists "are good at deciding to affirm basic moral values, it is difficult to see how the discourse is justified."[103]

---

[101]Jeffrey Burton Russell, *Mephistopheles: The Devil in the Modern World* (Ithaca, NY: Cornell University Press, 1986), 146-49.

[102]Hart, *Atheist Delusions*, pp. 229-40.

[103]Markham, *Against Atheism*, pp. 58-59.

Since both Christians and atheists can be immoral, is there any distinction in their behavior? Often not, but "as far as we can tell, very few of those carrying out the horrors of the twentieth century worried overmuch that God was watching what they were doing either. That is, after all, the meaning of a secular society."[104] In historical fact, the gentle values promoted by humanists and other secularists today are themselves based in Christianity.[105] Where did the idea of liberty, equality and fraternity come from? Not from the Greeks or Romans. Christianity was a giant rebellion against the pure power assertions of the ancient world.[106] Not from the Aztecs or the Mongols, either, but from the Enlightenment. And the Enlightenment came from what preceded it: Christianity. Christianity is the first philosophy to have enunciated and promoted these values. Christianity invented the idea of human rights.[107] There were no human rights in antiquity—in Egypt or Babylonia, Greece or Rome, China or India or Mesoamerica. There was only power. Christianity speaks truth to power, and it does so on the basis that there are rights inherent in every human being that are inalienable because they derive from the God who is both human and divine. Those who deny that there is truth can't use it to speak to power. If there is no God, there are no inherent rights—only temporary artificial "rights" imposed by pressure groups.[108] This is not a question of belief but of reality. As William Lane Craig put it, belief in God is not required for morality, since many atheists behave morally. It's much simpler: the actual *Being* of God is necessary for morality.[109] God the Creator is the basis of moral behavior.

35. CHRISTIANITY WARPS CHILDREN.

Some antitheists claim that teaching children Christianity is a form of child abuse.[110] In fact, they believe teaching children any religion at all is child abuse. What's more, they claim that teaching children any ideology

[104]Berlinski, *Devil's Delusion*, pp. 26-27.
[105]Hart, *Atheist Delusions*, pp. 29-31.
[106]Ibid., p. 115.
[107]Ibid., pp. 214-15.
[108]Mark D. Linville, "The Moral Poverty of Evolutionary Naturalism," in *Contending With Christianity's Critics: Answering New Atheists and Other Objectors*, ed. Paul Copan and William Lane Craig (Nashville: B & H Publishing, 2009), pp. 58-73.
[109]William Lane Craig, *On Guard: Defending Your Faith with Reason and Precision* (Colorado Springs: David C. Cook, 2010), pp. 127, 134-35.
[110]Richard Dawkins, *God Delusion* (New York: Houghton Mifflin, 2006), pp. 349-87.

is child abuse—but wait. No, they don't claim that. In fact they now run antitheist summer camps, as the Soviets used to do when they founded, supported and funded the League of the Militant Godless.[111] Still, contemporary radicals usually refrain from praising the U.S.S.R.; their ideology has to be tuned to just the right pitch.

Objectively there is no difference between teaching children secularist ideology and teaching them religious ideology. Atheists feel that they are a persecuted minority, even though American public education is already slanted toward materialism and relativism, and education departments promote what they call social constructivism. The classic meaning of "materialism" is that everything that exists is matter. But the term has become meaningless, because the universe includes not only matter, but also energy, antimatter, dark matter, dark energy, quantum fluctuations, the electromagnetic spectrum and more. "Naturalism" is the view that no being exists apart from the physical world of space-time; nature is all there ever was or ever will be. Subscribers to this view often hold that the mind and consciousness are essentially physical.

It is impossible to raise a child without any worldview at all. By the time a child is seven, he or she is wearing spectacles with some sort of coloring. The ideal might be to remove the coloring from the lenses for a clear view, but atheists persist in using colored lenses that they earnestly declare to be clear. If a child's psychological health is the chief concern, it is open to question whether it is better to teach children that they are responsible for their actions or to teach them that their lives have no meaning or purpose beyond what they happen to feel like doing or having. Antitheists consider any Christian education, whether at school or at home, a corruption of innocent minds, but exposing children to Christianity at least gives them some idea of the alternatives to the dogmatic materialism of the Western world, where public teaching of the idea of an intelligent planner is often against the law. Antitheists are unapologetic about indoctrinating their children into their own worldviews, which deny the true, good and beautiful. Some even boast about doing so. One scientific atheist proudly asserts that his "children have been thoroughly and successfully indoctrinated to believe . . . that belief in God is a form of mental weakness." The

[111]Robert Service, *Stalin: A Biography* (Cambridge, MA: Belknap, 2004), p. 268.

same person refers to faith as a viral infection and says that "religion is beyond irrelevant. It's evil."[112] Society is so permeated by materialism that it's hard to see how teaching (or even just allowing) children to think about the immaterial can be wrong.[113]

Once Christians move on to higher education, they tend to be witnesses for—or often against—their religion. They are seldom neutral. Where Christian education is weak, superficial and condescending, it gives young people the idea that Christianity is easy or simple or even silly. People who are exposed to weak Christian education in their early years tend to be inoculated against it and often consider it irrelevant. This is especially true of children whose "Christian education" stops at age twelve to fourteen. No one would assume that the level of math that they knew at thirteen was advanced, but many people believe that the level of religion they knew at thirteen is advanced. This is a problem with much Sunday school education. It is also a major problem with the religion taught in state schools in countries where Christianity is established. Such state religion classes are often taught by people whose own sophistication about religion is extremely low. The teachers themselves tend to be skeptical or even contemptuous of the lessons. In most European countries where religion is established, Christianity is dismissed with a shrug.

36. THE CHRISTIAN COMMUNITY HAS REPENTED FOR ITS SINS AGAINST OTHERS.

Some Christians think that they have repented enough already. But Christians regard themselves as being in one body united with Christ. No Christian is individually responsible for the crimes of others, but all Christians share responsibility for the crimes of the community. Crimes of the Christian community include African slavery, persecution of Jews and repression of free thought. Recently a number of Christian leaders and churches have apologized for such sins, but the community as a whole has not yet taken responsibility.

[112]Elaine Howard Ecklund, *Science vs. Religion: What Scientists Really Think* (New York: Oxford University Press, 2010), pp. 13, 19. Ecklund's work is useful but suffers from lumping the social scientists in with hard scientists, whereas hard scientists are more likely to be Christian. The sociologist Rodney Stark is always reliable: Rodney Stark, *What Americans Really Believe: New Findings from the Baylor Survey of Religion* (Waco, TX: Baylor University Press, 2008).
[113]Markham, *Against Atheism*, pp. 23-24.

Atrocities performed by Christians are not rare, nor are they limited to one denomination or another. No one ever served Christ by suppressing the truth, and the Christian community hasn't yet followed the path of reconciliation all the way to its end. On that path are acknowledgment of guilt, realization of the impact on those who have been hurt, acknowledgment that there is no adequate justification for the harmful behavior, willingness to accept the consequences of that behavior, and a request for forgiveness.

Recently, however, some Christian bishops and other leaders have gone so far as to apologize for converting people to Christ. They say that it is wrong to convert Buddhists, Hindus, Muslims and others, because everyone is on a separate but equal path to God. Whatever this idea may be, it is certainly not Christian. Christ asked his followers to teach him to all peoples (Mt 28:19; Lk 24:47). Recognizing the value in other religions is intelligent, fair, enlightening and fruitful, but denying the central beliefs of one's own is sterile. The good is not to reduce everything to the lowest possible denominator but to experience the full richness of all religions.

37. Kings, popes and other leaders used Christianity to justify their power.

It is the current fashion of historians to make power the main explanation for people's actions, which is a distortion of the way people actually think and behave, as if there were no love or loyalty, no commitment to justice or peace. To a large extent this tendency is a projection of current cynicism onto people in the past. Christ said that his kingdom was not of this world, but the church is a human institution. Like every other human institution, from the preschool PTA to the Kremlin, it is political and involved in power. A church with no relationship to power—unaffected by society outside it and free of politics within it—exists as an ideal but never in practice. Power struggles within the Christian community have always existed; merely to list them would take volumes. But the Christian community would not have survived if, over time, power had not been trumped by charity (Greek *agape*). Perhaps a new generation of historians may perceive that love is more a driver of human behavior than power.

The question, then, centers on the relationship of Christianity to authorities of "secular" power. Until the eighteenth century the very idea of separation of church and state was virtually unthinkable. From ancient

Egypt and Babylonia, through Greece and Rome, China and Japan, medieval and early modern Europe, Russia and Turkey—in all these cultures, spiritual and temporal leadership were either centered in one person (Pharaoh and Caesar were believed to be gods) or as closely conjoined as Siamese twins. So the question has to be more precise: To what extent did authorities wielding naked power use Christianity as a justification for that power, and to what extent were the spiritual authorities compliant? Here are just a few examples.

Roman authorities crucified Jesus and sporadically persecuted Christians for three centuries. The most vicious and violent persecutions, such as those under Nero (A.D. 54-68) and later Diocletian (284-305), were aimed at eradicating Christianity and its followers. Thus it was dramatic when the emperors Licinius and Constantine together decided on a policy of religious freedom in 312, culminating in 313 in the so-called Edict of Milan.[114] Constantine enforced the policy and began to favor Christianity above other religions. It is often thought that Constantine made Christianity the official religion of the Empire, but that is another historical myth. It was more than fifty years until the Emperor Theodosius the Great (r. 379-395) established Christianity as the official religion of the realm.

Whether Constantine was a sincere convert to Christianity has been debated, though historians tend to think that he gradually accepted it and died as a Christian.[115] But the state of Constantine's soul is not the point. His support of Christianity changed the whole relationship between it and the power of the Roman Empire. Before Constantine, Christians regarded the empire as the enemy, the Devil's chief tool on earth, and its rulers (Nero for example) as antichrists. Christians often refused to serve in the imperial army and to perform other civic duties such as sacrificing to the god-emperor. After Constantine, however, Christians tended to regard the empire as God's providential instrument for the spread of the faith. The emperor was transformed from an antichrist to "the equal of the apostles," as Constantine's biographer Eusebius put it. A practical effect of Constantine's favor of the church was that office seekers, who previously

---

[114]Beth DePalma Digeser, *Making of a Christian Empire* (Ithaca, NY: Cornell University Press, 2000), pp. 122-23.

[115]Harold A. Drake, *Constantine and the Bishops* (Baltimore: Johns Hopkins University Press, 2000), pp. 187-91; Peter J. Leithart, *Defending Constantine: The Twilight of an Empire and the Dawn of Christendom* (Downers Grove, IL: InterVarsity Press, 2010).

had profited from being either hostile or indifferent to Christianity, now began to embrace it as a means of securing imperial favor. So long as the emperors were hostile to the church, the church was threatened from outside; now it was threatened from inside by power seekers whose faith was often minimal and superficial.

Constantine, never a modest person (in his pre-Christian days he thought of himself as a manifestation of the sun god Apollo), exercised a greater and greater role in the church, convening meetings of bishops at his pleasure and using his authority to influence their decisions. Whatever Constantine's inner faith may have been, he saw that Christianity was a growing influence in the empire, so he channeled its energies to advance the unity of the empire under his personal leadership.

The decline of the empire in the fifth century did not mean the decline of Christianity. It is often assumed (another historical myth) that the "barbarians" who invaded the empire and eventually sacked Rome in 410 were pagans. The Visigoths, Ostrogoths, Lombards—even the Vandals—were already Christian before they invaded. Of the major invaders, only the Anglo-Saxons and the Franks were pagan. The Anglo-Saxons were gradually converted in the sixth and seventh centuries. The Franks, who were steadily becoming the superpower in Western Europe, converted under the reign of King Clovis (r. 481-511). A descendant of Clovis, Charlemagne ("Charles the Great"), united much of what is now France, Germany and Italy under his rule. In 788 Pope Hadrian I declared Charlemagne "the new Constantine," and in 800 Pope Leo III crowned him Roman emperor (the origin of the Holy Roman Empire). Meanwhile the power of the Eastern emperor in Constantinople continued to decline until in 1453 the Muslims completed their conquest of the modern Balkans, Turkey, the Near East and North Africa. In the West, the center of power was the alliance of the Franks and the papacy.

No one doubts that Charlemagne was a believing Christian, however unchristian many of his activities were. He saw the power of the empire and the power of the church as one. He advanced Christianity through force of arms against the Muslims in Spain and the pagan Saxons in what is now northwest Germany. And he advanced his empire by using the bishops and other Christian authorities to strengthen his powers. Charlemagne declared that the duty of the king-emperor was to protect "the people," by which he meant the whole Christian community. The king was God's representative on earth, symbolized by the anointing of each new king in imitation of the kings of Israel. Counts and bishops alike served as administrators of royal authority. When bishoprics fell vacant, the king took them over until he chose a new bishop. The king founded schools in order to create an educated clergy. Royal edicts were made known to the public by being announced in local churches. If Charlemagne or any of his counts or bishops had been asked where the line was between church and state, they would not have understood the question. The king's authority, derived from Christ, was over the entire community of his subjects.

Even in the so-called "investiture controversy" of the eleventh century, often presented as a struggle between popes and emperors, the idea of a division of powers in the community was unknown. During the great eleventh-century struggle between Pope Gregory VII (r. 1073-1085) and the emperor Henry IV (r. 1056-1106), Gregory had his own emperor, kings and counts while Henry had his own pope and bishops. Neither side had the slightest idea of a conflict between church and state. The idea of a single Christian community under the king led to the partition of Europe after the Protestant Reformation, when each country adopted the religion (Protestant or Catholic) of its ruler. The custom survives in a number of European countries today. For example, in the United Kingdom, at the queen's coronation in 1953, she was anointed and took an oath as head of the (Protestant Anglican) church to "defend the faith." The idea might seem quaint today, but it was the order of things in reality through most of Europe before the French Revolution of 1789. Beginning in 2000, the secularists in control of the European Union have been attempting to erect a barrier between religion and the state comparable to that in America.[116]

At present, even where in Europe church and state are technically united, everyone understands the distinction between temporal and ecclesiastical authorities, and Christianity has little influence in the corridors of power. However, in the United States the tension between church and state has become acute. The history of that relationship is long and complicated and tied to the First Amendment, which promises freedom of religion but does not mention separation between church and state, leaving

[116]Philip Jenkins, "Church-State Disconnect," *Christian Century*, February 23, 2010, p. 69.

the field open to endless legal contention. The media generally consider Christianity the antiprogressive mainstay of conservativism because of its moral objections to abortion and gay marriage. The alliance of the Christian conservatives with the (mostly non-Christian) neoconservatives during the Bush years was counterproductive, yet not so many years ago Christianity was identified with liberalism in the civil rights and antiwar movements and in the struggle against eugenic sterilization of the "unfit."

Whether Christianity is better "liberal" or "conservative" is open to question, or whether it is truest to itself by being neither. A 2009 survey of members of mainline Protestant denominations shows 48 percent declaring themselves liberal, 19 percent moderate, and 33 percent conservative (the most conservative were Baptists; the most liberal the United Church of Christ).[117] It is appropriate to render unto Caesar, but only what is appropriate to render unto Caesar.

Christians are often said to be either submissive or tyrannical. Inquisitions, religious wars and pogroms are alleged to prove the vicious nature of Christians; conscientious objection and obedience to authority are alleged to prove how cowardly they are. Some Christians really are lukewarm, despite the biblical warning: "As for the cowardly . . . their place will be in the lake that burns with fire" (Rev 21:8). Yet from the first to the twenty-first century Christianity has produced martyrs who suffer torture and death for the sake of Christ. These are real, individual persons with the usual human fears and feelings. Yet they underwent torments such as boiling oil, wild animals, sawing, stretching, stoning, crushing, shooting, emasculation, rape, roasting, beheading, hanging, drawing and quartering, burning at the stake, crucifixion, racking and gouging. Examples of modern martyrs are Dietrich Bonhoeffer, Franz Jägerstätter, Martin Niemöller and Martin Luther King Jr. Many others, such as Desmond Tutu, risked torture by decrying tyranny. And at the very beginning of it all, Jesus was taunted, beaten, mocked, flogged and crucified.

Some alleged Christians profess belief in Christianity yet behave abominably; other alleged Christians behave nicely yet deny belief in Christian teaching. Many Christians have been bloody oppressors, most recently Robert Mugabe of Zimbabwe and Slobodan Milosević of Serbia. However

[117]*Christian Century*, April 7, 2009, p. 13.

unchristian their behavior, they did profess Christianity, as did the apartheid rulers of South Africa. Though the horrors perpetrated by such alleged Christians do not compare with the horrors of anti-Christians such as Hitler, Stalin, Lenin and Pol Pot, Christians are supposed to hold themselves to a higher standard.

38. CHRISTIANITY IS EUROCENTRIC AND COLONIALIST.

Christianity was Eurocentric for centuries for the chief reason that it was decimated almost everywhere except Europe. Having been so closely developed within European culture, it was often spread by missionaries with European forms and values. But Christianity is no longer Eurocentric, and there is no single Christian culture.

For thirteen hundred years after the Arab conquest of Christian Africa and West Asia in the 600s, Europe was the center of Christianity. But the centuries before and after reveal a wider picture. Jesus, the apostles and almost all the earliest converts were West Asians. In the first six centuries Christianity spread northward and eastward from Palestine throughout Syria and Asia Minor and as far as Iran and even India. The earliest existing church building is in Iraq. As late as 600, the vast majority of Christians were in Africa and Asia. Westward, Christianity spread both to Europe and to North Africa.

In 600, most Christians lived in Africa and Asia, and most of the centers of Christianity were there. The five great centers of Christianity, led by the most important bishops—called patriarchs—were Jerusalem and Antioch in Asia, Alexandria in Africa, Constantinople (now Istanbul in Turkey) and Rome—the only one solidly in Europe. In the 600s, with astounding suddenness, the picture changed dramatically. All of North Africa and almost all of West Asia were subdued by Islam, overwhelming three out of the five patriarchates: Jerusalem, Antioch and Alexandria. Spain and the Mediterranean islands were taken by Islam, and northern and eastern Europe were for several centuries all that remained to Christianity. After 1453, when the Muslim Turks conquered Constantinople, the only ancient patriarchate left in Christian hands was Rome.

For a thousand years Europe was the center of Christianity, but that current is now reversing. About two-thirds of Christians now live in Africa, Asia and Latin America. The proportion of non-European Christians has climbed steeply in the past hundred years owing to the growth of the church in those areas and the decline of Christian belief and practice in Europe. An important question among Christian leaders today is to what degree the teaching and practice that evolved in Europe is essential and how much is merely cultural. Brazil, Nigeria, Congo, South Korea, Mexico, the Philippines, Peru and Kenya all have higher rates of adult baptism than the United States, let alone Europe. In Europe, Christianity is growing only in Russia. As the centers of Christianity shift to Asia and Africa, Christianity seems unlikely to be thought of as European in the future.[118]

39. The crusades were imperialist aggression.

For centuries in Western Society the crusades were generally considered a Good Thing. There were crusades against hunger, disease and crime, and many movies and books for young people made medieval crusaders heroic models to follow. President Eisenhower entitled his memoir of World War II *Crusade in Europe.* All that changed in the 1960s, since when the crusades started to be considered a Bad Thing. The historian Geoffrey Barraclough, for example, called them colonial exploitation.[119] But since humanity is complex, few historical events are simply good or bad. Two generations ago, a book called *1066 and All That* made fun of historians' tendency to divide events into Good Things and Bad Things, but many contemporary historians have gone back to doing so. It's more helpful to explore what happened.

For over three hundred years (roughly A.D. 350-650) the Mediterranean lands from the Atlantic all the way eastward to present-day Iraq were predominantly Christian. Since Islam did not exist before Muhammad (570-632), the religious differences in the region were primarily among Christians, Jews and polytheists. All the great centers of Christianity except Rome—Antioch, Alexandria, Jerusalem and Constantinople—were in what became predominantly Muslim regions. These centers (known as patriarchates) were central to Christian scholarship, theology, liturgy and education. Then, with amazing suddenness, from Muhammad's conquest of western Arabia in 632 to the conquest of Syria, Egypt and Iraq by 661, the Christian heartlands of Antioch, Jerusalem and Alexandria fell under

---

[118]"Sub-Saharan Africa Is World's 'Most Religious' Area," *Christian Century*, May 18, 2010, p. 19.
[119]Rodney Stark, *God's Battalions: The Case for the Crusades* (New York: HarperOne, 2009), p. 7.

Muslim rule. By 750 the Muslim empire stretched from what is now southern France to what is now Pakistan.

This was one of the most rapid and permanent changes in world history. If Charles Martel, "the Hammer," king of the Franks, had not defeated the Muslims in 732 at the Battle of Poitiers in central France, all of Christian Europe might have been subjugated. It was undoubtedly a good thing for Western Civilization that Charles won the battle, for it began a gradual retreat of Islam in Western Europe that was completed only in 1492 with the conquest of Granada by the Spanish monarchs. It was also undoubtedly a bad thing for Islam. Western historians until the twenty-first century considered the preservation of Western Civilization a plus, but the current revolt of the West against Western Civilization has produced the opposite opinion. One interpretation, now thoroughly debunked, went so far as to claim that the Christian defeat of the Muslim invasion of Western Europe set back economic, scientific and cultural progress.[120]

Be that as it may, the fact is that in the eleventh century Muslims occupied the holiest sites of early Christianity, including the holiest of all, Jerusalem. Some of the Muslim rulers of these Christian lands were harsh and some were lenient—but on the whole Christians were allowed to make pilgrimages to Jerusalem, where they worshiped primarily at the Holy Sepulcher, the traditional place where Jesus' body lay before his resurrection. It is hard for modern people to realize how important the Holy Sepulcher was to medieval Christians unless they compare it to the importance of Mecca today for Muslims. Muslims abhor the idea of a Christian power holding Mecca, and Christians felt as strongly about Jerusalem. When warring Muslim factions cut Jerusalem off to pilgrims during the 1080s and 1090s, Christians were truly and sincerely horrified. In addition, the Seljuk Turks were seizing Christian Asia Minor (now Turkey) from the Christian Byzantine Empire, and the emperor Alexius I asked Pope Urban II for help against them. Urban called the First Crusade in 1095, and from 1096 until 1291 Christian and Muslim armies battled for the narrow strip of land on the eastern Mediterranean in what is now Israel, Palestine, Lebanon and Syria.

---

[120]Hart, *Atheist Delusions*, pp. 49-53.

The motives of the crusaders were mixed. Some went out of piety: the naive Children's Crusade of 1212, for example, was spontaneous and ended horribly in the death or enslavement of the children.[121] Some went for plunder: the vicious sack of Christian Constantinople by Western Christian armies during the Fourth Crusade in 1204 was an unmitigated evil that undermined Byzantine resistance to Islam and still remains a vivid scar in the memory of Eastern Orthodox Christians. Many crusaders went for both piety and plunder.

Motives on the Muslim side were equally mixed. There is some truth in the idea that later kingdoms such as Spain and Portugal in the 1500s took the crusades as an example when they established foreign colonies, and the Romantic idealization of the crusades was still lingering when the British General Allenby triumphantly entered Jerusalem in 1917 during the collapse of the Turkish Empire. But to view the medieval crusades as "imperialist" or "hegemonic" is to impose modern concepts on a very different culture from our own and to forget that people take religion seriously. Distorting past cultures is no more helpful than distorting present ones. The medieval crusades have only the thinnest connection to the colonialism and imperialism of the 1800s and 1900s.

Today, the words "crusade" and "jihad" should be used with as much care as live hand grenades.

40. Christian Missionaries Degraded Indigenous Cultures.

This is a common criticism by people who believe that Columbus should be tried post mortem as a wicked exploiter of Native Americans and that the indigenous peoples of Mexico suffered more under the Christians than under the Aztecs. The source of such criticism is the Romantic fallacy of the noble savage. Humans are naturally good, it is claimed, and societies left untroubled will be happy. A glance at the ancient Assyrians might shake that assumption. To use a later example, it is easy to assume that before Western influence the Hawaiians were happy, peaceful people. How could they not have been in such a beautiful, fruitful, isolated environment? Yet in fact they were very warlike. Cruelty is common in all

[121]Gary Dickson, *Children's Crusade: Medieval History, Modern Mythistory* (New York: Palgrave Macmillan, 2008).

cultures. The Huron of North America held neighboring tribes in terror of their intense cruelty long before Europeans ever set foot in their forests.

That being said, how one evaluates Christian missions depends on one's point of view. If one holds that believing in Christ is good for people, one will have a different view from one who holds that it is bad for them. "Why can't Christians just let other people alone?" is a common question. Christians believe that they aren't permitted to, for Christ himself orders them to go out and preach the gospel to all nations (Mt 28:19; Acts 1:8).

As to particulars, the missionary efforts to get people to wear Western clothing and to have sex only in the "missionary position" are well-known and widely derided. On the other hand, the work of missionaries such as Albert Schweitzer in health, education and other social services such as orphanages are also well-known. Most important are basic changes in culture. It may be asked, for example, whether the Aztec custom of slitting open the bowels of slaves and prisoners for the purpose of removing their living hearts as sacrifice, or the Inca custom of sacrificing children and (it appears) flaying the skin off their bodies, were better for people than making them go to church on Sundays.[122]

How far it was proper for missionaries to adapt the Christian message to the culture in which it was being preached was an ancient question that became particularly acute in the 1500s with the conversion of the Americas. The powerful movie *The Mission* illustrates the efforts of Jesuit missionaries to protect the natives of Paraguay from the depredations of secularist exploiters, who were often backed by bishops whom they had in their pockets. Distinctions between what is essential to Christianity and what are cultural accretions are made by Orthodox, Catholic and Protestant missionaries.

Over the last few decades, as Europe has become more secularized, the nature of missionary effort has shifted. Missionaries are more American, or Korean, or African, than European. Pentecostals, rather than Orthodox, Catholic, or traditional Protestants, are the most vigorous missionaries. The question of culture remains, as Korean missionaries find that different people can be as uncomprehending of Korean culture as they

---

[122]The work of the anthropologist Guillermo de Anda is featured in "Into the Mayan Underworld," *Science Illustrated*, May/June 2009, pp. 46-47. See also Charles Gallenkamp, *Maya: The Riddle and Rediscovery of a Lost Civilization*, 3rd ed. (New York: Viking, 1985), pp. 74-75.

are of European culture. As China becomes more Christian, it may produce missionaries with yet another cultural dimension.

41. The great cathedrals were built with slave labor.

According to this new myth, the great European cathedrals were built by slaves, many of whom died in the work. It is also claimed that people starved because the money and energy put into the cathedrals' construction diverted funds from social needs. It is asked whether Jesus would have approved of such enormous places of worship. Though we don't know Jesus' architectural views, it is clear that he did not object to the Jerusalem Temple.

The purpose of cathedrals was to create a sacred space where a community of Christian people could join together in the presence of God to hear readings from the Bible and sermons and to participate in common rites such as baptism and the Eucharist (Lord's Supper). The earliest Christian services took place in what are today called "home churches," or else in synagogues where the congregations had decided to follow Jesus. As the number of Christians grew, buildings were set aside or constructed for worship. Naturally, larger communities constructed larger churches in order to accommodate their growing numbers. The leaders of these larger communities were usually called bishops (from Greek *episkopoi*), who were assisted by elders or priests (*presbyteroi*) and deacons (*diakonoi*). The large church where the bishop presided at services was called his chair or seat (*cathedra*). These large churches came gradually to be called cathedrals.

Given the relative poverty of the early church, the original cathedrals were unimpressive. But starting in the 300s, when Constantine the Great began to favor Christianity, powerful leaders began to finance the construction of vast and elaborate cathedrals. At the same time, Christianity began to emphasize the value of beauty as a gift of God and even an aspect of God's nature, so that architecture and artworks were seen as a form of divine worship. Cathedrals grew in size in proportion to the population of their cities. They were constructed with gifts and grants from the wealthy and with contributions and tithes (church taxes) from citizens. In places where bishops were also secular rulers, the construction and maintenance of cathedrals was part of the government's duties. As the physical center of the cities, cathedrals became centers of civic pride as well, and competition between cities ensued. Architectural styles of cathedrals varied widely according to time and place, the best-known being Byzantine, Russian, Romanesque, Gothic, neoclassical, modern and postmodern. The most famous cathedrals are in the Gothic style that began in France in the 1100s and dominated northern Europe into the 1500s (and was revived in the 1800s). The cathedrals were conceived as a mirror of the beauty of the cosmos, both in its mathematical proportions and harmonies and in all its diverse works and creatures.

As to the claim of slave labor: the fact is that there were virtually no slaves in medieval Europe—vastly fewer than exist in the world right now today. Medieval serfs were not slaves. They were bound to the land but had personal rights. Besides, there were few serfs—let alone slaves—constructing medieval cathedrals. Craftsmen working on cathedrals profited from displaying their skills publicly. They still do. And they were concerned not only for money and public relations: it was customary to place many works of craft and art unsigned and where they could be seen by no human eyes—only God's. The purely materialistic claim that cathedral-building caused poverty is defeated by the purely materialistic fact that the townspeople of cathedral cities profited enormously from the new jobs in construction and support that were generated.[123]

42. Christians burned down the Great Library at Alexandria.

It has been said that the ancient Library of Alexandria contained 700,000 books, until the Christian Emperor Theodosius ordered it burned down in 390. There was a Great Library at Alexandria, which may have contained tens of thousands of books, but Christians did not burn it down.

The library was established by King Ptolemy II (304-246 B.C.). The best sources indicate that it burned during the war between Caesar and Pompey forty-seven or forty-eight years before Christ. It may have been restored and, if so, may have burned again during the wars of the pagan emperor Aurelian in A.D. 272. Hart remarks, "In all likelihood, though, the original Great Library was very much a part of the distant (and somewhat legendary) past by that time. It was certainly no longer in exis-

[123]Jeffrey Burton Russell, *Medieval Civilization*, pp. 301-26.

tence in A.D. 390."[124] Ptolemy III (246-221 B.C.) constructed a temple to the god Serapis in Alexandria, a building that was torn down by Christians and imperial soldiers in 391. There may have been a small library attached to this temple (the Serapeum), and that library could have been destroyed along with the temple. "Of this, however, there is no evidence whatsoever," Hart observes. "None of the ancient accounts of the destruction of the temple says anything about the destruction of a library, not even the devoutly pagan rhetorician and historian Eunapius of Sardis."[125]

43. Christianity Has Nothing to Do with Law and Justice.

First of all, what is legal is not always just, and what is just is not always legal.

Most countries have complex legal systems. There are laws regulating everything from smoking to paying taxes to rape and murder.

But what is the basis of these laws? Some argue that it is pragmatic, or practical in a given social context. Over the past century the pragmatic idea that laws evolve through the contest of social forces against one another has come to prevail. In this view, laws properly shift according to the state of a society, so "justice" varies from time to time and place to place. This view has been characterized by Yale law professor Arthur Leff as "the grand Sez Who?" In practice this means that Bob's opinion is as valid as Betty's: it depends on who sez. In theory it means that pragmatists claim the right to "sez me" without any principle on which it can be demonstrated that their sez is better than any other sez.[126]

The main Western alternative to pragmatism is natural law (in China it's the Confucian rule of harmony; in Islam it's *sharia*). The Greek and Roman philosophers, notably Cicero (106-43 B.C.), argued that a universal natural principle of justice, *jus naturale*, underlies the laws of every culture. Civilizations have many different laws about small things, but almost all have some laws in common—for example, laws against rape and murder. Christian philosophers and jurists united natural law with divine law

[124]Hart, *Atheist Delusions*, p. 37.

[125]Ibid., p. 38.

[126]Arthur A. Leff, "Unspeakable Ethics, Unnatural Law," *Duke Law Review Journal*, December 1979, cited in Timothy Keller, *Reason for God: Belief in an Age of Skepticism* (New York: Dutton, 2008), pp. 153-55.

based on the Bible.[127] Because Christians believe that natural law is the human expression of divine law, they consider it immutable and permanent whatever the social context. Natural law, though already challenged in the 1700s, prevailed into the 1900s. Though currently most jurists are pragmatists today, others find natural law indispensable for justice.

A different distinction between two ideas of law affects the way justice is perceived.[128] Individual justice demands that a person be treated fairly; for example, he or she should not be punished for an offense he or she did not commit. Besides individual justice, there is also communal or distributive justice: the ideal of level opportunity for each human being. This sort of justice emphasizes special attention to the marginalized. In the U.S., the marginalized have included African-Americans, Catholics, Mexicans, homosexuals, victims of crime, the poor and the illiterate. In some places, such as North Africa and the Near East, Christians and Jews are the most marginalized. Christianity demands both individual and distributive justice. Both can be achieved without diluting the core of Christian Tradition. Currently, individual justice is often set aside in favor of distributive justice. When individual justice and distributive justice conflict, the relative merits of natural and pragmatic law need to be examined again.

What criteria separate just laws from unjust laws? Some cultures have laws that seem wrong. For example, in some countries an adulterous woman can be legally stoned to death, and U.S. laws not long ago used poll taxes to prevent African-Americans from voting. But on what basis are such laws wrong? Are they unjust, fundamentally wrong, because they violate natural law? Or did they only become unjust when power groups declared them so and had the power to enforce their views? If so, what happens when power shifts? If Hitler had won the war, antisemitism would be legally established as right and just. But would it then actually be right and just? That is something that pragmatism cannot answer. But natural law answers firmly and unequivocally that murder, rape, torture and persecution are always wrong under any circumstances in any society. A pragmatic jurist's response to the question of rights is to let the parties fight it out and see who wins. That is not the Christian answer. To the Christian, rights emanate from natural and divine law, not from power politics.

---

[127]Brian Tierney, "Natural Law and Natural Rights," in *Christianity and Law*, pp. 89-103.
[128]Witte and Alexander, *Christianity and Law*.

Christians believe that justice means the conformity of human law to God's law. Some things, Jesus taught, are always wrong and some are always right, no matter what the current social consensus may be. My late wife deliberately broke the segregation laws in the South in the 1950s by sitting with the African-Americans at the back of the bus. Luckily she was never arrested, but her behavior was not a ticket to popularity (with either whites or blacks). For her there was no hesitation: the law was stupid and unjust, so it was right—morally necessary by natural law—to disobey it. Christians in infinitely more dangerous situations (as in Nazi Germany or Soviet Russia) have deliberately disobeyed unjust laws that were wrong. Christian legal tradition says that we have the duty, as well as the right, to disobey orders that are contrary to natural and divine law.

Westerners squirm over the claims of some Muslims that *sharia* (Muslim religious law) should take precedence over secular law. But Christian Tradition too holds that divine law takes precedence over secular law. Martin Luther King Jr., made the point clear: "A just law is a man-made code that squares with the moral law or the law of God."[129] The other, pragmatic, legal view is decidedly non-Christian.

The idea of the unjust king goes back to the Old Testament, especially the books of Samuel and Kings. God was always regarded as the true king of Israel, but because of the people's desire for a human ruler, God permitted them to choose kings. However, there was no guarantee that the kings would be good. More often than not they were unjust and ruinous. Some New Testament texts counsel obedience to the authorities (1 Pet 2; Rom 13:1)—but then there was Nero, so Christians had to think about where to draw the line. Justice and law were carefully examined by Christian philosophers and jurists from the eleventh century onward. They said that when ruled by a just government, people should obey the laws, but if an unjust ruler promulgated unjust laws, it was the duty of the Christian citizen to ignore them. Christian jurists argued that if a ruler attempted to force people to obey unjust laws, they must refuse at whatever cost. They must also work to remove the unjust ruler—by peaceful means if possible or by rebellion if necessary.

The next question was who had the right to declare a ruler unjust and

[129]Martin Luther King Jr., *Letter from Birmingham Jail* (Philadelphia: American Friends Service Committee, 1963).

worthy of being deposed. Pope Gregory VII (r. 1073-1085) and his followers believed that the pope had that authority. Later, in the 1400s, "conciliarist" theologians argued that an ecumenical (universal) council had the right to remove an unjust pope.[130] In England, John of Salisbury (d. 1180) argued for the "right of resistance": the idea that the people had the right to remove a clearly unjust ruler. Marsilius (Marsiglio) of Padua argued in his book *Defender of Peace* (1324) that the "better part" of the people (those people with education, knowledge and responsibility) could make that decision. Such ideas were modified and passed down through Sir Edward Coke (1552-1634) and John Locke (1632-1704) to Thomas Jefferson. They are enshrined in the Bill of Rights of the English Revolution of 1688, the American Declaration of Independence of 1776, and the various declarations of the rights of man from the eighteenth century to the twenty-first century.[131] Legislatures and presidents can be as unjust as kings. The people—the majority, or the consensus of ruling power groups—can also be unjust. But there is no way of determining that in pragmatic law. If what is "right" and what are "rights" are determined by political power, then they will keep changing. If power falls to those who would deny freedom of speech to everyone who disagrees with them, pragmatic law may slow the destruction of freedom but has no principle by which to stop it.

Divine and natural law provide a basis for justice that pragmatic law cannot. If the universe has no meaning, then justice has no foundation and we can make of it whatever we like. It is argued that a fat lot of good natural and divine law have done for women, minorities and others who believe their rights have been violated. But the very idea that anyone has any right to just treatment comes from an inherent concept of natural law. The rights of women were affirmed by Christ and the early church, and there was no anti-African discrimination in the church before the 1500s. Sadly, Christians have often violated divine law by misinterpreting it, for example, in manipulating or forcing conversions. This is the failure of Christians but not of the principles of Christianity. Women's rights and minority rights come directly or indirectly from the Christian idea of divine, absolute justice.

---

[130]Francis Oakley, *Conciliarist Tradition: Constitutionalism in the Catholic Church, 1300-1870* (Oxford: Oxford University Press, 2003).

[131]The English Bill of Rights was the model for the American Bill of Rights (the first ten amendments to the Constitution).

Christianity Is Stupid

44. Bright people don't believe in God.

There is no evidence that intelligent people are more likely to be atheists than stupid people, but many atheists simply define belief in God as a sign of stupidity itself. People with bachelor's degrees are somewhat more likely to be atheists than those who do not go beyond high school, but people with advanced degrees are somewhat less likely to be atheists than those with only a bachelor's, and slightly more than half of college professors believe in God.[1] Correlation with income is firmer: those who earn more than $150,000 a year are more likely to be atheists.[2] Perhaps when you feel materially secure, you feel that you don't need God. Many Christians are anti-intellectual and make bizarre statements about both science and theology. At the same time, many scientists make ignorant arguments about religion. One academic finds it ridiculous to think that "there's some person sitting on a chair with a beard who has lightning coming out of his fingers or makes pronouncements about how people should live."[3] Of course it's ridiculous, as every Christian would agree.

Some of the dullards who have believed in God are the musicians Palestrina and Johann Sebastian Bach; artists such as Leonardo Da Vinci and Caravaggio; writers such as Dante and J. R. R. Tolkien; philosophers such as Augustine, Thomas Aquinas, John Calvin, René Descartes, Alfred North Whitehead and Antony Flew; and scientists (I list more of these because antitheists often claim that religion and science are incompatible) such as Louis Agassiz, André-Marie Ampère, Robert Boyle, Tycho Brahe,

---

[1]Amarnath Amarasingam, "Are American College Professors Religious?," *Huffington Post,* October 6, 2010 <www.huffingtonpost.com/amarnath-amarasingam/how-religious-are-america_b_749630.html>.

[2]*Christian Century,* June 16, 2009, p. 13.

[3]Elaine Howard Ecklund, *Science vs. Religion: What Scientists Really Think* (New York: Oxford University Press, 2010), p. 71.

Nicolaus Copernicus, Georges Cuvier, John Ambrose Fleming, Galileo, Pierre Gassendi, William Harvey, Werner Heisenberg, William Herschel, James Prescott Joule, William Kelvin, Johann Kepler, Carolus Linnaeus, Joseph Lister, Charles Lyell, James Clerk Maxwell, Gregor Mendel, Isaac Newton, Louis Pasteur, Max Planck, Bernhard Riemann and Nicolaus Steno. The antitheists retort that these people are too old and dead to have been aware that science disproves God. But here are brilliant people who believe in God today: Stephen M. Barr, Francis S. Collins, Simon Conway Morris, William Lane Craig, Owen Gingerich, Stanley Jaki, John C. Lennox, Alister McGrath, Kenneth Miller, Alvin Plantinga, John Polkinghorne, John A. Pople, Marilynne Robinson, Hugh Ross, Allen R. Sandage, A. N. Wilson and N. T. Wright. And that's just the beginning. At the world's leading research universities a much higher proportion of Christians is to be found in departments of natural science than in departments of humanities or social science. Among the leaders of the antitheist movement today, few are actually professional scientists.

45. Scientific evidence has shown that there is no God.

Many nonscientists believe this myth. In reality, science poses more problems for atheism than it does for theism.[4]

What would scientific evidence against God be? Science defines itself by its effort to explain the physical world of matter and energy. Since science properly prohibits itself from investigating the nonphysical, there can be no scientific evidence against God. However, physicalists shift from science to metaphysics when they assert that only what science can investigate is real. This is a simple declaration of a philosophical worldview, not a scientific proposition.[5] That science investigates only the physical in no way shows that there is nothing beyond the physical. If scientific evidence disproved God, the many first-rate scientists who believe in God would be atheists.[6]

---

[4]Ian S. Markham, *Against Atheism: Why Dawkins, Hitchens, and Harris Are Fundamentally Wrong* (Malden, MA: Wiley-Blackwell, 2010), pp. 74-79.

[5]Victor Stenger, *God: The Failed Hypothesis: How Science Shows That God Does Not Exist* (Amherst, NY: Prometheus, 2007), fails to understand that God is not a hypothesis.

[6]Francis S. Collins, *The Language of God: A Scientist Presents Evidence for Belief* (New York: Free Press, 2006).

46. Christians persecuted Galileo for saying Earth revolves around the sun.

The story goes that Galileo was imprisoned, tortured and forced to renounce his belief in the heliocentric view that Earth revolves around the sun. In fact, he was never imprisoned, never tortured and never forced to abandon heliocentrism; he was punished for refusing to alter his theological stance. Even in the mythology of Progress, Galileo wasn't the first "martyr" for science; that place is reserved for Giordano Bruno (1548-1600), who also defended the heliocentric view and was burnt at the stake on February 17, 1600.[7] Bruno, however, was not burnt for his scientific views but for the theological heresy of pantheism and his speculations about magic.

Galileo (1564-1642) has become a stereotype of the noble scientist struggling against the ignorant forces of Christianity. This portrayal is anachronistic and simplistic. For one thing, Galileo was a practicing Catholic. For another, in Galileo's time there were no set boundaries between what we now call "science," "philosophy" and "theology," and modern use of the word "science" did not appear until 1725. In Galileo's time, those whom we would now consider scientists were referred to as "natural philosophers," and that is what Galileo considered himself to be. The idea of a war between science and religion was invented in the late nineteenth century.

The "Galileo affair" is a complex story, with plenty of blame to share—if we are looking for blame rather than understanding. The overt issue was whether Earth moves in orbit around the sun. The concept of the solar system, which people today take for granted, was not physically proven until 1727. Until the late 1600s, the prevailing view among scientists was the Aristotelian-Ptolemaic geocentric system, which placed Earth in the center of the universe. Common sense, empirical observation and philosophy all held that the Earth was motionless. There is no point here in describing the Ptolemaic geocentric view other than to observe that it was

---

[7]Jole Shackleford, "That Giordano Bruno Was the First Martyr of Modern Science," in *Galileo Goes to Jail*, ed. Ronald L. Numbers (Cambridge, MA: Harvard University Press, 2009), p. 63. Stéphane Garcia, "Galileo's Relapse: On the Publication of the Letter to the Grand Duchess Christina (1636)," in *The Church and Galileo*, ed. Ernan McMullin (Notre Dame, IN: University of Notre Dame Press: 2005), pp. 265-78.

no superstition but rather an extremely accurate mathematical predictor of the movement of the sun, moon, stars and planets on the assumption that the globe of the Earth was the center of the system. The issues surrounding the geocentric versus heliocentric view had three major aspects: mathematical, philosophical and theological. Most scholars at Galileo's time were inclined to accept the mathematics, if not the theology, of the heliocentric world. The Ptolemaic system worked very precisely for all practical purposes. Its problem was that it was maddeningly complex. Could Occam's razor be applied—could a system be invented that would be at least as accurate as Ptolemy's and a great deal simpler? The first person to work one out in a precise manner was Nicolaus Copernicus (1473-1543). His book *De revolutionibus* ("On the Revolutions of the Heavenly Bodies") was published just before his death in 1543. By taking the sun rather than the Earth as the center, Copernicus made the complex Ptolemaic system unnecessary. His work, refined by Johannes Kepler (1571-1630), long remained known only to a few, and it stirred little controversy until Galileo pressed the argument.

Galileo was a brilliant mathematician and natural philosopher. He taught Ptolemaic astronomy at two universities, but beginning in 1597 he began to recognize the superiority of the Copernican hypothesis. In 1609 to 1611, Galileo's use of the newly invented (though not by him) telescope revealed the mountains of the moon, the satellites of Jupiter and the phases of Venus. His zealous defense of the Copernican view created a controversy that provoked complex political maneuvering and infighting. One of his political misjudgments was to waffle between the purely mathematical argument for placing the sun at the center and the assertion that this represented the actual physical reality of the cosmos. Many philosophers, such as Charles Borromeo (1538-1584), correctly argued that Galileo had not presented sufficient empirical demonstration of the heliocentric hypothesis. Still today, mathematical hypotheses about physical nature have to be confirmed by observation in order to become proper scientific facts, and physical proof of the sun-centered system did not appear before the 1700s.[8]

The philosophical controversy soon became a concern for Christian

---

[8]Dictionaries report more than sixty-six shades of meaning of the word "nature."

theology. So long as the heliocentric view was presented purely as a mathematical hypothesis, it was safe in both theology and philosophy. But when it was presented as physical reality, it seemed to be in conflict with the Bible, several passages of which speak of the motion of the sun and the immobility of Earth. Purely as a mathematical hypothesis it continued to be attractive, and in 1611 Galileo was honored and feted by Pope Paul V. Banking on this success, Galileo campaigned to have the church embrace the new system. Galileo made a theological argument that had been supported for over a thousand years from the times of Origen and Augustine. This argument, called accommodation, was that the infinite God, knowing human limitations, must address himself to people in terms they can understand. He does so in different ways, so that the Bible can be interpreted on a number of different levels. When the text says something that is contrary to sense and reason, it is to be read metaphorically. When Jesus said that he was a door, he did not mean that he was made out of planks. Jesus himself made it clear that he used metaphor: "I have said these things to you in figures of speech. The hour is coming when I will no longer speak to you in figures" (Jn 16:25). Thus Galileo could argue that the book of Joshua's statement that the sun delayed setting in response to Joshua's prayer could be taken metaphorically and accommodated to natural philosophy. Galileo's opponents agreed, but they insisted that if a physical hypothesis seeming to contradict the Bible had not been actually *proved,* the biblical text trumped it. Accommodation said that interpretations of the Bible could change according to scientific demonstration about nature but not by mere speculation.

Between 1611 and 1615, conservative Aristotelian philosophers outflanked Galileo politically, arguing that heliocentrism was theologically as well as philosophically false. Galileo would have been better off presenting his system in the 1300s than in the 1600s, because in the 1500s biblical studies in Western Christianity shifted strongly away from the metaphorical toward the literal. Metaphors convey a sense of what God is in human terms. God accommodates us by speaking in language that we can understand. That God is a king, or God is a shepherd, means that he acts as king and shepherd for us, but God's nature is not limited to "king," "shepherd" or any other metaphor. Martin Luther, John Calvin and other Protestant Reformers dismissed what they viewed as the excessive reliance of the Catholics on metaphor, tradition and reason and demanded a return to the primacy of the Bible. The Catholics responded by reemphasizing the Bible themselves and pulling back from metaphors that seemed to stretch too far. Thus by 1615 both Protestants and Catholics wanted to use the principle of accommodation sparingly.

In 1615 Galileo continued to defend his views,[9] but in February of that year a complaint had been lodged against him with the Roman inquisition. In December 1615 Galileo went personally to Rome to defend himself, but on February 26, 1616, he had a meeting with Cardinal Robert Bellarmine (1542-1621), who warned him not to press the heliocentric theory publicly. Galileo agreed not to, and that promise became the technical reason for his later downfall. On March 5, 1616, the Index of Prohibited Books declared the Copernican system physically undemonstrated (which was true at the time). It banned Copernicus' work until it could be corrected and proved, and it enjoined Galileo to stop promoting it.

Despite this, Galileo still had a large number of defenders, including Pope Urban VIII (r. 1623-1644), who admired his work and subsidized his research. But complex and tangled politics now interfered. Galileo's famous book *Dialogue on the Two Chief World Systems* was crucial. It received an imprimatur (church permission to publish), but in the course of the year in which it was published (1632) it was used against Galileo by his enemies. The *Dialogue* was aimed at refuting conservative geocentric arguments, and it featured a character named Simplicio, "Simpleton." This was a monumental political blunder on Galileo's part. During the summer of 1632 it was brought to Urban's attention that "Simpleton's" dialogue reflected some of the pope's own views. Urban felt betrayed and was especially upset that Galileo had violated his pledge to Bellarmine, so he founded a special tribunal to investigate Galileo for heresy. The tribunal presented its findings to the Holy Office (the Roman inquisition), which on June 22, 1633, found Galileo guilty of "vehement suspicion of heresy" (a technical term meaning something like "moderately bad heresy"), whereupon the pope banned the *Dialogue*, forbade him to write anything

[9]For example, his "Letter to Grand Duchess Christina," in Stillman Drake, ed., *Discoveries and Opinions of Galileo Galilei, Including: The Starry Messenger (1610), Letter to the Grand Duchess Christina (1615) and Excerpts from Letters on Sunspots (1613); The Assayer (1623)* (New York: n.p., 1957).

further about the Copernican system, and confined him to house arrest in his own villa near Florence for life.

The heresy for which Galileo was condemned was essentially that something could be true in natural philosophy that was untrue theologically. The always-sensitive question "what is truth" underlay the whole affair. Early church fathers had spoken of "the two books" in which God showed himself: the Bible and nature. Accommodation could harmonize them, but accommodation was out of fashion in 1633. When it regained theological respectability in the nineteenth and twentieth centuries, the issue abated, and Pope John Paul II formally rehabilitated Galileo in 1992.

Heliocentrism does not make humans insignificant. Modern physical cosmology says that the universe has no center, so any place in the cosmos—including Earth—is as much at the center as any other. And the existence of intelligent life on Earth makes it a rare or possibly unique place.[10] The Galileo affair was a painful one, but it was not a battle between science and religion.[11]

47. Christianity differs from atheism in being faith-based.

Atheists do not discover that life is meaningless; they simply declare it to be so. The dictionary properly gives the primary meaning of faith as "confident belief in the truth, value, or trustworthiness of a person, idea, or thing" and only the secondary meaning as "belief that does not rest on logical proof or material evidence." Sometimes faith is blind in the sense that some Christians and some atheists have blind faith in their views. This entry considers Christian beliefs about Christian faith, atheist beliefs about Christian faith, and atheist faith.

Christians believe there are two types of Christian faith. One sort of faith is intellectual assent to a proposition or system; the other is moral assent in personal trust. The first type of faith includes belief that Christ rose from the dead, or that Christianity as a system is true. The other sort of faith is commitment to Christ as a person in whom we have absolute

---

[10]Dennis R. Danielson, "That Copernicanism Demoted Humans from the Center of the Cosmos," in *Galileo Goes to Jail,* pp. 50-58.

[11]Maurice A. Finocchiarro, "That Galileo was Imprisoned and Tortured for Advocating Copernicanism," in *Galileo Goes to Jail,* pp. 68-78.

trust. Both types are necessary, though the latter is deeper. But these primary two types of faith have eyes wide open. They both require rearrangement of one's life and priorities, and they show themselves in the practice of good works promoted by grace, the divine "current" that God is thought to charge us with. Some Christian thinkers emphasize that the intellect leads people to faith, while others emphasize that faith leads to knowledge.

Atheist ideas about Christian faith are all based on the secondary definition of the word: belief in something intellectually unproven. Of course, blind assent to anything, whether Christian or atheist, is foolish. But antitheists ignore the role played by the intellect in Christian thought and interpret Christian faith as blind assent. They say that faith makes a virtue out of not thinking; that it's easy to believe in something not real if you don't stop to think that it couldn't possibly be true; that those who preach faith are intellectual slaveholders; that faith is believing something with no evidence. John Haught observes that the antitheist argument is a rhetorical strategy involving reduction of all Christians to biblical "literalists," seeing the social role of Christian community as centered on abuse, reducing faith to mindless belief, reducing the role of reason and evidence to the realm of science alone, reducing reality to what can be known by science alone, and reducing the idea of God to a "hypothesis" that (by definition) can't be demonstrated by science.[12] Atheists insist on presenting God and science as alternatives, which is factually incorrect, because God is not an alternative to science as an explanation of natural events. Everyone seeks physical explanations of physical things.

The "God of the gaps" procedure—introducing God to explain phenomena that science hasn't yet explained—is fatally weak. Although God "is the ground of all explanation: it is his existence which gives rise to the very possibility of explanation, scientific or otherwise," serious Christian thinkers know that making God the cause of "individual events explains nothing."[13] An old college friend of mine used to joke that the easiest answer to a history question about the cause of World War I was, "It was God's will." Some Christians really do think that faith is an act of pure

[12]John F. Haught, *God and the New Atheism: A Critical Response to Dawkins, Harris, and Hitchens* (Louisville, KY: Westminster John Knox, 2008), pp. 38-39.

[13]John C. Lennox, *God's Undertaker: Has Science Buried God?* (Oxford: Lion, 2007), p. 47.

will without basis in reason. This "fideism" has generally been rejected in the mainstream of Orthodox, Catholic and Protestant thought. Christians believe that the entire universe is contingent upon God, who sustains it. Events that we consider random may actually be contingent.

Atheism has its own "gap of a God."[14] Atheism, especially its current manifestation as antitheism, is no less based on faith than Christianity. There is no empirical proof of atheism. The antitheist assertion that there is no God is not a scientific statement but an ideological one. And since it is ideological in respect to religion specifically, it is a religious statement. Antitheists cannot avoid making religious statements. The American Humanist Association spent thousands of dollars plastering buses in Washington, D.C., with ads asking, "Why believe in a god?" The Freedom from Religion Foundation erected billboards that look like stained glass but declare "Beware of dogma" and "Imagine no religion."

Faith in anti-religion is as much faith as religion itself. True atheists (those who really think about it) assert a complete philosophy of life as much as Christians do. But most atheists may be simply imbued with current materialist attitudes, living a religion-free existence by not thinking about religion at all. Some atheists honestly admit that their beliefs are a matter of faith.[15] But most wear self-imposed blinders: Michael Devitt declares that "there is only one way of knowing, the empirical way that is the basis of science."[16] How could Devitt know that? Even the famous antitheist Carl Sagan (1934-1996) noticed that we can't scientifically "prove" that we love somebody. Most lives, including atheists' lives, have mostly to do with understandings that aren't scientific.

Materialist, atheist dogma is actually much more restrictive than religious dogma. As Stephen Barr notes, "While religious dogmas do not in fact limit the kinds of things one is able to think about, materialism obviously does. The materialist will not allow himself to contemplate the possibility that anything whatever might exist that [cannot be] completely describable by physics."[17] The materialist has put himself in his own strait-

[14]Michael Poole, *The 'New Atheism: Ten Arguments that Don't Hold Water* (Oxford: Lion, 2009), p. 55. Physicalism offers scientific explanations as a replacement for God.

[15]Lennox, *God's Undertaker*, pp. 34-35.

[16]David Berlinski, *Devil's Delusion: Atheism and Its Scientific Pretensions* (New York: Crown Forum, 2008), p. 57.

[17]Stephen M. Barr, *Modern Physics and Ancient Faith* (Notre Dame, IN: University of Notre

jacket.[18] His views banish God, souls, spirits, anything that is not part of the natural world, with the result that "there is nothing but nature. It is a closed system of cause and effect."[19] The materialist assumption is that there is not, cannot be, must not be anything beyond the physical. The materialist atheist says, "I don't believe in God," and he believes that that statement emerges solely from the kilogram of matter called a brain. If so, then the statement "I" is not meaningful. My kilogram of matter produces the reaction "there is no God," but my kilogram is only matter, like your kilogram—so what?

The buzzwords of physicalists are "nothing but," "only," "merely," "simply, "no more than." A human being is "nothing but" a collection of molecules. Francis Crick said, "You, your joys and your sorrows, your memories and ambitions, your sense of personal identity and free will, are in fact no more than the behavior of a vast assembly of nerve cells and their associated molecules."[20] However, the assembly of molecules called Crick didn't actually live that way. Barr, examining the ultimate circularity of physicalism, sums it up this way: "Materialism is true because materialism is true, because it must be true."[21] John Polkinghorne observes, "The very assertions of the reductionist himself are nothing but blips in the neural network of his brain. The world of rational discourse dissolves into the absurd chatter of firing synapses. Quite frankly, that cannot be right, and none of us believes it to be so."[22] Antitheists, who claim to have better minds than others, don't actually believe in minds at all.[23] In fact they are engaged in a "polemic against the mind."[24] The alleged mind is nothing but an illusion produced by complex physical activities in the brain.[25]

A note on vocabulary: The term "reductionism" is less useful than "physicalism" in defining this point of view, because mathematics and the natural sciences properly use a process called "methodological reduction," which involves taking a problem, separating out subproblems and trying to

Dame Press, 2003), p. 15.

[18]Ibid., p. 17.

[19]Lennox, *God's Undertaker,* pp. 28-29.

[20]Ibid., p. 55.

[21]Barr, *Modern Physics,* p. 256.

[22]Lennox, *God's Undertaker,* p. 56.

[23]Steven Pinker, *Blank Slate: The Modern Denial of Human Nature* (New York: Penguin, 2002).

[24]Marilynne Robinson, *Absence of Mind* (New Haven, CT: Yale University Press, 2010), p. 74.

[25]Ibid., pp. 111-12.

explain them in the simplest and most elegant terms that fit the empirical evidence. But atheist reductionists leap from methodological reductionism to reducing the cosmos to the sum of its material parts.[26] "Scientism" is also a confusing term because "science" is an excellent method, while scientism (parascience) is a metaphysical assumption not rooted in scientific method.[27] "Physicalism" is the word most often used for these concepts today. Physicalism implies that we should see the world with only one eye—the physical. If there is something beyond the purely "natural" or "physical" aspects of the cosmos, physicalism will never discover them, because it is by definition unable to discover them. The opinions of physicalists on the question are therefore empty of meaning unless they cease claiming to speak as scientists and speak solely as metaphysicians.

No physicalist I know of truly lives by his or her own expressed beliefs. To do so would be to become insane. To really and truly believe that there is no meaning, even for a few days, is more terrifying than death. I've been there. If a person doesn't, won't and can't live by his or her own worldview, how can anyone take it seriously?

A corollary of the physicalist view is that ideas are not "real" and have no effect. Rousseau's mind, Lenin's, Jefferson's, Hitler's, had no effect on reality? Lennox argues that faith is a foundational basis not only for ideological reductionism but for science itself.[28] The old Roman saying is "Whom the gods would destroy they first make mad"; they might have added that who would destroy the gods must first be made mad. The antitheists manifest theophobia, irrational fear of God, or at least fear of those who believe in God. While quoting statistics that show that smart people are atheists, they know that religion is growing worldwide at a more rapid pace than ever. Even if they were to be successful in eradicating traditional religion, what would likely emerge is probably not what they expect. When people stop believing in traditional religion, they do not end up believing in nothing; they end up believing in *anything*.

---

[26]Markham, *Against Atheism*, p. 66, makes the distinction between causal determinism and reductionism, both of which are outdated.

[27]Robinson, *Absence of Mind*, pp. 35, 129, coined the helpful term "parascience." She notes the crucial difference between real science and "parascience," which is almost opposite to science, since it has "the primary object of closing questions about human nature and the human circumstance." Poole, *The New Atheism*, pp. 60-61, notes that these parascientific positions violate their own verification principle.

[28]Lennox, *God's Undertaker*, p. 60.

Atheism and Christianity both rely partly on faith and partly on reason, so it is not faith against reason, but of two different faiths using reason against each other. As Einstein said, "What separates me from most so-called atheists is a feeling of utter humility toward the unattainable secrets of the harmony of the cosmos."[29] The evidence increasingly points to both harmony and directional purpose in the cosmos.[30]

48. MOST LEADING ATHEISTS ARE SCIENTISTS.

Among the leaders of the antitheist movement today, few are professional scientists. Most leading atheists have been poets, philosophers, journalists, politicians, novelists, playwrights, dictators or media celebrities. However, the reverse statement, "Most leading scientists are atheists," is supported by the statistic that ninety-three percent of the membership of the prestigious American Academy of Sciences say they are atheists or agnostics. But scientists often don't think about God any more than businessmen do. The answer to "Why aren't more scientists Christians?" might be the same as the one to "Why aren't more real estate agents Christians?" They go with the current, and the current flows where the going is easiest.[31]

49. MEDIEVAL CHRISTIANS BELIEVED EARTH WAS FLAT.

No doubt some Christians did believe Earth was flat, but not any educated people. A flat Earth seems to have been commonly believed in very ancient times. The ancient Egyptians thought it was flat. But most Greek and Roman philosophers and geographers—for example, Pythagoras (570-495 B.C.), Eratosthenes (276-194 B.C.) and Ptolemy (A.D. 85-165)—were confident that the Earth was round. Eratosthenes even measured its circumference to within 15 percent of the modern figure.

Then what happened? Did Christianity take over and suppress this ancient knowledge? Not at all. Over a hundred Christian writers discussed the shape of the Earth from the third to the fifteenth century A.D. During

---

[29]David Aikman, *The Delusion of Disbelief: Why the New Atheism Is a Threat to Your Life, Liberty, and Pursuit of Happiness* (Carol Stream, IL: Tyndale House, 2008), pp. 88-89.

[30]Simon Conway Morris, *Deep Structure of Biology* (West Conshohocken, PA: Templeton Foundation Press, 2008).

[31]Discussion of contemporary as well as earlier scientists who were open to Christianity can be found in Henry F. Schaefer, *Science and Christianity: Conflict or Coherence*, 4th ed. (Athens: University of Georgia Press, 2003).

this time, a period of twelve hundred years, there were just two who asserted that the Earth was flat and more than a hundred who attested that it was round. And the two dissenters had no followers. The whole cosmos as Dante (1265-1321) portrayed it in the *Divine Comedy* is based on the spherical Earth; medieval kings carried orbs (globes) as a symbol of their earthly power. An extant globe of the Earth dates from 1491, a year before Columbus's first voyage.

Still, the common story is that Columbus had to make his case for the round Earth against the opposition of benighted churchmen insisting that the Earth was flat and that ships would sail off the edge into the abyss. Columbus appears as a hero standing up against the Bible and the church. It's a gripping tale, but the evidence is all against it.

The fact is that Columbus did not have to overcome any flat-earth Christians at all. What he had to do was to persuade the king and queen of Spain to bet a large amount of their money on the idea that he could sail westward to Asia. This was a hard sell, not because anyone thought the Earth was flat, but because most scholars believed, correctly, that the globe was much larger than Columbus claimed. They were right; he was wrong; and he was the luckiest man in the world when the unknown Americas popped up in time to save him and his crew from perishing in a vast empty distance stretching west from Europe to the East Indies.

But where did the idea come from that Christians used to believe the Earth was flat? It was created in the late eighteenth century, especially by Washington Irving, the storyteller who gave us the headless horseman. In 1828 Irving published a largely fictional biography of Columbus that included a lively, lurid account of our hero courageously facing down his closed-minded Christian opponents. The event never happened. But it was too good a story. It gradually crept its way into other popular histories, and it was picked up by anti-Christian writers in the late nineteenth century in order to show that those Christians who opposed evolution at the time were just as stubbornly ignorant as those who had opposed the round Earth. The power of exciting fiction to overwhelm fact may not have been matched until *The Da Vinci Code* was published in the early twenty-first century. Let's sum up the logic: We know that medieval Christians were stupid. We know that they were stupid because they thought Earth was flat. Because they thought that Earth was flat, we know that they were stupid. Around and around, without benefit of historical evidence. It took well over a century to cut George Washington's fictional cherry tree out of the textbooks, so it may not be surprising that the flat-Earth myth still appears in some texts and teachers' manuals.[32]

50. Christianity represses free thought.

This has certainly been true at times. But other ideologies repress free thought too, so the question is whether Christians tend to be more or less repressive of dissent than other people. The current fact is that Americans of all persuasions are increasingly closed-minded to views other than their own. In contemporary culture, closed-mindedness is evident in identity politics, political correctness and physicalist reductionism. Scientific journals suppress evidence of anything that hints of intelligent purpose in any form, and even evolutionist professors can get into trouble for not being the right kind of evolutionists (atheists) or appearing to be "soft" on the question.[33] Meanwhile, Orwellian thought control is growing in the United States and is already established in Britain and Canada. The Canadian Human Rights Commission has been tireless in punishing (not just debating, not just censuring, but punishing) Christians and others who disagree with its doctrines.[34]

Relativism poses as freedom but is just another form of tyranny: You must believe that all religions are equal because we say they are. You must agree with us that everything is relative, or we will punish you. The only thing that isn't relative is the validity of our correctness. And that is based simply on what we and our colleagues happen to believe and what we have the power to enforce.

In reality, there is only one way that all religions can be equally valid, and that is if they are all wrong, which is the real subtext. Thought-control totalitarians feel the greatest need to suppress opinions precisely when those opinions are most persuasive, because then they are perceived as

---

[32]Jeffrey Burton Russell, *Inventing the Flat Earth: Columbus and the Historians* (Westport, CT: Praeger, 1991).

[33]Berlinski, *Devil's Delusion*, p. 220.

[34]Kathy Shaidle, *Tyranny of Nice: How Canada Crushes Freedom in the Name of Human Rights* (Toronto: Interim Press, 2008).

most dangerous to the ruling ideology. Here is a comment from the left-secular British newspaper *The Guardian*:

> There's an aspiring totalitarianism in Britain which is brilliantly disguised. It's disguised because the would-be dictators—and there are many of them—all pretend to be more tolerant than thou. They hide alongside the anti-racists, the anti-homophobes and anti-sexists. But what they are really against is something very different. They—call them secular fundamentalists—are anti-God, and what they really want is the eradication of religion, and all believers, from the face of the earth. But the fundamentalists saw an opening. Because we live in a multiconfessional society, they fostered the falsehood that wearing a crucifix or a veil or a turban was deeply offensive to other faiths. They pretended to be protecting religious sensibilities as a pretext to strip us of all religious expressions. . . . From everyone being welcome, it had become everyone but.[35]

Christianity is properly open-minded and reasonable. When it isn't, it isn't fully Christian. Christians want to look for truth whatever and wherever it is.

51. Christianity is irrational and unreasonable.

The 2008 movie *Religulous* proposed that religion is a neurological disorder, that it diverts man to destructive courses, that it must die for mankind to live, that we must choose between it and mass death, that humankind is in bondage to fantasy and nonsense, and that while it may appeal, we pay a terrible price for it in wars and torture. The underlying premise is that Christianity is inherently irrational and unreasonable. A distinguished chemist suggests, to the contrary, that Christianity is the most reasonable of any interpretation of the cosmos. There's obviously a gap in understanding here.

From the time of the Jewish philosopher Philo (25 B.C. to A.D. 45) Jewish and Christian thinkers have maintained that the mind can begin to understand the cosmos through the use of reason. The Christian Tradition emphasizes will and intellect. A growing number of people, Christian and

[35]Tobias Jones, "Secular Fundamentalists and the New Totalitarians," *The Guardian*, January 6, 2007, <www.guardian.co.uk/commentisfree/2007/jan/06/comment.religion1>.

otherwise, prefer emotion and even consciously oppose rationality. To prefer emotion to reason is to lose "the ability to follow an argument, detect a false premise, tell whether a conclusion is being drawn erroneously, and recognize the difference between a rational argument and a sentimental appeal."[36]

Dialogue is necessary: people need to exchange and discuss views and evaluate them, which is impossible on the basis of feelings and relativism. The foundational question is whether one believes in objective truth. If not, the conversation can't go anywhere. Even with the best wills in the world, it just means I feel this and you feel that, and so what? Pragmatic law doesn't help either: if you can convince a court that a pen is an orange, then it is legally an orange. It is possible that reason will be devoured by the pressures of interest groups and action committees of all political hues.

It helps to distinguish between rationality and reasonableness. The word "rationality" has been taken over by the physicalists, as the dictionary definition of "rationalism" shows: "the theory that the exercise of reason, rather than experience, authority, or spiritual revelation, provides the primary basis for knowledge." The exclusion of experience, authority and revelation leaves out immense swaths of human knowledge. It leaves room for a different term, "reasonableness," based on "reasonable," meaning "being in accordance with reason or sound thinking." The word "reason" means "good judgment, sound sense." It's obvious that in life reason is not limited to rationalism. Reasonableness involves the careful examination and evaluation of testimony—in personal experience, in law courts and in history.[37] Christianity is reasonable, and it may well be more reasonable than anything else: it is more open-minded than dogmatic relativism or physicalism because it allows for a variety of paths to truth.

52. BELIEF IN CHRISTIANITY IS INCOMPATIBLE WITH SCIENCE.

A person who declares that Christian beliefs won't stand up scientifically has failed to see the empty fallacy of his declaration. He sounds like the

[36]Melinda Symes, *National Catholic Reporter*, January 27/February 2, 2008, p. 7.

[37]Rick Kennedy, *History of Reasonableness: Testimony and Authority in the Art of Thinking* (Rochester, NY: University of Rochester Press, 2004).

Soviet cosmonaut who returned to Earth saying that he had been "up there" and hadn't seen heaven, or like the American surgeon who said that he had never seen a soul during any of his operations. Science by definition has no way to examine Christian beliefs because it properly limits itself to statements about the physical world. Science and Christianity examine evidence in different ways. Their methods are different, but their findings or results are compatible.[38]

Well into the nineteenth century belief in the union of science and theology was standard. But then, as Tina Beattie notes, "In the nineteenth century, the category of religion was . . . bracketed out of a scientific worldview."[39] This bracketing out—the refusal to consider realities beyond the physical—is not inherent in knowledge; the Latin *scientia* refers to all knowledge. The word "scientist" is first attested in 1834. Scientists define their fields as limited to the physical. This definition is reasonable and probably necessary. But it does not mean that entities outside their fields can't exist. Science is supposed to be based on evidence, and there is no evidence that every phenomenon is physical.

If it were true that Christianity and science were incompatible, there would be no Christians who were respected scientists. In fact, about forty percent of professional natural scientists are practicing Christians, and many others are theists of other kinds. Fewer than thirty percent are atheists. In the social sciences the percentage of atheists is higher because the social sciences are concerned with changing human behaviors rather than with discovering truths. In universities, more Christians are found in the natural sciences than in any other fields.[40] For more than a century an enormous number of brilliant contributions have also been made by Jewish scientists. For Judaism as well as Christianity God creates a rational universe and rational minds capable of understanding it.

Objections to Christianity raised by atheist scientists include these presumptions:

---

[38]General information on the relationship between Christianity and science is found at <www.st-edmunds.cam.ac.uk/faraday>.

[39]Tina Beattie, *New Atheists: The Twilight of Reason and the War on Religion* (Maryknoll, NY: Orbis, 2007), p. 39.

[40]Rodney Stark, *For the Glory of God: How Monotheism Led to Reformations, Science, Witch-Hunts, and the End of Slavery* (Princeton, NJ: Princeton University Press, 2003), pp. 193-94. Carlos Eire, *A Very Brief History of Eternity* (Princeton, NJ: Princeton University Press, 2010), pp. 201-4.

- Eventually science will make faith irrelevant.
- It's meaningless to waste time thinking about it.
- I don't understand it.
- The only questions worth asking are secular ones.
- I'm too busy.
- It's a threat to research and education.
- It's a threat to the separation of church and state.
- Religion is private and science is public, so religion ought to stay out of the public square.[41]

As Elaine Howard Ecklund notes, one of the most significant barriers is the fear that colleagues "will think you're nuts" if you express religious views.[42] As a result, "many give in to strong departmental cultures and practice a closeted faith."[43] Groupthink causes significant underreporting of religious belief by scientists for fear of negative sanctions by colleagues. Ecklund continues, "Religious scientists generally try to keep their faith to themselves because of the perception that other faculty in their departments think poorly of religious people."[44] It appears that scientists' attitudes toward religion are more the result of politics and peer pressure than of science. There's another fear at work too: if we think that physicalism is the one safe rock we can hold onto so as to avoid spinning off into the void, we can experience terror that it may fall and cling all the more tightly.

There's more to it than that. The findings of science now indicate that the existence of God is more likely than not. Even more important: "The scientific enterprise itself is validated by his existence."[45] If there were no cosmic order and regularity, there could be no science. Cosmic order derives from the principle that orders it. Physicalists respond that the laws of nature do not need anything to order them: they just exist in themselves. But the laws of nature are neither simple, nor necessary, nor self-evident, nor explained. As the great atheist philosopher David Hume (1711-1776)

---

[41]Ecklund, *Science vs. Religion*.
[42]Ibid., pp. 30, 120.
[43]Ibid., p. 76.
[44]Ibid., pp. 43-45.
[45]Lennox, *God's Undertaker*, p. 179.

showed, these laws are descriptive, not prescriptive. But scientists have to act as if they are prescriptive in order to make meaningful predictions. Imagine the impossibility of proceeding with scientific inquiry if it were not assumed that protons, say, behave similarly in ordinary circumstances. The practical necessity of using the laws often obscures the fact that the laws are human constructs that humans have derived from observing nature.[46] It is completely unknown why they are what they are or whether they may change.[47] Isaac Newton (1643-1727) observed that the laws of nature "are not laws of logic, nor are they *like* the laws of logic."[48]

Antitheists decree the absolute incompatibility of science with Christianity, but Christianity has not been the enemy of science; in fact, sustained scientific development originated in Christian Europe. The Christian view is that God creates the world rationally, mathematically, regularly, poetically and responsibly, and he creates humans with the ability to understand and love it. The alternatives cannot support science: (1) polytheism, with gods at cross-purposes; (2) Islam, with divine monolithic control over every event; (3) pantheism, a world soul with innate desires that cannot be explained rationally. The curious fact that we humans have minds capable of understanding the cosmos indicates that an intelligent mind created the cosmos.

53. Science did not originate in Christianity.

It's commonly assumed that science originated in secular thought. But the word "science" (Latin *scientia*) originally meant learned knowledge of any kind. Not until 1725 was the English word restricted to mean knowledge of the physical world obtained through reason, observation and mathematics. Before then, what today is called science was called natural philosophy (or sometimes natural history). Technology developed independently of natural philosophy and existed millennia before science. The inventors of flint tools did not have a theory about how their inventions worked; they used only trial and error. Science is often—particularly at

[46]Josef Zycinski, *God and Evolution: Fundamental Questions of Christian Evolution* (Washington, DC: Catholic University of America Press, 2006), pp. 114-15.

[47]Recent scientific evidence indicates that the "laws of nature" may not act the same in different parts of the universe: "Ye Cannae Change the Laws of Physics: Or Can You," *The Economist*, September 4, 2010, pp. 85-86.

[48]Berlinski, *Devil's Delusion*, p. 133.

present—aided by technology, but the origins of science do not lie in technology. They lie instead in a rational framework to explain nature.

The essence of what we call science is the union of theory and observation. The question is when and where this union was consummated. The ancient Babylonians made extraordinarily precise astronomical calculations but could not explain why the heavens moved. The ancient Greek philosophers were the first to develop logic and geometry, but they were more interested in speculation than in observation, and the underlying Greek polytheism in which many gods willfully disputed with one another inhibited science from getting purchase in the culture. The Romans had almost no interest in theory at all. The ancient and medieval Chinese developed the best technology anywhere in the world, but their view of many spirits operating in a cyclical cosmos provided them with no theory of science. Further, China closed itself off from the rest of the world for five centuries beginning in the 1400s. In medieval Islam from the 800s to the 1200s there was movement toward science, but it was hindered by the underlying belief that every event is caused directly by God. By 1300 Muslim science was being hobbled by the insistence that true knowledge came only from revelation—the Qur'an or Koran—from the *hadith* (traditions about Muhammad), and from the rules developed from them.

Science arose in Europe and in Christian culture. A recent article questioning this fact warns only against the exaggeration that Christianity was the *only* origin of science.[49] The objective, nonpartisan *History of Science and Technology* lists in its 719 pages very few ideas and discoveries after the year 1400 that originate anywhere but in Europe or areas educationally influenced by Christian Europe.[50] The enormous contribution of Jews to science in the past two centuries has come from Ashkenazi Jews whose education derived from Europe and America.

Until recently historians of science focused on a "scientific revolution" occurring in the 1600s and developing in the Enlightenment of the 1700s. The idea was that the religious wars of the 1500s and 1600s between Catholics and Protestants discredited religion in general, turning thinkers away from the "other world" to concentrate on "this world," or nature. The

[49]Noah J. Efron, "That Christianity Gave Birth to Modern Science," in *Galileo Goes to Jail*, pp. 79-89.

[50]Bryan Bunch, *History of Science and Technology* (Boston: Houghton Mifflin, 2004).

decline of ecclesiastical authority after 1700 permitted wider speculation than previously. Much can be said for this view, for the *History of Science and Technology* has 547 pages of entries dating from the year 1600 onward as opposed to only 172 dating earlier.

But there are also problems with the view. For one thing, Copernicus (1473-1543) was a devoted Catholic clergyman who lived a hundred years earlier than the alleged revolution. Galileo too was a practicing Catholic. For another, the great Enlightenment philosopher David Hume cast doubt on science as well as on religion. Finally, "revolutions" seldom come out of nowhere; they are based on what went on before, however much they may modify it. Historians of science increasingly find the origins of science in Christianity, and the evidence is strongly in favor of this view.[51]

As was proved by historians in the twentieth century, medieval Europe was vastly more technologically innovative than the Roman Empire. Still, as noted, technology can help science—or it can be irrelevant. What was needed was the union of reason and mathematics with observation. Greek philosophical thought with its emphasis on rationality was gradually subsumed into Christian thought from at least A.D. 100 onward. The crucial element in Christian thought was monotheism. Rather than many gods presiding over a semichaotic universe, and rather than an endlessly cyclical universe, there was one creator God who created, maintained and worked through the cosmos he created. And this was not a God directly exerting his unfathomable will in every moment and place. This was a rational God who created a universe with rational regularities, and who created creatures having enough reason and powers of observation to discover these regularities.

The physical and mathematical works of the ancient world were preserved and developed by medieval Christians, Jews and Muslims. The view that Christians demolished ancient science is historically false.[52] Natural philosophy continued through the Middle Ages, although it was secondary to theology.[53] Early theologians such as Augustine (354-430)

---

[51]Edward Grant, *Foundations of Modern Science in the Middle Ages: Their Religious, Institutional, and Intellectual Contexts* (Cambridge: Cambridge University Press, 1997); Stark, *For the Glory of God.*

[52]David C. Lindberg, "That the Rise of Christianity Was Responsible for the Demise of Ancient Science," in *Galileo Goes to Jail*, pp. 8-18.

[53]Michael H. Shank, "That the Medieval Christian Church Suppressed the Growth of Sci-

argued that there were two books by which humans could understand God. One was the Bible; the other was nature. One could approach God through learning the Bible; one could also approach God by learning the natural world through reason and observation. Both books were held to be true. Beginning with Anselm (1033-1109) and Abelard (1079-1142), medieval Christian scholastic theologians emphasized the use of critical reason so much that the Protestant Reformers later accused them of putting reason ahead of the Bible.

Still, one can't properly speak of science as early as the 1100s, because natural philosophy was still mostly theoretical, relying on reason and mathematics rather than on observation. The domination of medieval philosophy by the writings of the ancient Greek philosopher Aristotle in the 1200s and 1300s aided the development of theory but also stifled originality by making Aristotle's views standard and virtually unquestionable. The profound effort of Thomas Aquinas (1225-1274) to combine theology with Aristotelian natural philosophy was brilliant and monumental, but it accepted Aristotle as the last word on too many topics. The combination of reason and observation to produce true science began in the late 1200s and flowered in the 1300s and 1400s. Albertus Magnus (1200-1280) made intricate botanical observations. William of Ockham (1285-1347) is famous for "Occam's razor," the still valuable idea that the simplest explanation covering all known observations is usually the best.[54] But Ockham also made an important theological distinction that enabled the development of science in Christianity without the impediments that it had encountered in Islam. Ockham said that although God's power is absolute, God chooses to create a consistent system in which he rarely intervenes. This premise enabled Christians to believe in a cosmos constructed along rationally coherent, observable principles—without denying that God has the power to change anything if he wished. For example, God could choose to make a cosmos without planets, in which case he would not be "able" to make the cosmos with planets. To use the old, crude question, "Can God make a rock heavier than he can lift," the answer is no, he can't.

ence," in *Galileo Goes to Jail*, pp. 19-27.

[54]The original wording was probably *frustra fit per plura quod potest fieri per pauciora*. The version *entia non multiplicanda praeter necessitatem* does not appear in Ockham's published works. The meaning of both is "the best explanation is the simplest one compatible with the evidence."

God is logical: he is not bound by human logic but chooses to bind himself by his own logic.

Robert Grosseteste (1168-1263), Jean Buridan (1300-1358), Nicolas Oresme (1323-1382), Nicholas of Cusa (1401-1464) and others made observations of importance to astronomy, optics, medicine and the physics of motion. Buridan even anticipated Copernicus and Galileo in conducting thought experiments that indicated that the Earth was in motion. Again, this brings us to the time of Copernicus. The growth of science from the 1600s onward is one of the greatest phenomena of human existence, and it came out of Christianity. Destructive to both Christianity and science is the deconstruction and relativism that promotes the idea that anyone's science is as good as anyone else's because there is no objective reality. Combining hydrogen and sulfur will never produce ice cream. Deconstruction is a reversion to ancient mythologies that lack the idea of rational connections and regularities. Scientists and Christians prefer to pursue truth.

54. The evidence of evolution points away from Christianity.

This view has made its way into popular culture and even textbooks.[55] Here is one example: "Is there a divine purpose for the creation of humans? Evolution answers No. According to evolution, the adaptations of species and the adaptations of humans come from natural selection and not from design."[56] And another: "By coupling undirected, purposeless variation to the blind uncaring process of natural selection, Darwin made theological or spiritual explanations of the life processes superfluous."[57] According to such views, "biological evolution is incompatible with the existence of a Creator."[58]

But such views intrude ideology into science. The basis of most modern biology is neo-Darwinism, a synthesis of Darwin's natural selection with genetics. Almost all biologists base their scientific work on this synthesis. Many, though far from all, neo-Darwinists are atheists. However, con-

---

[55]Michael Poole shows that demanding a choice between evolution and Christianity is an example of the philosophical fallacy of the excluded middle. Poole, *'New' Atheism*, p. 9.

[56]Lennox, *God's Undertaker*, p. 85 quoting Monroe Strickberger.

[57]Ibid., p. 85, quoting Douglas Futuyma.

[58]Ibid., p. 86.

trary to the textbooks cited above, the pure science of biology does not answer, or even properly address, the existence or nonexistence of purpose in the cosmos. Antitheists have imposed their ideology onto biology education to the point where their metaphysical ideology is presented as science. Atheist evolutionists falsely imply that the "question of the involvement of an intelligent agency has been investigated and rejected when in fact nothing of the kind is the case."[59]

But what is "evolution"? The term has been successfully taken over by extremist antitheists (in much the same way that the term "creation" has been taken over by extremist Christians), so that when people say "evolution" they usually mean the atheist variety. It's important to look at what else the word can mean.

In the most general sense, it means development through time, and it can apply not only to biology but also to geology, human history and most other fields. Second, it can mean genuinely scientific concepts and procedures. In biology specifically it can mean the study of change and variation through random variation plus natural selection, microevolution (small genetic variations producing new subspecies), macroevolution (large-scale evolution producing new taxonomic groups over time), artificial selection (as in human-caused breeding of animals and plants), or molecular evolution (specifically the emergence of the living cell from nonliving molecules).[60] Essential concepts of evolution are mutations, mass extinctions and adaptive radiations. Third, evolution can be defined as a metaphysical ideology: capital-*E* Evolution.

Evolution in the capital-*E* sense, the way it is usually used by the media, is not a scientific theory or methodology but a metaphysical ideology specifically designed to exclude belief in purpose. This antitheist ideology is not based on science but on invented axioms. Atheists invent an axiom that no god can exist and then deduce from their own axiom that God does not exist. This isn't a proof; it isn't even an argument. It's nothing but a bald assertion. There is no reason to suppose that Darwin himself, equipped with today's evidence, would endorse atheism. Darwin was a great scientist, not an ideologue.

---

[59]Ibid., p. 89.

[60]Ibid., pp. 98-100; Tom Bethell, "The Cell Declares His Handiwork," *New Oxford Review*, July-August 2011, 18-22.

Atheists claim that it is *possible* to explain the origin and development of life without recourse to purpose, and that might possibly be so. From there it is a leap into the dark to insist that it is not only possible but extremely *probable* that there is no purpose.[61] And many go on to say that it is *impossible* that there is a purpose. The truth of this assertion has never been demonstrated, and some highly respected biologists and paleontologists challenge it. Since proof is impossible one way or the other, the question is whether the scientific evidence itself points more toward cosmic purpose or more away from it. This book does not rely on the specific theory called "intelligent design" but rather presents evidence for the general concept of intelligent purpose.[62]

While they condemn theists for using "God of the gaps" arguments, atheists use "evolution of the gaps." Instead of "God just did it that way," they say, "Evolution just did it that way." They bridge the gaps of the fossil record with what their theory says must have been there. The biggest gap is "the Cambrian explosion," the innovation, in a small moment of geological time about 542 million years ago, of almost all animal phyla. "The Burgess Shale [and the Chengjiang excavations of 1984 show] that, for the history of basic anatomical designs, almost everything happened in the geological moment just before, and almost nothing in more than 500 million years since."[63] Until, that is, the very rapid development of Homo sapiens.

In other words, more than four billion—four thousand million—years after the formation of the Earth, and after ninety percent of the history of life, almost all the basic forms of hard-bodied animals suddenly appeared. Where did the biological information for these new animals come from? According to neo-Darwinism, there must have been a slow evolution toward such animals in the late pre-Cambrian. The problem is that everyone since Darwin has been looking for forms that are transitional from pre-Cambrian to Cambrian, and few have yet been found. The explanation was that pre-Cambrian rocks don't show any hard-bodied animals because fossils in those rocks are so rare. But now intense

[61]Dale A. Russell, *Islands in the Cosmos: The Evolution of Life on Earth* (Bloomington: Indiana University Press, 2009).

[62]Ecklund reports that the intelligent design argument has lessened respect for religion among scientists: *Science vs. Religion*, p. 44.

[63]Stephen J. Gould, "Web of Tales," *Natural History*, October 1988, pp. 16-23.

investigation has made many discoveries of soft-shelled animals in pre-Cambrian deposits. If these deposits can show soft-shelled fossils they could certainly show hard-shelled ones—but they don't. Atheist evolution depends on "climbing Mount Improbable," to use Richard Dawkins's good analogy, by small steps rather than leaps and bounds.[64] That might eventually prove out, but so far there are too many unexplained leaps and bounds. The Cambrian explosion is explained neither by "God just did it" nor "Evolution just did it."

The metaphysical, antitheist side of evolution is based entirely on preselected axioms. Science defines itself so as not to deal with questions of ultimate Purpose, but that doesn't mean that ultimate Purpose doesn't exist. There are gaping fissures between the scientific evidence and atheism. It may turn out that it is more difficult to reconcile atheism with science than to reconcile Christianity with science. Even so, that doesn't prove the truth of either.

Instead, scientific evidence presently points away from atheism, which may explain why antitheists have been making a fuss lately. The origin of life is one of the universal questions. A single living cell is the most complex known machine in the universe—except, of course, for the life forms made up of numbers of cells. Once there is a living cell in existence, the neo-Darwinist synthesis might possibly be sufficient in itself for the development of more complex life, but there is a mountain of improbability that needs to be ascended to arrive at the first life.

Atheistic neo-Darwinism cannot explain the most dramatic discontinuity of nature: the emergence of a living cell from inanimate matter. Because chance mutations and natural selection can't occur in inorganic matter, there can be no evolution of inorganic matter toward living matter. We simply can not get to the origin of life with atheist neo-Darwinism. It is plausible that the first living cell was constructed from previously existing simple inorganic molecules, but as Paul Davies asked, "How do stupid atoms do such clever things"?[65] Either the information present in the DNA of living cells came from a previously existing plan or it emerged

---

[64]Richard Dawkins, *Climbing Mount Improbable* (New York: Norton, 1996). Stephen Jay Gould and Simon Conway Morris have disagreed with Dawkins (and with one another).

[65]Paul Davies, "Quantum Theory and the Ascent of Life," *New Scientist* 184 (2001): 28-32, cited in Russell, *Islands in the Cosmos*, p. 348.

by chance from inanimate matter.

"Emergence" is a recent idea in historical biology that "the basic building blocks of complex structures are available long before they are recruited for new and more sophisticated tasks."[66] Neither the human mind nor honeybees can be predicted from the inflation following the Big Bang. "The concept of emergence is one of the most mysterious, profound, and elusive phenomena in evolutionary biology."[67] It points to a plan imprinted on nature more than to purposeless change. And doesn't the world show purpose? The disproof of purpose would be a universe of pure chaos.

According to the Second Law of Thermodynamics there is not even remotely enough energy to assemble a cell out of proteins and other essential cellular constituents that themselves need to be assembled.[68] Take the constituents and shake them up in a test tube, and they will not produce life. "Left to its own devices, a concentrated solution of amino acids would need a volume of fluid the size of the observable universe, to go against the thermodynamic tide, and create a single small polypeptide spontaneously. Random molecular shuffling is of little use when the arrow of directionality points the wrong way."[69] And once you break open a living cell, it will not reassemble.

Some have argued that with enough time life could spontaneously appear. The old idea was that with enough time enough typing monkeys could produce the works of Shakespeare. But this myth has been disproved. It would take ten to the 80th power monkeys each making a keystroke once a second for the lifetime of the universe (3 x 10 to the 17th power seconds) to produce a two-line couplet of Shakespeare, much less all of his works. The chance of any hundred-word sentence appearing in any library on Earth by random typing is about one out of ten to the 690th power (1 with 690 zeroes after it). By comparison the whole universe

---

[66]Simon Conway Morris, *Life's Solution: Inevitable Humans in a Lonely Universe* (Cambridge: Cambridge University Press, 2003), p. 166.

[67]Dale A. Russell, *Islands in the Cosmos*, p. 350. Atheists consider emergent properties in physicalist terms, while theists consider them part of God's plan.

[68]Orin Hargraves, *New Words* (Oxford: Oxford University Press, 2004), p. 96. There are three laws of thermodynamics: (1) in a given physical system energy cannot be created or destroyed, (2) any given physical system (including the universe) tends to decreasing order, and (3) the rate of decreasing order declines as temperature approaches absolute zero.

[69]Lennox, *God's Undertaker*, p. 121.

contains about ten to the 80th power of elementary particles of all kinds (electrons, protons and so on) and about ten to the 90th power of photons and neutrinos. Another comparison is that the total number of bacteria on this planet is 5 x 10 to the 30th power.

Therefore the odds for true random assembly are vanishingly small and effectively zero. The astonishing fact is that life began on Earth as soon as life became possible, roughly four billion years ago, within only tens of millions of years after the end of major bombardments by interplanetary objects and the formation of liquid water. Early marine fossils have been found dating from 3,779 million years ago, only 21 million years after the late heavy bombardment.[70] A recent discovery of carbon-13 in diamonds that appear to be 4.25 billion years old indicates a possibility that life began even earlier. If that turns out to be true, it would mean that life appeared only about four hundred million years after Earth began to form out of the accretion disc that provided the raw materials for our solar system, and that would make the odds against random generation of life even greater.

It would require vastly more time than the whole universe has existed for life to originate in this random manner: it is about a hundred orders of magnitude too short. And that isn't even the biggest problem. In random assembly, vast amounts of unhelpful mistakes would have occurred, and nearly countless universes would be needed just to store them. The only answer would be to do it exactly right every time. Even in narrow fissures in thermal vents the odds against are fantastic. The famous Miller-Urey experiment of the 1950s to create life in an artificial "primeval soup" failed. Later it was argued that there must have been a vast primeval soup of RNA, but that idea had to be given up too because the information for the complexity of RNA had to come from somewhere. Far from being gibberish, "the roles of DNA, mRNA and protein are identical" in every living creature on earth from bacteria to humans.[71] The odds of life appearing randomly are the odds of winning the powerball lottery every week for a thousand years while buying only one ticket per week. Suppose Earth was seeded by life from outer space. That is remotely possible, but if it is true, it only pushes the essential question one step, for the question

[70]Russell, *Islands in the Cosmos*, pp. 41-53, suggests a possible origin of life.
[71]Lennox, *God's Undertaker*, p. 117.

remains whether life on other bodies could be generated truly randomly, and the answer is still no.[72]

A huge underlying problem is the ultimate nature of randomness. We may think that events are random merely because we don't understand the contingencies that bring them about. Einstein wondered whether there was a hidden determinism involved, a question remaining unsolved. Perhaps the hidden determinism is actually a hidden *determiner.*[73]

Another crucial question is the origin of consciousness: cognitive abilities that go beyond surviving and procreating. Numerous species (dogs, horses and so on) show levels of consciousness; chimpanzees, crows and dolphins show relatively high levels. The development of rudimentary intelligence in species as diverse as crows and dolphins indicates that intelligence has developed along different lines and that intelligence may have been programmed to emerge on Earth. The time of origin of Homo sapiens is still unclear; estimates vary from seventy thousand to two hundred thousand years ago. Is there a continuum between animal and human intelligence? Human intelligence seems to be qualitatively beyond the highest level of animal intelligence in that it is (or can be) self-reflective, reasonable and rational.

As one professor of evolutionary biology remarks, "There are signs that animal evolution passed along some capabilities, 'and then something dramatic happened, a huge leap that enabled humans to break away. . . . Things just took off. Precisely how and when this happened, we may never know.'"[74] In other words, something radical happened to the development of consciousness, something that separates human consciousness from that of even the most intelligent animals. Atheist evolutionists assume that emergence always arises from physical causes and that thought emerges from the material brain. Whether robots can ever achieve freedom beyond what they are programmed to do is a perennial question. Victor Reppert makes an important distinction between the view that mental states are physical states (which they seem to be) and the view that mental states *arise from* physical states. The fact that they correlate does not prove that one

[72]The latest claim to interplanetary origins was made by Richard B. Hoover. Andrew Couts, "NASA Scientist Finds Evidence of Alien Life," *Digital Trends,* March 5, 2011, <www.digitaltrends.com/international/nasa-scientist-finds-evidence-of-alien-life>.

[73]Zeeya Merali, "Physics of the Divine," *Discover,* March 2011, pp. 49-52.

[74]Marc Hauser, *Harvard Magazine*, November/December 2008, p. 12.

causes the other; the assumption that the physical causes the mental is purely gratuitous.[75] Christians more open-mindedly suggest that emergence arises from both physical and non-physical causes.[76]

Atheist neo-Darwinists say there is no progress in the development of life, since there's no plan or goal for it. But they, like the rest of us, can't avoid acting as if their own consciousness is better than nonconsciousness, and they usually presume that their own minds are better than those of the rest of us. Once one admits that consciousness is better than nonconsciousness, one is saying that there is a pattern of improvement in evolution, and improvement entails a goal toward which we are improving—which atheists deny. We cannot progress unless we are progressing toward something. If we set out for Buenos Aires, then every minute we get nearer to Buenos Aires is progress. But without a goal, then every moment we get nearer to Buenos Aires is as meaningless as every minute we get nearer to Chicago, Minsk or Saturn. The philosophical concept of moving toward an endpoint is called teleology, and atheists vehemently reject it, for it implies intelligent purpose. Teleology—the idea that some intelligence is drawing evolution toward a planned end—is seldom explored by biologists, not because there's no evidence for it, but because it's ruled out beforehand by their metaphysical assumptions.[77]

Now, however, some prominent biologists are departing from the conventional wisdom and advancing the idea of convergence: the premise that there is in fact progress, as measured by directionality in accelerating adaptivity and fitness. Evolutionary convergence implies a direction, which indicates a plan. There is a "predictable destination" of biological evolution. An example is the reptile ichthyosaur and the mammal porpoise, which developed entirely independently but acquired strikingly similar features.[78] A deep question is one of information in the scientific sense. The genetic information in a cell is famously comparable to the

[75]Victor Reppert, "Confronting Naturalism: The Argument from Reason," in *Contending with Christianity's Critics: Answering New Atheists and Other Objectors*, ed. Paul Copan and William Lane Craig (Nashville: B & H Publishing, 2009), pp. 26-46; Michael J. Murray, "Belief in God: A Trick of Our Brain," in *Contending with Christianity's Critics*, pp. 47-57, especially pp. 55-56.

[76]Lennox, *God's Undertaker*, pp. 50-51.

[77]Simon Conway Morris, *The Deep Structure of Biology: Is Convergence Sufficiently Ubiquitous to Give a Directional Signal?* (West Conshohocken, PA: Templeton Press, 2008), p. 222.

[78]Ibid., p. 19.

letters in a book. How did the DNA get written?[79] Where did the new information come from to produce a living cell and, eventually, consciousness? The physicalist idea is that the information in DNA "emerged automatically out of matter *by a mindless, unguided process.*"[80]

But matter cannot inform itself. Someone or something has to inform it. And if something does inform it, where did the something get its information? Infinite regress never solved any problem; it provides no reasonable way of discussing problems in the universe. Only in pure mathematics do actual infinite sets exist, not in nature.[81] If a thing gets information from another thing, and that thing gets it from another, where does the original information come from? Information never comes from nowhere. The idea that it may have come from a different planet solves nothing because it only removes the question of origin to another place and then on to yet another. Thomas Aquinas (1225-1274) already recognized this fact when he concluded that causes in nature could not form an infinite series.[82] William Lane Craig puts it succinctly: if the universe caused itself, then it "would have to exist before it came to exist."[83] Self-contradictory statements are logically impermissible, so there can be no time before time and no space beyond space.

Free thought about the evidence has produced theistic views of evolution. Of these there are two sorts. (1) Preprogrammed: At the outset of the universe, God knew all the details of how he would develop it through time. (2) Guided: God did not order each detail but guides development continually to achieve his purpose in ways that cannot be predicted from what has gone on before. For example, when it first became possible, God enabled the necessary proteins to combine to make life. God guides the cosmos rather than frontloading the detailed directions. In either (1) or (2), the information that forms the cosmos and life itself comes from outside the physical universe. Unguided evolution in itself would come from nowhere and would lead only to blind alleys.

---

[79]Lennox, *God's Undertaker*, pp. 139-53, 164-75.

[80]Ibid., p. 55.

[81]Craig, *Contending with Christianity's Critics*, pp. 78-87.

[82]Berlinski, *Devil's Delusion*, pp. 68, 88-89.

[83]This is the "kalam" argument revived by William Lane Craig, *On Guard: Defending Your Faith with Reason and Precision* (Colorado Springs: David C. Cook, 2010), pp. 74-78, quotation from p. 104.

Barring an intelligent planner, the emergence of life is so unlikely that an infinite number of other universes must exist and we just happen to be in the one that got lucky. This is purely hypothetical.[84] The known fact is that this universe exists and that life arose under the most unfriendly circumstances as soon as the early Earth would sustain it. Which fits Occam's razor better: one conscious planner whose existence cannot be proved scientifically or an infinite number of physical universes whose existence cannot be proved scientifically? As Stephen Barr says, "It seems that to abolish one unobservable God, it takes an infinite number of unobservable substitutes."[85] And from David Berlinski: "The whole gargantuan structure is scientifically unobservable and devoid of any connection to experience."[86]

Recently computer science has offered another option: what appears to be our universe is actually a virtual universe designed by a programmer. But it is difficult to see how we could distinguish whether this universe was "virtual" as opposed to "real," or indeed how the virtual universe would not itself be equivalent to real. And a virtual universe would still have to have been programmed by an intelligent entity.[87]

Until the last few years, evolutionary theory has been guided by the idea of contingency—the idea that one tiny change in evolutionary development radically changed outcomes for all species following it. If we could rewind the tape of evolution, the famous zoologist Steven Jay Gould suggested, and change one frame millions of years ago, we might have a completely different outcome today: the fall of one Triassic insect could have led to a world without humans. Recently, however, scientists including Simon Conway Morris, professor of evolutionary biology at Cambridge University, have argued instead for convergence, the idea that certain characteristics are in the cards in the sense that DNA space and the information built into it constrains the possibilities from the beginning. Eyes,

[84]Dale A. Russell, *Islands in the Cosmos*, p. 27, suggests ways such evidence might possibly be found, but Paul Davies, *Cosmic Jackpot: Why Our Universe Is Just Right for Life* (Boston: Houghton Mifflin, 2007), pp. 172-76, finds it unlikely.

[85]Barr, *Modern Physics*, p. 157.

[86]Berlinski, *Devil's Delusion*, p. 153.

[87]Vlatko Vedral, *Decoding Reality: The Universe as Quantum Information* (Oxford: Oxford University Press, 2010); S. Gill Williamson, "Multiverse Properties Impossible to Prove or Disprove using Physics," University of California San Diego, Department of Computer Science and Engineering <cseweb.ucsd.edu/~gill/MultUnivSite/>.

for example, have developed independently and analogously in different phyla, suggesting that eyes would occur regardless of what frames in the history of the development of life were altered. The same can be said, Conway Morris argues, for cognitive abilities and consciousness, and crows and chimpanzees obviously developed their relatively high levels of intelligence independently. Convergence implies directional, value-added change in evolution, an idea that atheists reject. They admit value-added properties in microevolution: a cat with sharper claws is "better" than a cat with dull ones (except for mice and furniture). But in macroevolution—the whole pattern of life through time—atheists distrust the idea of progress, because progress implies purpose.

The classical neo-Darwinist view that evolution always proceeds gradually in small incremental changes has been widely displaced by Gould's theory of punctuated equilibrium. Gould, an agnostic, noted that "most species exhibit no directional change during their tenure on Earth. A species does not arise gradually by the steady transformation of its ancestors; it appears all at once and 'fully formed.'"[88] There are tipping points in Earth's history when sudden changes appear in rapid cascades. Gould's punctuated equilibrium, like Neo-Darwinism, assumes a tree of life where life begins at the root and then branches off into new species, genera, families, classes and phyla. Conway Morris's convergence, on the other hand, argues for a variety of roots, strongly suggesting that there is directionality in biological development, which in turn suggests a patterner. The existence of a patterner is no proof of Christianity, but it makes Christianity much more likely than atheism.

55. Christians Are Creationists Who Deny Evolution.

All Christians believe in evolution in the sense that no one denies that the breeding of rams or roses produces changes through time. As early as George Abbot (1562-1633), one of the translators of the King James Bible, Christians speculated that creation developed through time under the influence of the environment and sexual selection.[89]

All Christians believe in creation: the idea that God creates the cosmos.

---

[88]Stephen Jay Gould, "Evolution's Erratic Pace," *Natural History* 86 (May 1977): 12-16.

[89]Adam Nicolson, *God's Secretaries: The Making of the King James Bible* (New York: HarperCollins, 2003), p. 160.

Some Christians believe in creationism, the belief that the first verses of the book of Genesis (as well as the rest of the Bible) intend a literal scientific statement.[90] These Christians believe that the universe was created in six days less than ten thousand years ago. Creationism has spawned "creation science," the use of evidence to demonstrate that this interpretation of Genesis is scientifically and historically true. For example, creation science argues that fossils are deposits laid down by the biblical flood and deny that humans evolved through time.[91] Creationists do not believe in the Big Bang because it implies that the cosmos is billions of years old, but before 1965 the dominant model was a steady-state universe infinite in time and space, a belief that reinforced atheism. The discovery since then that the universe really did have a beginning has created a new scientific model much more compatible with Christianity.

Most observers say that creation science is a "deformation of science."[92] Nonetheless, forty percent of all Americans think creationism should be taught in schools instead of evolution, and sixty-five percent think that the Old Testament creation story should be taught along with evolution.[93] No wonder a scientist who knows almost nothing about Christianity has said that he would confront a Christian with, "God did not just invent beavers! Beavers arose from a common ancestor."[94] Young Earth Creationists are doing a disservice to both Christianity and science with their easily refutable ideas.

The media promote a war of science versus religion, and everyone is urged to line up on one side or the other. But this is a false dichotomy. After Darwin and Wallace's breakthrough in 1859, theologians accepted Darwin's ideas more readily than scientists did. In the late 1800s Christians who accepted them greatly outnumbered those who did not, but T. H. Huxley (1825-1895) and others chose to declare war on Christianity.[95] Then in the 1920s George McCready Price and his followers declared war against Darwinism by arguing for a literal scientific interpre-

[90]Ronald L. Numbers, *Creationists* (New York: Knopf, 1992).

[91]"Go Figure," *Christianity Today* (November 2011): 13; "Religion and Evolution," *Christian Century* (November 15, 2011): 9.

[92]Zycinski, *God and Evolution*, pp. 38, 63.

[93]Ecklund, *Science vs. Religion*, p. 8.

[94]Ibid., p. 15.

[95]Harold W. Attridge, ed., *Religion and Science Debate: Why Does It Continue?* (New Haven, CT: Yale University Press, 2009), p. 36.

tation of Genesis, producing Young Earth Creationism. The noise made by extremists on both sides since then obscures that fact that most Christians still find evolution and Christianity compatible.

The real contest is not between science and Christianity but between two incompatible worldviews: atheism on the one hand and theism on the other. The focus on evolution by both extremes may be a red herring leading us away from the path of examining the evidence reasonably and dispassionately. Both sides may be rejecting evidence out of fear. Scientists are afraid that science will be buried. Given the enormous amount of money needed to keep most cutting-edge experiments going, scientists fear that the public might become so offended, ignorant or uninterested that money will be available only for narrow technological improvements. Science and Christianity can unite in rejecting fear.

56. Christians object to evolution on the basis of a literal reading of the Bible.

First off, most Christians do not object to evolution. But the extent to which parts of the Bible are literally true has been disputed throughout the history of Christianity. From at least the time of Origen (A.D. 185-254), the majority of Christian theologians have held that the Bible is properly interpreted on a number of different levels—literal as well as metaphorical. The account of creation in Genesis must be true, they have argued, because the Bible is God's revelation. But it can be true in ways other than the scientific and the historical. The Bible comprises songs, meditations, prayers, parables, stories and many metaphors. Christians do not believe that there exists only one true way to interpret any given passage of the Bible. Even the most thorough literalists can't believe that when Jesus said he was "the gate," he meant that he was a apparatus of bars and leather (Jn 10:7-9).

Belief in a historically and scientifically literal interpretation of the Genesis account was in decline as education spread from the 1100s onward, and in the nineteenth and twentieth centuries the decline became sharp. But literal creationism was revived and codified in the mid-twentieth century and given wide publicity by *The Genesis Flood* (1961) by John C. Whitcomb and Henry Morris. It was further spread by Hal Lindsey's book *The Late Great Planet Earth* (1970) and then by the immensely popular "Left Behind" series of books and movies. Catholics, Orthodox and mainline Protestant denominations do not subscribe to Creationism, but it is widespread among American evangelicals. Young Earth Creationists believe that the Bible supports a view of the world as being only a few thousand years old. It's extremely doubtful that that was the original intention of the biblical writers. Insisting that fossils are the result of the biblical flood, asserting that light from the Andromeda Galaxy only appears to be light-years away, and building a Creation Museum showing prehistoric human children romping with triceratops: such ideas encourage mockery of Christianity. Why would God create a six-thousand-year-old planet that gives every evidence of being billions of years old?

Creationism has spread to other countries such as Korea and is now so widespread in the United States that it has become a focus of public dispute. Reasonable people agree that science needs to be taught scientifically by scientists. The definition of science is the study of the physical world; the methods of science include observing accurately, inferring, predicting, classifying, developing questions and hypotheses, and constructing controlled experiments. Neither the definition of science nor its methods include formulating and imposing metaphysical worldviews. Such views are beyond the boundaries of science. Science can't demonstrate what it is unable to investigate. Young Earth Creationists and atheist evolutionists both rely on preconceived dogmas. Antitheists exacerbate the problem by classifying everyone who believes in creation as a Creationist. This underlies the popular myth that the Scopes Trial and the Wilberforce-Huxley debate showed Christians to be stupid.[96]

As most Protestant denominations have declared, and as modern popes have repeatedly taught, there is no conflict between Christianity and evolution when each is reasonably defined. Pope John Paul II said that "a belief in creation, rightly understood, and a rightly understood doctrine of evolution, do not stand in each other's way."[97] God creates and sustains the world and dwells in it as the immanent Word.[98]

---

[96]Edward J. Larson, "That the Scopes Trial Ended in Defeat for Antievolutionism," in *Galileo Goes to Jail*, pp. 178-86; David N. Livingstone, "That Huxley Defeated Wilberforce in Their Debate over Evolution and Religion," in *Galileo Goes to Jail*, pp. 152-60.

[97]Quoted in Christoph Cardinal Schönborn, *Chance or Purpose: Creation, Evolution, and a Rational Faith* (San Francisco: Ignatius, 2007), p. 30.

[98]Zycinski, *God and Evolution*, pp. 60-63.

The standard Christian view is that biological change occurs through time, and that it is a process infused with God's creative purpose. Most Christians believe in the development of life forms through time over a period of millions of years. Most accept that the universe was created about 13.7 billion years ago and Earth about 4.6 billion years ago. To equate belief in creation with belief in Creationism is common but entirely false. Christians believe that God creates, develops and sustains the universe, including Earth and life on Earth. Most Christians affirm biological development planned or guided by God. That is theistic evolution. Only one definition of evolution is incompatible with Christianity: the one that claims it is unplanned and unguided and caused by purely random and mechanistic events. That is atheistic evolution. Christians believe in evolution—when evolution is not defined in a purely physicalist way that makes it impossible for them to believe in it. The war is only between dogmatists on both sides. The evidence is that there is directionality and Purpose in the universe and that it comes from outside.

57. The Legal System and the Media Understand the Relationship of Christianity to Evolution.

Misunderstanding of Christianity and evolution is rife in public and judicial opinion because the distinction between science and worldview is blurred. Creationists argue that "creation science" should be taught in schools along with evolution science, but "creation science" is not pure science. Rather, it's the use of selective evidence to bolster a peculiar worldview. Scientists properly maintain that Creationists have a legal right to their ideas but not the right to teach them as science in the public schools; Christians properly maintain that atheist biologists have a legal right to their ideas but not the right to teach antitheism in public schools. So far, Christians are losing the argument in the courts, but on the other hand, many prominent scientists absolutely opposed to "creation science" point out the evidential problems of the currently dominant view that life has no purpose. Since antitheist evolution is questioned by many scientists, there is no honest reason why their questions should be censored out of the schools.[99]

The legal question is who has the "right" to teach what in the schools,

[99]Jerry Bergman and Kevin H. Wirth, *Slaughter of the Innocents* (Southworth, WA: Leafcutter Press, 2008).

and on this question democratic legislation and the courts are sometimes at odds. The courts have generally rejected anything but atheist biology. Judicial opinions rubber-stamp atheist presentations or simply plagiarize them. The courts have tended to prohibit the introduction of the scientific evidence against the antitheist neo-Darwinist view. It is difficult to understand why one view should be imposed on schoolchildren without allowing them to hear any evidence against it. Some judges have sarcastically queried whether belief in a flat Earth should then be taught along with belief in a spherical Earth, but the comparison is entirely specious. First, almost no educated persons have ever believed in a flat Earth; second, the spherical Earth theory has, unlike purposeless evolution, no credible counter-evidence. The prohibition of different opinions is the result of the power of antitheists in the establishment to use the prestige of science as leverage in the courts. The science of evolution needs to be taught, not the metaphysics of atheistic evolution.

58. THERE IS NO EVIDENCE FOR THEISTIC EVOLUTION.

Creation, or the Big Bang, happened about 13.7 billion years ago; Earth is about 4.57 billion years old. It's helpful to include geological dates:

Approximate years ago	**Event/era/developmennt**
13.7 billion	Big Bang, creation
4.57 billion	**Hadean Time:** accretion, bombardment, possible collision with another planet
3.8 billion	**Archaean Eon:** end of late heavy bombardment; earliest life
2.5 billion	**Proterozoic Eon:** first multicellular life
2.2 billion	Bacteria
1.89 billion	Colonial bacteria
1.4 billion	Complex marine life
575 million	Ediacaran biota
542 million	**Phanerozoic Eon**
542 million	***Paleozoic era***
542 million	Cambrian period
488 million	Ordovician period
448 million	Silurian: first land plants
416 million	Devonian
359 million	Carboniferous
299 million	Permian

251 million	***Mesozoic era***
251 million	Triassic period
200 million	Jurassic
146 million	Cretaceous
66 million	***Cenozoic era***
66 million	Tertiary period
66 million	Paleocene epoch
58 million	Eocene
40 million	Oligocene
23 million	Miocene
5 million	Pliocene
1.8 million	Quaternary period
1.8 million	Pleistocene epoch
12,000	Holocene (the present)[100]

For the first 800 million years or so of Earth, life was virtually impossible because the planet was in the process of accretion out of debris and later frequently bombarded from space by enormous meteorites that rendered it unstable and frequently molten; it is likely that at one point during this time it collided with another planet about the size of Mars. During these 800 million years, changes in the solar system gradually led to a relatively stable Earth with fewer collisions with big meteorites. There was and could be no evolution in prebiotic times, because natural selection by definition can play absolutely no role before life exists. Therefore neo-Darwinism cannot explain the origin of life. Whatever may have happened at the origin of life, we cannot explain it with evolution.

Life began astonishingly quickly after water appeared on Earth. This life consisted of one-celled organisms. The cell, once thought to be simple, is actually the most complicated entity known to science. Then for 3.2 billion (3,200 million) years all life continued to be unicellular. Suddenly, 542 million years ago, at the beginning of the Cambrian era, all the basic anatomical features of vertebrate life appeared all over the ocean—an event known as the Cambrian explosion. No such innovation has occurred since. The evidence here points less to Darwinian gradual development than to rapid change followed by periods of quiescence, what Steven Jay Gould called "punctuated equilibrium": usual stasis with occasional sudden appearance. The Burgess Shale fossils, whose existence challenges Dar-

[100]The chart is mostly derived from information in Dale A. Russell, *Islands in the Cosmos: The Evolution of Life on Land* (Bloomington: Indiana University Press, 2009); Benedict XVI, *Creation and Evolution: A Conference with Pope Benedict XVI* (San Francisco: Ignatius, 2008).

winian gradualism, were hidden for eight decades after they were discovered, stored away in the Smithsonian until the 1980s. The Chengjiang fossil discoveries indicate that the Cambrian explosion occurred even earlier than the date of the Burgess Shale fossils, making gradualism even less plausible.

Whatever the physical processes, the *information* for DNA and life had to come from somewhere. Atheists often admit that it appears as though there were some Purpose and plan for life, but they rule out the possibility on the basis of their baseless assertion that a Purpose cannot exist. Some propose that life must have come from another planet in outer space ("panspermia"), which advances the question not at all, because the information for life on that alleged planet would also have had to come from somewhere. Others propose a vast-to-disappearing (almost infinite) number of universes, among which this particular one happens by random chance to have life. Such proposals violate one of the oldest and most respected guidelines for knowledge: Occam's razor, the fundamental principle that the best answer is usually the simplest answer that fits all the evidence.[101]

Where does the original information for biology come from? Either from pure chance (which is vanishingly improbable), or else from a planner. Did the planner "frontload" all the information into the cosmos at once and then let it alone, as old-fashioned deists said? If so, then for all practical purposes it's irrelevant whether the universe is created or not: God is an unneeded hypothesis. The Christian view is that he is continually with the cosmos, creating, maintaining and developing it. He built time as well as space into the cosmos. God is beyond the cosmos, yet the cosmos is in God as a sponge is in water: distinct from the water yet suffused with it.

59. SCIENCE IS ABOUT FACTS, RELIGION ABOUT VALUES.

The late, beloved biologist Stephen Jay Gould declared that Darwinism was compatible with religion as well as with atheism but that the two occupied different spheres. His idea of NOMA (no overlapping magisteria) asserts that science is concerned exclusively with facts and religion exclusively with values.[102] But this idea doesn't work. Many scientists don't like

[101]Davies, *Cosmic Jackpot*, pp. 261-269, summarizes seven possible explanations for life and the cosmos.

[102]Stephen Jay Gould, *Rocks of Ages: Science and Religion in the Fullness of Time* (New York: Bal-

to derive their values from religious sources. And though science is theoretically supposed to be free of value judgments, it makes them all the time: which theory deserves investigation, which proposals deserve financial support, which research deserves to be published, and so on. And when science morphs into physicalism (the metaphysical claim that nothing science can't investigate is real), it makes a gigantic value judgment. As for religion, restricting it to values is against anthropological and historical evidence. Christianity claims to aim at truth as well as behavior and to be based on reasonable evaluation of evidence.

Both science and Christianity are about truth.

60. There is no evidence in nature for intelligent purpose in the cosmos.

The *Economist* newsmagazine got it wrong:

> Can something come of nothing? Philosophers debated that question for millennia before physics came up with the answer—and that answer is yes. For quantum theory has shown that a vacuum (ie nothing) only appears to be empty space. In fact, a vacuum is not nothing but something. Actually, it is full of virtual particles of matter and their antimatter equivalents, which, in obedience to Werner Heisenberg's uncertainty principle, flit in and out of existence so fast that they cannot usually be seen.[103]

To the contrary, an "it" that is "full of" particles can't be nothing. Every attempt to explain the origin of the cosmos in purely physical terms ends up postulating a precedent something (such as a sea of potential particles) that also must come from something. If something exists, something must have imparted existence to it, and something else must have imparted existence to that something. Infinite regression in explaining the origin of the cosmos is a tattered old idea because no physical thing can come into existence all by itself. Some physicists argue that the universe may have begun with quantum fluctuations. Where did the fluctuations come from? This is not the same as asking where did God come from. God is a simple,

---

lantine, 1999).

[103]"The Casimir Effect: Much Ado about Nothing," *The Economist*, May 22, 2008, <www.economist.com/node/11402849>.

nonmaterial entity which by definition has no beginning, whereas quantum fluctuations are physical and must have a beginning.

John Lennox observes, "Some scientists and philosophers . . . think that we should not even ask [the] question. For them there is no point in looking for a reason for the existence of the universe since, according to them, there simply isn't one."[104] That is a curious lack of curiosity. E. Tryton said that "our universe is simply one of those things which happen from time to time."[105] Like spilling milk? A universe where milk doesn't get spilled. One with purple cows. One without carbon. One without suffering. One without physicalists. Stuff happens? The combination of a universe with creatures capable of observing it is fantastically unlikely to "happen from time to time."

About 500 B.C. the Greek philosopher Heraclitus realized that "everything is in flux" but added that there has to be an organizing principle—the Logos, the Word—behind the flux. If there were no Logos, there would be mere chaos. The physicalist quantum vacuum is the "lowest energy state," but the lowest energy state isn't nothing; it's still something. Nothing at all, including fluctuating energy states, can physically come from absolute nothing. Nothing isn't something that we happen to call nothing: it is absolute nothingness. "Absolute nothingness means no laws, no vacuums, no fields, no energy, no structures, no physical or mental entities of any kind—and no 'symmetries.' It has no properties or potentialities."[106] Absolute nothingness cannot produce something given endless time, because there can be no time in nothingness. The Hindu Rig Veda agrees with the Judeo-Christian Bible that "before" the beginning there was neither existence nor non-existence. That is why it is better to say that the Logos (or God) *subsists* rather than that it *exists,* because "existence" suggests a physical existence in space and time such as a shirt or a star. (Latin *subsistere* means to "lie under"; *exsistere* means to "emerge, appear.") To go from absolute nothingness to something—anything—is the most inconceivable event possible.[107] It has recently been shown that

---

[104]Lennox, *God's Undertaker,* p. 62.

[105]E. Tryton, "Is the Universe a Vacuum Fluctuation," *Nature* 246 (December 1973): 396, quoted in Lennox, *God's Undertaker,* p. 62.

[106]Antony Flew, *There Is a God: How the World's Most Notorious Atheist Changed His Mind* (New York: HarperOne, 2007), p. 170.

[107]Berlinski, *Devil's Delusion,* p. 95.

the Big Bang is not repeatable: the universe does not undergo cycles of expansion and contraction but only expands.[108] The effects of the Big Bang are part of physics, but its origin is not. The Big Bang, when something came out of absolute nothing, demands a nonphysical origin, a Logos, an ultimate principle.

Christians by definition believe that the cosmos displays intelligent purpose. Atheists by definition believe the contrary. The question is in which direction the evidence points. There are three main choices: (a) the Logos created it, (b) it just happened and that's that, or (c) it didn't come from nothing but from something that existed before.[109]

The atheist problem with (a) is that it requires admitting that a nonphysical being subsists beyond physical time and space. The problem with (b) is that it makes the assumption that anything physical science can't investigate is beyond investigation. The problem with (c) is that it only puts the problem one step back on an infinite staircase. The antitheists insist that a Logos would have to be the most complex conceivable being. If anything physical preexists the universe, they say, it must be physically complex itself and produced by something even more complex and so to infinity. But God, according to Christianity (along with Judaism and Islam), is by definition uncreated, uncontingent and absolutely simple in himself. God isn't any-*thing*.

Antitheists use Sir Fred Hoyle's image and call the likelihood of God's assembling the cosmos the equivalent of a tornado tearing through a junkyard and assembling an operative Boeing 747. The likelihood of that happening is, as Hoyle originally suggested, nil. But God is not a physical force. The example actually shows the opposite of what the atheists claim: the likelihood of random physical forces assembling the cosmos is as close to zero as we can get. Atheists dismiss the classical argument that the cosmos shows planned order and purpose, but this argument has recently been revised and revived by sophisticated philosophers.[110] An organizing principle exists, since we observe organization. An informing principle exists, since we observe information. Either the principle comes from

---

[108]Barr, *Modern Physics*, p. 131. A few physicists do still work on models of cyclical expansion from Big Bang to Big Crunch. See "Big Crunch" <en.wikipedia.org/wiki/Big_Crunch>.

[109]Davies, *Cosmic Jackpot*, pp. 261-69, offers seven possibilities.

[110]Lennox, *God's Undertaker*, p. 82.

outside the universe or from inside. If from inside, what is it? It can't be evolution, because evolution is restricted to living beings and can't be applied to the study of inanimate matter.

Now the physical evidence. First, it's odd that anything exists at all.[111] Hugely odder is the fact that a universe producing life exists. And odder still is the fact that humans have the ability and power to observe and describe the actual workings of the universe from quarks to quasars. Every knowledgeable person from the most committed Christian to the most committed antitheist agrees that the odds against a cosmos producing intelligence are vanishingly huge.[112] The universe and the earth are fine-tuned for life in hundreds of diverse ways. Here are some of the conditions that permit humans to exist:

- The universe has a beginning, around 13.7 billion years ago.
- The universe contains slightly more matter than antimatter.
- The four constants—electromagnetism, gravity, and the strong and weak nuclear forces—must fall within a narrow range for atoms to exist.[113]
- The universe must be close to its present age and size. If it were ten times younger, there would not have been time for carbon to build up; if it were ten times older, the main sequence of stars and their planetary systems (including ours) would already have died out.
- If the total mass density of the universe were less, only hydrogen and helium could exist.
- The sun is a lately developed, metal-rich star with the appropriate mass and a relatively stable output of energy.
- A planet with life must be in a narrow life zone between areas too cold and areas too hot to support life. A change of only three percent of the distance between the sun and the Earth would likely extinguish life.

---

[111]Gottfried Wilhelm Leibniz (1646-1716) asked, "Why is there something rather than nothing?" Craig, *On Guard*, p. 53. On pp. 64-64, Craig summarizes Leibniz's argument for the existence of a mind transcending the universe.

[112]Davies, *Cosmic Jackpot*, pp. 222-60.

[113]These examples are overwhelming: for example, if the value of the weak force varied by 10 to the 100th power (1 with a hundred zeroes after it), life could not exist. This number is in a sense bigger than the universe: by comparison, the number of particles in the whole universe is estimated to be about 10 to the 90th power.

- A planet with life must be between the dense arms of a galaxy, or it would receive too much radiation from nearby stars, and/or the nearby stars would make the planetary orbit too irregular.
- "The planet must rotate at the right speed: too slow and temperature differences between day and night would be too extreme; too fast and wind speeds would be disastrous."[114]
- A large planet such as Jupiter is needed to sweep in comets and asteroids, but if Jupiter were closer to Earth, more massive than it is, or in an unstable or eccentric orbit, it would pull Earth out of the life zone.
- Without a large, single moon, the tilt of Earth's rotation would become unstable.
- The Earth needs a molten interior to generate a magnetosphere that herds destructive solar particles away from its surface.
- If there were more ozone in the atmosphere, the nutrient cycle would not work. If there were less ozone, life would be sterilized by ultraviolet radiation.[115]

What are the possible explanations for the existence of this miniscule fine-tuning of the cosmos in such a way that intelligent life exists? William Lane Craig presents them succinctly: "The fine-tuning of the universe is due to either physical necessity, chance, or design."[116] Here are the options.

1. A being with a Purpose did it. This fits Ockham's razor as the simplest explanation. It is not a scientific explanation, because God does not fall within the definition of science. The universe obeys certain regularities, and intelligent creatures (humans and possibly others) exist who observe the regularities. This conjunction points to a program and Purpose of some sort. Most informed atheists allow that the universe appears to be designed with a Purpose, but they insist that it's nothing but appearance, that Purpose is impossible for the reason that they say it's impossible.

There are properties of the universe that cannot be derived from other properties. For example, there is no explanation for the existence of ele-

[114]Lennox, *God's Undertaker*, p. 70.

[115]See especially Davies, *Cosmic Jackpot*; Peter Ward and Donald Brownlee, *Rare Earth* (New York: Copernicus, 2000); Martin Rees, *Just Six Numbers: The Deep Forces that Shape the Universe* (New York: Basic Books, 2000).

[116]Craig, *Contending with Christianity's Critics*, p. 111.

mentary particles, nor can the charge of particles be explained by any other part of the system. There is no explanation for the existence of matter, energy and time. There is no explanation for the existence of the four fundamental forces: gravity, the electromagnetic spectrum, the weak nuclear force and the strong nuclear force. Such parts of the cosmic system seem to be irreducible and therefore unexplainable by science. It is absolutely essential to realize that the fine-tuning argument is not a God-of-the-gaps argument.[117] There aren't any gaps in the evidence: it is exactly the discovery of this information, unknown a century ago, that has revealed the fine-tuning. Current atheism is based on knowledge almost a hundred years out of date.

2. It happened by chance. This is called the anthropic principle: the fine-tuning does not need explanation because if the universe weren't fine-tuned for life, we wouldn't be alive to observe the tuning.[118] Here are the odds. Suppose we shuffled a deck of cards thoroughly, and when we dealt them out they appeared in the exact order from ace of spades to deuce of clubs. The probability of the shuffled cards coming out this way once is one in 4.5 times 10 to the 66th power (1 followed by 66 zeroes). Now suppose that they turned out that way consecutively time after time. As the chemist John Kennedy pointed out to me, in order to match the odds of the universe being so finely tuned, the cards would have to turn out in perfect order somewhere between ten and one hundred times in a row.[119] Even if those odds could be beaten, the anthropic principle is insufficient. As William Lane Craig notes, "The fact that we can observe only a life-permitting universe does nothing to eliminate the need of an explanation for why a life-permitting universe exists."[120]

3. The universe is not physically real but a virtual reality. In that case some intelligence had to program the virtual reality.

4. Multiple universes exist. This is a corollary of the anthropic principle asserting that we have the good fortune of existing in this particular uni-

---

[117]Superstring physicists work at constructing a theory that explains every physical thing in the cosmos, including electric charge and the four fundamental interactions.

[118]At least four varieties of the anthropic principle can be found in these sources: *The Penguin Dictionary of Philosophy* (London: Penguin, 1997), p. 27; Markham, *Against Atheism*, p. 68; on the unlikelihood of the strong anthropic principle, James Daniel Sinclair, "At Home in the Multiverse," in *Contending with Christianity's Critics*, pp. 6-25, especially pp. 24-25.

[119]See Davies, *Cosmic Jackpot*, pp. 138-39.

[120]Craig, *On Guard*, p. 116.

verse. Multiple universes (the multiverse) are necessary when any non-physical explanation is ruled out as impossible to begin with.[121] Atheists are unwilling to accept the consequence of their theory. If their theory is right, there have to be a limitless number of universes.[122] Sometimes they say that they don't necessarily mean that multiple universes actually exist, just that the hypothesis fits their current theoretical physics.[123]

In point of fact, it is philosophers more than theologians who have a problem with the multiverse. There is no reason why God should have contented himself with only one universe. God could create a multiverse. In fact, the possible plurality of worlds has been repeatedly discussed in both Christian and scientific thought.[124] There can be no proof that there weren't an infinite number of Big Bangs.[125] Suppose there really is a multiverse. Suppose the Big Bang is the origin of only this particular universe: does that solve anything? What is the multiverse contingent on, and what caused it to be tuned in such a way that even one universe would support life?

The fundamental objection to multiple universes is that there is no evidence for them either in revelation or science. The idea of the multiverse is almost pure speculation, though quantum mechanics offers a hint that it isn't impossible.[126] Reach for Occam's razor.

The main point of the idea of multiple universes is neither philosophical nor scientific but political: it is atheists' only alternative to God. The multiverse is an illusory weapon in the ideological armory of those who want to "finally get rid of God."[127]

If SETI (Search for Extraterrestrial Intelligence) scientists received a detailed plan for a sophisticated device from another planet, they would conclude that the signal was the result of some intelligent purpose. Perhaps the detailed plan for the genetic code is also the result of intelligent

---

[121]Poole, *'New' Atheism*, pp. 78-86.

[122]Markham, *Against Atheism*, p. 72.

[123]Craig, *On Guard*, pp. 113-17. The idea of a multiverse is not a complete fantasy, since there are some mathematical hints that would allow it. See Sean Carroll, "Out There," *Discover* (October 2011): 30-31.

[124]Andrew Cambers, "'But Where Shall My Soul Repose?' Nonconformity, Science, and the Geography of the Afterlife, c. 1660-1720," in *The Church, the Afterlife and the Fate of the Soul*, ed. Peter Clarke and Tony Claydon (Woodbridge, UK: Boydell, 2009), pp. 268-79.

[125]Poole, *'New' Atheism*, pp. 59.

[126]Davies, *Cosmic Jackpot*, pp. 81, 188, 209, 219, 229.

[127]Ibid., pp. 15, 268.

purpose. We look up at the stars and marvel at how insignificant we are. The stars, however, are incapable of looking at us or wondering about us. It is the stars, not we, who are insignificant. If there were no consciousness to comprehend the cosmos, who or what would say that it existed at all? Physicalists argue that consciousness is "nothing but" the movement of the chemicals in the brain. Even with the astounding advances in brain-imaging and neuroscience, they have difficulty with the basic problem.[128] I just now happen to be looking at a glowing "neon" sunset. The problem is whether chemical motions in my brain cause me to see the beauty of the sunset or whether my seeing the beauty causes the chemical motions in my brain.

The former atheist philosopher Antony Flew observed, "Five phenomena are evident in our immediate experience that can only be explained in terms of the existence of God. These are, first, the rationality implicit in all our experience in the world; second, life, the capacity to act autonomously; third, consciousness, the ability to be aware; fourth, conceptual thought, the power of articulating and understanding meaningful symbols such as are embedded in language; and, fifth, the human self, the 'center' of consciousness, thought, and action."[129] The scale of likelihood tips more strongly in the direction of Christianity now than it did a century ago.

Atheists create enormous and unnecessary problems by insisting that the universe and life are accidental. As Marilynne Robinson observes, the problems of the origin of the universe, of life, of the human mind, simply disappear if one adopts the Christian view.[130]

61. THERE IS SO MUCH CHRISTIAN ART BECAUSE THE CHURCH PAID FOR IT.

This idea has cropped up in recent movies, along with the notion that Christian artists weren't allowed to produce secular works and that Jesus would be appalled by the churches built in his name. In fact, Christian artists produced lots of secular works, and though Jesus' views on archi-

[128]Mario Beauregard and Denyse O'Leary, *Spiritual Brain: A Neuroscientist's Case for the Existence of the Soul* (New York: HarperCollins, 2007).

[129]Flew, *There Is a God*, p. 161.

[130]Robinson, *Absence of Mind*, p. 72.

tecture are unknown, he certainly did not object to the Temple in Jerusalem. Artists have always produced for people who paid them for their work in money and prestige, including clergy, nobles, bourgeois, workers' syndicates, snobs, investors, urban secularists, secular governments and antitheists.

In the past few decades artists have been richly rewarded for antireligious art, such as the "piss-Christ" or the Virgin Mary sculpted in elephant dung at the Brooklyn Museum of Art. Fanatics have banned Christmas displays and blown up the Banyan Buddhas of Afghanistan, and it is not impossible that fanatics may once again, as they did in the French Revolution, launch a purge of Christian art, sighing in satisfaction as the last Rose Window is shattered by the wrecking ball.[131] Marilynne Robinson notes the radical marginalization of arts and history in contemporary society.[132]

The fact is that most Christian art stems from the honest devotion and spiritual imagination of the artist. True, some of it was commissioned for propaganda, but the same can be said for royalist art, communist art, fascist art, activist art and so on. Some even propose that the Battle Hymn of the Republic (the stirring anthem of the Union Army in its fight against slavery and now banned from schools by the thought police) was not inspired by real religious feeling. Those incapable of understanding different cultures may claim that the *Divine Comedy* of Dante, the paintings of Giotto, the Masses of Palestrina and the cantatas of Bach were not inspired by Christianity. But Christian artists, including many Eastern Orthodox icon painters and medieval Western architects, often worked anonymously for the love of God. The purpose of an icon is to "capture the characteristics of a holy person or of the spiritual world as directly envisioned by the iconographer."[133] Almost all of the artwork in the great cathedrals is unsigned, for example, and some of it is visible only from above, where before aviation only God was supposed to see it. Painters of icons did not sign them. Art can be an act of worship of the beauty of the cosmos, or it can be an act of ego flung in the face of the cosmos.

[131]On iconoclasm see Michael O'Connell, *Idolatrous Eye* (New York: Oxford University Press, 2000).

[132]Robinson, *Absence of Mind*, p. 36.

[133]Personal communication to the author from Archbishop Chrysostomos of Etna, November 24, 2011.

Into the twentieth century the ancient union of the true, the good and the beautiful was assumed. The understanding was that God's love of truth and beauty encompassed artworks, poetry, science and music, that anything pointed toward God would eventually reach reality, and that anything not pointed toward God would reach nowhere. In the twenty-first century, atonality in music, self-referential artworks and superficiality of poetry all reflect the fact that when we lose the true, we also lose the beautiful, the good and the meaningful. Much in the contemporary arts is based on egotism, schmoozing and contempt for beauty and truth. The fashion for meaningless art (actually celebrated for being meaningless) will not last, but it serves in the meanwhile to blind people to reality. The best art today really comes from science, in its breathtaking depictions of galaxies, extinct animals, or molecules.

The arts, for Christians, are meant to express the infinite beauty of God with finite hands and voices. There are few known Christian artworks from the first three centuries, and music was limited and wholly subordinate to the text of the liturgy; its purpose was to make the words intelligible and memorable. The purpose of the chant, which was derived from Hebrew worship, was to instruct. If the aesthetic sense was awakened, fine, but that was not the point. In both the Eastern and the Western church, chants often became more complex (and aesthetically more interesting) but did not depart from the instructional purpose. The most commonly known today is the Gregorian plainchant. The introduction of polyphony did not itself detract from the purpose—witness the clarity of the text in the Masses of Palestrina (1515-1594)—but with the addition of the organ and eventually other instruments, the text could be overwhelmed by the musical setting. Even such a masterpiece as the B-minor Mass of Johann Sebastian Bach (1685-1750) may suit the concert hall better than a church. It is the word that is central, the music an exhilarating adjunct.

There are, however, other dimensions to the idea of beauty. One is that beauty can draw one closer to an understanding of God. If one is lifted up from the limitations of egotism and opened up to what is greater, more joyful and more true, that is a good in itself. Richard Viladesau remarks, "In great Christian art, the content is presented in a way that is replete with spiritual meanings and associations that both connect with the verbal message . . . and at the same time go beyond it."[134] And also, "Beauty is the capacity to produce joy through perception."[135] Beautiful music and artworks can open the senses to what is good, holy and true. This process is an aspect of what the Eastern church calls *theosis*, the permeation and transformation of the human being by the divine. For Dante, music and dance are integral parts of heaven.

Music and art can of course lead in the other direction: to egotistic pride and greed. My musical friends comment gloomily on the emphasis of technique over meaning, on the fierce competition among performers, and on the power games played to advance self-interest. An icon painted with malicious or ironic intent is an abomination. Skill and technique without heart or meaning are empty. But when music and art are produced rightly, they can be transformative, opening one up to joy. Experience of God's beauty comes directly in his works of nature and indirectly in art, which God creates through his creatures. As Viladesau notes, "Beauty [is] an intrinsic element of both revelation and tradition,"[136] and "The innate sense of beauty is ultimately identical with the natural human dynamism toward being and goodness."[137] No doubt this paragraph will excite contempt among those contemporary artists and musicians who are as eager to promote themselves in contemporary cynical society as any other group of people. The Garden of Eden was beautiful; one of the consequences of human alienation from God may be the inclination toward ugliness.

Yet another dimension of beauty is the nature of God himself. God is truth and love; is he not also beauty? The Old Testament writers thought so, as do Viladesau and many other scholars and writers: "God is desirable, lovable, glorious, and the ultimate font of the order, beauty, and joy of existence."[138] The opposite of truth is complete lack of truth—the lie. The opposite of beauty is lack of beauty—ugliness. Both lies and ugliness are plentiful. In God there is no ugliness at all, only the perfection of beauty, which he loves in himself and loves to offer us to share.

---

[134]Richard Viladesau, *Theology and the Arts: Encountering God through Music, Art, and Rhetoric* (New York: Paulist, 2000), p. 151.
[135]Ibid., p. 227.
[136]Ibid., p. 146.
[137]Ibid., p. 220.
[138]Ibid., p. 219.

62. THE RENAISSANCE PREVENTED CHRISTIANITY FROM STAMPING OUT THE CLASSICS.

This is threadbare myth that one doesn't encounter much anymore. The word "renaissance" means rebirth, and the idea was that after a thousand years of darkness, classical literature was revived in the 1400s and 1500s. The intervening period is often called the Middle Ages or even the Dark Ages. Just a simple fact: Almost all (not just most, but almost all) of the works of ancient mathematics, science, philosophy and literature that still exist come from manuscripts painstakingly made and preserved during the supposed thousand years of darkness. For another thing, educated people in the Middle Ages were vastly more familiar with classical works than are educated people today. For yet another, medieval advances in science and technology went beyond the level of the ancient Greeks and Romans. The Middle Ages invented bound books, eyeglasses, stirrups, windmills, the heavy wheeled plow, horseshoes, the horse collar, whisky and the lowercase letters you are reading on this page.[139]

[139]Thomas A. Brady Jr., Heiko A. Oberman and James D. Tracy, eds., *Handbook of European History, 1400-1600: Late Middle Ages, Renaissance, and Reformation* (Grand Rapids: Eerdmans, 1996); Jeffrey Burton Russell, *Medieval Civilization* (New York: Wiley, 1968).

Jesus and the Bible Have Been Shown to Be False

63. The original Bible exists.

In July 2009 the media reported that "the original Bible" had been found, computerized and made available on a website, codexsiniaticus.org. This is a remarkable site displaying the oldest known manuscript of the New Testament and about half of the Old Testament. The manuscript is in Greek, dates from the A.D. 300s, and has been known since the 1800s as the *Codex Sinaiticus*, "the Sinai book," because it is preserved in the monastery of Saint Catherine's at Mount Sinai. Making the book available online is an important feat, but only breathless reporters claimed that it had been "discovered" or was an original Bible.

Many people believe that the King James Bible, also known as the "Authorized Version," is the original Bible. Far from it. The King James Version is so called because King James I of England (r. 1603-1625) authorized about fifty scholars to make a new English translation of the Bible.[1] The scholars were organized into six groups, each responsible for a section of the Bible. They translated from the original Hebrew and Greek. Each scholar in each group worked separately, after which the group met to discuss and agree on the translation of their assigned section. Later the sections all met together to discuss and agree upon the full text. The translation they produced from 1604 to 1611 is the most glorious work ever produced by a committee. It is beyond comparison the most beautifully written of any English version, but it was not the first.

Partial translations of the Bible had been made as early as the 800s to 1000s. The first complete English Bible was made by John Wycliffe's fol-

[1]Adam Nicolson, *God's Secretaries: The Making of the King James Bible* (New York: HarperCollins, 2003).

lowers in 1380-1392, but that was from Latin, not the original languages. A variety of English translations from the original Hebrew and Greek appeared in the 1500s under the influence of the Protestant Reformation, the most important of which was by William Tyndale (1494-1536), on which the King James Bible heavily relied. The Catholics produced the Douai version from 1582 to 1610. Nor was the King James Bible the last English translation, for many later versions have been produced, including some contemporary ones that clarify the obsolete English and correct the mistranslations in the King James.

It does not disparage the brilliant work of Tyndale or King James's translators to observe that since their time there has been much improvement in understanding the original languages and in the accuracy of the texts. On the other hand, some modern translations lack the richness of imagery and meaning of the King James, and some are flat and banal. A good modern translation that corrects errors but keeps much of the power of the King James is the New Revised Standard Version (1989). Neither the Old Testament nor the New Testament was written as a whole but rather as a number of separate books composed over time. The word "Bible" comes from the Greek *biblia* (plural of "books").

The original Bible is not in English. Jesus and his disciples did not live in England in the 1600s. The English language was not even in existence in the first century A.D. when he did live. If this seems obvious, bear in mind that I have had doctoral students in history who didn't know it. English is hardly the only language into which the Bible has been translated: the Bible now exists in all current written languages. The first language into which the whole Bible was translated was Latin, but Latin is also not the original language of the Bible. The language of the original Old Testament is Hebrew, a small amount of Greek, and a tiny amount of Aramaic; the language of the New Testament is Greek with a tinier amount of Aramaic. Before attempting any "literal" reading of any translation of the Bible, one needs to know a bit about languages.

The Bible consists of a number of books written over a time span of six hundred to a thousand years. Jews accept only the Old Testament (the Hebrew Bible), while Christians accept both the Old and New Testaments.

No original manuscripts (handwritten texts) of either the Old or the New Testament exist. That is not surprising: no original manuscripts of any ancient authors exist because the materials (mainly papyrus) used by ancient scribes almost all deteriorated through time. The growing use of parchment (sheepskin), which is much more durable than papyrus, accounts for the numerous surviving manuscripts from A.D. 300 onward. The earliest known manuscripts of an ancient classic, Virgil's *Aeneid*, are not much earlier than A.D. 500. Almost all knowledge of ancient writers derives from the work of later copyists, particularly those in the Middle Ages.

The manuscripts of the Bible are more reliable than those of the classics. Here's why: (1) A vast number of manuscripts of the Bible predate manuscripts of any other ancient writing. Compare the 5,700 manuscripts of parts or all of the New Testament with the twenty or so manuscripts of a classic such as Thucydides's *Peloponnesian War* or the seventy-five of Herodotus's *Persian Wars*.[2] (2) Whereas the earliest known manuscripts of classical works date from nearly a thousand years after the originals, the earliest New Testament manuscripts date from less than a hundred years after they were written. Existing manuscripts of parts of the New Testament date as early as the 100s A.D.; manuscripts containing substantial parts of the New Testament date from the 200s; and a nearly complete New Testament text survives from the 300s. (3) The closeness in time between the composition of the New Testament and the earliest manuscripts is unique among ancient works.

There's yet another reason that biblical texts leave less probability for error than classical texts: (4) Manuscripts of parts of the Old Testament found in the Dead Sea Scrolls date to about 100 B.C. The earliest complete Hebrew manuscript of the first five books of the Bible, also called the Pentateuch, the Torah or the Five Books of Moses, dates from A.D. 800-850. The idea that Moses himself wrote the five books is rejected by most modern scholars on a variety of grounds, including the fact that these books describe the death of Moses and the fact that there are strong linguistic differences among the texts. The actual books seem to date from the 600s to 500s B.C. On the other hand, the traditions on which the

---

[2]J. Ed Komoszewski, M. James Sawyer and Daniel B. Wallace, *Reinventing Jesus: How Contemporary Skeptics Miss the Real Jesus and Mislead Popular Culture* (Grand Rapids: Kregel, 2006), pp. 65-82; see also Paul D. Wegner, *Student's Guide to Textual Criticism of the Bible* (Downers Grove, IL: InterVarsity Press, 2006).

books were based go back to Moses, who lived sometime around 1200 B.C., and a recent archeological discovery of a written fragment shows that at least parts were written as early as the tenth century B.C.[3] The first known extant Hebrew manuscripts of most of the Old Testament are the Masoretic texts from the 800s to 900s A.D. Surprisingly, the first complete Old Testament, dating from the 200s B.C., is not in Hebrew but in a Greek translation called the Septuagint, and other old reliable Greek texts also exist.

Although the original manuscripts have perished, the text of the Bible—what the original compositions probably said—is now reasonably certain, owing to linguistic and textual studies. The text of the Old Testament is almost completely reliable. The differences in the various manuscripts of the Old Testament are few, testifying to the enormous care exercised by the scribes in translating sacred texts.

The text of the New Testament, though less completely settled than that of the Old Testament because of the much greater number of manuscripts, is also remarkably reliable. In addition to the New Testament manuscripts themselves, many of the church fathers (Christian writers up to about A.D. 600) provide extensive quotations from the New Testament that help confirm the text. There are numerous variations in the Greek manuscripts, but only a few are significant and none affects the teaching of the New Testament as a whole. The two big questions are the ending of Mark (Mk 16:9-20), which was evidently added to that Gospel later, and the placement of the story of Jesus' saving the woman from stoning (Jn 7:53–8:11).

Recently many new versions of the Bible, including graphic novel and video versions, have appeared with the intention of capturing the attention of generations more attuned to visuals than to texts.[4] These have their place, but the Bible remains fundamentally a text. New translations with serious and careful effort to reflect the text are more accurate than earlier ones. Owing to the scrupulous efforts of thousands of years of scribes, hundreds of years of textual criticism, and years of careful translation, most contemporary English Bibles are quite reliable.

---

[3]Clara Moskowitz, "Bible Possibly Written Centuries Earlier, Text Suggests," LiveScience (January 15, 2010) <www.livescience.com/8008-bible-possibly-written-centuries-earlier-text-suggests.html>.

[4]Sarah Skidmore, "Jazzy New Bibles Alter Form, Not Word," *Los Angeles Times*, October 9, 2008, p. C6 (the business section!).

64. Christians worship the Bible.

No Christians before very recent times have done any such thing. The Protestant Reformer and theologian Martin Luther (1483-1546) taught *sola scriptura* ("the Bible alone"), meaning that the Bible, although not the only source of truth, is the authority over the other of the "four pillars" of Christianity: tradition, reason and experience. Luther also taught *sola fides* ("faith alone") *sola gratia* ("grace alone"), *soli Deo gloria* ("glory to God alone") and *solo Christo* ("by Christ alone"). Neither he nor any other Protestant Reformer had the least intention of worshiping the Bible.

However, during the past hundred years or so, a few Christians, particularly in North America, have identified "the word" (the Bible) with the Word of God (Jesus Christ). It is hard to believe that the English Bible should be taken word for word, because it is a translation of Hebrew, Greek and Aramaic words. The Bible never calls itself "the Word." For Christians the Word is Jesus Christ, the second person of the Holy Trinity (Eph 2:18). It is not belittling the Bible to put it in its proper place in Christianity. Since Christianity rejects the worship of any object or even the idea of any object, worshiping the Bible is bibliolatry. The authority of the Bible is contingent upon the authority of Christ.

During the lifetime of Jesus, there was only one Bible: the Hebrew Bible or Old Testament. When Jesus quoted Scripture, the Old Testament was what he was quoting. The New Testament was written by his followers between about A.D. 50 and 90. The canon of the Bible was not completely set until nearly A.D. 400.[5]

Christians believe that the Bible is God's revelation to humanity. Many human artifacts can be said to be "inspired"—Dante's *Divine Comedy,* for example, or Bach's cantatas, or Tolkien's *Lord of the Rings*, or the physics of Newton and Einstein—but the Bible is not only inspired, it is revealed. A variety of interpretations exist as to what that means.

One is that God dictated the text of the Bible to the various human writers who acted as scribes taking down his words. In this view, the human authors of the Bible wrote exactly what God told them to regardless of their personality or social context. But whereas Muslims believe that the Qur'an (Koran) was dictated by God to Muhammad through an angel,

---

[5]Komoszewski et al., *Reinventing Jesus*, pp. 126-33.

the primary revelation of God for Christians is not a book but a person: Jesus Christ. Jesus said, "All authority in heaven and on earth has been given to me" (Mt 28:18).

Another idea is that the Bible is "inerrant," a view resembling the Muslim belief that God dictated the Qur'an through an angel, as opposed to the traditional Christian view that the basis of Christianity is not a book but the person of Jesus. Inerrancy also makes the experiences and settings of the actual biblical writers "nearly meaningless."[6] The strongest version of inerrancy is that the Bible cannot be wrong in anything, including what appear to be scientific or historical statements. According to this view, the Bible is infallible in that none of it is false and must be interpreted as "literally" (overtly) as possible.

Still another view is that the "literal" interpretation is what the author intended, rather than what a modern reader assumes the text to mean. The famous example is the first chapter of Genesis. The Bible says that God created the world in six days, and Christians cannot consider this false, but the meaning of "day" may be taken metaphorically, making the six days compatible with the 4.6 billion years that scientists estimate the age of the Earth to be. From the first century onward, Christian theologians such as Origen (185-254) and Augustine (354-410) have maintained that the Bible can be read on several different levels. When this approach is not taken, difficulties arise, as when the Bible is held to be true word for word in a scientific and historical sense that the authors did not intend. Traditional theologians have argued that when the text says something contrary to a proven physical truth, it is better to take it metaphorically.

In Christianity, Jesus Christ is the revelation of God to humans, and the New Testament is the chief witness to him. Is the Bible a personal guidebook or sacred wisdom to be understood within the tradition? Perhaps both and more, for there have been many interpretations of the text over the centuries to the present. It is naïve to think that one can read it "straight" without interpreting it. Augustine pointed out that when the meaning of a passage is in doubt it needs to be interpreted in the most charitable (loving) sense.

---

[6]Mark A. Noll, *Scandal of the Evangelical Mind* (Grand Rapids: Eerdmans, 1994), p. 133.

65. Christians take the Bible literally

The Bible itself says that it is inspired by God (2 Tim 3:16). Contemporary humanists strangely claim that "biblical illiteracy . . . has been at the heart of the Christian faith throughout its history,"[7] but in reality the main purpose of Christian scholarship has been to enhance the understanding of the manifold dimensions of the Bible.

The term "literal" can mean that every sentence of the Bible is to be taken as revealed and unquestionable in every sense; when it makes a statement regarding what we today call science or history, the statement must be true scientifically or historically. That view is held by a small minority. A much larger number interprets "literal" as meaning that every statement is revealed in one way or another without claiming that every statement is true in every possible sense. Many contemporary Christians prefer to avoid "literalism." But the question is unavoidable: if the text is revealed by God, what does God mean by it? All the earliest Christian writers had to grapple with the problem.

They were not all in agreement. The question of what books and passages of the Bible were to be included in the approved canon was still unsettled. Extremists such as Marcion (about A.D. 150) excluded many of the Epistles and all the Gospels except Luke, which he edited to fit his own view that the God of the Old Testament was not the true God but an evil secondary spirit ("demiurge"). Still, although the final canon was not set much before 400, it was well-enough established before 200 that most theologians could concentrate on exploring the meaning of the whole. By that time, Christian writers understood that the Bible was to be read both "literally" and metaphorically.[8]

Some statements can indeed be read in an overt sense; one among thousands of examples is, "Jephthah sent messengers to the king of the Ammonites" (Judg 11:12). Many such historical statements have been confirmed by modern history and archeology. But "A garden enclosed is my sister, my spouse; a spring shut up, a fountain sealed" (Song 4:12 KJV) is

---

[7]Thomas Mates, "School Spirit," *The Humanist*, May/June 2009, p. 17.

[8]John Mark Reynolds gives a helpful brief summary of hermeneutics (how to read ancient texts) in Phillip E. Johnson and John Mark Reynolds, *Against All Gods: What's Right and Wrong About the New Atheism* (Downers Grove, IL: InterVarsity Press, 2010), pp. 72-75. On pp. 12, 17 and 23, Johnson mentions notices in the general media such as *Time, Wired* and *The Wall Street Journal.*

meaningful neither historically nor scientifically. It had to be taken as a metaphor. That in no way implied that it had less meaning than the historical: indeed, it is vastly more important than Jephthah's messengers. But if God often spoke through the biblical authors in metaphor, two questions remained: which texts were best taken metaphorically, and what were the permissible meanings attached to the metaphor—how far could it be extended?

Origen (185-254) was the founder of the tradition of treating the Bible as truth in three ways: the "literal" (corporeal or overt) meaning, the moral meaning and the spiritual meaning. Multiple levels of meaning were accepted in both the Eastern and Western churches. Augustine's (354-430) influential system included four meanings, which became standard: literal (overt), allegorical, instructive practically, and meaningful in light of the end and final purpose of the world. These and other systems are all reducible to the distinction between literal (overt) and metaphorical truth. During the Protestant and Catholic reformations of the 1500s, stringent efforts were made to rein in metaphor and to emphasize the literal whenever possible.

A modern use of the term "literal" considers the intent of the various authors of the Bible. None of them operated under definitions placed on history and science in the nineteenth, twentieth and twenty-first centuries. The Bible can be read literally when literally means getting as close as possible to the meaning intended by the authors who were inspired by God, and the authors expressed their message in prayers, poetry and metaphor as well as facts.

66. The Text of the Old Testament (Hebrew Bible) is Uncertain.

The text of the Hebrew Bible or Old Testament is incomparably the most certain of any document written before printing was invented—and more than many since. For example, there are enormously more variations in the texts of Shakespeare's works than in the Hebrew Bible. The Old Testament text itself is, with few exceptions, nearly certain. Scribes, who regarded the duty of copying sacred and holy texts with the utmost seriousness, were extremely careful. Mistakes were inevitable, but almost all variants are simply a matter of spelling or grammar. No original manuscript of a biblical book exists, but modern scholarship has produced critical editions of the Hebrew Bible showing that the text has been preserved about ninety percent free of variation and that the variations that do exist almost never affect the intrinsic sense.

For example, in Isaiah 39:1, the Masoretic text (the standard Hebrew text dating from the A.D. 800s to 900s) uses the word *hazaq* to mean "get well," whereas the Dead Sea Scrolls (mostly first century B.C.) use *haya*, "recuperate." Only extremely rarely would a scribe deliberately change the text to clarify what he took to be its intention. For example, Genesis 18:22 may originally have read "and God remained standing before Abraham," whereas later scribes, believing that standing implied a subordinate posture, changed the wording to "and Abraham remained standing before the Lord." Especially given the length of the Old Testament, the degree of purity in the transmission through more than twenty centuries is astonishing. One might choose to hate the Old Testament, as some Christians have done since the time of the heretic Marcion (about A.D. 150), and as antitheists do now, but one has no evidence for challenging the reliability of the text in any serious way.[9]

67. The New Testament can be understood without the Old Testament.

One antitheist describes Judaism as "originally a tribal cult of a single fiercely unpleasant God, morbidly obsessed with sexual restrictions, with the smell of charred flesh, with his own superiority over rival gods and with the exclusiveness of his chosen desert tribe."[10] Christians consider the Old Testament, along with the New Testament, the unique revelation of the word of God. They believe that other texts such as the Upanishads or Dante's *Divine Comedy* may be inspired by the spirit of God, but that only the Bible is revealed, its truth guaranteed. Scholarly disputes over the status of certain passages continue to exist, as do disputes about how much the text is to be read "literally" and how much metaphorically. As a clergyman I know says, the opposite of literal is not false.[11] To deny that the

[9]Paul D. Wegner, *A Student's Guide to Textual Criticism of the Bible* (Downers Grove, IL: IVP Academic, 2006); Komoszewski et al., *Reinventing Jesus*.
[10]Richard Dawkins, *God Delusion* (Boston: Houghton Mifflin, 2006), p. 58.
[11]Personal communication to the author from Tim Vivian.

Bible is revealed is to cut oneself off from Christianity.

Some feel comfortable separating "the Old Testament God," whom they perceive as wrathful and warlike, from "the New Testament God," whom they perceive as kind and merciful. Atheists focus on the apparent dissonance between the two parts of the Bible. Certainly many people are shocked by the violence they find in the Old Testament. But as one writer notes, "God's anger is not like ours. It is infused with holy purpose," the pursuit of justice.[12] Dislike of the Old Testament is not just a recent phenomenon. In the first few centuries of Christianity, Gnostics split themselves off from the community by condemning the Old Testament and even suggesting that the God of the Old Testament was really Satan. Later, from the earliest days of printed Bibles, Christians often bought and carried a "Testament," by which was meant the New Testament alone, though often accompanied by the Book of Psalms.

But many of the words of the New Testament are quotations or citations from the Old Testament, and there are few words or actions found there that are not rooted in the Old Testament. The very words of Jesus on the cross—"My God, my God, why have you forsaken me?"—are a quotation from Psalm 22. The New Testament cannot be fully understood without its Jewish context. "Christ" means "Messiah, anointed king." Much if not most of the New Testament is associated with types in the Old Testament. A type is a person or event that prefigures another person or event and has the same spiritual meaning. A few examples: the passage of the Israelites through the Red Sea is a type of baptism. The chosen people of Israel are a type of the church. Israelite Temple sacrifice is a type of the Eucharist (Lord's Supper). The false charges against Susanna are a type of those against Christ, and Christ in his anguish even speaks the same words that Susanna spoke in her own anguish.[13]

Some readers fault the Old Testament as legalistic as well as violent. There are over six hundred identified commandments in the Torah (the five "books of Moses"), and recent parodies distort and make fun of them as if all were intended to be of equal validity. Such parodies avoid a number

---

[12]Linda Falter, "A Beautiful Anger," *Christianity Today*, April 2011, p. 36.

[13]Catherine Brown Tkacz, "*Aneboesen phone megale*," *Gregorianum* 87 (2006): 449-86; Tkacz, "Susanna and the Pre-Christian Book of Daniel: Structure and Meaning," *Heythrop Journal* 49, no. 2 (2008): 181-96.

of crucial points. First: Although the laws specified in the Torah resemble the laws of other contemporary Middle Eastern societies, they are much more humane. The Torah also insists on obedience to divine law. It does not exempt anyone, not even the king, on the basis of status: the prophet Nathan publicly humiliated King David himself for his sins. It requires care for the weak. It distinguishes (unlike most ancient religions) between voluntary and involuntary acts: one could not offend God involuntarily. Second: Many of the commandments refer either to regulations about worship at the Temple, which has not existed for over nineteen hundred years, or to prescriptions for life in a nomadic society. In other words, such commandments make sense only in a certain (now rare) sort of society. Third: Other commandments resemble natural law and the moral law of other societies, such as prohibitions against murder, incest, lying and theft.

The key to the Christian attitude toward the Old Testament law is the attitude of Jesus himself. He said that he did not come to change even the tiniest bit of the law, and also that that law must be superseded when love and charity demanded it. Jesus did not subtract from the law but added a new dimension to it. It took the apostles a few years to sort that out: some demanded that converts abide by the letter of Torah law, while others emphasized the new dimension; the latter position became that of Christianity.

An even more important connection between the Old and New Testaments is that the New Testament is firmly rooted in the Old. Jesus reads from the Hebrew Bible and frequently quotes it. When Jesus refers to "Scripture" he means the Old Testament. The God that Jesus calls Father is the God of the Old Testament. Jesus says that he has come to fulfill the prophecies of the Old Testament. He is the new *Mashiach*—Messiah, anointed one, king—of Israel. The sacrifice of Jesus fulfills and transcends the ancient tradition of sacrifice at the Temple. Even the Gospel-makers' words describing the Passion of Jesus are drawn from the words of Susanna in the book of Daniel.

The New Testament is based on the Old Testament and cannot be understood without it. The God of the Old Testament is the God of the New Testament is the God of Christianity. That raises an interesting question. Where, then, does Jesus appear in the Old Testament? The human Jesus cannot appear in the Old Testament because it was completed before he was born. But Christians regard a number of prophecies in the Old Testament as referring to him (Is 7:14; 40:3; Mic 5:2; Zech 9:9; 12:10; Mal 3:1). The prophecies are ambiguous: sometimes the one who is to come is a military leader, a king; sometimes he comes in triumphant glory; sometimes he comes as a victim; sometimes he comes as a shepherd. But they all seem to refer to the future coming of someone who would radically transform the people of Israel and the whole world. Jesus himself claimed to be the fulfillment in person of the prophecy of Isaiah:

> The Spirit of the Lord GOD is upon me,
> because the LORD has anointed me;
> he has sent me to bring good news to the oppressed,
> to bind up the brokenhearted,
> to proclaim liberty to the captives,
> and release to the prisoners. (Is 61:1; see Lk 4:17-21)

Luke's Gospel and the letters of the apostles suggest that the world has been looking for Christ since its beginning (Lk 1:55, 70; 2 Pet 1:21).

Christians have regarded the appearance of the three angels to Abraham and Sarah in Genesis 18 as representing the Trinity. Christianity declares that the Trinity consists of the Father, the Son and the Holy Spirit, a society of three equal Persons bound in perfect love and truth, one and inseparable in all eternity.[14] The Son became fully human and fully God in the person of Jesus of Nazareth, the Christ. Jesus both occupied a certain place in space and time, and also is the eternal incarnation of the Son. The Trinity exists beyond time and in all time, both when the New Testament was written and when the Old Testament was written. The two testaments, the two covenants, cannot be separated. For Christians, the New Testament adds a fuller dimension to the Old Testament and is the fulfillment of revelation.

68. THE APOCRYPHA ARE NOT PART OF THE BIBLE.

The dictionaries apply "erroneous," "inauthentic" and "secret" to the words "apocrypha" and "apocryphal," which have acquired a sense of the mysterious as well as the dubious. This sense of mystery may come from the fact

[14]Today the word "person" is so often used as a synonym for "human being" that some students mistakenly think that the Trinity means that the three Persons are human. The Latin *persona* and Greek *hypostasis* for "person" carry the connotations of "character" and "essence."

that the Apocrypha do not appear in modern printings of the King James Version of the Bible, although they did so in its original 1611 edition. The main sense of the word (Greek *apocrypha*, "hidden") refers to a number of ancient books, including Tobit, Judith, the Wisdom of Solomon, Ecclesiasticus (also called the Wisdom of Sirach), Baruch, two books of Maccabees, and longer versions of the canonical books Esther and Daniel.[15] Almost all the Jewish Apocrypha were included in the first complete Old Testament, the Septuagint, a Greek translation from Hebrew and Aramaic made about 200 B.C. Most of them were accepted as part of the canon by both the Christian and Jewish communities until about A.D. 100. At that time the rabbis excluded them on the grounds that they were composed late (200 B.C. to A.D. 70) and that some were originally written in Greek rather than in Hebrew. But the fact that they were no longer in the Jewish canon hardly removed them from Jewish consciousness. One of the important Jewish feasts, Hanukkah, is based on the books of Maccabees.

Until the 300s A.D., the Christian community accepted the Apocrypha almost universally, but in that century the great biblical scholar Jerome argued that they should be distinguished from the more obviously canonical books such as Genesis and Exodus. When the canon of the Christian Bible was formalized at the end of the 300s, the Apocrypha were included as part of the canon, a decision that Saint Augustine approved. But in the 1500s, Protestants adopted the Jewish canon, partly on the grounds that the Apocrypha had been challenged over the centuries. Some Protestant Bibles include them, placing them between the Old and New Testaments while cautioning that they are not canonical; other Protestant Bibles, including the King James Version, leave them out entirely. The Roman Catholic, Greek and Russian Orthodox, and some other churches have always included them in the canon.[16] Whether canonical or not, their value as sources is immense.

A number of other Jewish books written from about 200 B.C. to A.D. 100 also claimed to be revealed. The term for these books (for example the Books of Enoch) is "pseudepigrapha": false writings that were never

[15]The "canon" of the Bible refers to those books properly included in it. Recent research has shown the integrity of the entire book of Daniel: Tkacz, "Susanna," pp. 181-96.

[16]The Eastern Orthodox usually accept as canonical Esdras, Tobit, Judith, addenda to Esther, addenda to Daniel, the Wisdom of Solomon, Ecclesiasticus (Sirach), all four books of Maccabees, Baruch, the letter of Jeremiah, and the prayer of Manasseh.

included in anybody's canon. Very confusingly, the term "apocrypha" is also applied to a number of Christian books that were never accepted into any canon. These date from the second century, later than the New Testament. They include gospels, acts and letters written under pseudonyms, such as the so-called Gospel of Thomas, Gospel of Peter, Acts of Peter, and Letter to the Laodiceans. These second-century books often have a Gnostic slant.[17]

69. MODERN SCHOLARSHIP DEBUNKS THE BIBLE.

This widely believed myth is based on a number of errors, including the notion that there's little historical and archeological evidence for places and events in the Bible; that there are hundreds of thousands of variant readings of the Bible; that the Gospels contradict one another; that little or nothing is known about Jesus; that the truth about Jesus was suppressed by early Christians following the Apostle Saint Paul; that there were many "Christianities" in the first century; that truth is more likely to be found in secret documents than in open tradition; and that modern scholars are in agreement as to these points.[18]

Archeology since 1900 confirms much of the evidence in the Bible and disconfirms some.[19] A great deal of archeological data are lacking and may never be found, but because new major discoveries of written material are unlikely, archeology will continue to be the chief source of new information about the context of Israel and of Christianity. The most important modern discovery was that of the Dead Sea Scrolls in 1947-1960, which confirmed the traditional text of Isaiah. No New Testament materials are among the Dead Sea Scrolls.

If we total up all the variant readings in Bible manuscripts, there are indeed more than a hundred thousand, but almost all of them are trivial. There are several reasons for the existence of these variants. One of them

---

[17]Larry W. Hurtado, *Lord Jesus Christ: Devotion to Jesus in Earliest Christianity* (Grand Rapids: Eerdmans, 2003), pp. 427-85.

[18]Lee Strobel, *Case for the Real Jesus: A Journalist Investigates Current Attacks on the Identity of Christ* (Grand Rapids: Zondervan, 2007), pp. 65-100; Ben Witherington III, *What Have They Done with Jesus: Beyond Strange Theories and Bad History—Why We Can Trust the Bible* (New York: HarperOne, 2006).

[19]Disconfirmations are noted in Israel Finkelstein and Neil Asher Silberman, *Bible Unearthed: Archaeology's New Vision of Israel and Its Sacred Texts* (New York: Free Press, 2001).

is the great number of manuscripts, each hand-copied from another. There were no copy machines then, no scanners. Even if in electronic times we retyped a book on our computer, we would inevitably end up with mistakes, and the people copying from our copy would make even more mistakes. This process always occurs in the development of every manuscript tradition, even when people are striving to be careful. The reason that more variants are found in the New Testament manuscript tradition than in many other manuscript traditions is the sheer number of manuscripts created. Compare the 5,700 Greek manuscripts of the New Testament with the manuscripts of the most famous Greek historians Herodotus (seventy-five) and Thucydides (twenty).[20] One reason the text of classical works seems so settled, with few variants, is that there are few manuscripts. Almost all the variants in the enormous number of New Testament manuscripts are tiny and irrelevant, consisting of scribal errors with accent marks or letters or at most words. The substantial variations are in the last verses of the Gospel of Mark (Mk 16:9-20) and in the placement of the scene with the woman caught in adultery (Jn 8:3-11).

Christians complain that the critics apply doubts about the reliability of the Bible—a "hermeneutics of suspicion"—far beyond that applied to other ancient works.[21]

70. Jesus is ________ (fill in the blank).

Jesus has been seen through as many different lenses as there are people who have imposed their own ideological or idiosyncratic patterns upon him. I am not making any of these up. Jesus has been described as:

- A CEO.
- A political king.
- A philosopher influenced by the Greeks.
- An entrepreneur.
- The ticket to worldly prosperity.

---

[20]Wegner, *Textual Criticism*; Komoszewski et al., *Reinventing Jesus*.

[21]Michael Poole, *"New Atheism": Ten Arguments that Don't Hold Water* (Oxford: Lion, 2009), p. 46. Hermeneutics is the study of interpreting ancient texts.

- Another good guy who was killed for being nice, like Socrates, Gandhi and Martin Luther King Jr.
- A social revolutionary approving armed resistance against oppression.
- A meek model for obedient children.[22]
- A tough superhero.
- A guy in old times who ran around doing miracles.
- A transsexual woman.
- An Aryan.
- A myth based on ancient dying and rising gods.
- One of a number of great moral teachers such as Buddha.
- A fraudulent magician.
- The bastard son of Mary's fornication with a coarse Roman soldier.
- A homosexual.
- A pure spirit who only appeared to have a physical body.
- An Essene.
- A Gnostic.
- A Catholic.
- A Mormon.
- A Protestant.
- A con man.
- A sage who learned his wisdom in the Far East.
- A European.
- A great salesman.
- A liberal rabbi.
- A socialist.
- A communist.
- A hallucination of the disciples, who were perhaps on drugs.
- The ancient equivalent of a rock star.

---

[22]"Meek" in English has two distinct meanings: (1) patient and gentle, and (2) submissive. Parents telling their children to be meek usually mean (2). In the Bible, (1) is meant.

- A democrat.
- A monarchist.
- Deluded or crazy.
- An implantation in the human mind by space aliens.
- A space alien.
- A Manga hero.
- A sinner.
- A philosophical Cynic.
- Married with children, even married twice with children.
- A conservative.
- A liberal.
- Human, not divine.
- Divine, not human.
- A student of Buddhism in Egypt (or Tibet).
- Someone who never existed.
- Add to the list as you please.[23]

As Mark Sullivan puts it, "To ask who Jesus is in my life has the danger of turning the question inside out. Suddenly we're not talking about Jesus anymore. We're talking about ourselves."[24] Different views are possible, but those that fit the evidence of the ancient and continuous tradition of the churches are the most reliable. The book of Hebrews observes that "Jesus Christ is the same yesterday and today and forever" (Heb 13:8).

71. The Jesus of history is different from the Christ of faith.

This statement raises the question of what the Jesus of history really is.[25]

---

[23]Jaroslav Pelikan, *Jesus through the Centuries: His Place in the History of Culture* (New Haven, CT: Yale University Press, 1985); Michael Green, *Lies, Lies, Lies! Exposing Myths about the Real Jesus* (Nottingham, UK: Inter-Varsity Press, 2009), pp. 175-81. Hurtado, *Lord Jesus Christ*, p. 54, observes that it is "now difficult even for professional scholars in the New Testament and Christian origins to keep fully current on all the latest books on Jesus."

[24]Mark Sullivan, "Defying Easy Categorization," *Catholic World Report*, June 2010, p. 37.

[25]Scot McKnight, *Jesus and His Death: Historiography, the Historical Jesus, and Atonement Theory*

Beginning in the 1700s, scholars such as Gotthold Ephraim Lessing (1729-1781), David Friedrich Strauss (1824-1881) and Joseph Ernest Renan (1823-1892) claimed that the historical Jesus was different from the Christ of faith. The classic study of this movement is Albert Schweitzer's *Quest of the Historical Jesus*.[26] The core of the argument is that the New Testament presents a legendary or even mythical Jesus—the Christ of faith—rather than an accurate picture of the life of Jesus—the Jesus of history. Much of the biblical criticism of the last century was based on this view, with many claiming that the historical Jesus was an eccentric Jewish preacher.

There are many varieties of this view, which many scholars continue to advance. However, they disagree sharply among themselves: they dispute what kinds of historical criticism are appropriate, and they disagree over which passages of the Bible their criteria should exclude. According to the media's excited reports, the so-called "Jesus Seminar," a group of about seventy biblical scholars meeting in 1986, demonstrated that only a small number of the words and deeds attributed to Jesus could be considered authentic. It isn't as often reported that the seminar represented a small percentage of biblical scholars and that they proved little if anything. But the seminar revived itself in 2009, and one of its founders, John Dominic Crossan, was elected president of the Society of Biblical Literature.[27]

Many efforts have been made, most famously by Thomas Jefferson, to recover the allegedly real Jesus by purging the New Testament of Christ's divinity and miracles. This is like purging Beowulf of its battle scenes or excising liberty from the Declaration of Independence. It misses the whole point. The point of the New Testament is that Jesus is Christ, the Messiah, the Son of God, a supernatural being with supernatural powers. Without that, the New Testament is a flat tire.

The serious effort at purging began with the "form criticism" of the Tübingen School of the early 1800s, which excised miracles from the Scriptures and applied nineteenth-century literary and historical criticism to them.[28] In the twentieth century anthropology and sociology invented

(Waco, TX: Baylor University Press, 2005).

[26]Albert Schweitzer, *Quest of the Historical Jesus* (New York: Macmillan, 1950).

[27]Michael J. Wilkins, "Who Did Jesus Think He Was?" in *Contending with Christianity's Critics*, ed. Paul Copan and William Lane Craig (Nashville: B & H, 2009), pp. 167-81.

[28]Strobel, *Case for the Real Jesus*, pp. 23-63.

the ideas of collective memory and group identification.[29] Collective memory refers "to the traditions of a group about events not personally recollected by any of the group's members."[30] Most sociologists use the term in a way that makes individuals of little if any importance. According to this view, Christianity formed in the same way as religions that are based in a sense of timelessness without history. But as great scholars such as Mircea Eliade have pointed out, the myths of other religions place events in some other dimension of space and time, such as the Aborigines' "dreamtime."[31] The Jewish and Christian religions are entirely different from these myths, for Jews and Christians intend the events they describe to have taken place in normal time.

What does the term "historical Jesus" as used in the 1800s and 1900s mean? The skeptics maintain that the Gospels are true only to the extent that historians have independently verified them. Most historians today accept the physicalist view that the laws of nature make miracles impossible. This is to forget that the laws of nature are not prescriptive but descriptive: they are based on human descriptions of regularities in nature. The phrase "laws of nature" really means "regularities of nature." Historians denying miracles define history within a physicalist paradigm resting on the unproven axiom that natural regularities can never be suspended. They deny that miracles can be real because miracles don't fit their current definition of history. That definition excludes the eyewitness testimony of witnesses about miracles, although the testimony of witnesses is exactly what history is based on. Historians tend to present a Jesus reconstructed to fit their own present-centered, unhistorical way of thinking about history.

Modern critics differ widely among themselves, creating a plethora of "historical Jesuses." At best, the historical pictures they create constitute "no less a construction than the Jesus of each of the gospels."[32] It's more likely that the historical Jesus and the Christ of faith are the same: in other words, the Christ of tradition *is* the historical Jesus.

The twentieth-century search for the historical Jesus produced a great

---

[29]Richard Bauckham, *Jesus and the Eyewitnesses: The Gospels as Eyewitness Testimony* (Grand Rapids: Eerdmans, 2006), pp. 310-312.
[30]Ibid., p. 314.
[31]Mircea Eliade, *Cosmos and History: The Myth of the Eternal Return* (New York: Harper, 1959).
[32]Bauckham, *Jesus and the Eyewitnesses,* p. 4.

deal of valuable information about Near Eastern culture, and discoveries are continuing, especially in archeology. However, the historical-critical approach yields many questionable results. For example, it assumes that the New Testament was the product of oral community tradition. Given the undisputed early testimony of Paul and the book of Acts, this assumption is suspicious. Such oral tradition surely existed, but it was constantly corrected by the eyewitnesses to Jesus' life, death and resurrection. The Gospels were the product of carefully evaluated eyewitness testimony. All historical knowledge relies on testimony. There can be good reasons for trusting or distrusting a witness, but these are precisely reasons, not assumptions. The Gospels are an account of the way certain eyewitnesses perceived the history unfolding around them.[33] The same cannot be said for the writers of the noncanonical gospels, because they were written later than the canonical Gospels and because they were rejected by those who kept the eyewitness testimony relatively pure. The canonical "Gospel texts are much closer to the form in which the eyewitnesses told their stories or passed on their traditions than is commonly envisaged in current scholarship."[34]

Although oral traditions obviously existed, they seem to have mostly affected the false gospels. The canonical Gospels were written not out of a long and ever-changing oral tradition, but "within living memory of the events they recount." What's more, they were constantly checked and supervised by eyewitnesses of those events and their followers.[35] Written drafts or at least notes probably preceded the Gospels in their final form, but these "should not be imagined as proto-gospels."[36] Plus, early Christian writings refer to individual authors rather than to an anonymous community.[37] Like the Gospel writers, the best classical historians also relied on eyewitnesses as much as they could.

The letters of the Apostle Saint Paul show "that the early Christian movement did practice the formal transmission of tradition . . . specific practices employed to ensure that tradition was faithfully handed on from

---

[33]Ibid., p. 5.
[34]Ibid., p. 6.
[35]Ibid., p. 8.
[36]Ibid., p. 289.
[37]Ibid., p. 297.

[eyewitnesses] to others."[38] The names of those who wrote the Gospels are uncertain, but there is no evidence that the books themselves ever went by names other than those they go by now. As soon as the Gospels were in circulation among the churches, they had their current names attached to them.[39] They were taken to be direct eyewitness reports, as with John, or once-removed, as with Mark, who relied on Peter's eyewitness. No matter who the Gospel writers were, they were not anonymous, and they would never have been believed if they had sprung up without the authority of witnesses behind them.

The authorship of the Gospel of John is sometimes questioned. The author was likely John the son of Zebedee mentioned in the other Gospels, but arguments have been made for John the Elder.[40] What matters is that John's Gospel is an eyewitness account accepted widely in the earliest community. Some scholars have questioned its reliability on the grounds that it may have been written much later than the other Gospels. The theologian Irenaeus (A.D. 130-200) said that John was the latest evangelist. Yet John's placement of the Last Supper on Thursday is more likely than the other three Gospels' placement of it on Friday at a Seder.[41] John's theology was deemed too "advanced" to be early. Yet his theology is closely congruent with that of Paul, whom everyone dates as early as the 50s. It also used to be said that John borrowed much from Greek thought, but aside from the word *Logos* in the first verse, John not only doesn't sound like a Greek philosopher, he doesn't sound Greek at all. He sounds Jewish.[42] His Gospel follows the pattern of Israel's calendar of religious festivals.[43] Further, John's Greek is the easiest and simplest of all the Gospels, which would be strange if he was theologizing the other Gospels, as is often claimed. His Gospel does not mention the destruction of Jerusalem in A.D. 70. A Jewish historian after A.D. 70 who did not mention the destruction of Jerusalem would be comparable to a Jewish historian after

---

[38]Ibid., p. 264. An example is 1 Cor 15:3-4.

[39]Ibid., p. 304.

[40]Ibid., p. 463.

[41]Benedict XVI, *Jesus of Nazareth: Holy Week: From the Entrance into Jerusalem to the Resurrection* (San Francisco: Ignatius, 2011), pp. 106-15.

[42]However, Hurtado, *Lord Jesus Christ*, pp. 644-647, points out that by the time of Justin Martyr (100-165), theologians were already assimilating the Greek philosophical *logos* with the *Logos* of John.

[43]Benedict XVI, *Jesus of Nazareth*, p. 236.

1945 not mentioning the Holocaust. For various reasons, John probably cannot be dated earlier than A.D. 60, but the real date is probably much earlier in the first century than most scholars have assumed.

Scholars of the "historical Jesus" create their own Jesus or, more precisely, their own Jesuses. What historians actually know is Christianity; an alleged Jesus different from Christ has no historically convincing existence.[44]

That's the "Jesus of history." Now "the Christ of faith."

The word "faith" has many meanings. The primary two are: (1) To have faith in something is to believe in it without proof, and usually without analysis, as when we read in a book that Caesar was assassinated and accept that on the authority of the author. (2) To have faith in someone is to rely on that person's character, as when I trust you with my child or my life. Sense (1) is not as important as (2). For Christians, believing in the words of the creeds or the words of the New Testament is secondary. What is primary is faith in the person of Jesus Christ the Son of God. The Christian faith is, clearly and simply, trust in Jesus. The individual and the community give up self and replace self with Christ. The creeds of the 300s and 400s, based on the New Testament, confirm faith of both sorts in Christian thought, making it clear that Jesus is God.

Some contemporary Christians show a reluctance to embrace Christianity. Relativism and materialism, along with honest sensitivity to other religions, incline such people to believe that all religions are on the same plane. One even hears that it is fanatical to believe otherwise; some clergy preach that the Jesus story is one of a number of stories (such as those about Buddha) that are equally valid.

Christians certainly can learn a great deal from other religions. Most religions (those who say "all" might consider Satanism) are valuable, but the only way they can all be equal is if they are all equally false and meaningless. Advocating the equality of religions is a cover for the rejection of all religion. Attempts to compel Christians to accept the equality of all religions are really attempts to force Christians not to be Christians. The basic rule of logic is: *a* cannot be *not-a*. Either Christ is God or he is not God. That doesn't depend on what we feel. The basis of Christianity is that Jesus Christ is the only human who is God. It is illogical for people

---

[44]It is sometimes valuable to steer a middle passage between the radical historical-critical, history-of-religions course and the opposite anticritical, defensive course.

who disbelieve that to call themselves Christians.

The current downplaying of the uniqueness of Jesus is reminiscent of the religious syncretism of the late Roman Empire. Syncretism was the system in which you could add any deity from any culture you chose and combine it with deities you already had. For example, Egyptian Re (Ra) was Zeus, and Zeus was Jupiter, and so on. The more gods the better, as long as they were recognized as one pantheon guaranteed by the Roman emperor, who was himself considered divine. This political foundation for religion was challenged by Jews and Christians who refused to believe that the one God was only one of a number of gods. Monotheism is the basis of Judaism and Christianity, and it is logically impossible to be a Christian while denying it.

The idea that Jesus is God is embedded in the New Testament, especially in the letters of the Apostle Saint Paul and the Gospel of John. Skeptics have objected that the texts of the New Testament must have been substantially altered by the generation following Jesus. Except for small details, there is no convincing evidence supporting this objection. Paul wrote only twenty years after the death of Jesus and only after consulting thoroughly with the surviving disciples. Other skeptics object that the disciples and apostles got it all wrong themselves, that they thoroughly misunderstood Jesus. This is of course remotely possible, but that all the disciples and apostles who knew and heard Jesus all got it all wrong is quite improbable. The final objection is that Jesus himself got it wrong. If that's true then there is no basis for being a Christian at all. It may seem strange that the premise of Christ's divinity is not clearer and stronger in the Gospels than it is, but there are reasons: the claim is shocking, then and now, and to Jews it was utter blasphemy, so the evangelists may have played it down. Contrary to what some moderns suppose, more early Christians doubted that Jesus was human than doubted that he was God.[45]

Throughout the New Testament Jesus shares the honors, attributes, names and deeds of God. A few examples out of many:

> The Father and I are one. (Jn 10:30)

> No one knows the Son except the Father, and no one knows the Father

---

[45]Komoszewski et al., *Reinventing Jesus*, p. 174.

except the Son and anyone to whom the Son chooses to reveal him. (Mt 11:27)

I am in the Father and the Father is in me. (Jn 14:10)

Our great God and Savior, Jesus Christ. (Tit 2:13)[46]

Among the most powerful texts are the "I am" statements. In the Old Testament God reveals his own name when he tells Moses, "I AM WHO AM" (Ex 3:14; or I AM BEING or I AM AND SHALL BE), implying eternal Being (not the banal I AM WHO I AM that appears in many translations). "Thus you shall say to the Israelites," God says, "I AM has sent me to you" (Ex 3:14). This name, YHWH (Yahweh), has always been so sacred to believing Jews that it is seldom pronounced or written, being replaced by *Adonai* ("Lord"), *Ha Shem* ("the Name") or, in Greek, *to on* ("Being"). Jews and Christians who understand this are very cautious about pronouncing or singing the word "Yahweh" aloud.[47] Jesus' statement "Before Abraham was, I AM" (Jn 8:58) was the most blasphemous thing anyone could say.

The New Testament presents Christ as God, the Son of God, or at the minimum a human being who stands in a unique and unparalleled relationship with the Father. The Greek translation of the sacred name YHWH is *Kyrios,* "Lord," suggesting that when the Bible applies *Kyrios* to Jesus, it is likely that its meaning is not just a respectful "sir" but may indicate his divinity. Two quite different groups at the time took such claims totally seriously: the Jewish authorities who accused him of blasphemy and the community of believers who accepted him as the Son of God. Everyone has the right to reject Tradition and the New Testament writers as all wrong, but it is impossible to do that and be a Christian.

72. THE APOSTLE SAINT PAUL INVENTED CHRISTIANITY.

"Christianity was founded by Paul of Tarsus"[48] is a shopworn idea still for sale in the hand-me-down shops. The story goes that Jesus was a moral teacher but Paul transformed him into a deity. The idea "lets Jesus off the hook," so that he can still be respected as a nice guy and shifts the blame to

---

[46]Some more New Testament examples of Jesus' divine identity and characteristics: Mt 16:16; Mk 14:61-62; Jn 1:1-3; 20:28; Col 1:15-20; 3:11.

[47]Benedict XVI, *Jesus of Nazareth,* pp. 306, 346.

[48]Dawkins, *God Delusion*, p. 58.

Paul, the deluded fanatic. But it ignores the fact that the divinity of Christ is repeatedly affirmed throughout the New Testament. To deny Christ's divinity one has to deny the New Testament as a whole, which is of course what those propagating this myth really intend. Whether the New Testament is true or a web of fictions, singling out Paul goes against the textual and historical evidence. The best sources about the earliest followers of Jesus are the letters of Paul.[49] They show him engaged with people who had been established worshippers of the divine Jesus for a long while. And these followers believed in the physical resurrection of Jesus, in his divinity, and in his redemption of humanity.[50] As a contemporary Jewish scholar puts it, "One cannot any longer say that [Paul] was the founder of Christianity.[51]

73. The earliest followers of Jesus did not believe him to be divine.

This idea, advanced by some scholars two centuries ago, still has many adherents, but it has been decisively and thoroughly refuted, most recently by Larry W. Hurtado.[52] The earliest followers worshiped with "no precedent or parallel" in an "intense devotion to Jesus, which includes referencing him as divine."[53] Though some groups such as the Ebionites may have denied it, the idea of Jesus as God was already standard soon after his death. What is most astonishing, even shocking, is that this absorption of Jesus into God himself occurred in the strictest monotheist religion in the world: the Temple religion of the Hebrew Bible. It is certainly not sur-

---

[49]The literature on Paul has always been, and still is, enormous. A few of the many recent useful books are Donald Harman Akenson, *Saint Saul: A Skeleton Key to the Historical Jesus* (Oxford: Oxford University Press, 2000); J. Murphy-O'Connor, *Paul: A Critical Life* (Oxford, Oxford University Press, 1996); Thomas R. Schreiner, *Paul, Apostle of God's Glory in Christ* (Downers Grove, IL: InterVarsity Press, 2006); Ben Witherington III, *The Paul Quest: The Renewed Search for the Jew of Tarsus* (Downers Grove, IL: InterVarsity Press, 2001). The lengths to which scholars can let themselves go in claiming Paul as the originator of Christianity is evident in Hyram Maccoby, *Mythmaker: Paul and the Invention of Christianity* (New York: Harper and Row, 1986). An excellent account of both the debates and the evidence is Hurtado, *Lord Jesus Christ*, p. 160 and throughout.

[50]Hurtado, *Lord Jesus Christ*, p. 136: "We cannot attribute the origins of the cultic worship of Jesus to Pauline Christianity."

[51]Arnold Jacob Wolf, "Jesus as an Historical Jew," *Judaism* 46 (Summer 1997): 377, quoted by Akenson, *Saint Saul*, p. 61.

[52]Hurtado, *Lord Jesus Christ*, throughout; William Lane Craig, *On Guard: Defending Your Faith with Reason and Precision* (Colorado Springs: David C. Cook, 2010), pp. 217-18, presents a summary of Jesus' "radical self-understanding."

[53]Hurtado, *Lord Jesus Christ*, pp. 2-3.

prising that many rejected it as blasphemous. Some scholars have gone so far as to say that the absorption would have been impossible, so that Jesus religion must have developed under the influence of the loose syncretistic circles of Roman religion.[54] On the contrary, Jesus' followers retained exclusivist monotheism, stretching and expanding it to include Jesus with God the Father.

Worship of Jesus as true God began virtually immediately, so again the alleged distinction between "the Jesus of history" and "the Christ of faith" is misleading. The evidence indicates that few early Jesus worshipers doubted that Jesus was God; many more doubted that he was human. Little room is left for Christians who want to see Jesus as merely a gifted prophet whose example can be followed but who is not to be worshiped. Hurtado's statement is conclusive:

> Devotion to Jesus as divine erupted suddenly and quickly, not gradually and late, among first-century circles of followers. More specifically, the origins lie in Jewish Christian circles of the earliest years. Only a certain wishful thinking [on the part of some scholars] continues to attribute the reverence of Jesus as divine decisively to the influence of pagan religion and the influx of Gentile converts.[55]

However, in what way Jesus was divine had to be worked out by theologians over the following few centuries.

74. Early Christians suppressed the true religion of Jesus, and the truth about Christianity is found in secret codes and documents.

These ideas, nearly two millennia old, are now being presented in media specials, novels and movies as if they were new. The charges are that the early Christian community attempted to destroy the true facts about Jesus; that the real Jesus is radically different from the Jesus presented by the Bible and the church; that early Christians used compulsion to establish their views against those of a variety of other "Christianities"; that the suppression of these Christianities culminated at the Council of Nicaea in 325 under the authority of the emperor Constantine; and that Jesus'

---

[54]Ibid., pp. 42-43.
[55]Ibid., p. 650.

identity was thus formulated by the church and imposed by the state. The true religion of Jesus, it is claimed, is the one that was secret, while the one that was openly, widely and repeatedly discussed and approved, and formulated in open meetings, is false.

The charges continue: The creeds—for example those accepted by the Councils of Nicaea, Constantinople (381) and Chalcedon (451)—were arrogantly and arbitrarily imposed by the Christian community. The early Christians allegedly imposed the canon of the Bible (the books formally included in the New Testament), so that the New Testament is riddled with falsehood. Christianity is invalid unless the secret Jesus replaces the open Jesus of the church. The Gospels and Epistles of the New Testament are, they say, largely false. They claim that the "hidden gospels" that were rejected during the years of open discussion in the church are at least equally valid, and possibly more valid, than the canonical Matthew, Mark, Luke and John. People love secrets and conspiracies.[56]

According to these exhumed ideas, instead of one Christianity in the first century, there were multiple Christianities. (No one says that the occasional disagreement among apostles such as James, Peter and Paul is evidence of multiple Christianities; that would stretch the term so thin as to be meaningless. No one ever argued that the early Christians all agreed on every point.) Rather, the idea of multiple Christianities is that in the first century (A.D. 1-100) there were strongly divergent views on the central core of Christian teaching, for example, Christ's crucifixion and resurrection. Such divergence did occur in the second century (100s A.D.) but not in earliest Christianity. "The only way someone can come up with a divergent 'Christianity' is to import a second-century writing or teacher into the middle of the first century."[57] Every effort has been made by modern neo-gnostics (contemporary writers claiming the legitimacy of second-century Gnostic gospels) to do this, but the evidence is against them. The secret, "hidden" gospels and letters are simply part of a wide

[56]Among the best-known books shedding light or darkness on the question of alternate Christianities are Elaine Pagels, *Gnostic Gospels* (New York: Random House, 1979); Willis Barnstone and Marvin Meyer, *Gnostic Bible* (Boston: Shambala, 2003); Bart D. Ehrman, *Lost Christianities: The Battles for Scripture and the Faiths We Never Knew* (New York: Oxford University Press), 2003. On Nicaea, see Lewis Ayers, *Nicaea and its Legacy: An Approach to Fourth-Century Trinitarian Theology* (Oxford: Oxford University Press, 2004), esp. pp. 430-35.

[57]Craig A. Evans, *Fabricating Jesus: How Modern Scholars Distort the Gospels* (Downers Grove, IL: InterVarsity Press, 2006), p. 202.

variety of alleged scriptures produced in the second and third centuries and later. It is harsh to call them forgeries, as some scholars do, for their authors may have felt them to be genuine, but lumping them into the same category as the canonical materials is special pleading in favor of contemporary intellectual agendas.

Consider some of the objections to the canonical Gospels. It's been known from the beginning that texts of the New Testament vary owing to the enormous number of manuscripts, many of which still exist. But for a very few exceptions, such as the ending of Mark (Mk 16:9-20) and the placement of the scene with the woman taken in adultery (Jn 8:7-11), they are minor and insignificant. Some discrepancies do exist: the Gospel of Mark 1:2-3 attributes to the prophet Isaiah words that were actually written by the prophet Malachi, and the Gospel of Matthew 27:9-10 conflates the prophets Zechariah and Jeremiah. These differences are explainable in that the evangelists drew upon several different Greek translations of the Old Testament as well as the original Hebrew.

These are not questions that can be dismissed by appealing to nonliteral interpretation. If a canonical book contains a simple factual error, then the inerrancy of the Bible seems to be in question. On the other hand, these anomalies did not escape the early thinkers of the church as they considered the texts. One solution is to understand the Bible in terms of its intent rather than its exact words. Christian thinkers have long distinguished between the *ipsissima verba* (the exact words) and the *ipsa vox* (the true "voice" or meaning itself). Only those from extreme literalist backgrounds think that any discrepancy in the Bible destroys the whole Bible. Reading each individual element in the light of the whole and in the light of Christian Tradition is more productive. One of the earliest post-apostolic writers, Papias (A.D. 60-130), made it clear that the Christian community carefully weighed writings with reference to their authority and eyewitnesses. Between the contending contemporary historians on the one hand, and on the other hand the open consensus of the community for two millennia, including the open debates over the books and texts in the first four centuries, it's a safer bet to "give the ancient Christian writers the benefit of the doubt."[58]

[58]Komoszewski et al., *Reinventing Jesus*, p. 149. But scholarly skeptics such as John Dominic Crossan lend the appearance of academic credibility to their views. See Crossan, *Jesus: A Rev-*

Questions about the canonical books are small compared to the enormous questions surrounding books that some contemporary writers argue are of at least approximately equal value with those in the canon. Some of these have long been known; others were found in the discovery of the Nag Hammadi manuscripts in 1945-1946.[59] As many as twenty different gospels exist (including the four canonical ones), such as the Gospel of Thomas, the Gospel of Mary, the Gospel of Judas and so on, but only the canonical four were discussed in the early church. One reason is that some of the false gospels are preposterous on the face of them—can it be taken seriously that as a child Jesus used his supernatural powers to smite a clumsy playmate dead or amused himself by making birds out of clay and causing them to fly? Another reason is that they were written after about A.D. 100, after the standards for inclusion in the Bible had already been set by the Christian community.

The effort to date the "hidden" gospels to the first century by some scholars is extremely dubious, and at least one of the so-called secret gospels, the Secret Gospel of Mark, is thought to be a twentieth-century forgery by Morton Smith.[60] But the apparent novelty of these ideas has penetrated public consciousness through such books as the pseudo-history of Michael Baigent and the fiction derived from it.[61] These are not merely technical problems, for the issue is whether the Jesus of the Bible is the "real, historical Jesus." On balance, the biblical Jesus is a lot more likely to be true than the Jesus of contemporary revisionists.[62] Here, what's new is not what's true.

75. Gnostics are Christians.

Gnostic ideas derived from a combination of Persian Zoroastrianism and

---

olutionary Biography (New York: HarperOne, 2009).

[59]Robert J. Miller, ed., *Complete Gospels: Annotated Scholars Version* (San Francisco: HarperSanFrancisco, 1994); Robert W. Funk and the Jesus seminar, *Five Gospels: The Search for the Authentic Words of Jesus* (San Francisco: HarperSanFrancisco, 1997). The Nag Hammadi scrolls are mainly Gnostic in origin.

[60]Morton Smith, *Secret Gospel: The Discovery and Interpretation of the Secret Gospel According to Mark* (New York: Harper and Row, 1973); Stephen C. Carlson, *The Gospel Hoax: Morton Smith's Invention of Secret Mark* (Waco, TX: Baylor University Press, 2005); Evans, *Fabricating Jesus*, pp. 94-98.

[61]Michael Baigent, *Holy Blood, Holy Grail* (New York: Dell, 1983); Dan Brown, *The Da Vinci Code* (New York: Anchor, 2003).

[62]Evans, *Fabricating Jesus*, pp. 59-62, 77.

Greek Orphism. Each of these two traditions was dualistic in its own way. The Zoroastrians believed in a duality of two independent, warring gods: the god of light and goodness versus the god of evil and darkness. The Orphics believed in a duality of spirit, which is good, and matter, which is evil. The Gnostics interwove the two ideas, tying spirit to the god of light and matter to the god of darkness. Gnosticism is the gnosis (secret knowledge) of doctrines claimed to come either from a secret tradition of the apostles or from personal revelation. Whereas the open tradition of the apostles existed by at least A.D. 50, the alleged secret tradition did not appear until about A.D. 100. Gnostics were originally part of the Christian community, but they were extruded from it around A.D. 150-200, either by coercion (as modern gnostics say), or by the community's general recognition that Gnostic doctrines were incompatible with the real Jesus—or by the choice of the Gnostics themselves.

"Christian" Gnosticism was a movement that flourished from about A.D. 150 to about A.D. 250. Its basic belief was that the material world was created by the evil Old Testament God for the purpose of imprisoning human spirits inside flesh. The spirit's job was to liberate itself from its loathsome body by means of secret gnosis. Sex was bad, and the worst sex was procreative, since the conception of each new child entombed yet another human spirit. Jews, who worshiped the evil Creator deity of the Old Testament, were particularly wicked. Jesus did not have a real body, since bodies were disgusting; he had only the appearance of a body. As he had no body, he did not die on the cross, did not rise from the dead, and did not suffer in order to free people from sin. The point of Jesus was to teach people how to free themselves from matter through gnosis.

Over the past couple of decades, some writers have been promoting the view that original Christianity was actually Gnostic. They argue that what we now think of as Christianity is false and that Gnosticism is real Christianity. Some have been beguiled by this idea because it ties vague versions of Gnosticism together with pop spirituality. The characteristics of modern gnosticism fit contemporary "me-ness" and New Age, adding a pinch of Jesus so as to attract Christians. The characteristics include seeking the divine within, rejection of the past and a break with tradition, conspiracy theory, freedom of spirit against rules of conduct, women's leadership against patriarchy, sexual permissiveness, self-centeredness instead of community, intellectual elitism, secret knowledge, and exclusion of the "ignorant" from the circle of the "enlightened." Modern gnostics fail to confront the unpleasant characteristics of Gnosticism: it was dualistic, anti-material, anti-sexual, anti-woman, anti-child, anti-nature and anti-semitic.[63] The myth of neo-gnostics is that the Gnostics were "spiritual egalitarians, environmentalists, feminists, mystical pantheists—indeed, practically anything but what they actually were."[64] Larry Hurtado sums up the Gnostics' real worldview: "the world as a vain and pointless realm to be treated with disdain and the elect as an inner circle of aliens whose only hope could be to escape from the world and return to their celestial home."[65]

Many people are allured by the idea of some sort of secret truth or secret tradition as opposed to the open truth available to all. It is this temptation that Dan Brown and similar authors exploit. But even if Gnosticism were true, it would be unreasonable to call Gnosticism Christianity. A few churches now honestly call themselves Gnostic instead of pretending to be Christian. The historical development of Christianity from about A.D. 50 to the present is openly attested, whereas there is little evidence for "Christian Gnosticism" before about A.D. 150. Open Christianity—not secret codes—has been Christianity for twenty centuries. Whether Christianity is right or wrong, that's what Christianity is, by the standards of history, philosophy and common sense.[66]

76. Little or nothing is known about Jesus.

The small number of scholars who agree with the tiny, hyperskeptical "Jesus seminar" maintain that the New Testament contains little if any valid evidence.[67] The Gospels, they say, consist mainly of sayings and words of Jesus that Christians made up long after his death. Skeptics outdo

---

[63]N. T. Wright, *Surprised by Hope: Rethinking Heaven, the Resurrection, and the Mission of the Church* (New York: HarperOne, 2008), pp. 88-91.

[64]David Bentley Hart, *Atheist Delusions: The Christian Revolution and Its Fashionable Enemies* (New Haven, CT: Yale University Press, 2009), p. 137.

[65]Hurtado, *Lord Jesus Christ*, p. 559.

[66]Ibid., pp. 523-48; Hurtado discusses the ancient Gnostics and their most influential sect, the Valentinians.

[67]Andreas J. Köstenberger and Michael J. Kruger, *The Heresy of Orthodoxy: How Contemporary Culture's Fascination with Diversity Has Reshaped Our Understanding of Early Christianity* (Wheaton, IL: Crossway, 2010).

one another in order to continue to attract attention, with the result that skepticism becomes ever more extreme, with some saying that virtually nothing is known about Jesus. At the opposite extreme are the credulous people who also deny the evidence of the Bible but invent fantastic scenarios instead. On the basis of alleged secret codes in the Gospels and Dead Sea Scrolls they propose that Jesus learned Buddhism in Alexandria, that he was married (twice!) and had children by both wives, survived his crucifixion, and afterwards taught in various places in Asia and Europe.[68] Such writers have no inkling of the spectrum of probabilities in dealing with evidence; they promote infinite improbabilities—tiny quirks of evidence or no evidence at all. This is tabloid history: the weirder it is, the more it sells. A similar pattern of far-out speculation has surrounded William Shakespeare since 1800, with thousands of books and a movie claiming (with no plausible evidence) that Shakespeare did not write the works of Shakespeare.[69] A still popular scenario has space aliens building the Great Pyramids.[70]

Is there early evidence about Jesus outside the New Testament? Did the evangelists and other New Testament writers intend to tell the truth, or were they engaging in deceit? Were they able to tell the truth? In what manner did they intend to tell the truth? What does the term "historical Jesus" mean?

The existence of Jesus as a religious leader is attested by ancient non-Christian sources, such as Josephus (A.D. 37-100), Pliny the Younger (61-112), Suetonius (writing about 110) and Lucian of Samosata (115-200). Demands for further evidence from outside misses the point that any such evidence would almost certainly be less reliable than the earliest sources: the Gospels and Epistles. On the whole, the evidence for Jesus' life is stronger than that for all but the most famous ancient figures. The fact is that "there is no historically credible source outside the New Testament that calls into question the portrait of Jesus painted in the Gospels."[71] Only the most extreme skeptics accuse the Gospel writers of deliberate falsification.

---

[68]Evans, *Fabricating Jesus*, pp. 205-6.

[69]James Shapiro, *Contested Will: Who Wrote Shakespeare?* (New York: Simon and Schuster, 2010).

[70]Eric von Däniken, *Chariots of the Gods: Unsolved Mysteries of the Past* (New York: Putnam, 1969), one of the most preposterous books of the twentieth century and a best-seller.

[71]Craig, *On Guard*, p. 187.

Instead, the argument is that the Gospel writers were unable to tell the truth. They thought they were telling the truth, but they were mistakenly accepting old oral traditions. However, in fact the writers were either eyewitnesses or relying on the eyewitness accounts of people who knew Jesus intimately themselves. The oral tradition that did develop was based on recent events and always subject to correction by the witnesses. Some also argue that the New Testament is unreliable because there are discrepancies in the Gospels. But that is subjecting the Testament to impossible standards; any four accounts of any set of events by any four different people will be different. The assumption seems to be that if Christianity is true every word of the New Testament must be an equal statement of truth. This assumption is impossible. Only extreme literalists can be shocked into disbelief by the fact that the Gospel accounts differ. Each Gospel writer presented revelation from his own point of view, and none claimed to have written down everything fully (Lk 1:1-4; Jn 20:30; 21:25). The best criteria for the reliability of the Gospels are coherence of purpose, multiple attestations, dissimilarity, and the use of Semitisms and Israelite cultural background.[72]

In what manner did the evangelists intend to tell the truth? Christians, unlike Muslims, do not believe that God dictated scriptures. They do not believe that God revealed the New Testament word for word but rather that the intent of the writers was to impart as fully as they could what God had revealed to them. One discrepancy in the Gospels is between the timing of the Last Supper in John and that in the synoptic Gospels (Matthew, Mark and Luke). Another is that John reports the resurrection appearances of Christ differently from the Synoptics (Jn 20:11-18). This validates the Gospels by showing that they usually did not copy from one another. Instead of evidence against the reliability of the Gospels, the differences among them show that they are reports by eyewitnesses (or at least secondhand from eyewitnesses), each of whom saw events in a somewhat different way, just as eyewitnesses to events today each report them differently. If the Gospels did agree on every point, then collusion or parroting could properly be suspected.

Are the Gospels historically true? That depends on how one defines

---

[72]Evans, *Fabricating Jesus*, p. 51.

the term "historical." The first thing to note is that no historian can ever write entirely objectively for the simple reason that historians have human limitations. They come from personal and social backgrounds that always create a point of view. Even the best historians—those who strive for dispassionate accounts as opposed to propaganda—cannot describe "what really happened." Imagine trying to write a dispassionate and complete account of the Iraq war. One would have to know not only every small military or political move but also the thoughts and feelings of all the participants. Impossible. One has to select what is most important from the welter of details, and the selection will depend on one's point of view. Historians accept that they have a point of view, but good historians try to avoid bias by constantly watching out and correcting for their presuppositions.

The modern way of studying history according to certain defined criteria did not emerge before the late 1700s. In the ancient world the word "history" (Greek *historia*) simply meant any sort of investigation. No one in the ancient world intended to write history in the modern sense. The evangelists did not claim to write history or even think that they were writing history. They were writing testimony. They were describing events that they had observed personally or that eyewitnesses had reported to them. They related eyewitness details as correctly as they could within their human limitations. The authors' statement of intent was to present Jesus in accordance with the evidence (Lk 1:1-4). Early critical examination of the accuracy of the authors is displayed in the writings of Ignatius of Antioch (35-107), Papias of Hieropolis (60-130) and Polycarp of Smyrna (69-155).

The modern so-called "search for the historical Jesus" imposes contemporary criteria on people writing nineteen centuries ago. It is dominant in many theological circles today, but it is based on dubious assumptions. However much useful information it has contributed about the details of early Christian history, it makes certain presuppositions that have led to the fabrication of a fictitious Jesus.[73] The diverse opinions of a few skeptical scholars today do not outweigh the open testimony of Christianity from its outset.

---

[73]Evans, *Fabricating Jesus*, pp. 51-59.

77. Jesus was illiterate.

It's sometimes assumed that Jesus was illiterate. The first point is that, until the latter nineteenth century, illiteracy—inability to read and write—was not equated with ignorance. Many learned persons memorized, reasoned, managed, debated, theorized and organized without knowing how to read. Indeed, illiterate people, not having notes to rely on, often produce more reliable testimony than literate people. The evidence shows that Jesus was well-educated and almost certainly literate as well. It is difficult to imagine an illiterate Jesus debating with scholars or, especially, reading aloud from the scriptures in the Nazareth synagogue: "He unrolled the scroll and found the place where it was written" (Lk 4:16-20). Jesus said that not a letter or a stroke of the Law would disappear (Mt 5:17-18)—not a metaphor that would spring to the mind of an illiterate. Several times Jesus asked his followers whether they had read passages of Scripture.[74] John reports that Jesus knew his letters, and he was frequently called "rabbi" (Hebrew) or "rabbouni" (Aramaic), meaning a teacher learned in Scriptures (the Old Testament). The idea of an illiterate rabbi attracting disciples is "hardly credible."[75] Jewish law ordained that boys be taught to learn the Hebrew Bible, so it is likely that at least some of his disciples could read as well.[76] Finally, Nazareth was not so remote as is sometimes claimed, being within walking distance of Sepphoris, a multicultural town regionally important enough to have been the starting point of one of Herod the Great's military campaigns. The degree to which Jesus was literate is open to question, but "the evidence . . . favors literacy."[77]

78. The New Testament was composed long after the death of Jesus.

It is claimed that no one who knew Jesus wrote the Bible. This is false. Saint Peter the Apostle wrote at least the First Letter of Peter, and Peter knew Jesus in person. The Gospel and Letters of John were probably written by the Apostle Saint John, the son of Zebedee, who knew Jesus. In

[74]For example, Mt 19:4; Mk 2:25; 12:10, 26; Lk 10:26; in Mt 12:10 the noun *graphen* is used, denoting "a writing," not a "speaking."

[75]Evans, *Fabricating Jesus*, p. 38.

[76]Ibid., pp. 37-38.

[77]Ibid., p. 35.

any case, whoever wrote the books, the fact that the books were generally and almost universally accepted by A.D. 100 and that they were accepted in the final canon indicate that they were considered authentic.

The authorship and date of the four canonical Gospels—Matthew, Mark, Luke and John—have always been of special interest, for they offer the most detail about the life and teachings of Jesus. Scholarly views vary enormously. Radical scholars maintain that the four Gospels are no more reliable than as many as sixteen other gospels dating from the second century, such as the Gospel of Thomas, the Gospel of Peter and the Gospel of Mary Magdalene. But there are marked differences between the four and the others. First is the dating: the alleged gospels are all later than the four, despite assiduous and failed efforts to shoehorn them into the first century A.D. Second is the authorship: whereas the false gospels trumpet their claim to apostolic authorship, the canonical Gospels are modest in their claim. Matthew and John may have been direct eyewitnesses, but Mark and Luke never claim to be. Mark is reporting the eyewitness of Peter. If the early Christian community had wanted to give ironclad authority to Mark's Gospel, they would surely have claimed that the author was Peter himself. The tradition of writing something and attributing it to some well-known celebrity was common and even acceptable in the early centuries, so it required an extraordinary degree of honesty on the part of the earliest Christian community to refrain from calling the Gospel of Mark the Gospel of Peter.

Scholarship also varies as to the dates of the canonical Gospels. The most commonly accepted chronology is that Matthew dates from 65-85, Mark from 60-75, Luke from 65-95 and John from 75-100; it is possible that a hypothetical lost text, "Q," preceded Matthew and Luke. The accepted date of John (whoever was the author) is based partly on tradition and partly on modern scholarship, but it is likely that John may have been written as early as 60. His theology is very similar to that preached by Paul as early as the 50s A.D.; he does not mention the fall of Jerusalem in 70; and he indicates that he is "the beloved disciple" who was especially close to Jesus.

79. THE GOSPELS CONTRADICT ONE ANOTHER.

Antitheists believe that the Gospels are contradictory and that they were constructed by a conspiracy. The Gospels were written within a few decades of one another, and if the writers had been conspirators they had the opportunity to make sure to resolve inconsistencies in their accounts. Inconsistencies exist, and that fact is strong evidence that the Gospels are reports of direct eyewitnesses or of people who knew the eyewitnesses. Anyone who has been in a law court knows that honest eyewitnesses report events somewhat differently. If all the witnesses in a trial said exactly the same thing, collusion would be suspected. From honest witnesses we would expect both similarities and variations—and that is exactly the case with the Gospels. The differences indicate the independence of the reports.

In Mark 6, the arrest of John the Baptist occurs after Jesus has begun his ministry, while in Luke 3 it occurs before. The words of the Sermon on the Mount are somewhat different in Matthew 5 from those in Luke 6. The location of the place where Jesus cast demons into swine differs in Mark 10 from Matthew 8. In the Gospels of Matthew, Mark and Luke, Jesus usually speaks in short, pithy statements, whereas in the Gospel of John he speaks in longer discourses. It's likely that sometimes he spoke one way and other times another way, just as everyone does. It's also likely that some witnesses remembered some things differently from others.

It is not a recent discovery that differences exist. Beyond the fact that they would have been obvious from the beginning, early Christian writers such as Tatian and Irenaeus (130-200) discussed them carefully. Tatian tried to reconcile all the canonical Gospels in one narrative account about A.D. 150, an attempt made many times again down into the twentieth century. Such efforts were rejected by the early community; if it had followed Tatian, there might be a single Gospel without discrepancies, but that would have been at the cost of forcing eyewitness accounts into a single mold that would inevitably present a false picture of Jesus. Irenaeus believed that the differences were to be welcomed as different aspects of revelation, and his opinion was approved by the Christian community. The early community also rejected the opposite extreme of adding the later, apocryphal gospels to the four accepted ones.[78] The four Gospels present "a 'public' Jesus . . . resting upon the multiple witness of these texts, not upon esoteric revelations."[79] The Gospels were accepted by the com-

---

[78]Hurtado, *Lord Jesus Christ*, pp. 578-88.

[79]Ibid., p. 587.

munity before A.D. 150 and are complementary rather than contradictory.

80. CHRISTIANITY IS A REMODELED PAGAN MYSTERY CULT.

It has been claimed that Christianity, particularly Christ's death and resurrection, is based on the ancient myths of dying and rising gods such as Osiris, Attis and Adonis. The idea was popular about a century ago, particularly from 1890 to 1930, owing to the widely read *Golden Bough* by the anthropologist Sir James Frazer. Frazer (1854-1941) influenced a whole generation, including Carl G. Jung and T. S. Eliot.[80] By the 1960s Frazer's derivation of Christianity from the fertility cults and dying-rising myths had already been debunked by every serious scholar. It's necessary to mention this antiquated idea because it has reemerged in popular culture.

It's also false to lump the many different "pagan" religions into one single "pagan religion"—which never existed. If one lumps them all together with their myriad myths and practices, one can dig out parallels between paganism and every religion on Earth.[81] To the extent that some feature dying-rising gods (or goddesses such as Persephone), these divinities symbolize the eternal cyclical course of the seasons. Their worshipers take them as cyclical myths, whereas Christians regard Christ's death and resurrection as events that happened in real time and only once. Whereas the mystery religions, like Gnosticism, were open only to those who possessed secret knowledge, Christ was believed to lead all humans toward truth.

From the 200s and 300s Christianity began to adapt some of the mystery myths to its own purposes, such as the date of Christmas, which was also the birthday of the god Mithras and, most fundamentally, the winter solstice. Christianity also often turned legends about local gods or heroes into legends about local saints. But the virgin birth of Christ is different from those of Athena, Perseus, Aphrodite, Dionysus and Heracles, whose births were understood to be mythological, not historical. One popular misconception is that Mithras was supposedly born of a virgin; in fact he was supposed to have been born from a rock. The virgin births of myth result from the sexual lust of deities, of which there is no trace in the

---

[80]James G. Frazer, *Golden Bough* (New York: Macmillan, 1900).

[81]Komoszweski et al., *Reinventing Jesus*, pp. 219-58; Lee Strobel, *Case for the Real Jesus: A Journalist Investigates Current Attacks on the Identity of Christ* (Grand Rapids: Zondervan, 2007), pp. 157-87.

New Testament.[82] Finally, some scholars have invented parallels by using Christian terms to describe aspects of fertility myths, thus making the argument for parallels circular: for example, if one imports the Christian term "baptism" into the bull's bloodbath of Mithraism, then, lo and behold, Mithraism had baptism.

81. Christmas is the main Christian holiday.

There is a one in 365 chance that Jesus was born on December 25. Some Eastern churches celebrate the Nativity on January 7, which makes a one in 183 chance that one of those two dates is right. The day and month are absolutely unknown. He was not born in the year zero, for there never was such a year: the last day of 1 B.C. (Before Christ) is followed by the first day of A.D. 1 (Anno Domini: the year of the Lord). Nor was Christ born in A.D. 1, because the standard calendar, set by Dionysius the Little (500-545), was a few years off. The likely year of Jesus' birth is 4 B.C.

Christmas, or Nativity, is not the chief Christian holiday (holy day), though it is the most widely celebrated, now often in unrecognizably secular form. Easter—the day of Christ's resurrection—has always been the highest holiday. The date of Easter is also not known, and the day of its celebration is calculated each year not by date but astronomically, like the Jewish Passover, whose date similarly varies. Christmas was not widely celebrated until the 300s. Placing the birth of Christ each year near the winter solstice, when the days are just beginning to lengthen, fit the pattern of Easter, which is celebrated at the growing light of daybreak.[83] The date also seems to have been used by the Christian community in order to supplant pagan celebrations centering on the solstice.[84]

82. Christians believe that the book of Revelation predicts the future.

The End of the World Is Near. Quite possibly, but the date for the end has been set hundreds of times, irrespective of Jesus' warning that "about that

[82]Komoszweski, *Reinventing Jesus*, pp. 239-47.

[83]"New Calendar" Orthodox Christians adopted the Western calendar for Easter in 1922, but "Old Calendar" Orthodoxy prevails in Russia, Belarus, Serbia and among some Greeks.

[84]See "Christmas" in *Oxford Dictionary of the Christian Church*, 3rd ed. (Oxford: Oxford University Press, 1997), pp. 335-36.

day or hour no one knows" (Mk 13:32; see also Mt 24:36–25:13; Lk 12:46). A few examples of predicted dates include 968, 1010, 1033 and 1260; in modern times 1910, 1957, 1975, 1981 and every year from 1988, including 2012.[85]

The book of Revelation—the Apocalypse of John—is the most difficult book of the Bible. "Apocalypticism" (Greek *apokalypsis*; "unwinding" or "revealing") means belief that the end of the world is at hand. Many early Christian theologians thought the book should not be included in the canon, and some important Eastern Orthodox theologians such as John Chrysostomos (347-407) excluded it from their own lists of canonical books. Nonetheless, its place in the canon was secure by 400, and since then it has provoked centuries of disputed interpretation. Its historical context is the large number of Jewish apocalyptic visionary books of the period 200 B.C. to A.D. 100, and it is similar in language and image to many of them. Its author wrote on the island of Patmos about A.D. 90. The author was traditionally identified with the author of the Gospel of John, but they were not the same person. The author of the Gospel is most likely the Apostle Saint John, son of Zebedee, whereas nothing secure is known about John of Patmos. Differences in language, tone, image and theology between the books preclude common authorship.

The theology of Revelation is eschatological, relating to the *eschata* (Greek: "last things"), the events at the end of the world. Fewer theologians have believed that the lurid imagery of the book is to be taken "literally" in the sense of actual, historical descriptions of events either in the past or future than those who interpret it metaphorically. From ancient times, seven has been a mystical number, and there was an ancient notion that there are seven ages of the world, an idea fortified by the seven days of Genesis along with the seven seals and seven heads of the dragon in the book of Revelation. Augustine (354-410) supported it, and it regained influence from the twelfth century.

The author of Revelation intended it as an allegory or extended metaphor. The most important metaphors are the seven seals, the four horsemen, the 144,000 faithful, the seven trumpet calls, the woman per-

---

[85]Sharan Newman, *Real History of the End of the World: Apocalyptic Predictions from Revelation and Nostradamus to Y2K and 2012* (New York: Berkley, 2010); Yuri Rubinsky and Ian Wiseman, *History of the End of the World* (New York: Morrow, 1982).

secuted by the dragon, the war in heaven between Satan and Michael the archangel, the beast from the sea, the ruin of Babylon, the harlot, the wedding feast of the Lamb, the final battle, the destruction of the beast and the false prophet, the punishment of Satan, and the resurrection and judgment of the dead at the end of the world. The question has always been what these metaphors are metaphors *of.* What events did the author intend to symbolize with his imagery? The main approaches are discussed here.

One approach is simply to accept it word for word as an immediate divine revelation to each individual, who can find his or her own meaning in it. This approach obviously engenders an infinite number of views.[86] Another view widely held by scholars is "realized eschatology." In this view, the metaphors are for historical events of the first century A.D. In other words, the events had already occurred when John wrote about them. The great persecutor of the church that John refers to is often thought to be the emperor Nero, who cruelly persecuted Christians in A.D. 64, or possibly another persecutor, the emperor Domitian (r. 81-96).

Another view is that the book describes future events yet to occur. In this view, widely embraced today by dispensationalists, who make up a large proportion of American evangelicals, one can actually predict the future by interpreting the metaphors correctly. In this view, each metaphor is a piece of data to be fitted into others like a jigsaw puzzle. The idea of the seven ages of the world has recently been revived by the dispensationalists. They believe the present age is the sixth age, and the seventh—the end times—is at hand. According to dispensational doctrine, humanity is tested during seven great "dispensations" (divine ways of dealing with humanity). The seven dispensations are innocence (before the fall), conscience (from the fall to the flood), civil government (from the flood to the tower of Babel), patriarchal rule (from the tower to the Ten Commandments), Mosaic law (from the Ten Commandments to the crucifixion), grace (from Pentecost to the second-coming) and finally, the kingdom of God (still to come). In every age humans fail the test that God has set before them, though each age has its faithful remnant. The faithful remnant will be in heaven with God, while God's ultimate purpose on

[86]John J. Collins, Bernard McGinn and Stephen J. Stein, eds., *Encyclopedia of Apocalypticism* (New York: Continuum, 1998).

earth will be fulfilled in an exclusively Jewish state that will rule the earth in righteousness from David's eternal throne in Jerusalem, where the Temple of Solomon will be restored.[87] In 1909 Oxford University Press published the dispensationalist Scofield Reference Bible, which promulgated these ideas as legitimate biblical criticism, and which became a major influence in the evangelical movement. These views, supported by the Moody Bible Institute, Dallas Theological Seminary and the International Christian Embassy in Jerusalem, and by pastors and writers such as Jerry Falwell, John Hagee, Hal Lindsey and Tim LaHaye, have millions of followers around the world and affect United States foreign policy.

The Bible consistently teaches historical change from the beginning to the end of the universe or at least of human existence. Christians believe that Jesus will come again at the end, and the study of the end times (eschatology) has occupied many thinkers throughout the history of the church. Curiously, Christian eschatology was translated into secular terms by the philosopher Georg W. F. Hegel (1770-1831) and later by the founders of Communism, Marx and Engels, who foresaw the ultimate triumph of the proletariat, the withering away of the state, and the end of history.

Yet another view is that the events occur outside of normal time. For example, the defeat of Satan by the archangel Michael represents the cosmic victory of good over evil, as do the final punishment of the Devil and the resurrection of humanity. The point is the struggle between good and evil that is manifest in every period. In this approach, Revelation may refer to events before, during, and after John's time as events beyond historical time. Related to this view is the idea that the end times already began with the advent of Christ and that the transformation and restoration of the world by Christ is always occurring in the present.

The book of Revelation also led to millenarianism (Latin *millennium*: "a thousand years"). Millenarianism is based on Revelation 20:2-3, which reports that an angel seized the Devil "and bound him for a thousand years, and threw him into the pit, and locked and sealed it over him, so that he would deceive the nations no more, until the thousand years were ended."[88] Vastly diverse sorts of millenarians have existed from at least

---

[87]Stephen Sizer, "Orchestrating the End: The Prophetic Quest of Dispensationalism," *SCP* (Spiritual Counterfeits Project) *Journal* 32 (2008): 52-70.

[88]Mathew 24–25 is another source of millenarianism.

the second century to the present. The two main sorts have been pre-millennialists, who maintain that the thousand years are a peaceful kingdom on earth that will follow the second coming of Christ, and post-millennialists, who maintain that the thousand years will be a period of preparation before the second coming.

In the first two centuries of the church millenarianism was thoroughly debated, and the most influential theologians, such as Origen (185-254), Jerome (345-420) and Augustine (354-430), dismissed it. It was revived from time to time during the Middle Ages, when various dates were proposed for the second coming. Joachim of Fiore (1135-1202), an Italian Cistercian monk, was the most influential medieval millenarian. Millenarianism was repeatedly and soundly rejected by Catholics as heretical, but it appeared again in various Protestant movements of the 1500s and 1600s, notably among the Anabaptists. Having simmered down again, it boiled up again in the 1800s. In Britain, it was expressed variously by Robert Benton Seeley (1798-1886), Anthony Ashley Cooper Lord Shaftesbury (1801-1885) and Thomas Rawson Birks (1810-1883).

Millenarian thought took strong root in North America in groups such as the Millerites. William Miller predicted the end of the world on October 22, 1844, which only somewhat deflated his group on October 23, but the Seventh-Day Adventists, who adopted Miller's views if not his date, were founded in 1861. John Nelson Darby (1800-1882) introduced "dispensational pre-millennialism," which became established in the Plymouth Brethren denomination. In the latter part of the twentieth century millenarianism found renewed influence with the best-selling success of Hal Lindsey's book *The Late Great Planet Earth*, published in 1970. Lindsey claimed he had received a personal revelation from God. Since then, proposed dates for the end of the world have continued to multiply. The failure of each prediction is followed by trust in the next.[89]

Dispensationalists believe that the territory of Solomon's Israel from the Sinai to the Euphrates must be restored and that a final battle (Armageddon) must be fought for that to happen. They believe God is always

[89]Martin Spence, "The 'Restitution of All Things' in Nineteenth-Century Evangelical Premillennialism," in *Church, the Afterlife and the Fate of the Soul,* ed. Peter Clare and Tony Clayton (Woodbridge, UK: Boydell, 2009), pp. 349-59. Spence shows the enormous variety of millenarian thought.

pursuing two distinct goals, one relating to this world (Judaism), the other relating to heaven (Christianity). At the end of this world, faithful Christians will be in heaven; God will have no further need for the church on earth and will replace it with the state of Israel. This belief has led to an alliance between dispensationalists and Zionists. Dispensationalists also believe that the degeneracy of modern society is moving us quickly toward the final tribulation, when Satan's spawn, the Antichrist, will rule for seven years. This will be followed by the second coming and the battle of Megiddo (Armageddon), where armies will confront Israel in a last vain effort, probably a nuclear one, to destroy it. After a last successful battle against Satan, the end of history—the end of time—will occur. As the tribulation begins, the faithful followers of Christ on earth will be "raptured": taken up to heaven immediately to join Christ and the angels.[90] Whether or not one finds this plausible, the fact is that there are believers in more than eighty countries. It has consistently supported Zionism against Palestinians.

Millenarians have always searched the Bible for clues about the future end of the world. They have always identified contemporary events with the metaphors of Revelation and predict tribulation and trial in the immediate future. Trials and tribulations always occur, but so far all predictions about the end have been wrong. Traditional Christians of all denominations flee from such speculation. They point out that the Gospels categorically declare that no human being can predict the day or the hour of the end, and they regard using Revelation to predict the future as mistaken (see again Mt 24:36). However, millenarianism has become a very important aspect of recent Christian history, for much of the recent growth of Christianity comes from millenarians of one kind or another.[91]

83. The Canon of the Bible Preceded the Creeds.

Most Christians assume that the Bible precedes the creeds. The creeds

[90]Belief in the rapture is based largely on 1 Thessalonians 4:16-17: "For the Lord himself, with a cry of command, with the archangel's call and with the sound of God's trumpet, will descend from heaven, and the dead in Christ will rise first. Then we who are alive, who are left, will be caught up in the clouds together with them to meet the Lord in the air; and so we will be with the Lord forever."

[91]David Goodhew, "Life Beyond the Grave: New Churches in York and the Afterlife, c. 1962-2007," in *Church, the Afterlife and the Fate of the Soul*, pp. 404-12.

(from Latin *credo*, "I believe") are the concise theological statements of Christian truth formulated in A.D. 325-451. The idea that the Bible precedes the creeds is mostly, but not entirely, true. The times of the biblical writings vary. The oldest material in the Old Testament originated about 1100 B.C., possibly earlier. It was passed on orally, and recent discoveries indicate that parts were written down as early as the tenth century B.C. in the reign of King David.[92] When the writings were assembled and organized as books (for example, Genesis or Deuteronomy) is also uncertain. Probably many of them existed from the time of King Josiah of Judah (r. 640-609 B.C.), but a body of written texts of the Law and the Prophets may not have been formed before about 530 B.C. Some of the books were written as late as the second century B.C.

Although books of the Bible in Hebrew existed earlier, the earliest complete Old Testament is in Greek, not Hebrew. The first complete known Hebrew-Aramaic Old Testament is the Codex Cairo from about A.D. 895, a thousand years after the Greek Old Testament, which was translated from Hebrew and Aramaic about 200 B.C. This Greek translation is called the Septuagint (LXX: seventy); the story is that it was composed in Alexandria (fact) by seventy scholars (fiction). The Jewish community in Egypt at the time was large, learned and distinguished. The Septuagint seems to be a translation of a lost Hebrew recension (version) made in Egypt drawn from an earlier, also lost, recension made in Palestine as early as the 500s B.C.

The Septuagint includes books included in the modern Protestant canon, plus the books known as the Apocrypha ("hidden things"). Around A.D. 90, the Pharisees drew up a new canon that excluded the Apocrypha, and that has remained the official Jewish list. The basic meaning of "canon" is "a measure"; the canon of the Bible is the standard list of the books to be properly included. The Septuagint canon (with small variations) was accepted by the whole Christian church prior to the Reformation and remains canonical in Western and Eastern Catholic and Orthodox Bibles. The Protestants chose the rabbinical canon. The books considered apocryphal by Jews and Protestants include Ecclesiasticus (Sirach), Esdras, Judith, Maccabees, Tobit, the Wisdom of Solomon, and

---

[92]Fragment discovered by the archeologist Yosef Garfinkel of the Hebrew University of Jerusalem in 2010. Garfinkel, "Prize Find," *Biblical Archeology Review* 36 (2010): 51.

parts of Daniel. Scholarship now indicates that the original Daniel was the complete version and that the view considering parts of it uncanonical appears to be wrong. The Septuagint and other old Greek Bibles deserve renewed attention to their authority.[93]

Most of the books that make up the current Bible—the Old Testament and the New Testament—were originally written in the period 600 B.C. to A.D. 100. In that sense the Bible preceded the creeds. But until the 300s and 400s it was not certain what books the Bible consisted of. In addition to books now considered canonical, many pseudepigrapha ("false writings") dating from about 200 B.C. to A.D. 150 purported to be by ancient writers, such as the Books of Enoch.

Fragmentary manuscripts of the New Testament exist from the early second century A.D. The first known complete New Testaments date from the 300s. From the 400s onward vast numbers exist in Greek and many other languages. In order for the Bible to be authoritative, the leaders of the Christian community needed to decide which books were actually revealed and so properly to be included. They had to set a canon, a rule, authoritatively establishing which Scriptures were valid. By about A.D. 130 there was a mostly agreed view of what books were to be included, although questions remained about Hebrews, Jude, 2 Peter, 2 John and Revelation. The three criteria for excluding material are the same now as they were in the early church: forgeries, later productions of the second century (the 100s), and "those that did not conform to the orthodoxy of the core books already known to be authentic" were rejected.[94] The canon of the Bible was not finally settled until A.D. 367-382. That means the leaders of the Christian community set the canon of Scriptures at the same time they issued the great creeds of Christianity. The Christian community guaranteed the truth of both at roughly the same time and in roughly the same way: by the decisions of bishops in the ecumenical (universal, meaning "for the entire church") councils. [95]

---

[93]Tkacz, "Susanna," pp. 181-96; Tkacz, *Aletheia Hellenike: The Authority of the Greek Old Testament* (Etna, CA: Center for Traditional Orthodox Studies Press, 2012).

[94]Komoszewski et al., *Reinventing Jesus*, p. 149.

[95]Leo Donald Davis, *The First Seven Ecumenical Councils (325-787): Their History and Theology* (Wilmington, DE: Michael Glazier, 1983).

Christian Beliefs Have Been Shown to Be Wrong

84. The church changed the Bible to fit its doctrines.

This claim is often made on two different (and incompatible) grounds. Some modern writers feel that the church presented a false Jesus from the beginning; others feel that the church of the fourth century (300s A.D.) invented Christianity by tampering with the Bible.[1]

One argument is that the church, including the apostles, distorted the personality of Jesus to fit their preconceptions and suppressed people who had different views. This is not supported by the evidence. First, eyewitnesses of Jesus continued to be alive for a generation or even two generations after his death. Christians abided by the eyewitness accounts, and there is no evidence of substantial disagreements among them before A.D. 100 or later. Second, there is no evidence that theological disagreements split the community until after 100. The "rule of faith" (*regula fidei*), consisting of formulas of correct teachings, circulated widely before the councils crystallized them.

Another argument is that the church drove Gnostics out from its midst in the second century (100s). This is plausible, because it's exactly in the second century that the Christian community was becoming organized enough under the bishops to make "the church" a meaningful term. By 150-200 there was a deep, fundamental difference between orthodox Christians and Gnostic Christians. To some extent the churches excluded the Gnostics, and to some extent the Gnostics left voluntarily to set up their own communities. The church followed the eyewitness

[1] *Cambridge History of the Bible,* 3 vols. (Cambridge: Cambridge University Press, 1963-2008).

accounts of Jesus, while the Gnostics proclaimed radical doctrines such as that matter is evil and that Jesus was completely spirit and only looked as if he had a body.

Yet another argument is that the church changed the Bible in the fourth century under the leadership of the emperor Constantine the Great. By the time of Constantine (r. 306-337) the church was a large and organized institution under the bishops. In the Councils of Nicaea (325), Constantinople (381) and Chalcedon (451) the church firmly defined Christian doctrine on the basis of the theology of the preceding centuries. Some scholars argue that in doing so they departed from earlier tradition, and that's a subject for honest debate. That was certainly not their intention, and the creeds (formal statements of belief) have always been accepted by Catholic, Orthodox and most Protestant churches as compatible with the Scriptures and fundamental to Christianity. As for the Bible, the church confirmed the canon (the list of books properly to be included in the Bible) after three centuries of discussion about where to draw the line separating divinely revealed books from false books. The church did not change the words of the Bible.

Thus the claim that the church changed the Bible to fit its doctrines fails on at least two counts: it is both incoherent and inconsistent with the facts.

85. The creeds are irrelevant to modern Christianity.

The creeds are statements of common belief. They derive from the New Testament, clarifying its teachings, and became a standard for later Christian belief. Most of the creeds were originally in Greek and began with the word *pisteuo*, "I believe," the Latin for which is *credo*, the source of the word "creed." The creeds arose from thorough discussions in the early Christian community, especially about the nature of the Trinity and the nature of Christ. Many different opinions were proposed during the process, and some of these old views have resurfaced recently under different names. The formal creeds were efforts to establish a meaningful consensus of what could be called true Christianity.[2]

[2]J. N. D. Kelly, *Early Christian Creeds*, 3rd ed. (New York: Longman, 1972); Kelly, *Early Christian Doctrines* (London: Adam and Charles Black, 1958); Leo Donald Davis, *First Seven Ecu-*

The apostles issued no creeds themselves, so the so-called Apostles' Creed is a misnomer, but elements of the creeds exist in the New Testament itself (for example, 1 Cor 4:13-14; 15:3-8; 1 Pet 3:18-19; 1 Tim 3:16). Creeds appear in embryonic form in the letters of the Apostle Saint Paul, for example: "that Christ died for our sins in accordance with the scriptures, and that he was buried, and that he was raised on the third day" (1 Cor 15:3-4). By A.D. 100, various communities used creedal professions of belief, many of them based on "baptismal interrogations" of converts.[3] They differed in detail but coalesced gradually into a coherent Rule of Faith.[4] Hippolytus (A.D. 170-236) cited a common baptismal formula: "Do you believe in God the Father Almighty? Do you believe in Jesus Christ, the Son of God, who was born by the Holy Spirit of the virgin Mary, and was crucified under Pontius Pilate, and was dead and buried, and rose again the third day and ascended into heaven?"[5] By 200 the Rule of Faith began to stabilize around basic doctrines.[6] One of the most important formulas was the Roman creed, which later was adapted into the Apostles' Creed.[7] Theologians important in the formation of the early creeds were Polycarp (69-155), Justin Martyr (100-165), Irenaeus (130-200), Tertullian (160-225) and Origen (185-254), as well as Hippolytus.[8]

The reality of the Trinity was accepted by almost everyone on the basis of the Scriptures. The three Persons (Father, Son and Holy Spirit) are all mentioned in the New Testament, though the words *trias* and *triados* first appear in the writings of Theophilus of Antioch (about 150). Theologians agreed that God's internal nature is beyond human understanding and formulation but also that God gave minds to humans in order to understand him within the boundaries of human limitations.[9] The Trinity is true in the sense that it expresses the dynamic nature of God within himself in contrast to a static deity.

---

menical Councils (325-787): Their History and Theology (Collegeville, MN: Liturgical Press, 1990); T. F. Torrance, *Trinitarian Faith* (London: T & T Clark, 1991).

[3]Kelly, *Early Christian Creeds*, p. 96.

[4]Ibid., pp. 63, 76, 83-85.

[5]Ibid., p. 91.

[6]Ibid., pp. 98-100.

[7]Ibid., p. 167.

[8]Ibid., pp. 62-99.

[9]Later, Dionysius the Areopagite would put it this way: God is so far above us that we cannot express what he is, but only what he is not (for example, he is not limited).

The standard creeds were issued by ecumenical (universal) councils, consisting of bishops from various parts of the Christian world. The four most essential councils were held at Nicaea in 325, Constantinople in 381, Ephesus in 431 and Chalcedon in 451. The Eastern Orthodox church and many Protestant churches also accept the second council of Constantinople (553), the third council of Constantinople (680) and the second council of Nicaea (787). The Roman Catholic Church accepts these and fourteen other councils down through the second Vatican Council of 1962-1965.

The relationship of the Son to the Father was decided in 325 at the First Council of Nicaea after heated debate between the followers of Arius (d. 336) and those of Athanasius (296-373). Both accepted the Trinity, but Arius denied the equality of the three Persons. The use of the term "persons" in English is terribly confusing, since we often use the term to denote a number of human beings (as in "room capacity: 75 persons"). Nothing was further from the thought of any of the Fathers, for whom the terms *hypostases*, *onoma*, *prosopa* and *personae* referred to the modes or aspects of the undivided essence (*ousia*) of God with no reference to human beings.

Arius taught a view that later came to be known as subordinationism: the Father produced both the Son and the Holy Spirit in the beginning (Greek *en arche*). For him, there was a time when the Son and the Holy Spirit did not exist. He believed that all things are made by the Son, who was the first creature produced by the Father and thus was almost a created intermediary between God and the rest of creation.

Athanasius, on the other hand, taught that God creates things from nothing but produces the Son out of his own nature; the Son is not the same Person as the Father but is absolutely equal and eternal with the Father.[10] Athanasius said the Son is of the same nature with the Father, not merely of similar nature.[11] The ecumenical council of bishops at Nicaea in 325 supported the position of Athanasius and issued the Nicene Creed.[12] That creed begins with "I believe in one God, the Father almighty, maker of heaven and earth, and of all things visible and invisible. And in one

[10]Ibid., pp. 50, 78-80.

[11]Kelly, *Early Christian Creeds*, pp. 234-54: *Homoousios* means "same in being"; *homoiousios* means "similar in being." There is just one iota of difference, but it is a significant one.

[12]Technically the title is the Nicene-Constantinopolitan Creed Revised According to the Council of Constantinople, but it is usually nicknamed the Nicene Creed.

Lord Jesus Christ, the only begotten Son of God, born of the Father before all ages; God from God, light from light, true God from true God; begotten not made, of one essence with the Father."

Though a variety of lesser creeds continued to proliferate, a gradual consensus emerged that the formal creeds issued by the councils were the "tests of orthodoxy" about absolutely essential beliefs.[13] The creed of Nicaea established that the Son is not a creature at all but of one and the same substance as the Father.[14] The universe is made, whereas the Son is begotten, not made.[15] "Begotten," the standard English word, is perhaps not the most helpful translation of the Greek and Latin, because along with "conception" it conveys a false connotation of sexual relations. "Produced" is an alternative, for Christians have always believed that Jesus is the spiritual Son of God. The point of the wording is that whereas things are made in space and time, the Son is produced by the Father out of his own being and essence, so that the Son is as truly and eternally equal with the Father and of the same nature as the Father. The creeds reinforced that idea by calling the Son the "only begotten" (or better "only produced") Son of the Father.[16] Further, though the whole undivided Trinity willed the creation of the universe, it did so in the mode of the Son, "through whom all things were made."[17] Arius himself eventually accepted the Nicene Creed, but Arianism had a later, temporary revival owing to the politics of Byzantine emperors.[18]

In brief, the Nicene Creed established that God is three equal Persons in one Being. Some Christians today unwittingly hold the subordinationist view that the Father is somehow more God than the Son or the Holy Spirit is, and they find it odd that anyone should pray to the Son or to the Holy Spirit as well as to the Father. Subordinationism detracts from the *Triunity* and is not a traditionally Christian view.

---

[13]Kelly, *Early Christian Creeds*, pp. 92, 205.

[14]Athanasius settled on "one being, three persons" (*mia ousia kai treis hypostases*). Torrance, *Trinitarian Faith*, pp. 236, 310-11.

[15]Forms of the Greek verb *ginomai* of *gignomai* ("to be born") appear throughout the creeds—*e.g.*, *gennemenon*, *gennethe*, *gennethenta*, Latin *genitum*. "Begotten, not made" comes from *gennethenta ou poiethenta* (from Greek *poieo*, "to make"; Latin *genitum, non factum*). Kelly, *Early Christian Creeds*, pp. 182, 218.

[16]Ibid., pp. 103, 139, 147.

[17]Torrance, *Trinitarian Faith*, pp. 91-93.

[18]Kelly, *Early Christian Creeds*, pp. 283-95.

The doctrine of the Holy Spirit was well-established but ill-defined in both the Old and the New Testament.[19] The Council of Nicaea, while understanding the nature of the Holy Spirit, left it vague in its creed, but the Council of Constantinople in 381 clarified it.[20] The council confirmed the Nicene understanding that the unity, equality and eternity of all three Persons make up the one substance of God. Like the Son, the Spirit is eternal with the Father, and there was no time before the Spirit was.[21] Some theologians suggested that the Holy Spirit proceeds from the Father and receives through the Son, others that the Spirit proceeds from both the Father and the Son.[22] The Nicene-Constantinopolitan Creed simply says, "And I believe in the Holy Spirit, the Lord and giver of life, who proceeds from the Father, who together with the Father and the Son is adored and glorified."[23] This creed was established as the standard of Christian belief by the Council of Chalcedon in 451 and has remained so ever since.[24]

The Western church later adjusted the phrase "from the Father" to "from the Father and the Son" (Latin *filioque*).[25] This term originated in Spain about the time of the Council of Toledo in 589; from Spain it spread through Gaul to Rome, where in the 800s it was established and then by 1100 became standard for the Western church.[26] The Eastern church has always used the original wording. The difference does not affect the basic theology of the Trinity, since the phrase "from the Father" could be (and was) developed in a number of ways that do not exclude double procession. The real objection is that the original creed should not be altered at all.

After the nature of the Trinity, the nature of Jesus Christ needed defining. The earliest Christians accepted the divinity of Jesus, though a small sect may have denied it.[27] At the opposite extreme, Gnostics and other Docetists (from Greek *dokeo*, "to seem") argued that Jesus was not human: God despised flesh, and the divine Jesus only seemed to have a

---

[19]Torrance, *Trinitarian Faith*, pp. 192-93 on Old Testament, pp. 197-98 on New Testament.
[20]Kelly, *Early Christian Creeds*, p. 262.
[21]Torrance, *Trinitarian Faith*, p. 222.
[22]Ibid., pp. 231-36, 244, 309.
[23]Ibid., pp. 193-251; Kelly, *Early Christian Creeds*, pp. 322-31.
[24]Kelly, *Early Christian Creeds*, pp. 332-48.
[25]Torrance, *Trinitarian Faith*, p. 246.
[26]Kelly, *Early Christian Creeds*, pp. 358-67; Torrance, *Trinitarian Faith*, p. 246.
[27]Little is known of these so-called Ebionites.

real body. This view was rejected by the Christian community as early as it appeared; it has few adherents today, whereas the opposite unchristian view that Jesus was only human has again become common.

The Christian view of Jesus' nature was thoroughly threshed out in the 200s to 400s. One school of thought was Nestorianism, from the patriarch Nestorius of Constantinople (352-452). The Nestorians argued that Jesus Christ has two different natures: Jesus is completely human and completely divine, but the human nature and the divine nature are separate. In this view, Mary is the mother only of the human Jesus, and the title *Theotokos* ("mother of God") is inappropriate. Another main school was that of the Monophysites, who maintained that Jesus has only one nature, the divine one. This view implied that Jesus was not fully human and did not suffer. The majority of the Christian community rejected both views as extreme and false. The Council of Ephesus in 431 condemned Nestorianism and deposed Nestorius as patriarch. The Council of Chalcedon (451) decided that the Son of God and Jesus Christ are one and the same Person, perfectly God and perfectly human, true God and true man. Chalcedon also insisted on the term *Theotokos* for Mary. Importantly, the eternal birth of the only-begotten (*monogenes*) Son from the Father was distinguished from the physical birth (*genesis*) of Jesus from Mary, an event in time.

To summarize simply: the Monophysites held a one-person, one-nature (1P1N) view; the Nestorians a two-persons, two-natures (2P2N) view; and Catholic, Orthodox and Protestant Christians a one-person, two-natures (1P2N) view. The orthodox view is that Jesus is "not God *in man* but God *as man*."[28] As God, the Son suffered both in his human nature and his divine nature, thus reconciling God and humans.[29] The Trinity, which cannot suffer itself, experiences human suffering in Jesus. If God did not share suffering, he would be entirely remote from his creation.[30]

Chalcedon validated the creeds for the great majority of the Christian community. However, not all Christians accepted the decisions of Chalcedon.[31] Nestorians persisted in the Middle East, especially Persia (Iran)

---

[28]Torrance, *Trinitarian Faith*, p. 150.
[29]Ibid., pp. 184-86.
[30]See "Patripassianism" in the *Oxford Dictionary of the Christian Church*, 3rd ed. (Oxford: Oxford University Press, 1997), p. 1233.
[31]J. N. D. Kelly, *Early Christian Creeds*, 3rd ed. (Essex, UK: Longman, 1972), pp. 348-51.

and Iraq. These Christians have been subject to heavy persecution, especially since the U.S. invasion of Iraq in 2003. Monophysites also persist as what are now known as the Oriental Orthodox Churches: the Armenian, Coptic (Egyptian), Ethiopian and Jacobite (Syrian) churches. These are not to be confused with the Eastern Orthodox churches, which are fully Chalcedonian.

Other important creeds are the Athanasian Creed dated about 380-430 and accepted in the West; and the Apostles' Creed, accepted in the Western church from the 700s. These creeds, though antique, were composed neither by Athanasius nor by the apostles. They have four basic elements: belief in God the Father, belief in God the Son and his incarnation in Jesus Christ, belief in the Holy Spirit, and belief in the church.

The creeds have frequently been disused in contemporary worship for a number of different reasons. Radical theologians of many denominations reject the authenticity of both the Bible and the creeds. Some liberal churches consider the creeds old-fashioned and not adaptable to contemporary society. A number of pastors, both Catholic and Protestant, quietly let them drop on the grounds that they might confuse people. What, they ask, would people make of the statement that Christ "sits at the right hand of the Father"? Is Christ sitting on a chair somewhere? Does the Father have hands? Such difficulties arise when words are taken as overtly literal instead of in the metaphorical sense that they were intended. Some pastors prefer to explain the creeds instead of dropping them from the service. Most evangelicals wish to rely directly on the Bible, and the creeds do not appear fully in the Bible. A number of evangelical churches are "non-creedal" churches, basing themselves on personal, individual commitment to Christ. Nonetheless, if most evangelicals were asked to affirm the statements in the creeds they would, since the creeds have been the basic statement of Christian theology in Orthodox, Catholic and Protestant theology. They are irrelevant only if they are not understood both in themselves and in the development of Christian doctrine.

86. Christians believe that God is found only in church.

Christians believe that God is best found where people worship in community. God is present in everything in the cosmos and can be worshiped anywhere. An individual can find God on the sea or in the mountains: any opening up to the truth, goodness and beauty of God is a valid religious experience. But the fullest Christian worship is individuals coming together in communion, where religious experiences can be understood through Scripture and tradition. Religious experiences cannot be retained or possessed, and they should be sought not for their own sake but in the service of charity.[32] Jews and Christians have known that any humble activity such as washing the windows can be an act of worship because every action offered to God is a holy act.

87. Christians believe in three gods.

Christians believe in only one God. Muslims and Jews accuse Christians of being tritheists (worshipers of three gods) on the basis of the Christian doctrine of the Trinity. Muslims revere Jesus as one of the three greatest prophets but, like Jews, strenuously deny his divinity—for example, Sura 5:76 of the Qur'an: "They do blaspheme who say: God is one of three in a Trinity, for there is no god except the one God." The Christian doctrine of the Trinity is so complex that Muslims may misunderstand the Trinity as dividing God into three. As Miroslav Volf observes, "The oneness of God (*tahwid*) is the principle at the very heart of Islam."[33] Muslims stress the unchanging omnipotence of the one God; Christians stress the internal dynamism of the one God. These two ideas are not incompatible.

The Christian Trinity consists of one God in three aspects or names: the Father, the Son and the Holy Spirit. They are aspects of the one, eternal, indivisible God. The earliest written appearance of the word "Trinity" (from Greek *trias*, "three") is from about A.D. 180, but Jesus had already said, "Go therefore and make disciples of all nations, baptizing them in the name of the Father and of the Son and of the Holy Spirit" (Mt 28:19). Some readers remember the term "Holy Ghost," but since "ghost" sounds weird today, "spirit" is a better choice. Beginning with Tertullian (160-225), traditional Christian theology has called the three aspects of God "Persons" (Greek *prosopa* or *hypostases*, Latin *personae*). In contemporary English "person" is commonly used as a synonym for "human indi-

[32]Ian S. Markham, *Against Atheism; Why Dawkins, Hitchens, and Harris Are Fundamentally Wrong* (Malden, MA: Wiley-Blackwell, 2010), pp. 53-58.

[33]Miroslav Volf, "Allah and the Trinity," *Christian Century*, March 8, 2011, pp. 20-24.

vidual," but that is absolutely not the sense of the word in the idea of the Trinity. Different theologians have offered different ideas about the relationship among the Persons, but it is certain that they are not three gods.[34] The three Persons are one in all eternity; there was never a "time" or a "state of being" when they did not exist as one.

Christians believe that God is one and dynamic. One author has described the Trinity as "a dynamic, pulsating dance of joy and love."[35] This dynamism expresses itself in relationship: relationship among the Persons, relationship with creatures, and the relationship among creatures. God's most fundamental attributes are thought and love. The three Persons are eternal and inseparable. God the Father thinks, and this perfect thought is itself God. It is the Son, one with and equal to the Father. God loves, and this perfect love is itself God. It is the Holy Spirit, one with and equal to the Father and the Son. "God is love" can be taken as a vague cliché, but it means that love is the essence of God's being, a love of the three Persons for one another, a Trinity in a mutual society of love and a model for human society. God revealed himself to Moses as I AM, and he revealed himself to Christ as I LOVE. Since no human can understand the interiority of God, the Trinity must be taken as a metaphor revealing God's nature as perfectly as he can explain it to creatures with limited understanding and language. The reason that God creates the universe, Christians believe, is to extend the love of the three Persons for one another to beings with intelligence and free will. All traditional Protestant Christian denominations agree with the Catholic and Orthodox churches on the basic nature of the Trinity.[36]

Recently a number of metaphysical games have been played with the Trinity. For example, the great twentieth-century psychiatrist Carl Jung at one time suggested a quaternity including the Virgin Mary and at another time a quaternity including the Devil. However ingenious they appear, such inventions have nothing to do with Christian belief.

---

[34]See entry 85, "The creeds are irrelevant to modern Christianity," for a further account of the Trinity.

[35]Timothy Keller, *Reason for God: Belief in an Age of Skepticism* (New York: Dutton, 2008), p. 215.

[36]Thomas F. Torrance, *Christian Doctrine of God: One Being, Three Persons* (Edinburgh: T & T Clark, 1996).

88. Christians are dualists.

This abstract misconception is held only by a few scholars who suggest that Christianity supports one or another of two kinds of dualism: (1) between spirit and body, and (2) between good and evil. (1) Imagine a spectrum of views from the idea that spirit and body are absolutely separate, to the idea that they are absolutely one and the same. Gnostics held for absolute separation, believing that the spirit was imprisoned in the body by an evil deity and longed for its freedom. Materialists held the view that spirit or mind was simply the product of neurochemical motions in the physical brain. Christianity takes a holistic view. Spirit is different from body, but spirit and body combine to make soul, the complete human being. Spirit can be separated from the body temporarily at death, but spirit and body are reunited in the resurrection where they are one in the presence of God. (2) Imagine a different spectrum of views. At one end is the idea that there are two gods, one of absolute evil and darkness, the other of absolute good and light, eternally at war with one another. This was the view of the Mazdaist (Zoroastrian) religion of ancient Iran. The Gnostics were similarly dualistic, but added to the equation: the evil god was the lord of matter and the good god the lord of spirit. At the other end of the spectrum is the relativist view that there is no such thing as good and evil other than as purely human constructs that vary from person to person. Christianity takes a middle view. There is absolute good and absolute evil; there is a principle of good and a principle of evil against which all human activities can be measured. But these are not gods at war with one another. Everything is the creation of the one God, who is good. The existence of evil in the world is owing to the fault of humans in falling away from love of God and neighbor.[37]

89. Christians believe that Jesus is a son of God just as we are all sons and daughters of God.

In a real sense, we are all sons and daughters of God. Christians go further: they believe that Jesus is the Son of God in a unique way ("unique" means "sole, only," not just "unusual"). The Nicene Creed accepted by all tradi-

[37]Jeffrey Burton Russell, *Satan: The Early Christian Tradition* (Ithaca, NY: Cornell University Press, 1984), pp. 30-79.

tional Christians says, "I believe in one Lord Jesus Christ, born of the Father before all ages: God from God, light from light, true God from true God, begotten not made, one in being with the Father." Christians believe that Jesus Christ was a great prophet, and a warm friend, and a healer. They also believe that he is the incarnation of God, true God in real human flesh.

Many people assume that Christians obviously can't believe such an absurd thing. Rather, they think, Jesus was a wise man, like Gautama Buddha or Moses or Gandhi; Jesus' disciples couldn't really have believed that he was God; Jesus himself couldn't have believed that he was God. Such people feel that we are too advanced nowadays to believe that any human was ever God.

A technical discussion of the philosophical and theological details involved in the question of whether Jesus is God is beyond the scope of this book. But what people thought about Jesus' being God during his life and after is a historical question for which there is real evidence. There are some people who dismiss the evidence on the grounds that the Bible and other early Christian documents cannot be trusted, so they construct their own Christianity according to what they feel is up-to-date twenty-first century thinking. They are left with no basis on which to believe anything about Christ other than what current social preconceptions permit.

Sincere people involved in the ecumenical movement, which strives to bring all Christians and even all religions together, sometimes say that traditional Christianity is narrow and that Christ is not necessary to salvation. This sort of religious relativism amounts to practical atheism, for the only way all religions can be equally true is if they are equally meaningless. Honest dialogue that allows for differences, yet respects and explores them, is constructive. But a Jew who doesn't believe in Torah, a Muslim who doesn't believe in the Qur'an, and a Christian who doesn't believe in the divine Christ bring nothing to dialogue but empty hands.

The New Testament affirms the divinity of Jesus: "There is salvation in no one else" (Acts 4:12); "No one knows the Son except the Father, and no one knows the Father except the Son" (Mt 11:27). That is certainly an extraordinary idea, and Christians debated the exact manner in which Christ is the incarnation of the second Person of the Trinity until the Council of Chalcedon in 451. But the New Testament, the earliest Christians, theologians, councils, scholarship, and even the Gnostics agreed that he was God.[38]

90. The Christian God killed his own son.

Christians believe that Jesus Christ is the only Son of God the Father and that Jesus died a terrifying death on the cross. Most people naturally find it revolting that a father should send his son to be tortured and murdered. But this is a misunderstanding of the relationship of Jesus to God in Christian teaching.

The Christian God is a Trinity: three Persons in one—not three separate gods, but one God whose eternal dynamism is expressed in the eternal mutual relationship of the three who are one.[39] In the Trinity, the Son is eternal with the Father and the Holy Spirit, existing from the beginning of the cosmos to its end and beyond all space-time. Since the three are one, the Father did not sacrifice another deity or being called the Son.[40] Rather, the Son participated in the common and indivisible will of the Trinity to become incarnate, even though it was the Son rather than the Father who suffered, died, was buried and rose from the dead.[41] Even though the Father is not the Son and the Son is not the Father, they are wholly and essentially God and have the same eternal will. It is as accurate to say that the Son sacrificed the Son as to say that the Father sacrificed the Son.

But why did Jesus choose to suffer at all? Out of perfect love: "No one has greater love than this, to lay down one's life for one's friends" (Jn 15:13). Christ didn't *have* to die; he chose to die for the purpose of atonement (at-one-ment), bringing humans into full communion with God. But couldn't he have saved humans without suffering and dying? Christians believe that Christ was fully human as well as fully divine, and to be fully human means to experience suffering as well as joy. No human escapes suffering: if Christ had not suffered, he would not have been

---

[38]Larry W. Hurtado, *Lord Jesus Christ: Devotion to Jesus in Earliest Christianity* (Grand Rapids: Eerdmans, 2003).

[39]Torrance, *Trinitarian Faith*, pp. 302-40.

[40]Michael Green, *Lies, Lies, Lies! Exposing Myths about the Real Jesus* (Nottingham, UK: Inter-Varsity Press, 2009), pp. 157-61; Gustav Aulén, *Christus Victor: An Historical Study of the Three Main Types of Atonement* (London: SPCK, 1931).

[41]Torrance, *Trinitarian Faith,* pp. 185-86.

human. And a God who does not suffer with us is insufferably remote.

91. Christianity is about dogma.

In current English, "dogma" and "dogmatic" carry the connotation of narrow-mindedness, but that is not their basic meaning. The word "dogma" (Greek *dogma*, a belief that is accepted and taught) is a strong version of the word "doctrine" (from Latin *doceo*, "to teach"). Christian doctrine derives from both reason and revelation. A dogma is a doctrine that a group holds to be basic: "In the accepted Christian meaning the term signifies a religious truth established by Divine Revelation and defined by the Church."[42] The basic dogma of Christianity was established by 451 and includes the Trinity, the divinity of Christ, Christ's redemptive suffering for humanity and his resurrection.

From the 1100s, efforts were made to define smaller and smaller details of Christian belief. The medieval scholastics usually approached this process by stating contrasting views and texts and trying to resolve them. From the 1500s through 1900s, questions were replaced by statements that acquired the aura of dogma. Thus both Protestants and Catholics issued articles, confessions, catechisms and the like, which Christians were supposed to accept without question. This process deformed dogma and led to the use of the word in its pejorative sense. By the end of the twentieth century, however, the idea had spread that anybody's doctrine was as good as everyone else's. The middle way recognizes that the teachings that have been threshed out are true, but they are also open and living, not fossils.

An underlying question is whether dogma or imitation of Jesus is more essential to Christianity. Which is closer to God: a person who accepts the doctrines of the community but fails to love God and neighbor, or a person who denies traditional doctrines yet loves God and neighbor diligently? Assent to doctrine is assent to certain statements about God; it is an act of the intellect, a statement of truth. Love of others is an act of will resulting in action. The latter is morally better, but that does not mean that dogma is unimportant. It not only holds Christians together but is necessary to make Christianity a meaningful term. How is Christianity different from

[42]"Dogma," *Oxford Dictionary of the Christian Church*, 3rd ed. (Oxford: Oxford University Press: 1997), p. 495.

Islam or Judaism or Buddhism or atheism? That can be answered only by defining these religions in terms of their beliefs—their doctrines. An atheist may be kind and loving, but his or her conception of truth is quite different from a Christian's conception of truth. It is philosophically and practically necessary to distinguish the belief system of one group from that of another, and doctrine does that.

92. Christianity is about rules and rituals.

According to a recent survey, large numbers of people feel that Christianity focuses too much on rules and rituals.[43] But these rules and rituals are not arbitrary; they are aimed at connecting humans with God. There are Christian churches that are strongly based in traditional ritual called liturgy (formulas for public communal worship) and Christian churches in which ritual plays little part. Opinions differ as to which is closer to the practice of the early Christian community. It is likely that the liturgy or services of the earliest communities were small, relatively informal, and focused on the Eucharist (the Lord's Supper) and baptism. Baptism and the Eucharist were the distinguishing marks of Christianity from the first century. Liturgy and doctrine influenced one another as they developed.[44] By the time of Hippolytus (170-236), standard liturgies had become common.[45]

The liturgy always focused primarily on the Eucharist or Lord's Supper. Early liturgies included baptismal formulas, the Lord's Prayer, psalms, homilies (sermons), chants and acclamations, especially the "trisagion"—the "holy holy holy" (Latin *sanctus, sanctus, sanctus*; Greek *hagios hagios hagios*; Hebrew *qadosh qadosh qadosh*). The liturgy also included readings from the Old Testament, the Psalms separately, the Epistles and the Gospels. The liturgies were transmitted in a combination of tradition and vitality through the churches. Though the liturgies all contained the essential elements, there were varieties of traditions and forms.[46] Apart from

[43]Eric Gorski, "America: A Nation of Religious Drifters," Associated Press, May 2, 2009.

[44]The traditional "rule of what to believe," *lex credendi,* developed as much from the liturgy as from theology.

[45]Marcel Metzger, *History of the Liturgy: The Major Stages* (Collegeville, MN: Liturgical Press, 1997).

[46]For example the Eastern liturgies—Byzantine, Alexandrian, Antiochene and Milanese—and Western liturgies, such as the Roman, Celtic and Mozarabic. Languages used in liturgies in-

the eucharistic liturgies were daily prayers at certain times of the day, standardized in the Divine Office (Daily Office, Book of Hours). Another mark of liturgical churches is the use of formal seasons throughout the year in order to focus on elements of Christ's life. Advent, for example, is the season before Christmas, a time of waiting for the arrival (advent) of the Lord; Lent is the season of penance culminating in Good Friday, the commemoration of the crucifixion, followed by Easter. The point of all these elements is to correlate human time with cosmic time: to link human time with God's.

The Catholic, Orthodox and traditional Protestant churches continue to be liturgical churches, whereas evangelical and Pentecostal churches mostly eschew traditional ritual.

93. CHRISTIANITY IS BASED ON FEELINGS.

Christianity is based on love, divine love for humans and human love for God. Often the relationships of Christians with Jesus are intensely emotional and based on encounters with the divine. A few examples of people who had ecstatic experiences of God are Francis of Assisi (1181-1226), Julian of Norwich (1342-1417), Teresa of Ávila (1515-1582), George Fox (1642-1691), John Wesley (1703-1791) and C. S. Lewis (1893-1963). Still, when this emotional love is cut loose from the intellect and the will, it can be unreliable and even dangerous. Obviously some emotions such as love and empathy are positive and others such as hatred and rage are negative. But feelings are fluid. They easily shift and wax and wane, and when we privilege them above intellectual analysis, logic and reason, we risk deception by political and religious leaders who appeal to our emotions and passions.[47] Noise, shows, games and drugs can overwhelm thought with feelings. Emotions and reason can be in proper balance, but some theologians have neglected the place of aesthetics and feelings, and on the other hand contemporary society values feelings over reason. Consciousness, intellect, free will and conscience are based on intelligent consideration—not on sentiment or how we happen to feel at the moment.[48]

---

cluded Greek, Latin, Syriac, Coptic, Slavonic and vernacular languages including English.

[47]Douglas G. Campbell, "The Classroom Without Reason," *Academic Questions* 22 (2009): 204.

[48]Eva Brann, *Feeling Our Feelings: What Philosophers Think and People Want* (Philadelphia: Paul Dry, 2008).

The dominance of feelings over reason began with Jean-Jacques Rousseau (1712-1778) and was promoted by Friedrich Schleiermacher (1772-1829) in a Romantic revolt against Enlightenment thought. Schleiermacher emphasized feelings in an effort to rescue Christianity from growing skepticism by using intuition. William James (1842-1910) also valued religious experience over theology. Recently Pentecostals have weighed feelings heavily, relying on the guidance of the Holy Spirit within. But if the Spirit isn't discerned according to reason, revelation and tradition, feelings easily go astray and sometimes lead to evil.

Happiness for Christians is living in community with one another and with God in joy more than in transitory pleasures. Over the past fifty years a novel idea has taken over contemporary Western thought. This is the idea that our thoughts and actions are—and should be—governed by our feelings. This sentimental idea has roots in Romanticism, in psychoanalytic thinking, and most of all in the spread of hedonistic materialism, which justifies itself (when it troubles to do so) by the "pleasure principle."

Never before has any society maintained that feelings rule. The idea has crept slowly and almost silently through Western society, so that it has hardly been noticed. Yet it constitutes a revolution more effective and pervasive than the other revolutions of the late twentieth century. Its effect on Christianity has been immense. It produces the idea that if one accepts Christianity without feeling it, one is either a hypocrite or self-deluded—a knave or a fool. A fuss was once made about the fact that Mother Teresa, who devoted her entire life to helping the poor and the sick, had long periods in which she felt the absence of God. Many people argued that this fact made her inauthentic. How could she teach Christ by word and example if she didn't feel his presence? Her answer was that she was enabled by an inner conviction and commitment based on reason and will that underlay whatever her feelings might have been at one time or another. A sense of God's absence is also often a source of longing for his presence.

The emphasis on feelings has given rise to an even more revolutionary idea: that Christianity *ought* to be based on feelings more than reason. The idea is that our view of the world must be constructed to fit our feelings rather than fitting our feelings to external reality. Psychology is right that one should "own one's feelings," recognizing them and working with them or through them instead of denying them; early Christian writers such as

Evagrius of Pontus (346-399) knew as much.[49] But to imagine that our feelings should determine how other people feel—or even crazier, to imagine that our feelings change the reality of the external world—is at best childish and at worst insane.

Some people feel that their emotions arise from something deep and true within them. Their idea is that we become authentic when we are in touch with our deepest feelings. That makes sense if our deepest feelings are in the Holy Spirit, but where did the secular version of the idea come from? Not from Darwinism and physicalism: molecules and genes have no moral or intellectual views, or feelings either. Certainly not from deconstructionism, which declares that there is no truth or goodness. Rather, it derives primarily from the Romantic movement, which promoted the idea that "if it feels good, then it is good." This has now become almost a dogma. But feelings often arise from distortions and are easily manipulated, as cult leaders have shown again and again. They can make people feel good (for a while)—Jim Jones made his followers feel good before they drank his poisoned Kool-Aid. Does one's experience encourage us to think one's emotions are reliable?

Some people go further and claim that our feelings are what we essentially are. If we believe that we essentially are our feelings, then what we essentially are keeps changing. Whether in religion, politics or love—or anything else—our feelings fluctuate. Sometimes we feel deeply about nature, other times less so. Sometimes we feel more deeply toward our parents, spouse or child than other times. Sometimes we feel the presence of God, sometimes we don't. The belief that we are our feelings easily leads to the feeling that any questioning of the reliability of what we feel is a personal attack on us. "I happen to feel that . . . " is no demonstration of anything but the insecurity of the person who utters it. It blocks our perception of what is right and wrong. Neither history nor biology nor psychology provides any basis for the idea that good consists of feeling good.

The most bizarre aspect of the current age of feelings is that it leads us to think that the reality outside us changes to fit the reality inside us. If we feel that God exists this week, he does; if next week we don't, he doesn't. If we feel drawn to an ideology, we may join up—for as long as we feel that

[49]Evagrius of Pontus, Archbishop Chrysostomos, *Guide to Orthodox Psychotherapy* (Lanham, MD: University Press of America, 2007).

way. If we feel that chemicals behave one way, fine; if we feel differently tomorrow, let's change our copy of the periodic table of the elements. Atheists counter that whereas people in Wyoming, India, Argentina and Russia may have differing views about religion, scientists in all those countries all agree on the periodic table of the elements. This is an unbeatable argument for the periodic table, a strong argument for science in general, and an example of how Christianity and science agree in searching for truth through evidence and in dismissing deconstruction and postmodernism as an ephemeral intellectual fad that exists mainly as rationalization for the underlying hedonism of the whole society.

Whether deconstructionist ideas are fundamentally insane may be debated, but the fact is that none of our ancestors survived thinking this way. A Neolithic human being attacked by a wolf could deconstruct the wolf into a walnut—and die—or he could bash the wolf with a club—and survive. Total absence of meaning entails total inability to communicate about anything but trivia. And trivia are very popular today.

There is not a word about "feelings" in the Bible. As for early, medieval and modern theologians, they are virtually unanimous in arguing that feelings are tumultuous movements that shift frequently and cannot be relied upon. It is one thing to recognize that I feel like hitting someone, quite another to encourage the emotion, let alone to carry the action out. For Christians, intense feelings about Christ are a gift to be enjoyed if and when they come, but they are not the point of Christianity, and the intensity of the experience never lasts. When the great spiritual writers felt ravished by beautiful experiences, they were surprised and grateful, and they did not expect them to continue. Some have sought "mystical" experiences for pleasure, but seeking the experience is a guarantee of never getting through the frosting to the cake. The ingredients of the cake are:

1. Reason: By the use of the reason we possess as humans, we construct a coherent view of the cosmos. Natural reason within our minds, unaided by revelation, constructs an internal reality corresponding to external reality. Some philosophers have always argued that unaided reason and observation lead to God. Others have always argued that reason and observation lead to the conclusion that God does not exist. Up until the 1950s, philosophers could argue that the scientific evidence of their times indicated that God was unnecessary and un-

likely. Since the 1960s the weight of scientific evidence has shifted in favor of the existence of an intelligent programmer of the cosmos.

2. Will: In addition to the current standard model of biology and psychology, which states that everything is nature plus nurture, Christianity has always insisted on the freedom of the human will. The will to find God accompanies reason in finding him. Theologians have argued whether the act of will to find God precedes the use of reason to do so, or whether reason precedes the will. In any case, the two work together. Paradoxically, the perfect act of the human free will is to accept God's will.

3. Love: the desire to find God: This love is neither lust nor a surge of good feelings. Rather, it is a longing, open attentiveness to the call of the divine that may come at any time. The Christian view is that feelings and moods are unreliable, and this may be one reason why Christianity is unpopular in a sensual society.

The heart needs the mind, and the mind needs the heart.

94. FUNDAMENTALISM IS ANCIENT CHRISTIAN TEACHING.

People like to call anyone who has deeper convictions of any kind than they do a "fundamentalist." In the proper sense of the word, fundamentalism began in America in the period 1895-1920 as a movement within American Protestant evangelicalism. The idea was to hold to the ancient, original essence of Christianity, especially the inerrancy of the Bible, the divinity of Christ, the virgin birth, Christ's atonement on the cross for the failures of humanity, and Christ's second coming at the end of the world. A close correlation, though not a complete identity, exists between modern fundamentalist teachings and those of the early church. By A.D. 100 the Bible was accepted as the revelation of God and therefore true, but well before 200 it was recognized as having different kinds of truth on different levels; by 300 few theologians believed that every passage could be taken as true historically and scientifically. Most modern evangelicals understand that, but some believe that it is inerrant and infallible in every respect. By 100, almost all Christians believed in the divinity of Christ, though the church did not clarify just how until 451. By 100, the virgin birth of Jesus was generally accepted, as was the atonement on the cross, though how atonement works has been debated for centuries. Again by 100, the end of the world and Christ's reappearance at the end was generally believed, though again the manner in which this will occur is still being debated.

The fundamentalist movement began in opposition to those who revised faith according to current intellectual and societal norms. Does the meaning of Christ appear most fully in the earliest ideas about him or in the development of ideas about him up till the present? Does the Christian community look backward or forward? At present, the division distinguishes the conservative and liberal wings of Christianity. Liberals consider fundamentalists ignorant and uneducated, while conservatives think that liberals sacrifice eternal values for cultural trends. There is a middle ground, of course: it is possible to develop doctrines properly so long as they do not conflict with their origins. A young tree is whole in itself yet grows true to itself so long as it is connected with its roots. The church is constantly being re-formed (formed again), but reformations that cut themselves off from the roots are problematic. The differences in current Christianity lie less between denominations than between radicals and conservatives.[50]

If the increase in physicalism and atheistic evolution in the late nineteenth century provoked fundamentalism as a reaction, fundamentalists in turn provoked the antitheist counterattack of the twenty-first century, which has already generated a strong Christian response. Polemics are of less use than reasonable examination of evidence. There are closed-minded Christian fundamentalists and closed-minded atheist fundamentalists. Nothing is as certain as either side would like.

95. Christians believe in the immortality of the soul.

It is important to clarify what the word "soul" means. The Apostle Saint Paul did not distinguish clearly between the Greek words *psyche* and *pneuma*, and the ambiguity carries on into translations. As a result, in English translations the words "soul" and "spirit" are often used inter-

[50]Jozef Zycinski, *God and Evolution: Fundamental Questions of Christian Evolutionism* (Washington, DC: Catholic University of America Press, 2006), pp. 32-38, discusses the origin and development of fundamentalism, but he misrepresents Phillip Johnson as a fundamentalist (p. 39).

changeably. The ambiguity has led to millennia of confusion. A wide variety of interpretations have been developed, and there is no consensus today. But in Christian theology soul and spirit have often had different meanings. The "soul" properly speaking is the entire human—body and spirit—so that we are our souls today, and at the resurrection of the dead we will again be our entire souls. In the time between our death and our resurrection, our spirit will be separated temporarily from our physical body, which decays. The spirit looks forward to reunion with the body at the resurrection, at which the two parts of the soul—body and spirit—are reconnected.

In this view, spirit and soul are immortal in different ways. Christians believe that a human's life begins with conception and terminates in bodily death, which separates the spirit from the body. While the body perishes temporarily, the spirit lives on immortally. Spirit never dies, because death merely separates it from the body. Though soul suffers temporary separation of spirit and body, soul is essentially immortal. The emphasis of Christian teaching about the "afterlife" is less on the immortality of the spirit than on the resurrection of the body. (It is less Platonic than Jewish.) It is also less on the afterlife than on eternal life. "Afterlife" (or "hereafter," which dates from 1546) is a word that became common only in the twentieth century. It implies that people are somehow in time and space after they die. Since heaven is not in the space-time of the physical universe but the state in which the soul is perfected, most theologians consider heaven a state of being rather than a place.[51] It is eternal life, the fullness of being in every *now*.

96. EVIL DOESN'T EXIST, *AND* THE EXISTENCE OF EVIL DISPROVES CHRISTIANITY.

According to both relativism and physicalism evil does not exist. True relativists believe that nothing can be considered better or worse than anything else, other than by continually fluctuating currents of social values. True physicalists, on the other hand, believe that no one has free will and that everything that happens is either the result of physical processes or is random. According to both views, evil is an old-fashioned idea; no one is evil; nothing is evil; evil doesn't exist. At the same time that relativists and

[51]Jeffrey Burton Russell, *History of Heaven: The Singing Silence* (New York: Oxford University Press, 1997), pp. 44-45.

physicalists argue that evil doesn't exist, they argue that the existence of evil disproves the existence of God because he allows it. But if evil doesn't exist, there isn't any evil for God to allow. The argument contains mutually contradictory statements. In any case, denial of the reality of evil is disconnected from the reality of a world where actual genocidal rape, torture and murder occur daily.

There is no incompatibility between an amoral deity (and deities) and evil. But there seems to be an incompatibility between evil and a deity that is all-knowing, all-powerful and all-good. Thus atheists argue that the Christian God and evil are incompatible. This "argument from evil," as it is technically called, has always been the strongest argument against Christianity. It is an emotionally persuasive argument: no normal person can think of a child being burned to death without horror. Rationally, though, the argument against the coexistence of God and suffering is not convincing.[52]

97. Christians believe in evil.

Christians believe in the reality of both good and evil.[53] Along with many philosophers, they distinguish three types of evil. The first, ontological evil, is completely abstract. Ontology is the study of the essence of being. The idea of ontological evil is that any cosmos created by a perfect God must be less perfect than God is, so imperfection is a necessary corollary of creation. Many philosophers have defined evil as lack of being—the cosmos is like Swiss cheese, and the holes are simply lack of cheese. Or it is like absolute cold, which is simply lack of heat. However, if one places a pencil perpendicular to the ground in the sunshine, it will cast a shadow. The shadow certainly is lack of light, but that doesn't mean that the shadow isn't there.

A great many theologians have held sophisticated versions of the privation theory of evil. In a hierarchical cosmology with a spectrum stretching from the greatest to the least, the top is "the One," ultimate perfection, infinite reality. Whatever is less than this has inherent defects. The created cosmos, being less than God, is defective. Within the created

---

[52]William Lane Craig, *On Guard: Defending Your Faith with Reason and Precision* (Colorado Springs: David C. Cook, 2010), pp. 153-69.

[53]N. T. Wright, *Evil and the Justice of God* (Downers Grove, IL: InterVarsity Press, 2006); Alvin Plantinga, *God, Freedom, and Evil,* 2nd ed. (Grand Rapids: Eerdmans, 1977).

cosmos, humans are higher than animals, which are higher than plants, which are higher than inanimate objects. Below inanimate objects and the bottom of the scale is unformed matter, nonbeing, infinite privation, an ontological nothing.[54] However, on a scale that is moral rather than ontological, "the one" is perfection and absolute good, and the bottom is total imperfection, which is evil. Mixing the two scales created a problem for Christian theologians.[55] In the last century, Karl Barth (1886-1968) proposed an original solution. In this solution, three elements exist: God, God's creation, and nothingness. Nothingness is neither God nor God's creation, but it exists in the sense in that it comes into being wherever God withdraws his creative power. Evil as nothingness does not lie in God or true being: it is negation, defect, chaos, opposition to real being, yet as a vacuum it has the power to draw creatures toward it and into it.[56]

The second sort of evil is natural evil, suffering brought about by natural forces such as droughts and tsunamis. There's no place on Earth where one can escape the danger of suffering. From earthquakes to bacteria, nature provides rich opportunities for suffering, but they are all necessary for life. Without the plate tectonics that cause earthquakes, volcanoes and tsunamis, there would be no circulation of the elements needed for life. There is no natural evil on the moon because there is no life there to suffer. God could have created a planet without natural evil. In fact, he did: he created lots of them—lifeless planets such as Venus and Jupiter.

The third sort of evil is suffering deliberately inflicted by creatures with high intelligence and free will: humans. Torture, rape, genocide and the billion trivial hurts that people cause one another are the fault of humans. God makes creatures with free will to do both good and evil. He could have created creatures with no moral choice, but the point of God's creating the cosmos was to create a good independent of himself, and a universe of marionettes or robots would be of no value. And there are limits to evil. From each evil act, ripples of evil spread and spread, but they don't

[54]On Christian views of evil through time, see the five volumes on the history of the Devil by Jeffrey Burton Russell: *Devil: Perceptions of Evil from Antiquity to Primitive Christianity; Satan: The Early Christian Tradition; Lucifer: The Devil in the Middle Ages; Mephistopheles: The Devil in the Modern World; Prince of Darkness: Radical Evil and the Power of Good in History* (Ithaca, NY: Cornell University Press, 1977-1988).

[55]Russell, *Prince of Darkness*, pp. 74-76; Russell, *Satan*, pp. 109-11 on Clement of Alexandria, pp. 202-203 on Augustine; Russell, *Lucifer*, pp. 194-96 on Aquinas.

[56]Russell, *Mephistopheles*, pp. 265-66.

go on forever and some good may eventually arise from them.

Christianity has always held that no one should wish for suffering. In the early centuries of Christianity, thinkers cautioned against seeking martyrdom. They said there was no value in rushing up to the Roman authorities and saying, "Look here, I'm a Christian, what are you going to do about it?" They said that this amounted to suicide and so was not martyrdom but an offense to the Creator of life. The word "martyr" means "witness," especially one who suffers torture and death for Christ because she or he is forced to. Only if one is forced to choose between Christ and death can one be a martyr.

Suffering is built into human existence.[57] Christians believe that people should not seek it for themselves and least of all seek it for other people. The Apostle Saint Peter said, "Beloved, do not be surprised at the fiery ordeal that is taking place among you to test you, as if something strange were happening to you. But rejoice insofar as you are sharing Christ's sufferings" (1 Pet 4:12-13). Some Christians expect that if God is good they will not suffer, but Christianity has always been centered on the atoning power of Christ's suffering, and martyrs have suffered for the faith from the first to the twenty-first century. The idea is not that suffering is good—it isn't—but that if we must suffer we can choose to suffer with God. It is possible in terms of God's absolute power that God could create a universe without suffering. But in terms of his ordered power he cannot, for he has ordered life, which depends on certain things, such as plate tectonics, which have painful side effects such as earthquakes.

Assuming that God exists, he hasn't yet put an end to suffering, so there is little reason to believe that he will. Assuming he does not exist, there's little reason to believe that human nature will change for the better given the monstrous cruelties attested from earliest known human times to the present day.

The intense reality of personal suffering should not be diminished by theory. Abstract philosophies don't usually help someone who is in pain, alone and terrified. The questions raised by the existence of evil are personal questions; they need and deserve a personal answer. The Christian answer to the problem is personal: God, in the human person of Jesus

---

[57]Ian S. Markham, *Against Atheism: Why Dawkins, Hitchens, and Harris are Fundamentally Wrong* (Oxford: Wiley-Blackwell, 2010), pp. 117-24.

Christ, himself suffers all the pain of each creature. God takes evil and suffering on himself and into himself, and he thereby transforms them into something they could otherwise never be. Absent that, evil wins. During intense suffering one is hardly able to think of anything other than pain. But the great spiritual writer Julian of Norwich (1342-1417) said that although our limited minds can't grasp the meaning of the world, God makes all things right. God told her, "See, I am God. See, I am in all things. See, I do all things. See, I never remove my hands from my works, nor ever shall without end. See, I guide all things to the end that I ordain them for, before time began, with the same power and wisdom and love in which I made them; how should anything be amiss?" She asked God about pain and suffering and "had no other answer from our Lord than this: 'I shall preserve my word in everything, and I shall make everything well.' . . . And He will make all well which is not well."[58]

98. Christians believe that everything that happens is God's will.

When an atrocity such as a child murder occurs, many people ask this most painful of questions: "How could God let this happen?" But unlike Muslims, Christians do not believe that every event is directly and immediately willed by God. And unlike deists, Christians do not believe that God set the universe in motion and let it run by itself; they do not believe he frontloaded all the information necessary into the universe at the moment of creation and then kept his hands off. They believe that God is deeply involved in maintaining and developing the cosmos. God chooses to set up a universe with natural regularities, and he retains the power to modify or suspend these regularities at any moment. He also creates some creatures with freedom to choose and whose choice he does not control. If there were no freedom and no nature there would be no pain. If there were no cosmos, there would be no suffering and evil—and no goodness or joy (see Mk 4:26-28).[59] Perhaps one moment of joy justifies creation more than a moment of agony makes creation an outrage.

[58]Julian of Norwich, *Showings* (Mahwah, NJ: Paulist, 1978), pp. 199, 233.

[59]Craig, *On Guard*, pp. 153-69; John L. Esposito, *What Everyone Needs to Know about Islam: Answers to Frequently Asked Questions from One of America's Leading Experts* (New York: Oxford University Press, 2002); Michael Poole, *'New Atheism': Ten Arguments That Don't Hold Water* (Oxford: Lion, 2009), pp. 73-75.

99. Christians believe in hell.

The common idea that the clergy invented hell to keep people in line is impossible because the idea of hell preceded the existence of the clergy.[60] On the other hand, clergy often used it for that purpose. Protestant sermons matched Catholic artworks in frightening people. Many Christian teachers and preachers now avoid mentioning hell so as to avoid distressing (and diminishing) their congregations. Conservative Christians continue to follow the tradition of taking hell overtly and literally. There are really three basic interpretations Christians can hold. One is the overt view that hell involves physical darkness, fire and torment. Another is that hell is just a poetic figure of speech without reference to actual reality. A third is to take hell as a true metaphor: the fiery lakes and are true in the sense that they represent the reality of the spiritual pain felt by those who are eternally separated from true happiness. Some say that not to love is to be in hell already; others say that hell is the meanest, nastiest place in your mind.

Many Christians dismiss hell as outdated superstition, repulsive as well as unbelievable. To them it seems an obstacle to belief and needs to be jettisoned. Rather few Christians of any sort believe in hell in the gruesome form in which it was portrayed in artworks, sermons and literature over the centuries. As Gregory of Nyssa (330-395) stated, "We regard falling from God's friendship as the only thing dreadful, and we consider becoming God's friend the only thing worthy of honor and desire."[61] Belief in hell has never been defined as necessary Christian doctrine, so one can be a Christian without believing in it. Since the third century, Christian views have historically varied between the literal and the metaphorical, but hell is too firmly rooted in the New Testament to be ignored.

The idea of an afterlife in the underworld is a common motif among cultures, although the word "afterlife" became common only in the twentieth century. The Hebrew Bible refers to an afterlife in two different terms. The earlier term is "Sheol," which, like Greek Hades, is an underworld where the spirits of the dead live a shadowy, blurry, almost ghostlike

---

[60] Alan W. Bernstein, *Formation of Hell: Death and Retribution in the Ancient and Early Christian Worlds* (Ithaca, NY: Cornell University Press, 1993).

[61] Quoted by Tracey Rowland, *Ratzinger's Faith: The Theology of Pope Benedict XVI* (Oxford: Oxford University Press, 2009), p. 83.

existence, neither happy nor suffering. The later term is "Gehenna," a fiery pit where evildoers unfaithful to the Lord suffer torment. From 200 B.C. to A.D. 150, a number of pseudepigrapha—books written under the assumed names of ancient patriarchs or prophets—appeared in the Hebrew-Jewish community. Although never accepted as part of the Bible, they had widespread influence. They tended to be luridly apocalyptic and featured many visions of Gehenna and even alleged visits to hell, whose torments were hideously and fiercely corporeal. These apocalyptic books influenced early Christianity.

The New Testament declares the existence of hell more than a dozen times. Jesus says, "You will be liable to the hell of fire. . . . It is better for you to lose one of your limbs than for your whole body to go into Gehenna" (Mt 5:22-30). He also says, "Fear him who can destroy both soul and body in hell" (Mt 10:28) and that it is better to lose an eye than "to be thrown into the hell of fire" (Mt 18:9; cf. Mk 9:47-48). The Second Letter of Peter speaks of hell as "chains of deepest darkness" (2 Pet 2:4) and the Gospel of Mathew repeatedly refers to hell as "the outer darkness" (Mt 8:12; 22:13, 25:30).

The early theologians and most subsequent Christian writers affirmed the reality of hell. By the 400s there was a standard view of hell that prevailed for centuries with only minor modifications. Hell was thought to be a huge pit at the center of the Earth inhabited by the Devil, his demons and the spirits of unrepentant evildoers. It was an eternal place of darkness, fire, stench and torture, best described by Dante in his *Inferno* ("Hell" in Italian). Such views were accepted in Catholic, Orthodox and Protestant traditions. Depictions of hell in literature, theology and artworks became more and more terrifying from the eleventh century onward, and infernal scenes decorated many churches. The intensity of the suffering varied according to the gravity of the sins: Dante saw various levels in hell down all the way to the frozen, motionless center where Satan was embedded in eternal and unyielding ice.

Since the time of Galileo and Kepler it has been obvious that hell is not literally in the center of the Earth. Most theologians today believe that it is not located anywhere in the universe of space-time. Rather, it is a state of existence for people who in this life choose to turn away from God and gratify their own egos. One does not "go to" hell. One constructs hell for oneself; it exists in the character one has formed for oneself in life. The idea is not that God damns, condemns, sends or drags people off to hell. One chooses to live in hell by denying and rejecting love; no one is in hell unless he or she chooses to be. God gives us humans the freedom to destroy ourselves and also the freedom to choose to turn away from destruction. The point of hell is to satisfy justice: the wicked may prosper in this life, but the faithful experience perfect joy. The essence of hell is believed to be eternal separation from God, light, love and life: a state of complete meaninglessness and hopelessness.

Hell is best seen in the whole context of the Christian concept of life after death, in which heaven is more important than hell.[62] It is possible to be a Christian without believing in hell, but not without believing in heaven.

Heaven is dynamic rather than static, so our intellects and love may continue to develop and grow. Most theologians consider heaven as a spiritual state rather than a place, and it can begin here on Earth. The Greek word *ouranos* means both "sky" and "heaven," and most Christians through time took that overtly, as in Christ's "descent from" and "ascent to" heaven. The idea was that the physical description of the cosmos fit its spiritual description, a concept most powerfully expressed in Dante's *Paradiso* ("Heaven"). In modern cosmology, however, the idea that heaven is astronomically up is as implausible as that hell is geologically down. Rather, it's believed that we are in heaven when we are completely suffused by grace and love, and that state is perfectly fulfilled after death. But although heaven is often thought of as an entirely spiritual state, the biblical and traditional view is that body and spirit will be united in the resurrection. The view is that at the end of the world God transforms this earth into heaven. Jesus says that he is bringing his kingdom, the rule of love, from God onto the earth. His words are usually translated in English as, "My kingdom is not of this world" (Jn 18:36), while a more accurate translation is "from this world," meaning that his authority does not derive from this world and that he is bringing true authority into the world.[63]

---

[62]Carlos Eire, *A Very Brief History of Eternity* (Princeton, NJ: Princeton University Press, 2010); John Casey, *After Lives: A Guide to Heaven, Hell, and Purgatory* (New York: Oxford University Press, 2010).

[63]The Greek *ek* is more likely to mean "from" than "of," and the word *enteuthen*, "from this place," confirms "from" as the better translation.

What this transformation of the world entails and when it will occur, if it isn't already occurring, remains a matter of Christian speculation. Does it entail the transformation of the entire universe or of the Earth? Is it fulfilled at the end of the human race, at the end of the planet, or at the end of the universe? Some analogy of the physical world continues to exist for resurrected bodies, but it will be transformed into "a new heaven and a new earth" (1 Pet 3:13; Rev 21:1), in which God will be all in all with ever more perfect healing, justice and hope (1 Cor 15:28). Meanwhile, a curious idea has arisen in the current emphasis on entitlement: do we now feel we have a "right" to heaven?

100. CHRISTIANS BELIEVE IN THE DEVIL.

Christians believe in God in two senses: they both believe in God's existence and trust him as a Person. Christians believe in the Devil only in the one sense that they believe he exists. Few if any Christians believe in the crimson character with the cloven hoofs, horns, pitchfork and tail. That stereotype has been reduced to cartoons. Christianity is based on the New Testament, and the Devil is prominent in the New Testament—and in Orthodox, Catholic and Protestant tradition. The Devil by definition is a powerful force of evil, either a real spiritual personality or a metaphor for human evil. Such a figure is extremely vague in the Hebrew Bible or Old Testament. The Devil, often named Satan, first attained real prominence in the period 200 B.C. to A.D. 100 in Jewish pseudepigrapha (anonymous writings falsely claiming to be by ancient Israelite figures such as Enoch).

In the New Testament, Christ is tempted near the beginning of his ministry by the Devil in the wilderness; there Satan claims the power to hand over all earthly riches and powers to Jesus, a claim and an offer that Christ refuses. Jesus frequently rebukes the Devil and casts out (exorcizes) demons from the victims they "possess." The word "Devil" appears forty times in the New Testament and the name "Satan" thirty-three times, making them difficult for Christians to ignore. One may choose to read them metaphorically, but the metaphor must be related to some reality unless one dismisses the whole New Testament. The metaphor is of radical evil, whether human or beyond human.

The Apostles Saints Paul and John developed a theology about the Devil: he was an angel created good by God, but through his own free will he chose to serve his own ego rather than to love God. As a result, he and the other angels who chose to follow him were cast out of heaven. It was the Devil who tempted Adam and Eve (representing all humanity) to sin and who continues to attack and tempt humans. The Devil has great power over humanity, though he can never compel anyone to sin. By dying for us on the cross Christ broke Satan's power, though we still retain our free will, including the option to sin, until the end of the world, at which point Christ returns to cast the Devil into hell forever.

Throughout its history Christianity confirmed these views, though further details developed through the years. The earliest church established hell as the Devil's dwelling place from the moment of his fall from heaven yet affirmed that he could go out and roam the world seeking the ruin and destruction of humanity. Most of the baptismal formulas of the early church included a formal renunciation of Satan, a ritual widely preserved to the present day. The presence of demons was intensely felt in the first few centuries of the church, particularly in monastic communities, members of which often believed their prime purpose was to help Christ wage war against Satan. Christ's power is always greater than Satan's, and the Devil never can claim anyone whose character is turned away from selfishness and toward love of God.

Orthodox, Catholic and Protestant theologians continued to develop the idea of Satan without changing the basic concept, and the Reformation of the 1500s maintained the basic theology of the Devil. However, beginning in the 1700s, Christian Europe was increasingly skeptical about religious authority, tradition and the Bible. This skepticism had two huge effects on the concept. One was the development of a "liberal Christianity" that had little room for the Devil. The other was the development of atheism rejecting Christianity and all religion.

Those two effects are felt mostly in Europe and to some extent in the United States, but in countries where Christianity is on the rise—Africa, Latin America and China, for example—biblical and traditional views continue to prevail. In Western countries the decay of belief in the existence of Satan can be observed in five different attitudes. Among the dominant intellectual elite, the Devil is a superstition, and belief in the Devil is one of a number of preposterous ideas that make Christianity absurd. Among the minority of the elite who are Christian, the assumption is that the Devil may exist, but probably as a metaphor for human evil. Among the clergy, most Catholic and mainline Protestants try to avoid mentioning either the Devil or hell. In popular culture, hedonistic materialism and feel-good self-esteem discourage thinking about the Devil, sin and death. Some Christians, however, especially evangelicals, teach that the existence of Satan cannot be questioned in the light of the Bible's frequent allusions to him.[64]

101. CHRISTIANS BELIEVE IN ORIGINAL SIN.

On the dust jacket of an otherwise fine book on the subject by Alan Jacobs, a blurb reads, "How the world's most repugnant idea became the cornerstone of our self-understanding."[65] Many Christians as well as other people do find the idea repugnant, so original sin may be the single most misunderstood Christian concept. For example, many people imagine that original sin is sexual. The term "original sin" has been so distorted that other terms such as alienation or indelible egotism may be preferable. Whatever term is used, it is a cornerstone of Christian belief.

The actual Christian idea is that God created the cosmos to be populated by creatures who loved one another and loved him. God might have chosen not to create the cosmos at all. Or he could have forced all creatures to not hurt one another—but such creatures would be robots without any capacity for real love. Real love requires free choice. Therefore God created humans on Earth (and maybe extra-terrestrials elsewhere) with freedom to choose between love and selfishness. This was the freedom God gave the first humans. They abused it by choosing their own egos rather than love of God and his cosmos. God created human nature good, but humans turned it bad. The Hebrew Bible (Old Testament) follows the account of Adam and Eve's sin with accounts of sin after sin after sin, generation after generation, among weak and poor, strong and wealthy, kings and peasants, Israelites and Gentiles (non-Jews). The tendency to sin is pervasive, and it has held humanity captive: "I was born guilty, a sinner when my mother conceived me" (Ps 52:5). "There is no one on earth so righteous as to do good without ever sinning" (Eccles 7:20).

---

[64]Russell, *Devil; Satan; Lucifer; Mephistopheles; Prince of Darkness.*

[65]Alan Jacobs, *Original Sin: A Cultural History* (New York: HarperOne, 2008); Gary A. Anderson, *Sin: A History* (New Haven, CT: Yale University Press, 2009).

The New Testament is even more specific than the Old about the human tendency to sin. The Apostle Saint Paul said that he was in "slavery under sin. . . . I do not do what I want, but I do the very thing I hate" (Rom 7:14-25). Without Christ to put humans in touch with God, they would be left with what's become known as "sin management": working hard to improve themselves rather than finding transformation in uprooting the ego and turning oneself over to Christ.

It would be tangential to go on about whether Adam and Eve were actual historical persons (and if so, when they lived), or whether they spiritually incorporate all humanity, or whether they are metaphors for humanity as a whole, or how old Homo sapiens is, but recent scientific research affirms the monogenist view that all present humans are descended from the same African ancestors (Europeans and their descendants also have a small touch of Neanderthal DNA). Whenever the first Homo sapiens appeared, "something terrible and glorious befell us, a change gradualism could not predict."[66]

The term "original sin" does not appear in the Bible. Eastern Orthodox Christians refer to "the ancestral curse" or the *prognostike hamartia* (Greek for "foreknown sin"). All humans are attached to evil and tempted by sin, say the Orthodox, but Christ gives us the power of freedom to resist sin—or else to embrace it. The simple irruption of a destructive thought is not a sin: only our consent to that thought is sinful. The early Western theologians, culminating in Saint Augustine (354-410), used the term *peccatum originale* (Latin for "original sin"). They tended to view it as biologically transmitted from one generation to another, and this led to the idea that it was transmitted by the sexual act. Augustine has recently been blamed for the idea of original sin along with many other things, but the doctrine preceded him by centuries.[67] The Orthodox—and many Catholics and Protestants—believe that all humans are spiritually present in Adam and Eve and share in their fault. Some theologians maintain that Adam and Eve lost their intellectual as well as their moral sense. In Eden, their souls were spiritually pure and intellectually illuminated. Their sin distorted their souls, so that they (and all humans) lost their ability to fully understand the world as well as to choose to live rightly in it.

---

[66]Marilynne Robinson, *Absence of Mind* (New Haven, CT: Yale University Press, 2010), p. 135.
[67]Jacobs, *Original Sin*, p. 32.

Christians believe that God gave humans freedom to love and that we often choose not to love, or to "love" only our own egos. Real love involves gratitude and generosity. Christian thinkers observe that although everyone has moral free will, everyone also has an innate tendency to turn away from love. Some people do it all the time; everybody does it some of the time. Human behavior varies among times and cultures, but the tendency to turn away from love is universal. That's the essential meaning of the idea of original sin: the choice to alienate ourselves from loving harmony.

Christianity does not say that Christ canceled human ability to sin. Instead, he canceled the obedience to sin that would otherwise exist in the whole human race. The idea is that justification by Christ renews our souls, thus allowing us to detach ourselves from sin. Sins by Christians are particularly noxious and ungrateful, for they ignore the very light they believe Christ has given them. The great Protestant reformer John Calvin (1509-1564) argued that both will and intellect were totally depraved by original sin. In recent years there has been a revival of Calvinism.[68] Currently among the firmest defenders of the doctrine of original sin are Catholics and evangelicals.

Some people insist that humans are essentially "good." If we imagine that our society is full of love, joy, harmony and happiness, then the idea of sin is silly and grotesque. But that is pure fantasy: every day there are new horrors and griefs. As has been said only partly in jest, humans treat one another so abominably that original sin is the only empirically demonstrated Christian teaching.

Neither deconstructionists nor physicalists believe in sin. Deconstructionists say they believe that good and evil are just human constructs, and each human being constructs them differently. Some think blowing up a town is OK, others don't, and there's no way of saying which is right—any principle that might be called on to resolve the question is itself merely a human invention. Why not rape, burn and pillage? Physicalists maintain that there are evolutionary reasons for constructive and unconstructive behavior. Unlike Darwin's early followers, they observe that it is often more of an evolutionary advantage to cooperate than to behave selfishly. Of

[68]J. Todd Billings, "Calvin's Comeback," *Christian Century*, December 1, 2009, pp. 22-23.

course, that applies to the behavior of humans cooperating in genocide as much as to the behavior of charitable or environmental organizations. Without a transcendent principle of good, there is no reason to believe that anything is good other than what we feel like at the moment.

Jean-Jacques Rousseau (1712-1778) declared the "natural goodness of man." Human nature, he thought, was created good but had been deformed by the wickedness of political, religious and educational institutions. Remove the obstacles to human goodness, and good will flower spontaneously. Voltaire (1694-1778) objected, not sharing this optimism, but Karl Marx (1818-1883) and others shared this idealistic and anti-evidential delusion of overall human progress. The great Protestant theologian Reinhold Niebuhr (1892-1971) observed that "under the bland influence of the idea of progress, man, supposing himself to be more and more the measure of all things, achieved a singularly easy conscience and an almost hermetically smug optimism."[69]

Original sin is actually a democratic idea. Without believing in original sin, one person might pride himself or herself on being better than another and one group or race or nation might claim to be better than others. The idea that absolutely everyone is a sinner makes it much harder to be arrogant and judge others.[70]

102. Christians believe in predestination.

Christianity categorically denies that there is any such thing as "destiny" or "fate." These are both quite different from predestination, since neither has anything to do with God. Most Christians today don't believe in predestination either, and among those who do the idea of predestination varies. There have been vast differences of opinion about it throughout Christian history from the first to the twenty-first century.

There is a theological basis for predestination and a biblical one. The theological basis is this: if God knows everything—all time and space at once—he knows the future; and if God is all-powerful, he commands the future. Therefore God knows and wills everything past, present and future. If some people are forever alienated from God, God must know who; if he wills everything as well as knows everything, he must will the

[69]Quoted in Jacobs, *Original Sin*, pp. 233-34.
[70]Ibid., p. 200.

alienation. The biblical basis is this: "For those whom [God] foreknew he also predestined to be conformed to the image of his Son. . . . And those whom he predestined he also called; and those whom he called, he also justified, and those whom he justified he also glorified" (Rom 8:28-30; see also Eph 1:3-11; 2 Tim 1:9). The meaning of the Greek *proorizein* ("to see ahead," often translated "to predestine") is debated, but the idea of some sort of predestination was assumed by the early Christian theologians and their successors, Orthodox, Catholic and Protestant.

Here, put simply, are the main positions. (1) In double predestination: the omnipotent and omniscient God chooses in eternity to have some people in heaven and others in hell. (2) God selects those whom he wishes to save. Thus God predestines only to heaven and ignores the rest, who follow their own path to hell. (3) The omniscient God knows in eternity who will be saved and who will not be. Though he knows who will not be saved, he does not will them not to be. He wills everyone to be saved, but he suspends his absolute power so as to allow everyone free will, and each person chooses whether to love God or to prefer his or her alienation. In this alternative, it is God's foreknowledge that is the point of the passage from Romans. Nonpredestinarian views are: (4) Christ died to open the door to everyone, but free will means that some freely choose to pass through and others freely refuse. (5) God neither wills nor knows who will be saved. Even God does not know the future of each soul but works with each in the present, guiding each who is willing to salvation. (6) The whole idea is best ignored.

Many believe that the first two alternatives—that God both foresees and forewills the damnation of some—limit both God's justice and his mercy. Christ is believed, after all, to have died for all. On the other side, many warn that extending God's mercy even to those who choose to reject him is itself a violation of justice. Double predestination—predestination to both heaven and hell—has never been viewed as a required doctrine except by the strictest Calvinists, and it was repeatedly rejected by the Catholic church both before and after the Reformation. Luther and a few Catholic theologians taught the modified versions (3) and (4) above. "Many are called, but few are chosen" (Mt 22:14) has usually been taken to mean that although God calls everyone to follow him, some refuse to do so, and God knows who refuse and thus does not choose them. Most

Christians emphasize the freedom of the human will: as Augustine said, there is no cause of a free will choice; the ideal use of free will is to freely submit to God's will to love God and neighbor.[71]

103. The diversity and number of denominations disprove Christianity.

The often bitter disagreements between denominations are a bad advertisement for Christianity. However, the mere existence of denominations—different points of view—is no evidence against Christianity. There is a core of Christian belief, but beyond that there are honest differences. Most Christians agree that the Bible and the teachings of the early church are central. And most agree that differences are consistent within the mutual love of Christ. Even a strongly hierarchical church such as Roman Catholicism and a church as strongly faithful to Tradition as the Orthodox church allow for considerable differences in liturgy, worship and teaching. Roman Catholics, Orthodox and some other churches claim a degree of fidelity to Christian Tradition that they find lacking in many Protestant churches. Protestants, on the other hand, believe that the Catholic and Orthodox churches have constructed doctrinal and liturgical practices that departed from biblical Christianity. Differences among Protestant denominations have blurred greatly since the 1950s, and now splits between "liberal" and "conservative" are more important than denominations.

It is impossible that every Christian should think exactly the same as every other: there is strength in diversity. Still, ignorance, clannishness and narrow-mindedness repel honest inquirers. The less one group of Christians knows about others, the more they tend to disparage them. On the other hand, anger also arises between people who have once been close and then find themselves in sharp disagreement, which they view as betrayal. Angry disputes have historically undermined the cause of Christianity. Two historical examples: disputes between Orthodox and Monophysites[72] in Syria enabled the Muslim takeover of that area in the 600s;

---

[71]William Lane Craig, *Divine Foreknowledge and Human Freedom: The Coherence of Theism: Omniscience* (New York: Brill, 1991); Peter J. Thuesen, *Predestination: The American Career of a Contentious Doctrine* (New York: Oxford University Press, 2009).

[72]The Monophysites believed that Jesus did not have a human nature but was completely divine.

disputes between Catholics and Protestants in the 1500s and 1600s led to a reaction against Christianity during the philosophical Enlightenment and the American and French revolutions of the late 1700s. Yet efforts to mend bridges can sometimes be counterproductive. Reducing differences between viewpoints to bland statements about unity tends to water everything down. Churches sometimes compete for "market share" by trying to be more cheerful, entertaining, inclusive and less demanding than others. This can amount to throwing out the tapestry instead of cleaning it. Peaceful, charitable, respectful and honestly open-minded dialogue among informed, differing views adds to the richness of the tapestry without tearing it. But the fact is that not many outsiders today remark what observers of the early church did: "They must be Christians; see how they love one another."

104. EASTERN ORTHODOX CHRISTIANS ARE A FRINGE GROUP.

Most Western Christians are unaware that the Eastern Orthodox church represents about twenty percent of Christians today and historically over time as much as thirty percent. There are also more than three million Orthodox in America today, outnumbering such better-known denominations as the Episcopal church. Even when people have heard of the Orthodox church they think of something remote. In fact, the Orthodox constitute a traditional, liturgical church continuous with early Christianity. In the 100s A.D., when individual Christian communities were melding into a broader community, that broad community considered itself Christian, Catholic and Orthodox. Catholic (Greek *katholikos*) means "general and universal," and Orthodox (Greek *orthodoxos*) means "teaching true doctrine."[73]

The unity of this Christian, Catholic and Orthodox church was largely preserved until 1054, when the Eastern and Western churches split. While each continued to consider itself both catholic and orthodox, the term Catholic became standard for the Western church and Orthodox for the Eastern church. Both maintained a continuous tradition of faith and

---

[73]Archbishop Chrysostomos, *God Made Man and Man Made God: Collected Essays on the Unique View of Man, the Cosmos, Grace, and Deification that Distinguishes Eastern Orthodoxy from Western Christianity* (Belmont, MA: Institute for Byzantine and Modern Greek Studies, 2010).

practice from earliest Christianity. The beginnings of the schism (division) between East and West began in the 600s and 700s. In those years, Muslims conquered most of the Christian territories in the Mediterranean, including three of the five patriarchates (the patriarchs were the leading bishops) of Christianity—Jerusalem, Antioch and Alexandria. That left only two in Christian hands: Rome and Constantinople.

By controlling the Mediterranean, the Muslims cut off communication between the two halves of the church. When that happened, practices began to differ markedly, with the Latin language dominating the West and the Greek language dominating the East. The two halves began competing with one another in sending separate missions to convert eastern Europe. The patriarch of Rome—the pope—held primacy in the West and began to claim it in the East as well, while the patriarch of Constantinople—the ecumenical patriarch—held primacy in the East. The patriarch of Constantinople worked closely with the Byzantine emperor, who also ruled from Constantinople, while the popes off in the west gradually detached themselves from the declining power of the emperors. It all came to a head in 1054 when an ugly quarrel at Constantinople ended in the bishops of Rome and Constantinople declaring one another "schismatics" (Greek *schisma*, "tearing"). Although beginning in the late twentieth century the churches have sewn up some of the rips, and in 1965 they withdrew the mutual excommunications of 1054, the fabric is still far from rewoven. The Protestant Reformation of the 1500s affected Western Catholic Christianity but had almost no effect on the East, whose traditions in both doctrine and practice are unbroken since the second century A.D.

There are many more similarities between the Eastern and Western churches than differences. Both claim "apostolic succession," the idea that the original apostles chose other people to take their place when they were dying or going away, so that those who took their places were successors to the apostles, who then named others down through the ages in an unbroken line to the present. The bishops are believed to stand in this line of apostolic succession. There are no essential theological differences between East and West, and their liturgies (public practices) both center on the Eucharist (Lord's Supper) and baptism. Still, there are some important differences. The Western church is centered on the pope, whether it is for him (Catholics) or against him (Protestants), whereas the Eastern church is centered in national and ethnic churches. The Eastern churches have no central authority. They honor the pope in Rome and the ecumenical patriarch in Constantinople as titular heads of the universal church but grant the pope no influence and the patriarch very little. The church divides itself along national lines: the Greek church, the Russian church, the Bulgarian church, the Serbian church and so on.[74] The Russian church considers Moscow the sixth patriarchate, and in practice the most powerful person in the entire Orthodox church is the patriarch of Moscow.

The Orthodox churches consider the ecumenical (universal) councils of all the bishops the highest authority, beyond that of any patriarch, but they accept the validity of these councils only through the Second Council of Nicaea in 787, whereas the Catholic church recognizes twenty-one ecumenical councils down through the second Vatican Council of the 1960s. The Orthodox emphasize tradition and practice (Greek *praxis*), with fidelity to the early church fathers being more important than historical development. Whereas in the Catholic church images of Christ and the saints are reminders, in the Orthodox church the images, when properly made, are considered windows to the other world in which the saint is immediately present spiritually. Orthodox Christians also venerate Mary more than Catholics (let alone Protestants) do, and Orthodox liturgy is full of praise for the *Theotokos* (Greek for "mother of God").[75] On the practical side, the Orthodox permit married priests; on the spiritual side, the Orthodox emphasize spirituality (communion with the divine) more than the Western churches, which incline to emphasize doctrine.

105. CATHOLICS ARE NOT CHRISTIANS.

Some Protestants assert that this is so, and significant hostility to Catholicism persists among secularists as well.[76] The word "catholic" (Greek *katholikos*) means "universal." From at least the time of Ignatius of Antioch (A.D. 35-107), the followers of Jesus were known as both "Christians" and

---

[74]The Oriental Orthodox churches, such as those in Georgia, Armenia, Egypt and Ethiopia, are distinct from the Eastern Orthodox church; they do not accept the ecumenical councils.

[75]Catherine Brown Tkacz discusses the many meanings of *Theotokos* in *The Ruthenian Liturgy* (Lewiston, NY: Mellen, 2012).

[76]Elaine Howard Ecklund, *Science vs. Religion: What Scientists Really Think* (New York: Oxford University Press, 2010), p. 117. On the other hand, Ecklund also notes a growing proportion of Catholics in the sciences, p. 24.

"Catholics," essentially synonymous terms.[77] The Christian community was also called "Orthodox" (Greek *orthodoxos*: "right teaching"). The community of the church (Greek *ekklesia*) remained generally unified until the break in 1054 between Western Christians, who emphasized the term Catholic, and Eastern Christians, who emphasized the term Orthodox. In the 1500s, Protestants broke with the Catholic church, essentially on the grounds that it had departed from biblical teaching. Some Protestants insisted that the pope is the Antichrist. Some churches retain this anachronistic view.

During the nineteenth century, the United States considered itself a Protestant nation. The large-scale immigration of Catholics beginning in the 1830s caused fears of foreign, un-American influence. In the 1830s to 1850s a political group called the American Party—unofficially called the Know Nothing Party because its members were supposed to say that they knew nothing about it—devoted itself primarily to combating Catholicism. In the 1850s riots against Catholics occurred in many American cities. The Civil War in the 1860s diverted attention, but the war was followed by the ascension of the Ku Klux Klan, an organization to suppress African-Americans. After a decline beginning in the 1870s, the Klan reinvented itself in 1915 as a "pro-American group" aimed against Jews and Catholics as well as African-Americans, and in this form its membership grew and achieved considerable power in the 1920s though declining again in the 1930s. My mother remembered large Klan parades in (of all places) the San Francisco Bay Area.

Anti-Catholic feelings continued after World War II, and in 1949 Paul Blanshard published his best-selling *American Freedom and Catholic Power*.[78] The Catholic church was perceived as a dangerous antidemocratic force comparable to the Nazis and the Soviets. Legends abounded that the pope was preparing to sneak into America on a submarine, that Catholic churches stocked weapons in their basements in preparation for an armed takeover, and that convents were centers of debauchery. In 1960, John F. Kennedy had to make great efforts to convince Protestant clergy that he would not take orders from Rome when he was in the White House. As late as the late twentieth and early twenty-first centuries, some Protestant

---

[77]Ignatius of Antioch, "Letter to the Smyrnans" 8.2.

[78]Paul Blanshard, *American Freedom and Catholic Power* (Boston: Beacon, 1949).

leaders have continued to preach anti-Catholicism. Bob Jones distributed anti-Catholic literature, Tim LaHaye called Catholicism a "false religion," Jimmy Swaggart declared that Catholics were going to burn in hell, and John Hagee, who endorsed (and was repudiated by) John McCain in the election of 2008, considered the Catholic church "the great whore," "a false cult system," and "the apostate church."[79]

Underlying this indignation is an idea that many Christians support: the idea that the Catholic church departed from the simple religion of the Bible, established bishops, introduced popery, worshiped images, repressed true Christians as heretics, worshiped Mary, formulated bizarre doctrines, created elaborate rites, and in general gave itself over to pomp, circumstance and corruption. Catholics thus became, it is said, apostates from pure Christianity: they had been Christians once but ceased to be. Protestants have disagreed as to the time when this apostasy occurred. Luther considered it to be in the 1400s. Others said it happened in 1050-1200 when the pope claimed sovereignty over Christendom. Still others say in the 700s, when the popes first obtained secular power.

Traditional Anglicans have also offered different dates, though they favor 1054, when the Eastern and Western churches split, and some have put it as late as 1870, when Pope Pius IX declared the infallibility of the pope in faith and morals. Evangelicals often date the apostasy to the first few centuries, on the grounds that no development in Christian teaching past biblical times is valid. But both the creeds and the canon of the Bible itself (the books properly to be included in the Bible) were confirmed by the bishops of the Christian, Catholic, Orthodox church in the 300s and 400s. And both Luther and Calvin drew strongly from Saint Augustine (354-410). If the alleged apostasy occurred before 400, there's no guarantee that the Bible as we have it contains the correct books; if it happened after 400, by then there was already an organized church under the apostolic authority of the bishops and patriarchs, including the patriarch of Rome (the pope).

Increasingly in the twenty-first century, Catholics and Protestants are finding their common devotion to Jesus more important than their differences.

---

[79]John Micklethwait and Adrian Wooldridge, *God Is Back: How the Global Revival of Faith Is Changing the World* (New York: Penguin, 2009), p. 106.

106. Protestants are heretics.

Protestants are Christians who broke from the Catholic church in the 1500s and those who have followed them since. Heretics are those who deliberately preach and teach contrary to accepted Christian Tradition. Who is a heretic depends in considerable part on point of view. Until the 1960s, Catholics called medieval dissenters heretics, while Protestants called them precursors of the Reformation.

Until the 1960s the Catholic church considered Protestant churches heretical. Some Catholics still imagine that Catholic teaching is exactly the same today as it was two millennia ago. Since the mid-1800s there has been growing realization that in fact the teaching of the churches—whether Catholic, Orthodox or Protestant—has evolved organically over time.[80] The more that understanding grows, the less tendency there is to condemn. Since the second Vatican Council of 1962-65, the Catholic church considers Protestants separated brothers and sisters who accept the truth yet not the full truth. Protestants find this new position less provocative but still condescending. Catholics continue to believe that Protestants needlessly broke the unity of Christ's church. The Orthodox church has taken a less dim view of Protestants because the Orthodox agree with Protestants in blaming Catholic corruption for provoking the Protestant Reformation.

Some Protestants consider other Protestants heretics. Mainstream Protestants often treat as heresy the feel-good idea of Christianity as the road to worldly prosperity.[81] The word "heresy" has popped up in the current schism in the American Episcopalian church. What was lost with the Protestant secession from Rome was a central controlling authority able to set enforceable limits to theological deviation. All of this illustrates the dilemma faced by the church as a human institution. As Brooks Alexander of the Spiritual Counterfeits Project says, a central authority can stop rot at the bottom, but if the top is rotten it can provoke insurrection. These days Christians are less inclined to condemn other Christians, but the urge has hardly disappeared. Efforts toward unity seem to falter for the

---

[80]John Henry Newman, *Essay on the Development of Christian Doctrine* (London: James Toovey, 1845).

[81]Mark Driscoll, "The Emerging Church and Biblicist Theology," in *Listening to the Beliefs of Emerging Churches*, ed. Robert Webber (Grand Rapids: Zondervan, 2007), p. 23.

crude reason that bishops, pastors and other leaders are seldom inclined to yield or even share power.

The church has needed both the spirit of prophets and the spirit of order: prophets to speak out what the Spirit seems to be urging and order to control the extreme swings of prophecy.[82] There is no objective definition of heresy, but to deny that the Bible is revealed and that the creeds express theological truth is in jarring disharmony with Christian Tradition.

107. Orthodox and Catholics worship idols.

One of the Ten Commandments is "You shall not make for yourself a graven image" (Ex 20:4). The veneration of images—statues, paintings, stained glass and other media—is sometimes considered idolatrous. The word "idolatrous" comes from the Greek meaning "worship of images." Common Christian images include the crucifix, scenes from Christ's life, other biblical scenes, and representations of saints or events from saints' lives. Protestant churches are sparing and sometimes devoid of such images on the grounds that they distract from hearing the Bible and the sermons based on it.

Catholic churches usually have many images and Orthodox churches even more. What are Catholics and Orthodox doing with such images?

The central point is technical, but it is an essential distinction between *latreia* (Greek for "worship") and *douleia* (Greek for "veneration" or "respect"). Worship is due only to God. Honor and respect are due to holy persons. Catholics and Orthodox reject *latreia* of anyone other than God and agree with Protestants that worship of images is idolatry. God's creation is holy and is owed veneration, but it is distinct from God, who alone can be worshiped. Catholics and Orthodox give honor (*douleia*) to the saint whom the image represents.

Various attitudes toward images exist within the Christian Tradition. An image may be simply a reminder. An image may remind viewers that Christ was born in a manger or that he died on the cross. Or that Luther was a great reformer. Going further, some believe that by concentrating their thoughts and prayers on an image, they form a certain connection with the person represented.

---

[82]Jeffrey Burton Russell and Douglas W. Lumsden, *History of Medieval Christianity: Prophecy and Order*, 2nd ed. (New York: Peter Lang, 2000).

The Orthodox belief about images centers on their use of icons. The original meaning of the word "icon" is a picture that represents a sacred person—a Person of the Trinity, a saint or an angel. It is "art attempting spirituality . . . [that] captures the characteristics of a holy person or of the spiritual world as directly envisioned by the iconographer" (the painter of the icon).[83] It is not merely a reminder or aid to prayer or meditation. The purpose is not aesthetic but to show the immanent presence of God or the saint. An icon may be beautiful, but its purpose is to convey transcendent power. When an icon is painted with reverence and prayer, it is an opening between the viewer and the holy person depicted, establishing a communion between them.

Historically, attitudes toward icons have varied widely. Christian icons, or at least sacred images, became common beginning in the 300s A.D. During the 700s and 800s in the Byzantine (eastern Roman) Empire, iconoclasts—"breakers of images"—rejected the use of icons and attempted to destroy all of them. Both the Eastern monks and the Western church in general rejected iconoclasm. Curiously, the West gradually ceased using icons, but once they were restored in the East, they became a central part of worship. The first thing that one notices in entering an Orthodox church is the number and beauty of the icons and the reverence that the congregation pays them. Traditional iconography portrays holy persons in a transfigured form. The creativity of the artist, who is usually anonymous, is always subsumed under the transcendent style, because the holy archetypes are considered direct spiritual visions of the other world.

Iconoclasm reappeared during the Protestant Reformation in the Western church in the 1500s and 1600s. Protestants destroyed large numbers of paintings, stained glass and other images that they felt to be idolatrous. Some were simply covered with whitewash, which has allowed some recent restorations.

Even more puzzling to Protestant and secular minds is the importance of relics in Catholic and Orthodox practice. Relics are physical and may consist of the whole body of a holy person or object, or parts of the body or object. Some are authentic, and the extent of fakery has been exaggerated.

---

[83]Personal communication to the author by Archbishop Chrysostomos of Etna, November 24, 2011; Leonid Ouspensky, *The Theology of the Icon* (Crestwood, NJ: St. Vladimir's Seminary Press, 1992).

The joke that there are enough relics of the true cross to build a stadium persists, but actually taking all the pieces even claimed to be from the true cross would produce only enough wood for, well, a cross. A piece of wood or the knucklebone of a saint may not seem to have anything to do with spirituality, but as with icons, the holy person is believed to be spiritually present.[84] There is biblical evidence for the use of relics (2 Kings 2:14; 13:21; Mt 9:20; Acts 19:12). Belief in the power of relics began very early in the church's history, notably in *The Martyrdom of Saint Polycarp* (A.D. 156-157). The use of relics in Christianity also helped refute Gnostic hyperspirituality and anchored Christianity to the inherent goodness of the physical world.

108. Orthodox and Catholics worship Mary.

Protestants often criticize Catholics for worshiping Mary, and Orthodox venerate her even more than Catholics do. To venerate is to honor or revere; to worship is to honor as a deity. Orthodox and Catholic theologians have always distinguished between veneration and worship. They *worship* God and *venerate* Mary and other saints. A few ardent supporters of Mary, particularly from about 1900 to 1960, seemed to go beyond Christian Tradition by calling her "co-redeemer" or otherwise exaggerating her significance to the point of what Protestants call Mariolatry.

Reverence of Mary is centered on her being the mother of Jesus. The Gospel of Matthew says that an angel revealed to her fiancé, Joseph the carpenter, that she was given a child by the Holy Spirit (Mt 1:20-25). The Gospel of Luke says that God sent the archangel Gabriel to announce this fact to her, a virgin engaged to marry Joseph. This is traditionally known as the Annunciation. Gabriel said, "Hail, highly-favored one, the Lord is with you. . . . You will give birth to a son, and you are to name him Jesus." Mary asked how that could be true, since she was a virgin. The angel replied, "The Holy Spirit will come upon you, and the power of the Most High will overshadow you; therefore the child to be born will be holy; he will be called the Son of God" (Lk 1:26-38). When Mary visits her cousin Elizabeth, Elizabeth says, "Blessed are you among women, and blessed is the fruit of your womb" (Lk 1:42).

---

[84]Eire, *Very Brief History*, pp. 54-56.

Mary was venerated as a saint in the earliest church, though not preeminently, but by the beginning of the third century at the latest, she was widely recognized not only as the mother of Jesus but the mother of God (Greek *Theotokos*). Reverence of Mary as God's mother continued to grow throughout the church, both East and West. The Orthodox and Catholics continued this tradition, while the Protestant Reformers believed that the honor due Mary should stop short of veneration.

Less important was her virginity. It is affirmed by the Gospels of Matthew and Luke and has always been taken to confirm that Jesus was the son of God rather than of Joseph (Mt 1:20-23; Lk 1:34). Over the past two centuries, some scholars have disputed her virginity, claiming that the Greek *parthenos* is better translated as "young woman" than as "virgin,"[85] but the normal meaning of the Greek word *parthenos* is "virgin" or "maiden," and in the society of Mary's time a young woman engaged to be married had to be a virgin. The Bible also indicates that Jesus had brothers,[86] but the universal church over the centuries asserted her virginity at the time she conceived Jesus. Theologians through the first few centuries focused on Mary as a model of obedience more than as a virgin, but the emphasis on virginity in the monastic movement of the 300s and 400s helped shift the focus. Since that time a number of theologians have argued that she was perpetually a virgin—that she never had sexual relations and bore no children other than Jesus. The references to the brothers of Jesus in the Bible were taken to mean "relatives" rather than actual brothers. That interpretation was generally accepted from the 400s on but is now doubted, since the exact meaning of the Greek *adelphoi* is not relatives but "brothers" or "siblings." It is possible that they were half-siblings, the children of Joseph with an earlier spouse (Mt 12–13; Mk 3; Lk 8; 21:16, which distinguishes between brothers and relatives; Jn 2; 7).

From at least the 400s it was commonly believed that when Mary died, her soul was immediately taken to heaven, and "soul" meant both her body and her spirit. Like Jesus, she is present in heaven body and spirit. This belief, known as the Assumption or Dormition, was common from the 300s throughout the universal church, which held that Mary was in heaven

---

[85]The Hebrew *almah* of Is 7:14 probably means a young woman who is engaged or about to be engaged.

[86]One is named James (Gal 1:19).

from the moment of her death. In 1950 Pope Pius XII declared it Catholic doctrine. Orthodox generally agree with the idea but have always believed that the Western church, both Catholic and Protestant, spent too much effort defining beliefs and too little time evoking spirituality.

The Immaculate Conception of Mary, a common belief from the 500s on, has been discussed in both the Western and the Eastern church. The Immaculate Conception does not refer to Mary's conception of Jesus. Rather, it refers to the conception of Mary by her own mother, and it does not imply that Mary's mother Anna was a virgin. The idea is that God would choose only a perfect woman to be the mother of his son, so Mary must have been sinless from the time of her conception. In 1854 Pope Pius IX defined the Immaculate Conception as Catholic doctrine.

Catholics and Orthodox have considered Mary the greatest of intercessors with Christ. This means that one can pray to Mary (and other saints) to ask her Son to help us. The rich veneration of Mary during the Middle Ages, especially from 1100 on, gave rise to great cathedrals dedicated to her (*e.g.*, Notre Dame de Paris), hymns to her, and the glorious presentation of her in Dante's *Paradiso* (1321). Protestants believe that this veneration was excessive, but no branch of Christianity permits worship of Mary.[87]

109. Orthodox and Catholics belittle the Bible.

Protestants sometimes think this is so because Catholics and Orthodox believe that the Bible does not stand alone as the guarantor of Christianity. Catholic and Orthodox hold that Christian doctrine developed over time, not in contradiction of the Bible but in opening it up. The Holy Spirit, they believe, protected this development from essential error. In this view, reason, Tradition and experience join with the Bible as the four pillars of the faith. Some Protestant churches—notably the Anglican, Methodist and Lutheran—have held similar views. Many evangelicals believe that the Bible should be followed directly and overtly without interpretation and that development of the tradition sometimes contradicts the Bible and distracts from authentic biblical Christianity.

[87]For a non-Christian view of the history of Mary, see Miri Rubin, *Emotion and Devotion: The Meaning of Mary in Medieval Religious Communities* (New York: Central European University Press, 2009).

Believing that the Bible must stand alone as the only Christian authority, they feel that any other view belittles it.[88]

110. The Catholic church discourages reading the Bible.

It doesn't anymore, but it used to.[89] The first thing to realize is that before about 1500 there were few Bibles to be read—by anybody. Until the invention of the printing press, Bibles had to be copied carefully by hand. A Bible is over a thousand pages in small letters. Through most of the history of Christianity, the only Bibles or portions of the Bible were those laboriously copied by monks. Although from the fourteenth century on there were numerous commercial writing shops employing scribes, even then only well-to-do people could afford to have a Bible.

Western European Bibles in the Middle Ages were usually in Latin. Eastern European Bibles were in Greek, Slavonic or modern languages such as Russian. In the West only educated people could read Latin, and until the fourteenth century almost all educated people were clergy. The clergy were supposed to read the Bible and interpret it in sermons in the language of the people. The effect was that few people could read the Bible for themselves, and the situation was encouraged by the medieval church for fear that ignorant people would mistranslate and misinterpret it. The enormous spread of biblical literacy from the 1500s onward was due to the Protestant emphasis on the Bible, to translations into modern languages, and to the invention of printing, which meant that Bibles could be owned by all.

Medieval Christians, though seldom possessing Bibles, were generally well-versed in the biblical message. Through sermons, liturgy, statues, stained glass, paintings, poems, drama and music such as chants, hymns and devotional songs, the ordinary Christian had a good grasp of biblical events—much more so than most literate people do today. I know of someone with a Ph.D. in medieval history who was utterly baffled by a literary reference to the burning bush, whereas most me-

[88]Jeffrey Burton Russell, *Paradise Mislaid: How We Lost Heaven and How We Can Regain It* (New York: Oxford University Press, 2006), pp. 15-16.

[89]Susan Boynton and Diane J. Reilly, *Practice of the Bible in the Middle Ages: Production, Reception, and Performance in Western Christianity* (New York: Columbia University Press, 2011).

dieval illiterates would have understood it immediately. In the Orthodox East, Bible stories were contained in icons. The Orthodox liturgy is a recapitulation of the words of the gospel. Because the Eastern church tended to celebrate the liturgy in the language of the people, scriptural readings in the liturgy were easily understandable. As for theological writing, in both the Eastern and Western churches the vast majority consisted of commentaries on the Bible (or commentaries on those commentaries) until the twelfth century.[90]

From the twelfth to the sixteenth century, Catholic authorities tried to restrict reading of the Bible to those who had been properly trained. This movement was influenced by the growth of universities and the logical philosophies associated with them. A person was obliged to have a license to teach or to preach, and such licenses, granted after years of study, were controlled by the universities. It was thought that only highly educated people should have Bibles because only they could interpret them correctly. The reason for the restriction was that many people who had read the Bible—or bits of it—were teaching ideas contrary to established orthodoxy. The more people who got hold of a Bible, it was thought, the more misinformation there would be.

In the Christian East, where Protestantism had little impact on popular piety or theology, the Bible was understood as a product of the authority of the church. Orthodox Christians affirm that the Bible and Tradition are not separate sources of authority; rather, they complement one another as organic features of Christianity. The reality of Scripture exists, they believe, in its recapitulation in each individual believer and in the life of the church.

111. THE CATHOLIC CHURCH IS MONOLITHIC.

The Catholic church never has been monolithic (solid and homogeneous), and it certainly isn't today. Some Catholics believe that the pope has always been the highest authority in Christianity, and some Protestants think the papacy had absolute power over the church before the Protestant Reformation, but neither view is correct. Until the year 1054 there was only one church: the Christian, Catholic, Orthodox and Apostolic church. But that

[90]See the series Ancient Christian Commentary on Scripture, ed. Thomas C. Oden (Downers Grove, IL: InterVarsity Press); for example, Alberto Ferreiro, ed., *The Twelve Prophets* (2003).

church was not monolithic. From A.D. 100-450 there were numerous dissenters, for example Gnostics, Arians, Monophysites, Nestorians, Manicheans, Donatists and more.[91] The Council of Chalcedon (451) settled the basic beliefs of the church—the Trinity and the nature of Christ as both fully human and fully divine—but a number of communities did not accept Chalcedon, and the Oriental churches in Egypt, Ethiopia, Armenia, Iraq and Syria still do not.

In 1054 a formal schism (Greek *schisma*, "tearing") occurred between the Western church centered in Rome and the Eastern church centered in Constantinople. The alienation between the two halves of the church had been growing ever since the Muslim conquests of Christian Africa and Asia had made communication through the Mediterranean difficult. In the 600s, the Byzantine emperor also maintained control over Rome, summoning disobedient popes to Constantinople, sometimes in chains. But by the 700s the Muslim invasions shattered both Byzantine power and church communications, and the imperial possessions in Italy were reduced to a few outposts, including Rome. The collapse of Byzantine economic and military power made it difficult to protect these possessions in Italy, so the citizens of Rome, tired of paying taxes to the emperor without getting the necessary protection in return, revolted and asked the pope to assume civil as well as religious authority. The alienation of Rome from Constantinople increased when the popes came to rely on a close alliance with the Franks (forerunners of the modern French and Germans). In 800, the pope crowned the Frankish ruler Charlemagne as emperor, a direct challenge to the emperor in Constantinople.

Beginning in the 1050s the popes launched a vast reform movement aimed at eliminating corruption and ignorance and repressing heresies. In order to advance this program, popes (especially Gregory VII, r. 1073-1085) increased their direct control over the churches in the West. It was the effort to bring Constantinople into this newly centralized papal system that was the final straw. The two patriarchs of Rome and Alexandria excommunicated one another in 1054, a mutual

[91]Monophysites believe that Christ has only one nature: the divine (1P1N); Nestorians believe that Christ has two separate natures, the human and the divine (2P2N); the orthodox view is that Christ has two natures in one Person (1P2N). Manicheans were dualists believing in a struggle between a good god and an evil god; Donatists believed that clergy who committed apostasy were never to be allowed to administer the sacraments again.

excommunication lifted only in 1965. Though both churches continued to be both Orthodox and Catholic, the Western church emphasized the term "Catholic," while the Eastern church emphasized the term "Orthodox." The Catholic church then remained relatively united (with many theological and jurisdictional disputes) until the 1500s. The excommunication of Martin Luther in 1521 marked the beginning of the third major part of Christianity, Protestantism.

The rise of papal authority was gradual from the beginning. There was no doubt in the early church that Rome was one of the five great patriarchates—Jerusalem, Antioch, Alexandria, Constantinople and Rome—and the patriarch of Rome was sometimes consulted by churches in the East as well as in the West. However, it was not until the Council of Chalcedon in 451 that the pope had pronounced influence on the ecumenical councils. From the 300s, the term "pope" (Greek *pappas*, "father") was commonly used for bishops in general (and is still used for priests in the Eastern church), but by the eleventh century in the West it was applied exclusively to the bishop of Rome.

Rome was naturally important because it had been the center of the Roman Empire and because the Apostle Saint Peter, the head of the Christian community, had been martyred and buried there. The biblical text most frequently cited as the basis of papal supremacy is Christ's statement to the apostle Simon Peter, "You are Peter, and on this rock [*petra*, Greek "rock"] I will build my church" (Mt 16:18). Some Protestants argue that "this rock" pertains to Jesus rather than to Peter, but that dismisses the intentional wordplay. It seems clear that Jesus meant the rock to be Peter. Catholics and Orthodox believe that Peter's successors are the bishops of Rome (the popes).

The authority of all the bishops derives from apostolic succession, the idea that the apostles chose others to replace them, and those chose still others, and so down through time in unbroken succession. "The church," said Bishop Cyprian of Carthage (d. 258), "is bound together by the cement of the bishops, who adhere together."

Bishops sometimes disagreed with one another, and no bishop had preeminent authority, though some were more influential than others according to the size of the city where they lived. Ignatius of Antioch (A.D. 35-107) and Irenaeus (130-200) suggested that special authority inhered in the Roman church. When the bishops of the whole church met in ecumenical councils (seven councils altogether, according to the Orthodox, and twenty-one according to the Catholics), their decisions were considered to be protected from error by the Holy Spirit. The first council of Constantinople in 381 declared the patriarchs of Constantinople and Rome to be co-equal, but Pope Innocent I (r. 401-417) argued that all the bishops derived their authority from the successor of Saint Peter—namely, the bishop of Rome. The same argument was made by the Roman delegation to the Council of Ephesus in 431, and it was asserted fully by Pope Leo I "the Great" (r. 440-461), who said that the bishop of Rome had power (*potestas*) over the other bishops; he also assumed the title *pontifex maximus* (in Christian context meaning the "greatest bishop"). "Although there are many priests and many pastors," Leo said, "Peter rules all whom Christ rules." By 1054 the popes had increased their practical power in the West to match their theoretical authority. The title "pope" had been commonly used for the bishop of Rome since the 600s; by the 1100s the Western church reserved the title to him exclusively.[92] The popes were also patriarchs of the West, bishops of the "apostolic see" (by 600), metropolitans of central Italy, defenders of the city of Rome, and dukes of Rome, and they held an increasing amount of land called "the patrimony of Peter." Powerful popes such as Gregory VII and Innocent III (r. 1198-1216) established what was almost a papal monarchy in the West.

However, by the time of Pope Boniface VIII (r. 1294-1303), the growing power of secular kings and princes shifted the balance, and the king of France was able to kidnap Boniface and begin a century of French control of the papacy, which was moved from Rome to Avignon in 1309-1377.[93] In the 1400s, the conciliar movement attempted to bring the pope back under the control of the ecumenical councils. In the 1500s, the Protestant Reformers denied the authority of the pope altogether. In England, William Tyndale in 1534 used the term "popery" for Catholicism, and Catholics were outlawed in the reign of Elizabeth I (r. 1558-1603); it is still illegal for a Catholic to be monarch of the United Kingdom. After the wars of religion in the 1500s and 1600s, Western Europe was divided by religion according to the will of the princes. Protestant rulers established

[92]In Greece, the term traditionally denotes any priest.
[93]Walter Ullmann, *Short History of the Papacy in the Middle Ages* (London: Methuen, 1972).

Protestantism in one form or another (for example Lutheranism in Scandinavia and Anglicanism in England) in their territories, and Catholic rulers (for example the kings of France and Spain) established Catholicism in theirs.

Meanwhile, the Catholic church launched its own reform movement at the long Council of Trent (1545-1563). In the 1800s and 1900s, disagreements continued in the Catholic church—for example, over the role of the pope and his alleged infallibility, over the degree to which the church should engage with contemporary non-Catholic thought, and over the degree to which it should isolate itself as a bastion against modern errors. Despite persistent arguments between conservatives and "modernists," the church achieved a relative degree of homogeneity from the time of the first Vatican Council (1869-1870) until the second Vatican Council (1962-1965). From the 1960s onward, tensions between modernists and traditionalists have grown, and Popes John Paul II and Benedict XVI have tried to achieve balance and restore order. The Catholic church has never been homogeneous.[94]

112. PURGATION IS NOT AN EARLY CHRISTIAN IDEA.

Purgatory (from Latin *purgare*, "to cleanse") is based on the idea of purgation, which is supported by some biblical passages (Mal 3:2-3; 1 Cor 3:11-15). A very few people are pure and whole enough to enter heaven immediately; many have corrupted themselves so much that they have destroyed their capability of ever experiencing God. The basic idea of purgation is that most people are in between: they love God but have flaws. If they are to experience the vision of the Lord of the universe, they must be without fault, so a moment of cleansing is necessary. Early on, this cleansing was usually thought of as a painful purification by fire. Saint Augustine (354-430) said it was more painful than any experience in this life, and Gregory the Great (r. 590-604) agreed. In the early church both East and West it was common practice for the living to say prayers for the deceased in order to mitigate this pain. The purification, however painful, made one clean and perfect enough to enter into the vision of God (beatific vision).

---

[94]Geoffrey Barraclough, *Medieval Papacy* (New York: Harcourt Brace & World, 1968).

Over the years Christians have disagreed as to what point in the human narrative from conception to union with God this cleansing occurs. Most of the earliest Christians believed that the end of the world, the second coming of Christ and purgation were imminent. The Bible allowed no doubt that fiery pain would accompany the end (among many examples, Mt 3:12; 13:40-50; Mk 9:43-49; Rev 10–21). A century later, after many people had died and been buried, it became clear that the end was not coming as soon as had been thought, so the early theologians had to consider the interim state between the deceased's death and the end of the world. One answer was that the body and spirit were separated until the last judgment; another was that the deceased would experience an immediate personal judgment at the moment of death. In this scenario, purgation could occur immediately or happen gradually until the last judgment.[95]

This last view, placing purgation in time, generally prevailed in the Western church. It implied that the spirits of the dead were still inside time and that therefore they were waiting for the reunion with their bodies. And since they were somehow in time, they were also in some sort of place. Since everyone agreed that purgation was painful, the idea predominated that the spirits of the dead suffered while they waited.

Ideas of purgatory were discussed as early as the second century.[96] From then onward, it was a common idea in both the Eastern and Western churches. In the 1100s and 1200s it became a fixed doctrine in the West, when the tripartite division of the other world into heaven, purgatory and hell became clearly defined. By that time, purgatory was linked closely with the idea of penance. Penance (Latin *poena*, "pain" or "punishment") is a combination of repentance and reconciliation. It is the means of getting right with God by confessing sins and praying to refrain from them in future. By the twelfth century it was increasingly believed that just as in this life people did penance for their sins, so the spirits of the dead did penance until they were purified. The "place" and "time" where they did so got the name "purgatory." Purgatory was one of the doctrines firmly

[95]Russell, *History of Heaven*, pp. 48-49.

[96]Josephine Laffin, "What Happened to the Last Judgement?" in *Church, the Afterlife and the Fate of the Soul,* ed. Peter Clarke and Tony Claydon (Woodbridge, UK: Boydell, 2009), pp. 27-30; Matthew Dal Santo, "Philosophy, Hagiology and the Early Byzantine Origins of Purgatory," in *Church, the Afterlife and the Fate of the Soul*, pp. 41-51.

rejected by the Protestant reformers in the 1500s.

The idea of purgatory was from the beginning intimately connected with prayers for the dead. It was believed that just as prayers for living persons were effective, prayers for the dead helped their spirits complete their sentences in purgatory. By doing penance here on earth you could reduce your sentence in purgatory, and you could even apply your own penance to release your friends and relatives. By 1300 purgatory was so established that Dante (1265-1321) could without hesitation divide his portrait of the afterlife in the *Divine Comedy* into three sections describing hell, purgatory and heaven.

Purgatory bridges the gulf between damnation and salvation. But the idea came to be misused. Different sorts of penances that you could perform for the dead developed, including pilgrimages, numerous prayers, abstinence from worldly comforts—and, eventually, payment of money. Money inevitably corrupted the whole idea. By the 1500s the abuse had reached scandalous proportions as clerical con artists promised release of loved ones from purgatory on payment of gold or silver.

The Protestant Reformers were revolted by such scandals. So were the Catholic Reformers at the Council of Trent (1545-1563), but the Protestant Reformers abolished the idea of purgatory altogether, observing that it did not derive clearly enough from the Bible. The abolition of purgatory removed indulgences from Protestantism. Still, the early Christians had changed the ancient separation of the dead and the living by bringing past and present into the one body of Christ: the dead are not remote but are always with us. The Protestant Reformation, while removing abuses, also had the effect of reducing the strong conviction people held of solidarity with the dead, their sense that they were in communion with their deceased friends and family and with the whole Christian community in space and time. "According to Protestant eschatology, the dead are no longer with us . . . 'gone beyond the reach of human contact, even of human prayer.'"[97]

The Eastern Orthodox church never had a defined idea of purgatory, and almost all Protestants continue to reject it. Recent Catholic theologians also tend to treat the time and space of purgatory metaphorically,

---

[97]Eire, *Very Brief History*, pp. 86, 104-56; Frans Ciappara, "Strategies for the Afterlife in Eighteenth-Century Malta," in *Church, the Afterlife and the Fate of the Soul*, p. 301.

preferring to think of it as a state of being. The "moment" of cleansing has been compared to the timeless quantum leap of a physical particle from one state to another. Most Christians continue to believe that some sort of cleansing is necessary before meeting God.

113. Catholics invented the sign of the cross.

Many people, especially American Protestants, believe that the sign of the cross—made by touching one's forehead, breast and shoulders while saying, "In the name of the Father, the Son and the Holy Spirit"—was invented by Catholics. Since the 1600s most Protestants have avoided using it for that reason. In reality, the sign of the cross (sometimes made on the forehead only) is ancient and was universal usage in Christianity from at least A.D. 200. It was used in daily prayer, at baptism and at other important events. The Catholic church in the West and the Orthodox church in the East continue this tradition, with the Orthodox touching their right shoulder first and the Catholics their left shoulder first. It indicates a prayer, a blessing, a commemoration, a recommitment, a sign of gratitude. It is a sort of body language, a gesture in lieu of speech, an act that is an outward sign of inward prayer and commitment.

114. Protestants had no reason to divide the church.

The church at its deepest level is the union of all believers in Christ in one indivisible community. On earth, however, there have been a number of important divisions. In 1054 the Eastern and Western halves of the church were divided, and in the 1500s the Western church was further divided when the Protestant Reformation renounced the authority of the pope. Both divisions persist at present.

The causes of the Protestant Reformation of the 1500s were diverse. Among the more important were the growth of cities, commerce and literacy; the invention of the printing press, which made the Bible available to many; the Renaissance emphasis on humanity more than on divinity; the legacy of the movement of personal spirituality that had flowered in the 1300s and 1400s; vivid exchanges of diverse theological ideas; popular movements such as those of the Lollards (followers of John Wycliffe, 1330-1384) and Hussites (followers of Jan Huss, 1372-1415) demanding a simpler, more democratic church; and the worldliness of the popes. The Reformation had almost no impact on Eastern Orthodox Christianity.

The 1400s and early 1500s witnessed a great growth of wealth and secular power in the church. By this time popes and some bishops had become not only spiritual authorities but also secular rulers and thus were responsible for the maintenance, administration and defense of their territories. Since the 700s, when Byzantine power collapsed in Italy, the pope had become ruler of a large swathe of central Italy called the Patrimony of Saint Peter or, later, the Papal States. The archbishop of Liège, as another example, governed a large section of what is now eastern Belgium. Lay rulers, such as the kings of England and France, were also increasing the size of their governments and demanding more money for administration and defense, so they reduced the amount of money the church could raise in their realms. This led the church to find other sources of revenue. To rebuild St. Peter's cathedral in Rome, the popes sanctioned the infamous sale of indulgences, while changes in politics and society undermined the power of the popes and made them defensive. Some (though not most) monasteries also had accumulated great wealth.

Catholic historians have maintained that the abuses could have been addressed and corrected within the structure of the church, as earlier abuses had been by the papal reform movement of 1050-1300. Protestant historians have countered that in the 1500s, unlike the earlier period, the papacy resisted reform instead of supporting it. Catholics have responded by pointing to the sweeping reforms that did occur within the church in that century. Protestants believe that the split was a positive good rather than a necessary evil; Catholics believe that it was not necessary at all. In the church, both prophecy and order are needed: prophecy in the sense of burning zeal, and order to restrain that zeal from extremism. Authority is necessary to prevent abuses, but when the authority is itself abusive, the right of resistance can be invoked.[98]

In the 1500s, the basic issue between Protestants and Catholics was authority. The authority of the pope, councils, bishops and priesthood was openly questioned for the first time since the second century. Until this

[98]Russell and Lumsden, *History of Medieval Christianity*; Steven Ozment, *Age of Reform 1250-1550* (New Haven, CT: Yale University Press, 1980); Lewis Spitz, *Protestant Reformation, 1517-1559* (New York: Harper and Row, 1985).

time the church both East and West had always depended on the bishops' apostolic authority—i.e., the apostles chose people to replace deceased apostles, and those apostles chose others down through the ages. Thus each bishop had authority deriving in an unbroken chain back to Christ. Any bishop could err, but when the bishops were in accord at councils, their authority was accepted. Both East and West accepted the authority of ecumenical councils through the second council of Nicaea in 787. In the Western church, the bishop of Rome, known as the pope, was considered chief among the bishops and had extensive authority.

The formal beginning of the Protestant Reformation is generally said to be the moment when Martin Luther (1483-1546) posted his ninety-five theses on the door of the church at Wittenberg in 1517. The theses centered on the sale of indulgences, but they implied a challenge to papal authority.

The Reformation took three forms. One was the conservative Protestant Reformation—the Reformation of Luther and Calvin—which retained most Catholic theology (including traditional Trinitarian and Christological beliefs), respect for the ecumenical councils and the theologians of the early church (especially Augustine), the nature of heaven and hell and the Devil, the retention of baptism and the Eucharist (Lord's Supper), the centering of worship on the Eucharist, the Bible as revelation (though the canon was altered), original sin, the virgin birth, free will (though modified by Calvin), and the atonement of Christ on the cross. To scholars familiar with late medieval theology, Luther and Calvin look very much like late medieval theologians. The great difference was the rejection of the Catholic structure of authority, particularly the authority of the pope over the church.

The second form was the radical Protestant Reformation characterized by the Anabaptists and Mennonites, who dismissed most existing theology as well as structure and even rejected the priesthood. The third was the Catholic Reformation, which sought to remove abuses without undermining the theology or structure of the church. The most important events of the Reformation were the posting of the Wittenberg theses in 1517, the papal excommunication of Luther as a heretic in 1521, the arrival of the radical Thomas Müntzer in Prague in 1521, the anti-Catholicism and anti-humanism preached by Ulrich Zwingli in Zurich in 1518-1531,

Calvin's publication of the first edition of the *Institutes of the Christian Religion* in 1536 and his subsequent theocratic rule in Geneva from 1541, the Catholic Reformation launched by the Council of Trent in 1545-1563, and the establishment of Anglican Protestantism in England by Elizabeth I (r. 1558-1603).

The most important results of the Protestant Reformation were an emphasis on faith instead of good works, predestination (in Calvin's case), the authority of the Bible over popes and councils, the rejection of bishops (by Calvin and the radicals though not by Lutherans or Anglicans),[99] the elimination of the requirement for clerical celibacy, the suppression of monasticism, limitation of the sacraments to two: baptism and the Eucharist, the elimination of purgatory, and the translation of the Bible into modern languages for everyone to read. On the last point, Luther has often been misunderstood: he did say *sola scriptura* ("Scripture alone") but also "faith alone," "grace alone" and "Christ alone." On most points Luther held to the theological tradition of the church. Lutherans and Anglicans continued to believe that Christ was truly present in the Eucharist, though Luther replaced the Catholic doctrine of transubstantiation with consubstantiation (the distinction is meaningful only in Aristotelian philosophy).[100]

The division of the church remains. It can be seen as a scandal of division or a sign of liberty. What is an obvious scandal and one of the more persuasive atheist arguments is the presence of rage and even hatred among Christians.

115. PROTESTANTISM IS PURITANICAL.

The word "Puritan" (from "purity") was coined in 1546 to apply to Protestants working to replace Anglican (Church of England) rituals with simpler worship, which they considered a purer form of Christianity. From 1571 on it referred specifically to Presbyterians, Scottish followers of the Protestant Reformer John Calvin (1509-64). By 1592 it connoted any Protestant especially strict in doctrine and morals. By the 1800s, American

[99]1 Pet 5:2 calls for *episkopoi* (Greek for "overseers"), or bishops. The word "bishop" derives from *episkopos*.

[100]Gary Macy, "Dogma of Transubstantiation in the Middle Ages," *Journal of Ecclesiastical History* 45 (1994): 11-41.

historians were using the word to refer to the early colonists of New England (who, by the way, consumed prodigious amounts of beer). Currently the word is generally applied to anyone living by a strict code of personal religious standards. Certain Protestant denominations have been called puritanical owing to their strictness about sex, alcohol and dancing; Irish Catholics, influenced by a long tradition of ascetic monasticism, have also been deemed puritanical. Though Puritanism exists in some denominations today, most churches have become more liberal—or more lax, depending on one's point of view.[101]

116. Rome's claim to be central to Christianity is a power play.

Recently the social sciences have established the axiom that the search for power explains human history. Religion is assumed to be "a mechanism by which people's thoughts and lives are controlled or meant to be controlled."[102] Given that axiom, the development of the pope's authority in Rome had to be, along with all other institutions, a power play. However, dominant axioms in the social sciences change every few generations. The power model is partly true, but only partly. All people, including popes, have various motivations. The belief that the pope is at least the nominal leader of Christianity is held by well over half of Christians.

Catholics often imagine that the authority of the pope is the same now as it was nearly two millennia ago, while Protestants suppose that there was a time when the pope broke with true Christianity. In fact, the authority of the pope was minuscule in the first three centuries, and on the other hand it developed without a break from then to the present. Authority developed over time as Christians searched for an authority that would legitimately represent Christ on earth. The underlying basis of papal authority is apostolic succession, the idea that the earliest bishops were chosen by the apostles and that they in turn appointed others in an unbroken line to the present. In this theory all bishops have apostolic succession, but since individual bishops can make serious mistakes, there must be an authority to supervise the bishops. The ecumenical (universal)

---

[101]John Morgan, *Godly Learning: Puritan Attitudes towards Reason, Learning, and Education 1560-1640* (New York: Cambridge University Press, 1986).

[102]Ecklund, *Science vs. Religion*, p. 21. On p. 123 Ecklund notes the power of elite scientists.

councils of bishops exercised this authority in the early centuries; later the bishops of Rome (popes) gradually claimed authority over other bishops. Catholics believe that papal authority began with Christ's words to the Apostle Saint Peter: "You are Peter, and upon this rock [Greek *petra*] I will found my church" (Mt 16:18). Since Peter was the leader of the Christian community of Rome, his successors were the bishops of Rome, who came to have primacy above all bishops and the whole church. Protestants argue that whatever legitimacy Peter's claim once had was forfeited by later popes. Orthodox grant the pope high honor but do not accept his jurisdiction.

Here are some important landmarks in the development of papal authority: Pope Calixtus I (r. A.D. 217-222) was the first pope known to cite the "Petrine theory" that the bishops of Rome had preeminent authority as successors of Peter. Innocent I (r. 410-417) said that all bishops derived their authority from Peter's successor, the pope. Gregory I (r. 590-604) decreed that the pope was to be elected by "the clergy, senate, and people." Gregory II (r. 715-731) and Gregory III (r. 731-741) freed Rome from the power of the emperor in Constantinople. Benedict II (r. 1032-1045) represents the low point of the papacy: chosen by Roman nobles, he wallowed in gross sins and abdicated only when bribed. Leo IX (r. 1048-1054) launched the movement of papal reform in morals and education; in 1054 the schism between the Western and Eastern churches began. Gregory VII (r. 1073-1085) asserted that the Roman church was the church and had universal authority over the whole Christian community, that the pope had the authority to depose bishops and secular rulers, and that there could be no legitimate council without papal approval. Innocent III (r. 1198-1216) represented the height of papal power, declaring that "the authority of the apostolic see [the bishop of Rome] is so extreme that nothing can reasonably be determined in all the affairs of the church except by the authority of the pope." Boniface VIII (r. 1294-1303) attempted to carry these claims even further but ended up being kidnapped and exiled by the French kings, who then controlled the papacy from 1309 to 1377.

Then came a forty-year schism between 1377 and 1417, when two (and at one point even three) popes claimed power. This schism was followed by the conciliar movement, which sought to establish the authority of the ecumenical councils over that of the pope.[103] In 1521, Leo X (r. 1513-1521) excommunicated Martin Luther, after which the split between Catholics and Protestants developed. In 1870, under the influence of Pius IX (r. 1846-1878), the first Vatican Council declared the pope infallible in matters of faith and morals. The second Vatican Council (1962-1965) reaffirmed papal authority but granted more independence to the bishops, clergy and laity. John Paul II (r. 1978-2005) and Benedict XVI (r. 2005-), though hampered by the failure of many bishops to remove sex offenders from the clergy, have sought to achieve moral reform and restore traditional doctrine.

117. Pentecostals, evangelicals, fundamentalists and Creationists are all the same.

These groups are not the same, though they are interconnected. And because they are in continual flux, any picture of them—including this one—can be only a blurry snapshot. In very rough terms, evangelicals produced fundamentalists, who produced Pentecostals, who became "Creationists."

The word "evangelical" was first applied to Lutherans, Lutherans and Calvinists together, or to Protestants generally. Evangelicals were devoted to the Bible and emphasized social justice, leading both missionary and anti-slavery movements, and made exclusive claims for Christianity relative to other religions. In the 1920s, the movement split between moderate and conservative factions, the moderates being open to modern culture and science and the conservatives suspicious of them. Conservatives such as Billy Graham (1918-) stressed personal experience, rebirth in the Holy Spirit (being "born again"), the inerrancy of the Bible, and individual reading of the Bible guided by the Holy Spirit. In America, conservative evangelicals were tied to political populism and distrust of government. Moderate evangelicals drifted toward the traditional Protestant denominations, while the conservatives moved toward fundamentalism.[104]

Fundamentalism in the strict sense refers to the movement beginning in 1895 and growing from 1900 to 1920. Reacting against modernism and

---

[103]Walter Ullmann, *Growth of Papal Government in the Middle Ages*, 2nd ed. (London: Methuen, 1962).

[104]Randall J. Stephens and Karl W. Giberson, *The Anointed: Evangelical Truth in a Secular Age* (Cambridge, MA: Belknap Press, 2011).

liberalism, it also connected with populist fear of "un-American" influences such as Jews, Catholics, big government, secularism and anything else that threatened the idea of America as a Protestant nation. Fundamentalists upheld the "fundamentals" (core beliefs) of Christianity: the inerrancy of the Bible, the divinity of Christ, the virgin birth, the atonement, the resurrection of Jesus, and the second coming of Jesus. There is no fundamentalist church, but fundamentalism strongly influenced Baptists, Presbyterians, Lutherans and other denominations. From the 1920s and 1930s fundamentalism became suspicious of science, especially of evolution, and that helped produced creationism.

All Christians believe that God created the cosmos, but the term "Creationist" has come to refer specifically to a variety of Christian belief that began in the 1920s. It is generally, and mistakenly, thought that Christians opposed Darwin's theory of evolution early on. They did not: the vast majority of Protestants and Catholics accepted the idea that evolution was part of God's maintaining and developing the universe in general and life in particular. Asa Gray, the great American botanist (1810-1888), called himself "a Darwinian, philosophically a convinced theist, and religiously an acceptor of [the Nicene Creed] as the exponent of Christian faith."[105] This continues to be the position of most Protestants today. As for the Catholic church, not only did it not condemn evolution, it specifically affirmed it.[106]

The "war" between science and Christianity is a myth. However, in the 1920s conservative fundamentalists began to reject evolution because it seemed to contradict the creation story in the book of Genesis. Creationism arose out of Seventh-Day Adventism and the works of George McCready Price (1870-1963), and it gained huge popularity after the publication in 1961 of *The Genesis Flood* by John C. Whitcomb Jr., and Henry M. Morris. This book claimed that the earth was less than ten thousand years old and that fossils were laid down by Noah's flood. Creationists

---

[105]Mark Noll, *Scandal of the Evangelical Mind* (Grand Rapids: Eerdmans, 1994), p. 179; Martin E. Marty, *Fundamentalism and Evangelicalism* (New York: K. G. Saur, 1993); George S. Marsden, *Fundamentalism and American Culture* (New York: Oxford University Press, 2006).

[106]Benedict XVI, *Creation and Evolution* (San Francisco: Ignatius Press, 2007); "Evolution Doesn't Contradict Bible, Cardinal Affirms," *Zenit*, Nov. 3, 2008 <www.zenit.org/article-24145?l=english>; Benedict XVI, "No Opposition Between Faith's Understanding of Creation and the Evidence of the Empirical Sciences," *Zenit*, Oct. 31, 2008 <www.zenit.org/article-24120?l=english>.

invented "creation science," which is based on the premise of a young earth, denial of evolution and rejection of the Big Bang. All this was inevitably and furiously refuted by the scientific establishment, which in turn became ever more radical in asserting an atheist view of evolution and denying the compatibility of religion and evolution. Enraged hostility between these two extremes has increased drastically ever since, widening gaps into chasms. The public attention paid to the extremes has obscured the moderates, and it has left much of the public with the false idea that one must choose between evolution and Creationism.

Pentecostal ideas began with John Nelson Darby (1800-1882), and the Scofield Reference Bible of 1909[107] became the theological basis of Pentecostalism. Pentecostalism may have sprung up independently in various places, but the most influential movement was the 1906 Azusa Street Revival in Los Angeles, initiated by William J. Seymour (1870-1922), an African-American lapsed Catholic, and popularized by Aimee Semple McPherson (1890-1944). The word *Pentecostal* is derived from Greek *pentekoste* (fifty days) based on ancient Israelite tradition and modified in Christianity to mean the seventh Sunday after Easter. That day traditionally celebrates the moment when the Holy Spirit came to the apostles in the form of "tongues of fire" (Acts 2:1-4). The crucial difference between fundamentalists and Pentecostals is that whereas fundamentalists emphasize the authority of the Bible, Pentecostals emphasize the direct illumination of the Holy Spirit within. They emphasize personal experience of Jesus and the Spirit, spontaneity, glossolalia (speaking in unknown languages), divine healings, exorcism and the immediacy of the second coming of Christ. The largest Pentecostal denomination in the United States is the Assemblies of God; others are the Church of God and the Church of God in Christ.[108] Pentecostalism also influenced Protestant and Catholic congregations in the 1960s to 1980s in what is known as the charismatic movement (from Greek *charisma*, "the gift of grace").

The belief that the end times are near has had a number of spin-offs, including belief in the rapture, in which faithful Christians will be taken

[107]*Scofield Reference Bible* (Oxford: Oxford University Press, 1909).

[108]William K. Kay, *Pentecostalism: A Very Short Introduction* (New York: Oxford University Press, 2011); Amos Yong, *In the Days of Caesar: Pentecostalism and Political Theology* (Grand Rapids: Eerdmans, 2010).

up bodily to heaven from their daily lives (based on 1 Thess 4:13-18). Another variety of the evangelical movement is dispensationalism, which claims that the end will come when all Christians are taken into heaven and the whole planet is ruled by the state of Israel.[109] This relatively small but vocal and growing movement affects American foreign policy. Pentecostalism and dispensationalism have been spreading rapidly in developing countries, and there are now hundreds of millions of Pentecostals and charismatics of other denominations.[110]

A new phenomenon, the "Emergent," "Emerging" or "Emergence" church, has appeared, but the term is being used in so many different ways that it resists definition.[111]

118. Christianity has no spiritual tradition as Eastern religions do.

Most young non-Christians regard Christianity as lacking in spirituality.[112] Spirituality appears in most religions of the world, certainly including Christianity. The word has an absolutely different meaning from spiritualism, which refers to contacting the dead through séances and other magical means. Spirituality emphasizes individual religious experience on a level deeper than that of the intellect and the emotions. It refers to the encounter with the divine that fulfills the meaning, purpose and being of the individual, rendering him or her holy and whole. In the 1960s and 1970s many young people sought visions or other manifestations, but in Christianity one does not seek to enjoy (much less boast about) experiences. Whatever manifestations may occur along the way are extra gifts and never to be sought in themselves. In Christian Tradition, spirituality is neither ego-centered nor (as in Buddhism) ego-eliminating. Whereas in Buddhism the ego is dissolved, in Christianity one is brought into the closest contact with God possible in this life. Christians believe that this

---

[109]Noll, *Scandal of the Evangelical Mind*; William K. Kay, *Pentecostalism* (London: SCM Press, 2009); R. G. Robins, *Pentecostalism in America* (Westport, CT: Praeger, 2010).

[110]Micklethwait and Wooldridge, *God Is Back*, p. 217.

[111]Scott McKnight, "McLaren Emerging," *Christianity Today* (September 2008): 59-66; Phil Snider, ed., *The Hyphenateds: How Emergence Christianity Is Re-traditioning Mainline Practices* (St. Louis: Chalice Press, 2011).

[112]David Kinnaman and Gabe Lyons, *unChristian: What a New Generation Really Thinks About Christianity* (Grand Rapids: Baker, 2007), p. 123.

contact is a state of pure joy. One prepares for it by prayer, meditation on Christ and the Bible, and contemplation, which is opening the soul completely to God without an agenda of any kind. The Eastern Orthodox call this *theosis* or *theopoiesis* "becoming God," which really means God becoming us: not the exaltation of ourselves but the complete filling of ourselves with God.

In Christianity, spirituality can be practiced by anyone, but historically it was centered in the monasteries and hermitages where people withdrew to focus on God. Some people claim that monastics are selfish, antisocial people, but monastics have always believed that their prayers were their labor for the entire community. *Orare est laborare*, "to pray is to work," is a Latin pun. Of course, if one believes that prayers are worthless, then prayer of any sort is a waste of time. For hundreds of years, from about 450 to 1050, monasteries also were the only refuge for the sick and the poor; they were the only places where ancient learning—both Christian and secular—was preserved and copied; they served as hospitals, schools, producers and distributors of food and clothing to the needy, and rest stops for travelers and refugees from war. Their work was long, intense and often grueling. Anyone living through a monastic week is unlikely to find it fun. Monasticism began with Anthony (A.D. 251-356), Pachomius (290-346) and other desert fathers and mothers—people who withdrew from society in order to struggle against the worldly preoccupations on behalf of bringing everyone closer to the reality of God. In Eastern Orthodoxy contemplation is called *theoria*, producing knowledge of God, closeness to God and union with God. Contemplation is constantly opening oneself to God until at last it is not us ascending to God but rather God descending to us.

The first great theologian of the contemplative tradition, Dionysius (about A.D. 500), called it "mysticism," but this word has been devalued and now connotes all kinds of weird ideas.[113] Besides Dionysius, great Christian contemplatives include John Climacus (570-649), Maximus Confessor (580-662), Bernard of Clairvaux (1090-1153), Bonaventure (1217-1274), Meister Eckhart (1260-1328), Gregory Palamas (1296-1359), the anonymous author of *The Cloud of Unknowing* (about 1340), Julian of Norwich (1342-1416), Teresa of Ávila (1515-1582), John of the Cross (1505-1560),

[113]Dionysius is usually known as Pseudo-Dionysius the Areopagite because his real identity is unknown.

William Law (1686-1761) and Thomas Merton (1915-1968).[114]

Bonaventure defined contemplative theology when he stated that God is not only what we know but that by which we know; it is by having faith that we can have true knowledge, and without faith knowledge is vain and easily twisted. The essence of contemplation is love—our love for other people, the cosmos and God as well as God's love for the cosmos. The author of *The Cloud of Unknowing* understood that between humans and God there is a thick cloud of unknowing that cannot be penetrated by the intellect, but only by the dart of longing love.[115] Despite the emphasis on the Bible and doctrine in both Catholic and Protestant churches, spirituality has always been a strong undercurrent and easily accessible with only a little effort; in the Orthodox churches it remains the mainstream.

119. Christians believe that they eat the body of Jesus.

The two actions that most characterized earliest Christianity were baptism and the Eucharist (also called the Lord's Supper, Holy Communion, the Mass and the Divine Liturgy). These two actions were known as sacraments (Latin *sacramenta*, Greek *mysteria*).[116] Augustine (354-430) famously called the sacraments "visible signs of invisible grace." A modern theologian observes that Christ is present everywhere but that there are some actions in which he is especially present, where the intersection of God and human is especially strong.[117] The word "Eucharist" comes from the Greek *eucharisto*: "to give thanks." It is based on numerous passages in the New Testament

---

[114]Lest these authors seem rare examples of Christian spirituality, here are more—both men and women as well as Orthodox, Catholic and Protestant, presented chronologically: Origen, Ephraim the Syrian, Gregory of Nyssa, Symeon the New Theologian, Hildegard of Bingen, Francis of Assisi, Hadewijch, Mechtild of Magdeburg, Nicholas of Cusa, Marguerite Porete, Ignatius Loyola, Martin Luther, Jacob Boehme, Francis de Sales, George Herbert, John Donne, Blaise Pascal and many others. Among contemporary books on Christian spirituality are Archbishop Chrysostomos, *Flowers from the Desert* (Etna, CA: C.T.O.S., 2003); Tim Vivian, *Journeying into God* (Minneapolis: Fortress, 1996); Richard Foster and Gayle D. Beebe, *Longing for God: Seven Paths of Christian Devotion* (Downers Grove, IL: InterVarsity Press, 2009). The most thorough study of western spirituality is Bernard McGinn, *Presence of God: A History of Western Christian Mysticism*, 3 vols. (New York: Crossroad, 1991-1998).

[115]*Cloud of Unknowing* (New York: Paulist, 1981).

[116]The total number of sacraments has ranged from two to seven, depending on times and denominations. The Roman Catholic Church has seven: baptism, the Eucharist, holy orders (ordination of priests), confirmation, marriage, penance (confession) and the anointing of the sick.

[117]N. T. Wright, *Simply Christian: Why Christianity Makes Sense* (New York: HarperOne, 2006).

(Mt 26:26-28; Mk 14:22-24; Lk 22:17-20; 1 Cor 11:23-26). At the Last Supper, Jesus says of the bread that he is handing round the table, "Take and eat: this is my body," and of the wine, "This is my blood." The original Greek is explicit: *touto esti to soma mou; touto esti to haima mou* (*esti* means "precisely is"). There was no doubt in the universal church from the beginning that Jesus was really present in the Eucharist: this belief in the "real presence" is the universal teaching of traditional Christianity.

How Christ is really present, though, is debated. The Orthodox church prefers to leave it a mystery and to consider the whole Divine Liturgy the manifestation of the presence rather than emphasizing a moment of consecration. Catholics and Protestants sought to define it more, and the more they did so, the more diverse opinions appeared. The Catholic Fourth Lateran Council (1215) and Thomas Aquinas (1225-1272) supported the doctrine of transubstantiation, which says that the substance of the bread and wine changes at the moment of consecration (when the priest says the words "This is my body. . . . This is my blood"). Although the bread and wine continue to appear to be bread and wine, their underlying substance has become the body and blood of Christ. In this view the Eucharistic host (consecrated bread) continues to be the body and blood even after the Mass is over.

Martin Luther (1483-1546) condemned transubstantiation and substituted the idea of "consubstantiation," in which the consecrated bread and wine are both bread and wine and the body and blood of Christ. Both interpretations depend on Aristotelian philosophy, so neither is a necessary way of defining how Christ is present. The Eastern Orthodox avoid both. Benedict XVI (r. 2005-) makes the point that the consecration is not a "quasi-magical command," but rather the church "praying in and with Jesus."[118] Ulrich Zwingli (1484-1531) considered the Lord's Supper as a memorial, for Jesus said, "Do this in memory of me" (Lk 22:19). John Calvin (1509-1564) denied both transubstantiation and consubstantiation, arguing that the bread and wine remained bread and wine, though Christ was spiritually present so that the person taking communion in good faith benefited. So many different views developed that some people could believe Christians ate and digested the physical body of Jesus.

---

[118]Benedict XVI, *Jesus of Nazareth: Holy Week: From the Entrance into Jerusalem to the Resurrection* (San Francisco: Ignatius, 2011), p. 128.

120. Christians believe that Jesus created the world.

This idea does not come readily to most Christian minds today, but before the Renaissance the Creator of the world was sometimes shown in artworks as Jesus rather than God the Father. The idea is that the Son of God is God, and the Son is the Word (the *Logos*), the creative principle, one of the Persons of the Trinity. According to the Gospel of John, "In the beginning was the Word, and the Word was with God, and the Word was God. He was in the beginning with God. All things came into being through him" (Jn 1:1-3). In the human sense of time, there was a time before Christ was born, but in eternity the Son and the Holy Spirit were always with the Father. Because the Son became human in Jesus, it is appropriate to think of Jesus as the Creator of the cosmos—not in his human nature but in his divine nature.[119] The creeds say that it is through the action of the Son that the Trinity pours forth the created cosmos: I believe "in one Lord Jesus Christ, the only begotten Son of God, born of the Father before all ages; God from God, light from light, true God from true God; begotten not made, of one essence with the Father, through whom all things were made."

121. Christianity adopted pagan practices.

According to a recent but already outdated vogue among historians, Europe remained largely pagan through the Middle Ages. There's roughly as much truth in that idea as that the United States remained largely monarchist after the Revolution. On the other hand, as Brooks Alexander remarks, neopagans today complain that Christianity "achieved its cultural triumph in Europe illegitimately by appropriating the sites and symbols of paganism and perverting them to Christian ends, renaming pagan festivals and integrating them into the cycle of the church's liturgical year, building physical churches on pagan shrines and sacred sites, and generally retaining forms of pagan piety while putting Christian labels on them." There is some truth in this, though Christians called it appropriate evangelizing. The terms "pagan" and "heathen" are derogatory terms (both

---

[119]Jaroslav Pelikan, *Jesus Through the Centuries: His Place in the History of Culture* (New Haven, CT: Yale University Press, 1985), pp. 57-70.

meaning "rustic" and "hick") that Christians pasted onto a miscellany of immensely diverse polytheist religions from Egyptians to Algonquins.[120] "Paganism" is a catch-all word for a lot of different beliefs.

The relationship of Christianity to paganism can be divided into several periods: the Roman Empire, the Middle Ages, and the modern colonial and postcolonial world. At the time of Christ almost everyone in the Roman Empire except the Jews were polytheist. Christianity first spread through the Jewish communities around the Mediterranean by way of its claim to fulfill the Jewish faith in the coming of the Messiah. At least by the 50s A.D., Christians were spreading their message to the Gentiles (non-Jews) as well. Early conversions to Christianity were achieved by individual persuasion or by acceptance by an entire family, village or neighborhood. From the 300s onward, these ancient means of persuasion were supplemented by the conversion of rich and ruling elites. Christianity continued to be a movement of the weak against the mighty, but now the mighty sometimes used it against the weak. Whereas before the time of the emperors Constantine (r. 306-337) and Theodosius (r. 379-395) it had been disadvantageous to be a Christian, it now became a road to power and wealth. Conversion of a ruler was the quick track to conversion of the ruler's people. King Clovis converted the Franks about 500; King Recared converted the Visigoths in 589; Prince Vladimir of Kiev converted the Russians in 989.[121] Conversion of the people following that of the ruler was not a practice unique to Christianity: the prince of the Khazars converted his people to Judaism about 700. Another means was conversion of a people by force, like Charlemagne's conquest of the Saxons in 780-804.

However much the people obeyed their rulers, though, they did not suddenly abandon their pagan beliefs and practices en masse. Monks and missionaries carried out the conversion of the "heathen" gradually. They used a variety of methods in addition to the traditional ones. One was to destroy pagan temples and shrines, as Saint Boniface (675-754) did when he cut down the Oak of Thor in Germany. Often a church was built on the ruins of a shrine. Another method was to adapt the pagan temples and shrines to Christian worship. (The Muslims later similarly turned churches

---

[120]There were a number of ancient pagan myths with accounts of creation, flood and doom. That fact is not a modern discovery but has been known for several centuries.

[121]Clovis's conversion is dated anywhere from 496 to 506.

into mosques.) When devotion to a local deity or hero had pervasive support from the people, it was replaced by devotion to a saint who was assigned characteristics similar to that of the original deity; this process was common from Ireland to the Mediterranean and later in the conversion of the Americas and Africa. Pagan festivals were often translated into Christian ones, as in the dating of Christmas at the winter solstice. But the process of conversion did not cease when Christian labels were pasted onto pagan practices. By employing ancient beliefs and customs as a way into a culture, Christianity usually replaced pagan beliefs within a few generations. Certain pagan customs—for example the Yule tree—lasted indefinitely, but monastic and other missionary activity gradually transformed them, and from the twelfth century Europe was thoroughly Christian.

Christian missionary movements have ranged over a wide spectrum as to how much they adapted to local cultures. Catholic missionaries differed radically from one another in their approaches during the 1600s and 1700s. As early as the 1600s the question of how far missionaries should incorporate indigenous beliefs was widely discussed. In the nineteenth and early twentieth centuries both Protestants and Catholics often imposed European practices with little adjustment to the indigenous cultures, but since the late twentieth and early twenty-first centuries indigenous practices have been encouraged so long as core Christian teachings are retained. Contemporary differences between, say, Korean worship and European worship are wide.

Since the 1950s a neopagan movement has claimed that Christianity unfairly suppressed paganism over the centuries. And recently a bizarre phenomenon has arisen: "Christo-paganism." Some Christians feel that their churches are bland and dry and turn to pagan practices to fill in the experiential gaps and then construct something new out of the amalgamation. When the Bible and Tradition are set aside, Christianity inevitably crumbles into personal opinions, which are virtually infinite. Christianity cannot go along with this if it is to retain its character.[122]

---

[122]Jeffrey B. Russell and Brooks Alexander, *New History of Witchcraft: Sorcerers, Heretics, and Pagans*, 2nd ed. (London: Thames and Hudson, 2007).

Miracles Are Impossible

122. Miracles are explained away by science.

The essence of Christianity is based on belief in two overwhelming miracles: the creation of the cosmos and the resurrection of Jesus Christ. Neither of these can be explained away by science. A miracle is a supernatural event, which in its very nature is inaccessible to science, and any scientist honestly open to inquiry into natural phenomena—which is his or her vocation—will admit as much. The statement that nothing can exist that can't be explained by science is not a scientific statement. As Thomas Crean asks, "What is the philosophical argument or scientific experiment that conclusively assigns to miracles this supreme degree of unlikelihood?"[1] There isn't one. Some atheists claim that miracles would make science impossible on the grounds that if there is a God who can intervene in natural events there can be no regularity in natural events.[2] But the rare suspension of natural regularities does not mean that natural regularities cannot exist. Some say God should submit himself to the scientific tests of people in the twenty-first century. Aside from the obvious fact that God cannot be scientifically tested, this idea of twenty-first century intellectual elitists is a form of chronological ethnocentricity, the arrogant assumption that "we" know better about everything than other people at other times. The idea of the regularities of God's ordered universe is compatible with science, and the Christian idea of such regularities is one of the most important sources of science. People who believe in miracles don't think of them as God's "breaking" the laws of nature but as God's being constantly attentive to his cosmos.

Antitheists argue that a universe made by God would be different from

[1]Thomas Crean, *God Is No Delusion: A Refutation of Richard Dawkins* (San Francisco: Ignatius, 2007), p. 53.
[2]Ibid., pp. 52-53.

one made by only natural occurrences. To them, the universe appears to have no signs of being made by a planner. But there are such signs: in the order of the universe, in the direction of time, and in the existence of miracles. The antitheists simply exclude the evidence beforehand without examining it.[3]

Statistics show that most Americans believe in miracles. Elitist atheists reply that most Americans are dolts. Of people forty-five years of age and over, eighty percent believe in miracles, forty-one percent believe that they occur every day, and thirty-seven percent claim to have witnessed at least one. Eighty-five percent of women believe, and seventy-three percent of men (males being more inclined to the materially practical). Eighty-six percent of people with high school diplomas believe, and seventy-one percent with college degrees. As with other religious indicators, the big division is financial: eighty-six percent of people making less than $25,000 a year believe, as contrasted with seventy-eight percent of those making $75,000 or more.[4] The more comfortably off one is, the less likely one is to believe in miracles—or anything supernatural. But it may be that people working hard to support their families are more connected with actual reality than people patting one another on the back in expensive restaurants for being superior to the folks serving them.

The atheist Michael Shermer tried to reconcile science and miracles through "the law of large numbers," which states that "an event with a low probability of occurrence in a small number of trials has a high probability of occurrence in a large number of trials. . . . Events with a-million-to-one odds happen 295 times a day in America."[5] This view mistakes marvels or wonders for miracles. Strange marvels have occurred, such as rains of frogs, but these eventually have a scientific explanation. Small wonders are scientifically possible, but a gigantic wonder such as the resurrection of a truly dead person is outside the boundaries of science. Shermer's view relies on statistics about wonders, but miracles are immune to statistics. There are no odds on miracles. Miracles can be instantaneous or develop over periods of time. Scientifically the odds against a resurrection are ∞:1, but religiously

---

[3]Gregory E. Ganssle, "Dawkins' Best Argument Against God's Existence," in *Contending with Christianity's Critics: Answering New Atheists and Other Objectors,* ed. Paul Copan and William Lane Craig (Nashville: B & H Publishing, 2009), pp. 74-86.

[4]*AARP: The Magazine,* January/February 2009, pp. 50-64.

[5]Ibid., p. 52.

the chance of a miraculous resurrection is x:x. There is no way of predicting any odds of its occurring. It either occurs—or not. Therefore when one prays for a miracle one is not playing against the odds. Whether a miracle happens or not is entirely out of the realm of prediction. Christians, by the way, are usually cautious in reporting a miracle because reported miracles usually turn out to be mere marvels, hallucinations or frauds.

Christian theology doesn't say that "God can do anything" but that "God can do anything that isn't self-contradictory." An old question is whether God can create a stone heavier than he can lift. The answer is of course not, and this answer is no limitation on God's power but a statement of the internal logic of God. William of Ockham (1285-1347), the inventor of Occam's razor, made an important distinction between God's absolute power and his power expressed in the order of the universe he has created.[6] God has the absolute power to suddenly change the relation between the sun and the Earth, or to turn a senator into a duck. But God's "ordered power" prevents him from doing either. God's absolute power is absolutely unlimited, but he limits his own ordered power. Ockham's idea was, by the way, an essential step toward science as well as an essential basis of theology. People often pray for rain. It is within God's absolute power to bring rain to their locality without changing the weather patterns of the whole Earth, but it is not within his ordered power. If God suddenly drenched one field or town with rain, that would have an effect on the weather throughout the world.[7]

How, then, do Christians evaluate miracles; how do they separate miracles from marvels, delusions, frauds and mistakes? On the basis of the reasonableness of the testimony. Before the 1700s the truth of events was weighed according to testimony, a method still used in some fields such as the legal system. The reasonableness of testimony arose from the reliability of the witnesses. One of the greatest English historians of all time, Bede (673-735), poses a problem for historians. On the one hand, his

---

[6]*Potestas absoluta* and *potestas ordinata*.

[7]Christoph Cardinal Schönborn, *Chance or Purpose? Creation, Evolution, and a Rational Faith* (San Francisco: Ignatius, 2007), pp. 78-83, on contingency and continuous creation. Since new things appear every moment, creation is obviously developing, so God must be developing it. But this does not mean that God is himself developing, as process theology (which began with Alfred North Whitehead in 1928-1929) claims. Everything past, present and future is contingent on God, who is continuously creating. One might say he foresees every development in nature—or better, he acts with and in every development in nature.

history of the English people up to his own time has been confirmed in most details by modern history and archeology; on the other hand, it contains numerous accounts of miracles that Bede carefully examined and some of which he declared to be valid. How, modern historians fret, can Bede be so reliable in one way and so unreliable in another? Contemporary historians usually evade the question by patronizing Bede, saying that he was influenced by his culture, as if contemporary historians aren't influenced by theirs. Bede evaluated reported miracles on the basis of whether they were reasonably reported by reliable witnesses.[8]

In the eighteenth century rationality shouldered reasonableness aside and replaced it with narrower "rationality." Events were to be judged true or false not on the basis of testimony, but on the basis of repeatable experimentation. Rationality works well in the natural sciences but not well in history. Historians continue to judge events by the reliability of witnesses. Still, most contemporary historians now simply assume that a witness reporting a miracle (or even a wonder) is unreliable. Humans still observe miracles, but unlike other events, miracles are not allowed as evidence. Yet "it can't happen" is true only if nothing can happen except things explained by physicalism, and physicalism isn't a demonstration or even an argument, it's the axiom (the unsupported assumption) that everything real is physical, followed by the corollary that nothing that isn't physical is real.[9] No miracles are allowed because no miracles are possible. This undemonstrated flat assertion does not explain miracles away at all.

123. CHRISTIANITY IS FALSE BECAUSE MIRACLES CAN'T OCCUR.

Turning the previous entry around, does the alleged fact that miracles don't occur prove Christianity to be false? If this alleged fact were true, Christianity certainly would be false, absolutely and irretrievably.

---

[8]Rick Kennedy, *History of Reasonableness* (Rochester, NY: University of Rochester Press, 2004).

[9]"Ideas from information theory need to be taken more seriously by physicists. If our universe is a computer simulation running in some other reality, then the fascinating enterprise of combining increasingly sophisticated mathematical tools with increasingly complex narrative descriptions of the universe may never reach a satisfying end. In fact, foundational issues in mathematics might guarantee the lack of a 'satisfying end' for mathematical physics as long as our universe has a certain level of complexity." Communication to the author by S. Gill Williamson, who is working on the complex mathematics of multiple universes.

Christians who say they disbelieve in miracles are in step with contemporary physicalism but at odds with the Bible and Christian Tradition. A miracle is a work of God that does not fit the ordinary working of the natural laws that God makes for the universe. Christianity has been based on miracles from its very beginning, so if there are no miracles Christianity is false. A nonmiraculous Christianity is historically and philosophically not Christianity at all. Thomas Jefferson and other well-meaning people edited the Bible to take out the miracles or else to explain the miracles away in pseudoscientific terms. Snipping miracles out of the Bible is like taking battles out of *Beowulf* or liberty out of the Declaration of Independence. It misses the point. The Bible is about God's involvement with nature and human history. The idea that God wound up the universe and then let it alone is deism, which is practical atheism requiring nothing but an abstract nod to a vague and remote divinity. Christianity requires a God who is active in the cosmos, a cosmos where miracles can occur. If you're a deist, it doesn't matter whether God sets the universe off or whether it sets itself off—it would be the same either way. What matters is whether God is constantly involved in the cosmos.

The fundamental question is whether the cosmos we inhabit is one in which miracles occur or whether it is one in which they do not occur. Some people claim that this is a cosmos with miracles. Others claim that it is one without miracles. Some claim that they don't know, and that's fair enough. But still others claim that it depends on your point of view, and that is not fair at all. The most basic rule of logic is: *a* is not *not-a*. Call the cosmos with miracles *a* and the cosmos without miracles *not-a*. The cosmos can't be both *a* and *not-a*. It's one or the other. Postmodernists invent *c*, saying that the reality of the cosmos depends on what kind of cosmos you think it is. This tells something about postmodernists but nothing at all about the cosmos: choice *c* is pure fantasy. Supporters of both cosmos *a* and cosmos *not-a* argue from evidence, but supporters of cosmos *c* simply assert the uselessness of evidence.

Physicalists assert without doubt that we live in *not-a*, a cosmos without miracles. They offer a reason for asserting that miracles are impossible: miracles are impossible because they violate the laws of science. They say that regularities in science constitute "laws." But these laws are descriptive rather than proscriptive; they derive from observations rather than excluding observations. If a certain physical event changes *n* to *m* nine billion times, it is always possible that the nine billion and first time it will not do so. Science works very well—it couldn't work at all otherwise—when it proceeds on the basis that nine billion times (or less!) is enough to establish a regularity on which science can confidently rely. The chance that next time the event won't change *n* to *m* is vanishingly small and necessarily ignored in scientific research. But nothing excludes the possibility of exceptions, and speaking of "violating laws" makes an exception sound like an indecency. It is much more helpful to speak of exceptions rather than violations.

Scientists properly exclude the miraculous from their scientific work. They are entitled to draw the boundaries of science in such a way as to exclude miracles. Everyone can accept this. If a scientist tried to offer a miraculous explanation for something, he or she would not be doing science. Miracles are inadmissible as scientific evidence. The problem arises when those scientists who are materialists leap from excluding miracles from science to the position that only scientific knowledge can be knowledge—and then move on to declare that because there can be no scientific evidence for miracles there can be no miracles. This is like saying that "baseball is the only game you can play on this field" and then concluding that "football doesn't exist." This is not an argument. It is an invented, unprovable axiom, a principle "accepted as true without proof as the basis for argument," according to its dictionary definition. Simply put, the fact that no miracles are allowed in science is not evidence of any kind that miracles are impossible. Physicalism is not based on science but on the metaphysical assumption that the only reality is material reality.

Not every exception to physical regularity is a miracle. Marvelously unusual and bizarre events have been reported that, when verified, prove to have had natural causes. The nine billion and first time may indicate that our idea of the regularities needs to be modified. But a miracle is by definition an irregularity brought about through direct action by God. That miracles are very rare exceptions was already clear two thousand years ago—otherwise why would miracles have been reported as extraordinary events? People at the time of Jesus' birth were fully aware that virgins did not bear children, which is why Mary's fiancé Joseph at first planned to dismiss her quietly.

To say that the only kind of evidence that can exist is scientific evidence is an axiom that is completely unwarranted in human experience. All sorts of nonscientific evidence are rightly used as criteria for all sorts of human judgments. For example, juries are asked to decide cases on the weight of the evidence. Scientific evidence may enter, but the evidence of reasonable witnesses is usually an important part of a case. Most contemporary historians, like scientists, usually argue that miracles are not admissible as evidence. But they are on much thinner ice than scientists, for history, unlike science, usually relies on the testimony of witnesses. And there have been very many reasonable witnesses to miracles. Why are these reasonable witnesses dismissed by atheists? On the grounds that since they are reporting impossible events, the witnesses cannot be reasonable. This is just an unsubstantiated corollary of the original axiom.

Whether a miracle can justifiably be believed to occur partly depends on how reliable and how reasonable the witnesses are and partly on whether the alleged miracle has a constructive point—miracles usually have to do with things like healing, not turning frogs into princes. Unless the evidence is arbitrarily ruled impossible at the outset, the weight of the evidence offered by reasonable persons is that we live in a cosmos with miracles. I once was in a jury selection process in which a woman said she assumed before the trial that the accused was guilty. The astonished judge asked, "Ma'am, are you saying that before you hear a single word of evidence you assert that the accused is guilty?" She persisted in saying yes. And the judge sent her away. And so might we send away those who without hearing one word of evidence declare that witnesses to miracles are guilty of fraud or delusion. The Christian wants the case to proceed to trial so that it can be shown whether a claim of miracle is false or true. The person who allows for the possibility of miracles is open to evidence; the person who asserts from the outset that they are impossible is not open-minded.[10]

124. The Resurrection of Jesus Has Been Disproved.

The one certain thing about this statement is that it is false.[11] Atheists dislike saying "disproved," so instead of saying that the resurrection has

---

[10]Kennedy, *History of Reasonableness.*

[11]William Lane Craig summarizes the evidence for the resurrection and shows that the physical resurrection is the most likely of any of the proposed explanations for the empty tomb: *On Guard: Defending Your Faith with Reason and Precision* (Colorado Springs: David C. Cook, 2010), pp. 219-64, especially pp. 231-36 and 263-64.

been disproved, they say that it is scientifically impossible.[12] That is true, but the assumption that science is the only way to establish truth is an unscientific and philosophically undemonstrated claim, a metaphysical faith. It is also circular: something that science can't demonstrate can't be true; science can't demonstrate a resurrection; therefore a resurrection can't occur. If one adopts the premise on faith, then no other outcome is possible. But there is no sufficient reason to believe the premise true. Once we get off the carousel of "resurrections can't occur; therefore the Resurrection didn't occur" and get onto solid, unspinning ground again, we can examine the evidence without prefiltering it.

The resurrection of Jesus can be discussed reasonably on the basis of the evidence. The New Testament is primarily based on eyewitnesses: "We declare to you what we have seen and heard" (1 Jn 1:3). The resurrection can be evaluated not by science but instead in the way that most knowledge is evaluated: by the testimony of witnesses.[13]

The prior question, though, is whether it matters. Why didn't God perform a more generally useful miracle like stopping genocide? What, in other words, does Jesus' resurrection matter to anyone except, say, Jesus and his family and friends? But billions of people find that it does matter to them as evidence for hope past, present and future.

The historical question is divided into two parts: What did the earliest Christians think happened to Jesus? And how reliable is their testimony?[14] This entry will not go into specifics because the evidence has been so thoroughly—and variously—examined. The main points of evidence are the burial of Jesus, his empty tomb and his physical appearances after his death.[15] Belief in the physical resurrection of Jesus was almost universal among his earliest followers, and the claim that such belief began only with the Apostle Saint Paul has been demonstrated to be false.[16]

---

[12]Craig observes that the atheist statement "You can't prove a universal negative" undermines atheism: *On Guard*, p. 149.

[13]Lee Strobel, *Case for the Real Jesus: A Journalist Investigates Current Attacks on the Identity of Christ* (Grand Rapids: Zondervan, 2007), pp. 23-63.

[14]N. T. Wright, *Resurrection of the Son of God* (Minneapolis: Fortress, 2003), p. 6. Wright's book combines open-mindedness, analysis and thoroughness.

[15]William Lane Craig, in *Jesus' Resurrection: Fact or Figment? A Debate between William Lane Craig and Gerd Lüdemann,* ed. Paul Copan and Ronald K. Tacelli (Downers Grove, IL: InterVarsity Press, 2000), p. 163.

[16]Larry W. Hurtado, *Lord Jesus Christ: Devotion to Jesus in Earliest Christianity* (Grand Rapids: Eerdmans, 2003), pp. 168-71, 231.

The resurrection of Jesus is unique. Jesus raised Lazarus from the dead, but then Lazarus continued to live his life and eventually died a natural death. Jesus' resurrection was not a reanimation or resuscitation; it was "breaking out into an entirely new form of life, into a life that is no longer subject to the law of dying and becoming, but lies beyond it—a life that opens up a new dimension of human existence."[17]

125. The Resurrection of Jesus Was a "Resurrection Experience" Rather Than a Physical Resurrection.

This view is held by skeptical scholars who wish to preserve the moral teachings of Jesus while excising his miracles and thus evacuating the essential meaning of the New Testament. The problem with their view is that the New Testament writers and the earliest Christians definitely did not mean by resurrection some spiritual manifestation. They knew the difference between ghosts, dreams, illusions and physical bodies. The apostles were not asking people to believe that they had had visions or dreams or "experiences"; they were asking people to believe that Jesus' body, having died, lived again on earth. And they knew this to be the most extraordinary thing possible; people in the first century knew as well as we do that dead people do not reappear in their bodies alive again on earth. Dead people certainly do not eat fish, as the resurrected Jesus did (Lk 24:42). The proposition that Jesus of Nazareth—Yeshua the carpenter—rose from true death into true life in his body was as shocking then as now. Yet always and everywhere Christians have said, "For now is Christ risen, truly risen, *alethos anesti*."

The Apostle Saint Paul reports, "He was raised on the third day. . . . He appeared to Cephas [Peter] and then to the twelve. . . . Then he appeared to more than five hundred brothers and sisters at one time, most of whom are alive, though some have died. Then he appeared to James, then to all the apostles" (1 Cor 15:3-11).

These are the alternatives to the literal resurrection: (1) Someone had given Jesus a drug so he only looked dead; (2) The women at the tomb saw someone who looked like Jesus, not Jesus himself; (3) Jesus appeared only

[17]Benedict XVI, *Jesus of Nazareth: Holy Week: From the Entrance into Jerusalem to the Resurrection* (San Francisco: Ignatius, 2011), p. 244; on the ascension of Jesus, see pp. 278-93.

to those who already believed that he would reappear (which was virtually no one); (4) People began by saying, "He will be raised," and quickly transitioned to "He has been raised"; (5) the resurrection was not a literal, historical event but some sort of inexplicable "experience" among his followers.[18] A (6) appears remotely feasible: Saint Augustine said that a miracle is worked through natural processes speeded up. Perhaps it is also worked through natural processes slowed down. Recent medical research has proved that people can be brought back to life hours after apparent death by inducing a body temperature of 95 degrees Fahrenheit or lower, which can produce a state of suspended animation equivalent to hibernation.[19] At least, this state can be induced with the present techniques of medicine, but those were unavailable in the first century. When applied to Jesus, this is a physicalist stretch reminiscent of the pointless old nineteenth-century explanation of Jesus' walking on the water: he appeared to the disciples to be walking on the water but was actually walking on a hot beach where the heat waves produced a mirage. If Jesus' low body temperature had been induced (without modern medical means) and remained so low, that itself would be a miracle. There's no point in trying to keep the Bible while doing away with its entire basis: miracles.

The resurrection was physical if it was a resurrection at all. Either Christ actually rose as a full human being with his cells and his DNA, or he didn't. The Apostle Saint Paul put it succinctly: "If Christ has not been raised, your faith is futile and . . . we [Christians] are of all people most to be pitied" (1 Cor 15:17-19). There is absolutely no indication that any of the New Testament writers really meant a spiritual instead of a physical resurrection (see Acts 1:22; 2:31; Rom 1:4 and many other New Testament passages; the pre-Christian Maccabees and Pharisees also believed in physical resurrection).

---

[18]N. T. Wright, *Surprised by Hope: Rethinking Heaven, the Resurrection, and the Mission of the Church* (New York: HarperOne, 2008), pp. 61-62.

[19]Sanjay Gupta, "Another Day Cheating Death," CNN, January 2, 2011 <transcripts.cnn.com/TRANSCRIPTS/1101/02/se.01.html>.

Worldviews Can't Be Evaluated

126. Few people believe in God anymore.

This is true only in materialist Western culture. The uncritical assumption by elitists that God does not exist is mostly based on an incoherent combination of the theories of Sigmund Freud (1856-1939), Karl Marx (1818-1883), Charles Darwin (1809-1882), Friedrich Nietzsche (1844-1900) and B. F. Skinner (1904-1990).

Cultures have different views of God, and belief in one sort of god or another is increasing rapidly around the world. It's more useful to take the statement as meaning, "Few people believe in the Christian God anymore." The Christian view of God is that he created, sustains and develops the cosmos and that he became human in Jesus the Christ, died for us and rose from the dead. When elitists claim that few people believe in God anymore, they mean, "The people I know—that is, the bright sort of people who are naturally my friends—don't believe in God anymore." Although fewer people in Europe, Canada and the United States believe in the Christian God than did half a century ago, the number of people in Asia and Africa who believe in Christ is growing rapidly. Elitists assume that the growth of Christianity among non-Western people is a sign of their backwardness.

Not only is belief in God growing worldwide, but based on the discoveries of science over the past half-century, the existence of God appears more likely than it did a century ago. Many atheists rely on a view of the cosmos that is at least forty years out of date, and that is the view now generally taught in Western schools. However, the current evidence of physics, chemistry and biology points to the existence of a cosmic purpose more now than it did half a century ago.[1] This is denied by atheists on the

[1]This is currently debated: Stephen Hawking and Leonard Mlodinow deny it in *The Grand*

basis of an axiom and a corollary rather than evidence: If one adopts the faith-based axiom that the only reality is physical reality that can be measured by science, then the inevitable corollary is that God is not real. That is not an argument; it's simply a declaration. If one is a physicalist, God can not exist; if one is a Christian, God can't not exist. But that does not mean that the two worldviews are equally valid. Physicalists artificially limit their mental reality by disallowing evidence that does not fit their prefabricated worldview. The Christian, on the other hand, says that reality does not stop at the boundary of the physical; it opens out to the inexhaustible mystery of the cosmos.

Arguments have been marshaled against the Christian God since the beginning. Recently Richard Dawkins argued that if a God exists, he must be more complex than the complex cosmos he created. That might be true of a physical entity: Dawkins seems to regard God as a material object subject to natural laws.[2] The Christian view is that God is simple perfection and that he "knows all things in a single act by knowing Himself."[3] No physical being could possibly do that. Again this is a confusion of the physical with the material. Physical existence and divine existence are two different things. My shirt and Mount Everest once did not exist; they now exist; they will cease to exist. God is that in which all exists. "Subsists" ("lies under") is a better word than "exists" ("emerges") when speaking of God. His subsistence underlies everything, which no mere existence can do. Antitheists seem to have difficulty in grasping the principle of plurality of explanation.[4]

The question of who or what made God pops up from time to time,[5]

Design (New York: Bantam, 2010), but Hugh Ross affirms it in *Beyond the Cosmos: What Recent Discoveries in Astrophysics Reveal about the Glory and Love of God,* 3rd ed. (Orlando: Signalman, 2010).

[2]Tina Beattie, *New Atheists: The Twilight of Reason and the War on Religion* (Maryknoll, NY: Orbis, 2007), pp. 12, 109; David Berlinski, *Devil's Delusion: Atheism and Its Scientific Pretensions* (New York: Crown Forum, 2008), p. 142; Alvin Plantinga, "The Dawkins Confusion: Naturalism 'Ad Absurdum,'" in *God Is God, God Is Great,* ed. William Lane Craig and Chad Meister (Downers Grove, IL: InterVarsity Press, 2009), pp. 247-58.

[3]Thomas Crean, *God Is No Delusion: A Refutation of Richard Dawkins* (San Francisco: Ignatius Press, 2007), p. 32.

[4]Michael Poole, *'New Atheism': Ten Arguments that Don't Hold Water* (Oxford: Lion, 2009), pp. 54-55.

[5]John C. Lennox, *God's Undertaker: Has Science Buried God?* (Oxford: Lion, 2007), pp. 174-175; Ian S. Markham, *Against Atheism: Why Dawkins, Hitchens, and Harris Are Fundamentally Wrong* (Malden, MA: Wiley-Blackwell, 2010), pp. 10-11.

but it is completely meaningless. Christianity defines God as eternal and unmade. He simply is. A god that is not eternal and that was made by something else would not be God. Of course any material entity that produced the cosmos would have to be infinitely complex, but Christians believe that the entity producing the cosmos is spiritual, not material. Every material thing is contingent on some other material thing; no material thing can be uncontingent—deriving its being solely from itself. Therefore there must be an entity on which everything is contingent, and that entity cannot be material.[6] Indeed, without God, the very basis of science in cosmic regularities is undermined.

Some objections have more strength. If God is real, why doesn't he make truth clearer to everyone?[7] What about God and time? Does he know everything at one instant, or does he know things as they develop? Is God omniscient, or are there events that God does not know? It's easier to conceive of God's knowing the state of every particle in the cosmos at any given nanosecond than it is to imagine his knowing every pulse of human activity. Does God know the price of every share on the New York Stock Exchange at every moment of every day? Or the score of a basketball game before it is over? In other words, is God interested in trivia? Suppose God suspends his absolute omniscience for his ordered omniscience so that he knows only what he chooses to know?[8] How can God be both eternal and in time? Does he do things in time from our point of view, since we are in space-time, but from his point of view does he also act beyond space-time, where "space" and "time" are understood metaphorically? Time, like space, expands from the Big Bang, and God is beyond both as well as involved in both. Carlos Eire shows that definitions of eternity and infinity vary.[9] How does God's knowledge relate to human freedom?[10] All these questions are meaningful.

---

[6]Markham, *Against Atheism*, p. 79.

[7]Benedict XVI, *Jesus of Nazareth* (New York: Doubleday, 2007), p. 30.

[8]David P. Hunt, "What Does God Know? The Problems of Open Theism," in *Contending with Christianity's Critics: Answering New Atheists and Other Objectors,* ed. Paul Copan and William Lane (Nashville: B & H Publishing, 2009), pp. 265-82. "Open theism" is the idea that God does not necessarily know the entire past, present and future.

[9]Carlos Eire, *A Very Brief History of Eternity* (Princeton, NJ: Princeton University Press, 2010), pp. 229-32. It is hard to see how God could avoid at least "Cambridge change" in his relationship to the changing cosmos. The relationship has to change as the cosmos changes.

[10]William Lane Craig, *Only Wise God: The Compatibility of Divine Foreknowledge and Human Freedom* (Eugene, OR: Wipf and Stock, 2000); Crean, *God Is No Delusion*, p. 49.

So the question is why belief in God is decreasing among the elite. Here's one possibility: in the approach-avoidance syndrome, desire draws us toward something that fear drives us away from. As Brooks Alexander says, people seek God but fear him and so construct ways to evade him. One way of evading him is to disbelieve in the existence of the true, the good and the beautiful. Encountering God causes urgent spiritual discomfort because he is so beyond us and so other than us, and this fear can create theophobia: aversion and fear of God.

127. God is the product of structural and chemical arrangements in the brain.

There are two bases for this statement. One is a circular argument based on the faith that everything is physical. In this view, the human mind is nothing but an elaborate physical entity of structural and chemical arrangements, so its thought about God must be explained in physical terms. This indemonstrable assertion is often clothed in scientific language: "Modern neuroscience rests on the assumption that our thoughts, feelings, perceptions, and behaviors emerge from electrical and chemical communication between brain cells: that whenever we recognize a face, read the newspaper, throw a ball, engage in a conversation, or recall a moment in childhood, a pattern of activity in our neurons makes such feats possible. . . . Neuroscientists can begin to explain how individual neurons link together to become a working mind. . . . How can a tangle of cells produce the complexity and subtlety of a mind?"[11] Actually, they can't, not without an intelligent plan. A mechanic may understand how the parts of an engine work together; he does not assume the engine planned itself. The undemonstrated axiom—note the phrase "rests on the assumption" in the quotation—is that physical reality is the only reality.

The other basis is more rational, since it is based on actual neurological investigation of how the brain works. Recently scientists have tried to explain the almost universal human belief in something beyond nature in terms of a "God gene" and then, when that hypothesis was exploded, a complex combination of neural patterns built into the normal human brain that draws us toward a sense of mystery. In other words, human beings

[11]Courtney Humphries, "Untangling the Brain: From Neuron to Mind," <www.harvardmagazine.com/2009/05>.

possess an innate tendency toward the divine in one sense or another.[12] This tendency can be explained in two basic ways: (1) It is there because there is something external that it actually refers to; (2) it is a web of irrational junk that somehow got stuck in the brain in the past, has no real use and will eventually fade. Neurologists have observed changes in the brains of people who are in deep meditation and prayer. Are physical causes the ultimate source of the spiritual experience, or does the spiritual experience cause the changes in the brain? These questions need to be explored with open minds.

128. If there is a God, he has a lot of explaining to do about suffering.

Your only child is killed in an automobile accident caused by a careless teenage driver. Or your spouse of forty years loses her mind to dementia. Or you go in for your yearly checkup and learn that you have terminal brain cancer. Or your adolescent son is present when your spouse crumples up and dies of a stroke before his eyes. Or your mother is driven out of her home by taxes. Or your friend is duped out of his estate, leaving his bipolar son without support. Or your mentally handicapped cousin sets herself on fire at the stove and burns to death. Or your son, only in his thirties, dies of cancer. Or you wake up one morning blind. Or you are forced to choose between the strong risk of having your child die during a tricky heart operation or letting him live a year or two longer without the operation. Or your children are molested. Or despite all your efforts, your son cannot free himself from an addiction that causes his death from an overdose. Or your spouse commits suicide. Or your baby dies. Or your spouse leaves you without warning. Or your child is in jail. Or your spouse is mugged. Or you lose your job because of economic cutbacks. Or you are persecuted by a racist. Or your spouse suddenly dies when your baby is six months old. Or a friend whom you trusted betrays you. Or you are deliberately cruel to another person.

I mention these in particular only because they are all events known personally to me. Other horrors happen daily, often on a much grander scale: towns are wiped out; people are tortured; children are prostituted

[12]Andrew B. Newberg, *Why God Won't Go Away: Brain Science and the Biology of Belief* (New York: Ballantine, 2001).

and beaten. And more, and more, and more. It seems to many that if the Christian God, all-knowing and all-powerful, permits such things to happen, he must be a monster, and it seems easier to believe that God does not exist than to believe in the monster. "God has a lot of explaining to do," as one of my friends put it. This has always been the most powerful argument against God. Since examples of suffering are endless, and since they have been so often recounted, we now pass from the personal and immediate to general and philosophical points.[13]

Philosophy recognizes three types of evil. The first is purely abstract: any created universe is less good than its creator, so evil (at least in the sense of absence of good) is inevitable. The other two involve things that we actually experience in life. Natural evil is suffering that is caused by natural events rather than human events. Moral evil is suffering caused by human actions.

Natural evil is the sort of evil where tsunamis and pandemics wreak destruction. God could have avoided evil by not creating a cosmos at all, or he could have avoided evil by creating a purely inanimate cosmos without any creatures capable of suffering. But could he have created an animate cosmos without natural evil? The cosmos we inhabit follows regularities such as the laws of thermodynamics. God has the absolute power to do whatever he wants, but he chooses to follow the regularities he has established. Tsunamis are the result of earthquakes or volcanoes caused by movements in the Earth's crust, and without such tectonic movement continually recycling elements, life could not be sustained. Life on planets without tectonic plates is relatively unlikely. Here on Earth, few kinds of life exist without eating other forms of life, and many eat other animals. As for the coyote and the cat, not to mention the human at the supermarket meat counter, if multicellular creatures had not devoured unicellular creatures, life would have remained at its crudest—if it had existed at all. Since God cannot contradict himself, he could not have made life without suffering. Without death, none but the most primitive life could ever exist. The universe follows the rules that are necessary to its existence, even if we often prefer them to be otherwise.

[13]Rabbi Harold S. Kushner, *When Bad Things Happen to Good People* (New York: Schocken, 1981); Rick Warren, *The Purpose-Driven Life* (Grand Rapids: Zondervan, 2002); C. S. Lewis, *The Problem of Pain* (New York: Macmillan, 1945).

As for moral evil, Christians believe that in important moral matters people have free will to do what they choose. They sometimes choose according to God's will and sometimes against it. God wills people to have the free choice that permits them to disobey his will. God could have created robots instead of humans, but robots have no freedom to choose; they would be incapable of love or hate, good or evil. Christians believe that a universe where creatures choose to love God is better than one in which God forces everyone to love him automatically—one in which "love" would be an empty word.

Here is the Christian view: God could have created a cosmos in which you are forced not to do wrong, or a cosmos in which you are forced to do good. But then why would he have created a cosmos at all? After all, he can think perfect thoughts in his own mind. But could he love if he kept it all to himself? So he pours out his love into the cosmos, and he loves the cosmos to return his love, which it could not do if it had no freedom to love. The reciprocity of love, even though it entails frequent failures to love, is the point of the cosmos.[14] The Christian view has always been to avoid suffering if possible—at almost any cost (1 Pet 4:12-19). To seek martyrdom is unchristian. But there are lines that cannot be crossed: for example, one must not betray Christ or fellow humans (or other creatures). God might seem intolerable if he had not experienced the fullness of human suffering himself in Christ, but he did.

William Lane Craig observes that atheists as well as Christians can be challenged about suffering. There is no explicit contradiction between these two statements: An all-loving, all-powerful God exists, and suffering exists.[15] Is God's power limited? He is certainly unable to do something self-contradictory such as making a round square. Nor is he able to make creatures with free will without the freedom to do wrong. Could God really have created a world without suffering? Craig observes that the chief purpose of life is not pleasure or even freedom from pain, "but the knowledge of God."[16] The Apostle Saint Paul said the knowledge of God is set in each person's mind: "What can be known about God is plain to

---

[14]Jeffrey Burton Russell, *Prince of Darkness* (Ithaca, NY: Cornell University Press, 1988).

[15]William Lane Craig, *On Guard: Defending Your Faith with Reason and Precision* (Colorado Springs: David C. Cook, 2010), pp. 154-55.

[16]Ibid., p. 163.

them, because God has shown it to them. Ever since the creation of the world, his eternal power and divine nature, invisible though they are, have been understood and seen through the things he has made" (Rom 1:19-20). When the great psychologist Carl Jung (1875-1961) was asked in a BBC interview whether he believed in God, he smiled and said, "I don't believe; I know." The argument against God based on suffering is more emotional than rational, and it can be turned around: "If God does not exist, then we are locked without hope in a world filled with pointless and unredeemed suffering."[17]

129. ATHEISTS OPPOSE CHRISTIANITY MAINLY ON INTELLECTUAL GROUNDS.

Some atheists oppose Christianity on intellectual grounds, and some Christians oppose atheism on intellectual grounds. Intellectual grounds sometimes produce "rationales . . . for convictions that are rooted not in reason but in a greater cultural will."[18] This is particularly true in a society that has rejected the idea of truth. As David Bentley Hart remarks, "The truly modern person may believe in almost anything, or even perhaps in everything, so long as all these beliefs rest securely upon a more fundamental and radical faith in *the* nothing—or, better, in nothingness as such."[19]

Atheism is a broad term embracing everything from antitheism (fierceness against anything that hints at the possibility of a supernatural planner), to humanism, to agnosticism, to rejection of the Judeo-Christian-Muslim God while being open to other spiritual entities, to practical atheism that simply doesn't care about the question and behaves as if God does not exist. Unlike philosophical atheism, which makes intellectual demands on its proponents, practical atheism is popular exactly because it makes no demands at all. This sort of atheism is cool, because it enables people not to take life seriously and to act as if God doesn't exist. In a hedonistic, rudderless society, admitting among the elite that you believe in God in any serious way loses you social points, friends and sometimes jobs.

---

[17]Ibid., p. 173.

[18]David Bentley Hart, *Atheist Delusions: The Christian Revolution and Its Fashionable Enemies* (New Haven, CT: Yale University Press, 2009), p. 19.

[19]Ibid., pp. 20-21.

As for intellectual atheists, there are two almost opposite sorts. First, there are the relativists and postmodernists who deny God by denying all objective truth and who claim that each person constructs his or her own reality. These people use the tool of intellect to prove that intellect demonstrates nothing. They believe that any claim to objective truth is merely a device to assert power and manipulate the weak. But the statement "I don't believe in anything" provokes the response, "Is that what you believe?" The terror of truly, actually, honestly believing that everything is meaningless is a bottomless horror that almost no deconstructionist dares face. And besides the personal suicide of deconstruction, there can emerge a "desire to master reality by the exercise of human power," the result being unlimited moral monstrosity.[20]

Deconstruction has even invaded science, when physicalism fades into practical deconstructionism. Some scientists no longer believe that science is about truth or even about nature; it's "a fierce fight to construct reality."[21] Here, like Hitler and Stalin meeting to divide Poland, the two mortal enemies, postmodernism and physicalism, embrace. But this view is rare; most scientists do believe that what they discover is true. One of the things that thinking Christians and physicalists have in common is a belief in objective reality, a firm conviction that God really either exists or does not exist.

The other kind of intellectual atheism is espoused by physicalists who deny God by denying that anything other than the purely physical can exist. The real world, they say, is one without anything supernatural. I have seen a distinguished physicist go into an uncontrolled, stamping rage at the suggestion by a distinguished philosopher that the scientific method is not the only way to truth. Physicalists are terrified that the moment the suggestion "there is something beyond" is introduced, the process of scientific investigation is blocked. This is based on a misunderstanding of Christianity. Christian thinkers believe that God made everything, including the natural regularities and the minds of scientists. Theologians are as eager as scientists to explore every aspect of the physical and biological universe; the difference is that they perceive it as a gift from God and worthy of respect and gratitude. Physicalists who fear other ways of

---

[20]Hart, *Atheist Delusions*, p. 231.

[21]Bruno Latour and Steve Woolgar, *Laboratory Life: The Construction of Scientific Facts*, 2nd ed. (Princeton, NJ: Princeton University Press, 1986), p. 243.

understanding the cosmos narrowly construct an artificial dichotomy between *either* and *both,* and prefer either/or to both/and.

But most people want to remain in their comfort zones. Atheists and Christians are equally prone to shut themselves away in cupboards. When people close their minds or put their reputations on the line, they tend to erect a steel wall against contrary evidence. Many intellectuals are seeking confirmation of their own models rather than practicing objectivity. The conflict of ideologies overwhelms open-minded discussion.

The question "Why in the world are some people Christians?" can be countered by the question "Why in the world are some people atheists?" There are many explanations, but few of them are scientific. Atheism is the current fashion in academia, law, the media and elsewhere. That means that in those fields one's friends are usually atheists, and one goes with the flow. Christians are the targets of mockery and often take cover, allowing atheism to advance into undefended territory. Atheism is so much easier than belief: it demands nothing of us, whereas Christianity commits us to a way of life and certain actions. Many people are God-deaf the way others are tone-deaf.

Early in the twentieth century the scientific evidence that was then known pointed away from God, and atheist views percolated down to the general public during the following century, with the result that atheism was assumed to be more likely than theism. Current scientific evidence on balance points the other way but has not yet been generally accepted. It is now known, to cite one example, that the normal human brain is constructed so as to respond to the divine. To cite another, the likelihood of life arising from nonlife without information from outside the physical approaches zero. But atheism has become the default position in elitist culture; while theists are required to defend their belief, atheists get a pass.

130. Christ couldn't have had any impact, since things haven't got better since his time.

Atheists reasonably ask why, if Christ is God and died to save humanity from ruin, the world isn't better now than it was before the time of Jesus. But it is untrue that Christianity improved nothing. Together with Judaism, it demands the qualities of mercy and truthfulness, the equality of all human persons, responsibility for the unfortunate, human rights for all women, children and men and racial equality.

131. "I don't know" is the most defensible position.

Well, I don't know. It's certainly the easiest. If we say we don't know, no one can argue with us about that. However, "I don't know" exposes society to real dangers, which is evident from the extremism on all sides today. While "I don't know" sounds soft and gentle, it offers no principle on which to resist whatever social forces are the most intimidating at any one time. One doesn't have to look far and wide to find intimidation: it is happening right now in Britain, Canada and the United States. Loud voices call for ostracism and punishment of those who express unpopular views. One can lose one's livelihood by expressing an unpopular view such as Christianity.[22]

Of course, no one (including a deconstructionist) really believes that he or she doesn't know anything at all. And if there's evidence that might help us know, why not look at it? If we choose not to, then it must be that we simply don't want to know. The defense that we can't know anything for absolutely certain is feeble. For instance, it is not OK to say, "I don't know whether the Holocaust happened," and the reason it is not OK is not political correctness but the overwhelming weight of the evidence. In some places it is politically correct to ignore the evidence and say that the Holocaust didn't happen. Truth, not political correctness of any sort, is the compelling criterion.

132. Christians believe that Christianity is one of a number of equally valid paths to God.

In 2008, seventy percent of Americans affiliated with a religion or denomination said they agreed that "many religions can lead to eternal life," including majorities among Protestants and Catholics. Among evangelical Christians, fifty-seven percent agreed with the statement, and among Catholics, seventy-nine percent did. The findings seem to undercut the conventional wisdom that the more religiously committed people are, the more intolerant they are. Americans generously think a majority of their fellow citizens will be in heaven, including Jews, Muslims, and atheists.[23]

---

[22]See the religious liberty accounts posted on the website of the Foundation for Individual Rights in Education (FIRE) <thefire.org/cases/religiousliberty>.

[23]Adapted from Neela Banerjee, "Survey Shows U.S. Religious Tolerance," *New York Times*, June 24, 2008 <www.nytimes.com/2008/06/24/us/24religion.html?ref=neelabanerjee>.

Still, it remains a fact that to be a Christian is to believe that Jesus Christ is the unique Son of God. It is impossible to believe in the equality of religions without ceasing to be a Christian. Because of that fact, some condemn Christianity as arrogant and exclusive. There's a comfortable feel to the idea that all religions are equal. But the only way all religions can be equal is if none of them has any meaning—that is, if none refers to reality. The idea implies that religions are a matter of taste. As David Bentley Hart puts it, "Religion has become indistinguishable from interior decorating."[24] Christianity is not based on preferences but on evidence. To take religion out of the realm of truth is to assert the underlying nihilism that there is no truth. Some philosophers are perfectly content to deny truth in science as well as in religion. But we must be aware that if there is no truth, then there is no truth. Including our own.

Without truth, there is no cosmic purpose, and everything slides down inexorably into nothingness. Nietzsche understood that and feared the results of his own philosophy. He knew that the existence or non-existence of God affected everything. If God is dead, everything changes. Progressiveness and inclusivity are well-intentioned, but they play into a political agenda aimed at the destruction of religion.[25] Does anyone really think that Buddhism and Satanism are equally valid? Honestly? There are criteria for measuring the likely validity of religions. On the positive side: trueness to type, experience by large numbers over time and place, continuity of principles, power of assimilation, richness and variety, admission of limitations, and a sense of the universe as a cosmos to be loved. On the negative side are self-righteousness, pride, cruelty, manipulation and exploitation of others, arrogance and unwarranted certainty.

Christians are often smug about their religion, but aware Christians know that there are a number of sacred texts and traditions—Hindu, Buddhist, Muslim, Jewish and others—from which wisdom and enlightenment can be drawn. They believe that many religions other than Christianity are valid yet lack the fullness of Christianity. They affirm that Christianity does not subtract from the truth of other religions: it adds. As for inclusiveness, Christians believe that Christ loves every single person who has ever lived or will ever live. Though we can each exclude ourselves

[24]Hart, *Atheist Delusions*, p. 24.

[25]Craig, *On Guard*, pp. 284-86, points out the incoherence of religious pluralism.

from love if we choose to, Christ wills to include everyone.

Though Christians have often used biblical texts to be exclusive, Augustine (354-430) remarked that when there are differences of understanding, it is best to take the most charitable interpretation. To cite the Apostle Saint Paul's letter to the Romans, Christians are to call people from "among the rest of the Gentiles" (Rom 1:13). Paul also declares the gospel to be "salvation to everyone who has faith" (Rom 1:16) and states that "ever since the creation of the world his eternal power and divine nature . . . have been understood and seen" (Rom 1:20). He warns, "In passing judgment on another you condemn yourself" (Rom 2:1) and predicts "glory and honor and peace for everyone who does good . . . for God does not show partiality" (Rom 2:10). The Gentiles, Paul says, "show that what the law requires is written on their hearts, to which their own conscience also bears witness" (Rom 2:15), and he warns his readers not to "boast of [their] relation to God" (Rom 2:17). Christians believe that it is not by their own merit or virtue but by the grace of Christ that they can find God.

133. What we believe about Jesus and God affects who Jesus and God are.

On first sight, this statement looks insane. It is like saying that what we believe about gravity or DNA affects what they are; it implies that our will and imagination exercise a magical power over external reality. On the other hand, many people actually claim to believe it and insist on the right to pick and choose what to believe about Jesus (or reality in general). The painful alternative would be to doubt themselves. It is common to hear the statement that everyone's idea of Jesus is equally true. The only way that this can be sane is on the assumption that there is no reality about Jesus and so we can each make up our own story. And if that is true, we get to create our own story about everything, including the reality of chalk or China. Some people say that the story of Christ is true for Christians, while others have different stories.[26] But Christianity is more than a story: it is a structure based on reasonable evidence. Christ cannot be the unique Son of God and also not the unique Son of God. It can be true; it can be

[26]Lee Strobel, *Case for the Real Jesus: A Journalist Investigates Current Attacks on the Identity of Christ* (Grand Rapids: Zondervan, 2007), pp. 229-34.

false; but it can't shift from true to false and back to true depending on how we feel. The statement "I happen to feel" simply can't be challenged, and to ask *why* a person feels such and such is not considered correct.

On first sight, the statement is insane. On last sight, the statement is, if not insane, at least irrational and unreasonable.

134. EXTRATERRESTRIALS ARE MORE PROBABLE THAN ANGELS.

When I presented the idea that angels are more probable than extraterrestrials at an interdisciplinary conference, a distinguished physicist gaped at me. And thereby hangs a worldview. First consider this scientific fact: although extraterrestrials (intelligent life elsewhere than on Earth) are perfectly possible, there is as yet no scientific evidence that they exist.[27] If they do exist, the likelihood of communicating with them is extremely low on the probability scale. There is a field known as astrobiology or exobiology that investigates life on other planets, but most of my scientific colleagues rate the likelihood of discovering any as approaching zero. Even so, the expensive search for such beings by SETI (Search for Extraterrestrial Intelligence) scientists may well be worth it, for if communication were established it would be among the greatest scientific discoveries ever. In a materialist scientific worldview, extraterrestrials are possible though improbable.

Angels, being supernatural, are completely outside the boundaries of physicalist scientific probability; if one bases one's view on the axiom that physical science is the only way to truth, the corollary is that angels are impossible.

But if one allows that there are other ways to truth than science, the evidence for angels is striking, for most religions have something resembling angels (Greek *aggelos*: messenger) between the divine and the human. The existence of angels is affirmed by Jewish, Christian and Muslim theology. In a spiritual worldview, then, angels rate extremely high on the probability scale.

Therefore, if spiritual and scientific worldviews are both allowed,

---

[27]The first exoplanets (exoplanets are planets of another solar system) found be in a "life zone" where somewhat earthlike conditions may prevail are Gliese 581g and Kepler-22b <www.wired.com/wiredscience/2011/12/kepler-22b>.

angels have a high probability and extraterrestrials a low one. Only to a physicalist is this proposition incredible. It makes no difference to Christianity whether extraterrestrials exist or not. If God created the Earth in order to produce an intelligent species with free will, he may elsewhere in the universe have produced other intelligent species. Literalists may object that revelation declares that the whole world will be transformed at the return of Christ, but "the world" may be taken to mean Earth rather than the entire universe.

In Christian tradition, angels are the most powerful of all creatures, and the cherubs and seraphs are the greatest and most worthy of awe. The amalgamation of cherubs with cute little cupids, an insipid invention of Renaissance art, is absolutely contrary to biblical and traditional views. In most theology, angels are held to be a whole order of being above humans.[28]

[28]David Albert Jones, *Angels: A History* (Oxford: Oxford University Press, 2010); Henry Mayr-Harting, *Perceptions of Angels in History* (Oxford: Clarendon, 1998).

What's New Is True

135. The latest religious theories are the best.

A common fallacy is to jumble up radically different beliefs, toss them all into one bag, and call it "religion." Christians are much less interested in "religion" than they are in Jesus. Another origin of this fallacy is the assumption that religious knowledge increases incrementally as it does in science. Natural science normally advances by testing hypotheses against external evidence, and what is new in chemistry is (usually) better than what is old. But Christianity is not a natural science; its evidence is based on testimony, and its center is the person of Jesus. Theology has opened up many ideas over the years, but these ideas are tested by their trueness to Jesus and evaluated without "privileging" (showing preference for) the present as opposed to the past and future. The idea that what most people believe today is truer than what most people believe at other times is chronocentrism, a variety of ethnocentrism.

Another source of the fallacy is that "sensationalism sells better than sense."[1] Media are not eager to broadcast an argument that Jesus is who Christians have been saying he is over the past two millennia. But claim, for example, that Jesus' body has been found frozen in the Greenland icecap, or any other idea for which alleged evidence can be manufactured or imagined, and immediately there's an audience. Partly this is the human wish (as strong among academics as anywhere) to be on the crest of any wave of fashion and partly, again, the unfounded assumption that what's new trumps what's true. There are many versions of the fantasy that Jesus was associated with some secret tradition that is now at last being unveiled by the latest clever and ambitious person.

[1]David Bentley Hart, *Atheist Delusions: The Christian Revolution and Its Fashionable Enemies* (New Haven, CT: Yale University Press, 2009), p. 220.

136. New Age and Christianity are compatible.

New Age is so vague and various a viewpoint that Christianity is certainly compatible with it in some respects—for example ecology, individual rights, respect for other creatures, peace, and belief in the harmony of the cosmos. A sense that there's something out there beyond oneself is more realistic than the sense there's nothing beyond oneself at all. It is possible to be a New Age Christian in the sense of being a Christian who shares many New Age feelings. In essence, however, Christianity and New Age are incompatible in their attitude toward truth. Christians claim that Christianity is objectively true, whereas New Agers design their own religions to suit their own tastes on the basis of what makes them feel harmonious and content. Over the past few decades some Christians have adopted New Age beliefs that are definitely non-Christian, such as reincarnation.[2] One also hears people repeating the cliché that they do not need so-called organized religion to be spiritual. A growing number of people including scientists believe that they are spiritual without being religious. Precisely because "spirituality" is generally lacking in content and therefore not susceptible to evidence, it is popular because individuals can tailor it to themselves. Forty-one percent of scientists consider themselves at least slightly spiritual.[3] However that may be, it is not a Christian point of view. "Religion reduced to personal opinion is diminished nearly beyond recognition, just as science is when creature comforts become the sole reason for studying and supporting it."[4]

137. Reincarnation is compatible with Christianity.

The compatibility is zero. Christianity (along with Judaism and Islam) has never believed in the idea of the transmigration of souls. Christianity's view is that humans will rise from the dead at the end of the world, judged

---

[2]"Many Americans Mix Multiple Faiths: Eastern, New Age Beliefs Widespread," *The Pew Forum on Religion and Public Life*, December 9, 2009, <ww.pewforum.org/Other-Beliefs-and-Practices/Many-Americans-Mix-Multiple-Faiths.aspx>.

[3]Elaine Howard Ecklund, *Science vs. Religion: What Scientists Really Think* (New York: Oxford University Press, 2010), pp. 51-68. On p. 64 Ecklund reports that scientists who are spiritual do more volunteer work.

[4]Mollie Ziegler Hemingway, "Faith Unbound," *Christianity Today,* September 2010, p. 74. See also Harold W. Attridge, ed., *Religion and Science Debate: Why Does It Continue?* (New Haven, CT: Yale University Press, 2009), p. 177.

according to their characters, and reside eternally either with God or without him. This life is the only life we have in which to develop our character. Reincarnation may seem comforting by providing some "other chance," but it is absolutely not Christian.[5]

138. Christianity leads to wealth.

In recent years a movement commonly known as "the prosperity gospel" has made advances throughout the world. It teaches that practicing Christianity will bring prosperity in this world. It fits neither biblical nor traditional teaching: none of Jesus' disciples lived or died rich or famous. Neither did the martyrs nor any of the most revered Christian teachers.

139. *The Da Vinci Code* is fact-based fiction.

Dan Brown's *Da Vinci Code* is false. Brown and his publishers admit that the book is a work of fiction, but that is easy to forget, because the first page of the book declares as "**FACT**" (in bold capital letters) that something called the Priory of Sion is a real secret organization founded by European crusaders in 1099. It goes on to state that in 1975 parchments known as *Les dossiers secrets* were discovered in the Bibliothèque Nationale, the French national library. The alleged "parchments" identified numerous famous figures of history as members of the Priory of Sion.

These "facts" are an almost total falsehood. In reality, the Priory of Sion is the name of a tiny French extremist group founded in the 1950s. Before then it had no existence at all. The *Dossiers secrets* were not discovered in the Bibliothèque Nationale at all. Instead, they were deposited there in 1967 by a twentieth-century French fantasist and fanatic named Pierre Plantard, one of the Priory's officers in the 1950s and 1960s. Plantard claimed to be the rightful king of France, a descendent of the Merovingian kings and ultimately of Jesus Christ. These dossiers include newspaper clippings, imaginary genealogies and "parchments" forged in the twentieth century. None of the documents are ancient or medieval. Plantard quit the organization himself in 1984. Nothing that Brown alleges of the Priory is true, and all the elements deriving from it are false.

---

[5]Paul Edwards, *Reincarnation: A Critical Examination* (Amherst, NY: Prometheus, 2002); Robert A. Morey, *Reincarnation and Christianity* (Minneapolis: Bethany Fellowship, 1980).

Brown's Sion myth is only the first falsehood on which the novel's pretensions to fact rest.

Brown's plot is ingenious and based on a few real facts (as is true in most novels). But fantasies dominate, linking Freemasonry, witchcraft, the Gnostic Nag Hammadi scrolls, Mithraism, Leonardo, Botticelli, Newton, tarot cards, Opus Dei, the crusades, the Merovingian kings, the Templars, the Louvre, the Holy Grail, Victor Hugo, Rosslyn Chapel, Jean Cocteau and other unrelated subjects. Historical evidence contradicts, among other things, that Jesus and Mary Magdalene had children, that Leonardo painted Mary (instead of the Apostle Saint John) in his *Last Supper*, that the grail is the cup used by Jesus at the Last Supper, that the Merovingian kings of the Franks were descendants of Jesus, that the Templars had anything to do with the grail, that there ever was a secret society dedicated to fostering the alleged descendants of Jesus, and so on and on. The novel is a tissue of misrepresentations that can barely be excused in a work of fiction and absolutely never in a work claiming even the slightest historical credence.[6]

Plantard's documents are among a long list of forgeries and fantasies about so-called ancient secrets from the seventeenth-century Rosicrucians through the antisemitic *Protocols of the Elders of Zion* through Madame Blavatsky's *The Secret Doctrine* and Gerald Gardner's *Witchcraft Today* to the neopagan present. The success of Brown's fraud is due to contemporary lack of concern for reason and evidence, credulity about vast conspiracies, relativism, the notion that "secret truths" are more likely than overt truths, and reliance on intuition and feelings instead of facts.

140. The real founder of Christianity was Constantine the Great.

This modern myth about the Roman emperor Constantine the Great (r. 306-337) has been popularized by novels and pseudohistories. It is one part true and nine parts false. Its versions range from the plausible—based on the emperor's undoubted influence on the church—to the nonsensical, such as the claims that he created a new version of the New Testament and

[6]Sharan Newman, *Real History Behind the Da Vinci Code* (New York: Berkley, 2005); Carl F. Olson and Sandra Miesel, *Da Vinci Hoax: Exposing the Errors in the Da Vinci Code* (San Francisco: Ignatius, 2004).

that no one believed Jesus was divine before the reign of Constantine.[7] Such nonsense could hardly be further off target, because previous theological debates about the nature of Jesus centered on the question whether he was actually human or whether he was divine.

The myth includes the following: Constantine made Christianity the established religion of the Roman Empire (false); he was not a Christian before he was baptized when dying (false); his baptism and faith were perfunctory (almost certainly false); he introduced the use of force by Christians against nonbelievers (false); he dictated one brand of Christianity and stamped out others (much exaggerated); he dictated the decisions of the Council of Nicaea in 325 (much exaggerated); and he arbitrarily decided on the canon of the Bible (false) since his predecessor Diocletian (284-305) had destroyed all copies of the New Testament (mostly false, though Diocletian did destroy some).[8]

The facts: in 312-313 Constantine and his co-emperor Licinius established a policy of toleration traditionally called the "Edict of Milan," assuring Christianity legal status along with other religions that "ensured reverence for the Divinity."[9] This, according to H. A. Drake, "was the first official government document in the Western world to recognize the principle of freedom of belief."[10] Constantine was always a monotheist who felt personally called by divine power to establish justice in the empire, and his conversion seems to have been a gradual conviction that Christ was the real manifestation of the one God, rather than his previous choice, Apollo, "the unconquered sun." He believed that Christianity would best bring consensus to the empire and that the Christian clergy should be favored. He made it possible for people to bequest land or money to churches, and he himself gave enormous gifts that allowed the building of elaborate cathedrals such as the Lateran Basilica in Rome. In 325 he summoned the

[7]David Aikman, *Delusion of Disbelief: Why the New Atheism Is a Threat to Your Life, Liberty, and Pursuit of Happiness* (Carol Stream, IL: Tyndale House, 2008), p. 204. The nonsense was propagated by Michael Baigent, Richard Leigh and Henry Lincoln in their pseudohistory *Holy Blood, Holy Grail* (New York: Delacorte, 1982).

[8]J. Ed Komoszewski et al., *Reinventing Jesus: How Contemporary Skeptics Miss the Real Jesus and Mislead Popular Culture* (Grand Rapids: Kregel, 2006), pp. 116-17, disposes of this nonsense.

[9]Licinius, quoted by H. A. Drake, *Constantine and the Bishops* (Baltimore: Johns Hopkins University Press, 2000), p. 194.

[10]Drake, *Constantine and the Bishops,* p. 194. See also Drake, "Intolerance, Religious Violence, and Political Legitimacy in Late Antiquity," *Journal of the American Academy of Religion* 79, no. 1 (2011): 193-235.

First Ecumenical Council at Nicaea, whose discussions he influenced and whose decisions he approved. He admonished bishops and sometimes appointed them. His unceasing advancement of his own career and power has been seen as a sign of hypocrisy, but this is because his relation to Christianity has been misunderstood by modern historians who think in terms of "church and state," a gigantic conceptual anachronism.

Separation of church and state was not conceived of before the 1600s at the earliest. Before then politics and religion were indistinguishable. The activities of bishops in politics and of emperors in religion were not intrusions but universal practice in societies that considered both as an inseparable whole. It is also untrue that the emperors had full control over the Eastern church. In fact, the great controversies in the church often pitted the monks and the church fathers against imperial authority. Saint John Chrysostomos (347-407) died in exile for his anti-imperialist stand. Sometimes the secular authority yielded to the spiritual authority, as when the powerful emperor Theodosius the Great (r. 379-395) was obliged to humble himself in penance before Ambrose (339-397), the bishop of Milan.

Christianity became the official religion of the Empire only in 395, over half a century after Constantine's death. One effect on Christianity and the conversion of the Empire was that it finally became respectable to be a Christian, thus terminating persecutions but drawing the lukewarm and the hypocritical into the church.

141. Christians believe in the Holy Grail.

Any Christians who may do so have been misled by the fiction that the grail was a dish or cup used by Jesus at the Last Supper. The basis for this notion is not Christian history or even Christian Tradition. European folk beliefs in a magical vessel like a horn of plenty existed by the twelfth century, and these beliefs were attached to the Last Supper in the entirely fictional stories about King Arthur that were popular in France and elsewhere from about 1190 into the twentieth century. The Holy Grail never existed, and it was never a Christian idea.[11]

---

[11]D. D. R. Owen, *History of the Grail Legend* (Edinburgh: Saint Andrews University Publications, 1968).

142. ARCHEOLOGISTS FOUND THE FAMILY TOMB OF JESUS.

Most archeological work is careful and valid. Some archeological claims are false, like the discovery of Jesus' family tomb. Some are frauds, like the alleged "sepulcher of James," the brother of Jesus.[12] Some are the result of leaping to conclusions. At any rate, no tomb of Jesus or any of his family has been found. The most famous object in controversy is the Shroud of Turin, which bears the startling image of an ancient crucifixion victim. Discussions of the shroud still abound, some citing evidence that it is the true burial cloth of Jesus and others citing evidence that it is not. The jury will probably remain out for quite a while.[13] In the meantime, Christian leaders have cautioned against basing commitment to Christ on any object.

143. RELIGION NEEDS TO BE REMOVED FROM THE PUBLIC SQUARE.

Censorship, which used to be condemned by liberals, has recently enjoyed a spectacular revival and success among people calling themselves liberals. Anything that might cause offense to any officially designated group is censored in the schools, universities, the press and even the law. Anything that offends a member of such a group (but not of other groups) is banned as hate speech. The term "hate speech" is parallel to the term "heresy" in medieval Catholicism: it presumes that some ideas are evil and must be suppressed. The intellectual background of this attack on free thought lies in the writings of Michel Foucault (1926-1984) and Herbert Marcuse (1898-1979). Marcuse argued that no speech against oppressed people should be allowed until complete equality is attained for everybody. This led to the imposture of diversity, where diversity can mean anything except diverse points of view. The idea is that everyone is free to believe what the reigning elite believe, but no one is allowed to believe anything else—or at least only privately without expressing it to others. A shift in rhetoric from "freedom of religion" to "freedom of worship" has occurred, with the subtext that one should keep one's religious beliefs to oneself. But religion

---

[12]Ben Witherington III, *What Have They Done with Jesus? Beyond Strange Theories and Bad History—Why We Can Trust the Bible* (New York: HarperOne, 2006), pp. 295-98; Michael Green, *Lies, Lies, Lies! Exposing Myths about the Real Jesus* (Nottingham, UK: Inter-Varsity Press, 2009), pp. 104-6.

[13]Robert K. Wilcox, *Truth About the Shroud of Turin: Solving the Mystery* (Chicago: Regnery, 2010); "The Real Face of Jesus" on MSNBC, February 12, 2012.

is about much more than freedom of worship. It is about the right to speak openly and to engage in public debate.

Censorship of free expression applies to religion in general and Christianity in particular but not to other ideologies. Elaine Ecklund interviewed a professor who "especially assumed that any sort of proselytizing on the part of faculty was not allowed."[14] The faculty I know proselytize every day for various ideologies, including Marxism, atheism, deconstructionism, feminism, Freudianism and materialism.[15] Ecklund notes, "It seems, ironically, that those . . . who most prize the vision of the university as committed to plurality are actually the most opposed to the entrée of diverse religious views into the fabric of the intellectual life of universities."[16]

The offense of such ideas against liberalism, education and the First Amendment is gross and ongoing. If liberalism means anything, it means freedom (Latin *liber* means "free"); if education means anything, it means learning how to think rather than being propagandized what to think; if the First Amendment means anything, it means that the government is not empowered to suppress religion.[17]

144. Christianity is different from what it is.

A late, distinguished colleague of mine used to say that all who call themselves Christians are Christians. That sounds liberal, but it makes the term meaningless: during the Nazi years, a great many German Christians claimed that Jesus was not Jewish but Aryan and that Hitler was God's representative on earth. An older example: Gnostics and other Docetists (from Greek *dokeo*, "to seem") claimed that Jesus was not human at all but only appeared to have a human form. But Christ entered history "not as some sort of furtive phantom, merely arraying himself in the outward appearance of a man."[18]

---

[14]Ecklund, *Science vs. Religion*, p. 98.

[15]Adam Bellow, ed., *New Threats to Freedom: From Banning Ice Cream Trucks in Brooklyn to Abandoning Democracy around the World* (West Conshohocken, PA: Templeton, 2010); Alan Charles Kors and Harvey A. Silverglate, *The Shadow University: The Betrayal of Liberty on America's Campuses* (New York: Free Press, 1998).

[16]Ecklund, *Science vs. Religion*, p. 99.

[17]Ted Olsen and Trevor Persaud, "'All Comers Only,'" *Christianity Today,* August 2010, pp. 17-19, on the bizarre Supreme Court decision in 2010 that prevents Christian groups from excluding non-Christians.

[18]Hart, *Atheist Delusions*, p. 209.

A thought experiment: Is a Muslim who claims that the Qur'an is not a revelation from God a Muslim? Is a Marxist who believes in the infallibility of the pope a Marxist? How is a Republican who always votes Democratic a Republican, and how is a Democrat who always votes Republican a Democrat? A Christian who denies that Jesus is the unique Son of God who was fully human, suffered death and rose from the dead might be a moral giant, but he is not a Christian. Many Christians seem not to really believe in the resurrection, or they imagine it to be a purely spiritual existence in an afterlife.[19] We have the legal right to call ourselves whatever we choose, but we do not have the intellectual and moral right to dissolve philosophical distinctions.

For several decades, many clergy have emphasized the "horizontal" people-to-people approach rather than the "vertical" people-to-God approach, making the church something like a club with a sanctuary, or the "holy church of Christ without Christ."[20] Recently some have realized where this emphasis has led and are changing back.[21]

As the term "Christian" is stretched thinner, many Christians are losing their commitment. Pastors and other Christian leaders describing their congregations as having a "clear mission and purpose" declined from forty-one percent in 2005 to thirty-six percent in 2008; congregations deemed "spiritually vital and alive" declined in the same period from forty-two percent to thirty-five percent.[22] The sociologist Rodney Stark has repeatedly shown that organizations demanding less of their members tend to lose members, and the surge toward inclusiveness has diluted Christianity without extending its appeal.

Christianity does change over time, as the oak develops from the acorn. It develops beyond its origin and core, but it must be true to its origin and core or it stops being what it is. When something is no longer what it is, it becomes something else or a hovering, amorphous cloud. The Apostle Saint Paul writes broadly to "all those who in every place call on the name

---

[19]Vigen Guroian, "Descended into Hell: The Meaning of Holy Saturday," *Christian Century*, March 23, 2010, pp. 26-29.

[20]Flannery O'Connor, *Wise Blood*, 2nd ed. (New York: Farrar, Straus and Giroux, 1962), p. 153.

[21]William H. Willimon, "Too Much Practice," *Christian Century*, March 9, 2010, pp. 22-25.

[22]"Faith Communities Today Study, A Report on Religion in the United States Today—Executive Summary, 2000," <http://faithcommunitiestoday.org/report-religion-united-states-today-executive-summary>.

of our Lord Jesus Christ" (1 Cor 1:2). By the word "Lord," Paul meant the divine Christ. A person who admires Jesus but rejects his divinity can be a follower of the teachings of Jesus but not a Christian. Teachings can be derived from the biblical core but cannot subtract from it. Jesus cannot be God and not God. The underlying cultural assumption that religions are subjective, so that any one statement about Jesus is as good as any other statement, is a recent invention.

There is a lot of room for both/and thinking—both science and Christianity have truths—but not for logically self-contradictory thinking.

145. Nothing is true.

The dictionary says that "truth is conformity to fact or actuality, . . . a statement proven to be accepted as true." Capital-T Truth is "that which is considered to be the supreme reality and to have the ultimate meaning and value of existence."

We easily understand truth as conformity to reality. We distinguish simple, practical truths from simple falsehoods. As children we learn that it is true that fire is hot and that a turnip is not an apple. Later we learn general truths such as that Earth is round, dinosaurs are extinct, Poland is not in Asia, and Mars is smaller than Jupiter. No sane person denies that practical, everyday propositions such as that the sun rises in the east are true, or that some elements have a greater atomic weight than others, or that the Holocaust occurred. If we tried a fact-free diet, we would die.

At a certain point, we begin to wonder whether there is Truth behind the unbounded variety of truths. We want to know because of our natural curiosity about the world and because how we live our lives depends on our understanding and knowledge, which come from our experience and our reasoning. We want to know that our lives mean something. At some point we may get discouraged and say, "I don't like to think about that stuff," or "It doesn't matter," or "It's not safe." When the pre-Christian philosopher Socrates said that "the unexamined life is not worth living" and went through the streets of Athens asking people to question their assumptions, they executed him. When Jesus told Pilate that he (Jesus) was truth, Pilate asked, "What is truth?" And executed him.

Denial of Truth is the deepest form of relativism. There are different sorts of relativism, some popular and some philosophical. There is polite relativism, recognizing that people have a variety of opinions and refraining from pushing them into a corner. There is lazy relativism, where we refuse to think things through and so avoid pushing ourselves into a corner. Lazy relativism is related to hedonistic relativism, where we consider only what gives us pleasure and reject anything that might disturb us. Then there is exploitative relativism, where we maintain and advance ideas to suit our own interests. The history of economic "derivatives" is an example of that. Me-ness can be simple selfishness, but some me-ness is intellectual, as when a scientist or scholar is content with specific results in a specific problem on which he or she is working. "I wouldn't say it was true, but it works" is the attitude of many who take refuge in narrow specialties and ignore the big picture. That satisfies the person who is nothing but a scientist or scholar and is uninterested in the meaning of his or her life.

Reference works distinguish among varieties of philosophical relativism.[23] The term "relativism" originated about 1865. Cultural relativism holds that one culture cannot judge the values of another. Ethical relativism holds that right and wrong depend on an individual's opinion in a given situation. Knowledge relativism maintains that there is no such thing as knowledge—only "knowledges" from different points of view. In knowledge relativism there are no facts, just interpretations. Truth relativism denies the existence of Truth and even truth, teaching that truths are relative to societies, ideologies, groups and individuals.

As widespread as these views are at the moment, they don't satisfy thinking people. Humans seem to have a "biologically anomalous craving for 'the truth' [and] desire to see and know far beyond the limits of any conception of utility."[24] In other words, we are born wanting to know Truth until we are intimidated or indoctrinated out of doing so. The basic question is whether there is a reality beyond our own mind. Some people, not all of them clinically insane, deny that there is. Obviously no one can know the whole truth, but we can have the intention of moving in the direction of truth as best we can. We do so by keeping our minds open to evidence. It is one thing to say, "Truth exists" and quite another to say, "I've got the truth."

---

[23]For example, see Thomas Mautner, *Penguin Dictionary of Philosophy*, 2nd ed. (London: Penguin).

[24]Marilynne Robinson, *Absence of Mind* (New Haven, CT: Yale University Press, 2010), p. 131.

The current intellectual fad is to deny any objective truth at all. The fad is called postmodernism or deconstruction, which metastasized from the thought of Friedrich Nietzsche (1844-1900) for whom "argument, logic, and truth itself have all become absurd."[25] The fatal flaw in Nietzsche's thinking and that of all his postmodernist successors is that they deny the basis of argument: you can't make an argument that argument itself is impossible.[26] Deconstruction has become common in literature, art, the social sciences and history, and it has even begun to affect natural science, where it is sometimes called postnormal science. Since deconstructionists reject the whole idea of definitions, definitions of deconstruction and postmodernism are unattainable. No logic or argument from evidence can shake them since they deny the value of argument and evidence. It happens that the chancellor of my university is a professor of engineering, and when I explained deconstruction to him he thought it was a joke: "Imagine deconstructing the idea of a dam." Deconstruction is not real philosophy but a political agenda aimed at correcting the alleged failure of modern, rational thought to produce a world without misery and suffering. It is increasingly accepted by those who find its lack of intellectual and moral principles comfortable; it dominates contemporary education and political discourse.[27]

Deconstruction and postmodernism eat away at both scientific atheism and Christianity. An Orwellian postmodernism was taught by Herbert Marcuse (1898-1979), who argued that the search for truth is an illusion and that all so-called truth and so-called rights arise from what those with power declare them to be. The establishment of white patriarchal males, he said, has through its power oppressed minorities of race, gender and ethnicity, so patriarchal ideas of objectivity, freedom and truth must be destroyed so the oppressed can reconstruct reality in their own terms. There can, according to Marcuse's followers, be no free exchange of ideas until all formulations of reality have attained equal power. Only by the censorship of unprogressive ideas can real freedom be achieved.[28]

People who deny truth have a logical problem, for they are saying that

---

[25]Ian S. Markham, *Against Atheism: Why Dawkins, Hitchens, and Harris Are Fundamentally Wrong* (Malden, MA: Wiley-Blackwell, 2010), p. 45.

[26]Ibid., p. 44.

[27]William Ayers, ed., *Teaching for Social Justice* (New York Norton, 1998) is a good example.

[28]Kors and Silverglate, *Shadow University*, pp. 68-71.

"it is true that there is no objective truth," or at least that "the idea that there is no truth is more true than the idea that there is." But since logic is one of the things postmodernists reject, their illogic does not trouble them. One of the many problems with denying truth is that it makes any conversation about reality impossible, and this destroys the human condition. If I affirm that there is no truth and deny that I have any access to it or intention toward it, how can you and I discuss the world? You feel this, and I feel that, and so what? To deny the existence of truth also discourages others from seeking it, depriving them of the means of constructing their minds rationally and coherently and leaving them open to infinite manipulation of their feelings and senses. Intimidation and indoctrination, and lazy submission to them, take the place of the always difficult search for truth. The ease with which ideologies can twist history to suit their purposes is clear in the career of Stalin. As Simon Sebag Montefiore asks, "Did Stalin really believe it [the false accusations] all? Yes, passionately, because it was politically necessary, which was better than mere truth. 'We ourselves will be able to determine,' Stalin told Ignatiev, 'what is true and what is not.'"[29] Attitudes in some universities today are not dissimilar. Denial of truth is convenient. Once a politician was asked whether he would change his mind if it were proved to him that his position was false; he replied that he would not, because then he would have to change ideas in which he was heavily invested.

Truth is reality. The pagan emperor Marcus Aurelius (r. 161-180) said, "You must one day realize at last of what universe you are a part and from what governor of the universe your existence comes, and that a limit of time has been set aside for you, and if you do not use it to clear away the clouds from your mind, it will be gone, and you will be gone, and it will never return again."[30] Christian philosophers believe that the truth, directionality, purpose and intentionality in the cosmos come from a mind outside the cosmos. The great theologian Thomas Aquinas (1225-1274) said, "And this all people call God." But today all people don't necessarily call it so. A number of scientists and philosophers believe in purpose without assenting to the traditional Judeo-Christian view of God. In this book, however, "God" is the Christian God. Truth is not dry and bloodless.

---

[29]Simon Sebag Montefiore, *Stalin: The Court of the Red Tsar* (New York: Vintage, 2003), p. 623.
[30]Marcus Aurelius, *Meditations* 2.1.

The origin of the word "truth," Old English *treowth*, means "loyalty," and truth involves loyalty as well as assent. It may take a while, but the true, the good and the beautiful will outlast relativism. The world is a bud about to burst into bloom.

Bibliography

Aikman, David. *The Delusion of Disbelief: Why the New Atheism Is a Threat to Your Life, Liberty, and Pursuit of Happiness.* Coral Spring, IL: SaltRiver, 2005.

Alexander, Dennis R. *Creation or Evolution: Do We Have to Choose?* Oxford: Monarch, 2008.

Anderson, Gary A. *Sin: A History.* New Haven, CT: Yale University Press, 2010.

Attridge, Harold W., ed. *The Religion and Science Debate: Why Does It Continue?* New Haven, CT: Yale University Press, 2009.

Ayres, Lewis. *Nicaea and Its Legacy: An Approach to Fourth-Century Trinitarian Theology.* Oxford: Oxford University Press, 2004.

Baggett, David, ed. *Did the Resurrection Happen? A Conversation with Gary Habermas and Antony Flew.* Downers Grove, IL: InterVarsity Press, 2009.

Barr, Stephen M. *Modern Physics and Ancient Faith.* Notre Dame, IN: University of Notre Dame Press, 2003.

Bauckham, Richard. *Jesus and the Eyewitnesses: The Gospels as Eyewitness Testimony.* Grand Rapids: Eerdmans, 2006.

———. *Jesus: A Very Short Introduction.* New York: Oxford University Press, 2011.

Beattie, Tina. *The New Atheists: The Twilight of Reason and the War on Religion.* Maryknoll, NY: Orbis, 2008.

Benedict XVI. *Creation and Evolution.* San Francisco: Ignatius Press, 2008.

———. *Jesus of Nazareth.* New York: Doubleday, 2007.

———. *Jesus of Nazareth: Holy Week from the Entrance into Jerusalem to the*

Resurrection. San Francisco: Ignatius, 2011.

Berlinski, David. The *Devil's Delusion: Atheism and Its Scientific Pretensions*. New York: Crown Forum, 2008.

Berry, Wendell. *What Matters? Economics for a Renewed Commonwealth*. Berkeley, CA: Counterpoint, 2010.

Blomberg, Craig L. *The Historical Reliability of John's Gospel: Issues and Commentary*. Downers Grove, IL: InterVarsity Press, 2001.

Bock, Darrell L. *The Missing Gospels: Unearthing the Truth Behind Alternative Christianities*. Nashville: Thomas Nelson, 2006.

Bowman, Robert M., Jr., and J. Ed Komoszewski. *Putting Jesus in His Place: The Case for the Deity of Christ*. Grand Rapids: Kregel, 2007.

Carter, Stephen. *The Culture of Disbelief*. New York: Basic Books, 1993.

Cimino, Richard P. *Shopping for Faith: American Religion in the New Millennium*. San Francisco: Jossey-Bass, 1998.

Clarke, Peter, and Tony Claydon, eds. *The Church, the Afterlife and the Fate of the Soul*. Woodbridge, UK: 2009.

Collins, Francis S. *The Language of God*. New York: Free Press, 2006.

Conway Morris, Simon. *The Deep Structure of Biology: Is Convergence Sufficiently Ubiquitous to Give a Directional Signal?* West Conshohocken, PA: Templeton Foundation Press, 2008.

———. *Life's Solution: Inevitable Humans in a Lonely Universe*. Cambridge: Cambridge University Press, 2003.

Copan, Paul. *How Do You Know You're Not Wrong?* Grand Rapids: Baker, 2005.

Copan, Paul, and William Lane Craig, eds. *Contending with Christianity's Critics: Answering New Atheists and Other Objectors*. Grand Rapids: Zondervan, 2009.

Copan, Paul, ed. *Jesus' Resurrection: Fact or Figment? A Debate Between William Lane Craig and Gerd Lüdemann*. Downers Grove, IL: InterVarsity Press, 2000.

Coyne, Jerry. *Why Evolution is True*. New York: Viking, 2009.

Craig, William Lane. *On Guard: Defending Your Faith with Reason and Precision*. Colorado Springs: David C. Cook, 2010.

Craig, William Lane, and Chad Meister, eds. *God Is Great, God Is Good: Why Belief in God Is Reasonable and Respectable.* Downers Grove, IL: InterVarsity Press, 2010.

Crean, Thomas. *God Is No Delusion: A Refutation of Richard Dawkins.* San Francisco: Ignatius, 2007.

D'Addio, Mario. *The Galileo Case: Trial, Science, Truth.* Leominster, UK: Gracewing, 2004.

Davies, Paul. *Cosmic Jackpot: Why Our Universe Is Just Right for Life.* Boston: Houghton Mifflin, 2007.

Davis, Leo Donald. *The First Seven Ecumenical Councils (325-787): Their History and Theology.* Wilmington, DE: Michael Glazier, 1983.

Dawkins, Richard. *The God Delusion.* 2nd ed. Boston: Houghton Mifflin, 2006.

———. *The Greatest Show on Earth: The Evidence for Evolution.* New York: Free Press, 2009.

D'Souza, Dinesh. *What's So Great About Christianity?* Chicago: Regnery, 2007.

Eagleton, Terry. *Reason, Faith, and Revolution: Reflections on the God Debate.* New Haven, CT: Yale University Press, 2009.

Ecklund, Elaine Howard. *Science vs. Religion: What Scientists Really Think.* New York: Oxford University Press, 2010.

Ehrman, Bart D. *God's Problem: How the Bible Fails to Answer Our Most Important Question—Why We Suffer.* New York: HarperOne, 2008.

———. *Lost Scriptures: Books That Did Not Make It into the New Testament.* New York: Oxford University Press, 2003.

Evans, Craig A. *Fabricating Jesus: How Modern Scholars Distort the Gospels.* Downers Grove, IL: InterVarsity Press, 2006.

Fodor, Jerry, and Massimo Piatelli-Palmarini. *What Darwin Got Wrong.* New York: Farrar, Straus & Giroux, 2010.

Gingerich, Owen. *God's Universe.* Cambridge, MA: Harvard University Press, 2006.

Goodspeed, Edgar. *Biblical Hoaxes.* Grand Rapids: Baker, 1956.

Green, Michael. *Lies, Lies, Lies! Exposing Myths About the Real Jesus.* Nottingham, UK: Inter-Varsity Press, 2009.

Harris, Sam. *The End of Faith: Religion, Terror, and the Future of Reason.* 2nd ed. New York: Norton, 2005.

———. *Letter to a Christian Nation.* 2nd ed. New York: Vintage, 2008.

Hart, David Bentley. *Atheist Delusions: The Christian Revolution and Its Fashionable Enemies.* New Haven, CT: Yale University Press, 2009.

Haught, John F. *God and the New Atheism: A Critical Response to Dawkins, Harris, and Hitchens.* Louisville: Westminster John Knox, 2008.

Hebblethwaite, Brian. *The Christian Hope.* 2nd ed. Oxford: Oxford University Press, 2010.

Hedges, Chris. *I Don't Believe in Atheists.* New York: Free Press, 2008.

Hitchens, Christopher. *God Is Not Great: How Religion Poisons Everything.* New York: Twelve, 2007.

Horton, Michael. *Christless Christianity: The Alternative Gospel of the American Church.* Grand Rapids: Baker, 2008.

Hunter, Cornelius G. *Science's Blind Spot: The Unseen Religion of Scientific Naturalism.* Grand Rapids: Brazos, 2007.

Hurtado, Larry W. *Lord Jesus Christ: Devotion to Jesus in Earliest Christianity.* Grand Rapids: Eerdmans, 2003.

Jacobs, Alan. *Original Sin: A Cultural History.* New York: HarperOne, 2008.

Jenkins, Philip. *Hidden Gospels: How the Search for Jesus Lost Its Way.* New York: Oxford University Press, 2001.

Johnson, Phillip E., and John Mark Reynolds. *Against All Gods: What's Right and Wrong About the New Atheism.* Downers Grove, IL: Inter-Varsity Press, 2010.

Kay, William K. *Pentecostalism: A Very Short Introduction.* New York: Oxford University Press, 2011.

Keller, Timothy. *The Reason for God: Belief in an Age of Skepticism.* New York: Dutton, 2008.

Kelly, J. N. D. *Early Christian Creeds.* 3rd. ed. London: Longman, 1972.

———. *Early Christian Doctrines.* London: Adam and Charles Black, 1958.

Kinnaman, David, and Gabe Lyons. *Unchristian: What a New Generation Really Thinks about Christianity.* Grand Rapids: Baker, 2007.

Komoszewski, J. Ed, M. James Sawyer, and Daniel B. Wallace, eds. *Reinventing Jesus: How Contemporary Skeptics Miss the Real Jesus and Mislead Popular Culture.* Grand Rapids: Kregel, 2006.

Lennox, John. *God's Undertaker: Has Science Buried God?* Oxford: Lion, 2007.

Lewis, C. S. *The Abolition of Man.* New York: Macmillan, 1947.

Licona, Michael. *The Resurrection of Jesus: A New Historiographical Approach.* Downers Grove, IL: InterVarsity Press, 2010.

Markham, Ian S. *Against Atheism: Why Dawkins, Hitchens, and Harris Are Fundamentally Wrong.* Malden, MA: Wiley-Blackwell, 2010.

McGrath, Alister. *Christianity's Dangerous Idea: The Protestant Revolution—A History from the Sixteenth Century to the Twenty-First.* New York: HarperOne, 2008.

———. *The Twilight of Atheism: The Rise and Fall of Disbelief in the Modern World.* New York: Doubleday, 2004.

McGrath, Alister, and Joanna Collicutt McGrath. *The Dawkins Delusion: Atheist Fundamentalism and the Denial of the Divine.* Downers Grove, IL: InterVarsity Press, 2007.

McMullin, Ernan, ed. *The Church and Galileo.* Notre Dame, IN: University of Notre Dame Press, 2005.

Metzger, Bruce M. *The Canon of the New Testament: Its Origin, Development, and Significance.* New York: Oxford University Press, 1987.

———. *The Text of the New Testament: Its Transmission, Corruption, and Restoration.* 4th ed. New York: Oxford University Press, 2005.

Meyer, Marvin. *The Gnostic Gospels of Jesus: The Definitive Collection of Mystical Gospels and Secret Books about Jesus of Nazareth.* San Francisco: HarperSanFrancisco, 2005.

———, ed. *The Nag Hammadi Scriptures.* New York: HarperOne, 2007.

Meyer, Stephen C. *Signature in the Cell: DNA and the Evidence for Intelligent Design.* New York: HarperOne, 2009.

Micklethwait, John, and Adrian Wooldridge. *God Is Back: How the Global*

Revival of Faith Is Changing the World. New York: Penguin, 2009.

Miller, Kenneth R. *Finding Darwin's God.* New York: Perennial, 2002.

Noll, Mark A. *Jesus Christ and the Life of the Mind.* Grand Rapids: Eerdmans, 2011.

———. *Protestantism: A Very Short Introduction.* New York: Oxford University Press, 2011.

Novak, Michael. *No One Sees God: The Dark Night of Atheists and Believers.* New York: Doubleday, 2008.

Numbers, Ronald L., ed. *Galileo Goes to Jail: And Other Myths about Science and Religion.* Cambridge, MA: Harvard University Press, 2009.

Pagels, Elaine. *The Gnostic Gospels.* New York: Vintage, 1989.

Pelikan, Jaroslav. *Jesus through the Centuries: His Place in the History of Culture.* New Haven, CT: Yale University Press, 1985.

Poole, Michael. *The 'New Atheism': Ten Arguments That Don't Hold Water.* Oxford: Lion, 2009.

Purnell, Frederick, Jr., Michael S. Petersen, and Mark C. Carnes. *The Trial of Galileo: Aristotelianism, the "New Cosmology," and the Catholic Church, 1616-1633.* New York: Pearson, 2008.

Roberts, Mark D. *Can We Trust the Gospels: Investigating the Reliability of Matthew, Mark, Luke, and John.* Wheaton, IL: Crossway Books, 2007.

Robinson, James M., ed. *The Nag Hammadi Library: The Definitive Translation of the Gnostic Scriptures Complete in One Volume.* 3rd ed. Leiden: Brill, 1988.

Robinson, Marilynne. *Absence of Mind.* New Haven, CT: Yale University Press, 2010.

Russell, Dale A. *Islands in the Cosmos: The Evolution of Life on Land.* Blooomington: Indiana University Press, 2009.

Russell, Jeffrey Burton. *A History of Heaven: The Singing Silence.* Princeton, NJ: Princeton University Press, 1997.

———. *Inventing the Flat Earth: Columbus and Modern Historians.* Westport, CT: Praeger, 1991.

———. *Paradise Mislaid: How We Lost Heaven and How We Can Regain It.* New York: Oxford University Press, 2006.

Shaidle, Kathy. *The Tyranny of Nice: How Canada Crushes Freedom in the Name of Human Rights.* Toronto: Interim Press, 2008.

Stark, Rodney. *Cities of God: The Real Story of How Christianity Became an Urban Movement and Conquered Rome.* San Francisco: HarperSanFrancisco, 2006.

———. *Discovering God: The Origins of the Great Religions and the Evolution of Belief.* New York: HarperOne, 2007.

———. *For the Glory of God: How Monotheism Led to Reformations, Science, Witch-hunts, and the End of Slavery.* Princeton, NJ: Princeton University Press, 2003.

———. *God's Battalions: The Case for the Crusades.* New York: HarperOne, 2009.

———. *One True God: Historical Consequences of Monotheism.* Princeton, NJ: Princeton University Press, 2001.

———. *The Victory of Reason: How Christianity Led to Freedom, Capitalism, and Western Success.* New York: Random House, 2005.

Stenger, Victor. *God: The Failed Hypothesis: How Science Shows That God Does Not Exist.* Amherst, NY: Prometheus 2007.

Strobel, Lee. *The Case for the Real Jesus.* Grand Rapids: Zondervan, 2007.

Swinburne, Richard. *The Resurrection of God Incarnate.* Oxford: Clarendon, 2003.

Taylor, Charles. *A Secular Age.* Cambridge, MA: Belknap Press, 2007.

Torrance, Thomas F. *The Trinitarian Faith: The Evangelical Theology of the Ancient Catholic Church.* London: T & T Clark, 1991.

Viladesau, Richard. *Theology and the Arts: Encountering God through Music, Art, and Rhetoric.* New York: Paulist Press, 2000.

Von Kamecke, Fred. *Busted: Exposing Popular Myths About Christianity.* Grand Rapids: Zondervan, 2009.

Ward, Peter, and Donald Brownlee. *Rare Earth: Why Complex Life is Uncommon in the Universe.* New York: Copernicus, 2000.

Wegner, Paul D. *A Student's Guide to Textual Criticism of the Bible: Its History, Methods, and Results.* Downers Grove, IL: InterVarsity Press, 2006.

Wiker, Benjamin. *The Catholic Church and Science: Answering the Questions, Exposing the Myths.* Charlotte, NC: Tan Books, 2011.

Willard, Dallas, ed. *A Place for Truth: Leading Thinkers Explore Life's Hardest Questions.* Downers Grove, IL: InterVarsity Press, 2010.

Williams, Thomas D. *Greater than You Think: A Theologian Answers the Atheists About God.* New York: FaithWords, 2008.

Wills, Garry. *What the Gospels Meant.* New York: Viking, 2008.

Witherington, Ben, III. *The Gospel Code: Novel Claims about Jesus, Mary Magdalene and Da Vinci.* Downers Grove, IL: InterVarsity Press, 2004.

———. *What Have They Done with Jesus? Beyond Strange Theories and Bad History.* San Francisco: HarperSanFrancisco, 2006.

Wright, Bradley R. E. *Christians Are Hate-Filled Hypocrites . . . and Other Lies You've Been Told.* Minneapolis: Bethany House, 2010.

Wright, Christopher J. H. *Knowing Jesus Through the Old Testament.* Downers Grove, IL: InterVarsity Press, 1995.

Wright, N. T. *Judas and the Gospel of Jesus: Have We Missed the Truth About Christianity?* Grand Rapids: Baker, 2006.

———. *The Resurrection of the Son of God.* Minneapolis: Fortress, 2003.

———. *Simply Christian: Why Christianity Makes Sense.* New York: HarperOne, 2006.

———. *Surprised by Hope: Rethinking Heaven, the Resurrection, and the Mission of the Church.* New York: HarperOne, 2008.

Persons Index

(Pages with dates of historical persons are in ***bold.****)*

Subject Index

*(Pages in **bold** contain definitions.)*